8. Victory in Africa

This is the eighth of twelve books which together make up the first complete paperback edition of Sir Winston Churchill's classic memoirs, The History of the Second World War. *Here, full and unabridged, is the greatest Englishman of our time, describing in unforgettable words the follies which brought about the most terrible war known to mankind, and the sacrifices, determination and matchless courage by which it was brought to an end.*

The Moral of the Work

In War: RESOLUTION
In Defeat: DEFIANCE
In Victory: MAGNANIMITY
In Peace: GOODWILL

Winston S. Churchill

THE SECOND WORLD WAR

8. Victory in Africa

CASSELL · LONDON

CASSELL & COMPANY LTD
35 Red Lion Square · London WC1

and at Melbourne, Sydney, Toronto,
Johannesburg, Cape Town, Auckland

Victory in Africa
was first published as Book 2 of 'The Hinge of Fate',
the fourth volume of Sir Winston Churchill's
The Second World War

First published 1951
All rights reserved
First published in this edition 1964

Set in 9 point Intertype Times and
printed in Great Britain by Cox and Wyman Ltd.,
London, Reading and Fakenham.
F.664

Preface

(From the Preface to the original edition)

I must regard these volumes as a continuation of the story of the First World War which I set out in The World Crisis, The Eastern Front *and* The Aftermath. *Together they cover an account of another Thirty Years War.*

I have followed, as in previous volumes, the method of Defoe's Memoirs of a Cavalier, *as far as I am able, in which the author hangs the chronicle and discussion of great military and political events upon the thread of the personal experiences of an individual. I am perhaps the only man who has passed through both the two supreme cataclysms of recorded history in high executive office. Whereas however in the First World War I filled responsible but subordinate posts, I was in this second struggle with Germany for more than five years the head of His Majesty's Government. I write therefore from a different standpoint and with more authority than was possible in my earlier books. I do not describe it as history, for that belongs to another generation. But I claim with confidence that it is a contribution to history which will be of service for the future.*

These thirty years of action and advocacy comprise and express my life-effort, and I am content to be judged upon them. I have adhered to my rule of never criticising any measure of war policy after the event unless I had before expressed publicly or formally my opinion or warning about it. Indeed in the afterlight I have softened many of the severities of contemporary controversy. It has given me pain to record these disagreements with so many men whom I liked or respected: but it would be wrong not to lay the lessons of the past before the future. Let no one look down on those honourable, well-meaning men whose actions are chronicled in these pages without searching his own heart, reviewing his own discharge of public duty, and applying the lessons of the past to his future conduct.

It must not be supposed that I expect everyone to agree with what I say, still less that I only write what will be popular. I give my testimony according to the lights I follow. Every possible care has been taken to verify the facts: but much is constantly coming to light from the disclosure of captured documents and other revelations which may present a new aspect to the conclusions which I have drawn.

One day President Roosevelt told me that he was asking publicly for suggestions about what the war should be called. I said at once 'The Unnecessary War'. There never was a war more easy to stop than that which has just wrecked what was left of the world from the previous struggle. The human tragedy reaches its climax in the fact that after all the exertions and sacrifices of hundreds of millions of people and the victories of the Righteous Cause we have still not found Peace or Security, and that we lie in the grip of even worse perils than those we have surmounted. It is my earnest hope that pondering upon the past may give guidance in days to come, enable a new generation to repair some of the errors of former years, and thus govern, in accordance with the needs and glory of man, the awful unfolding scene of the future.

WINSTON SPENCER CHURCHILL

Chartwell,
Westerham,
Kent.

March 1948

Acknowledgments

I have been greatly assisted in the establishment of the story in its military aspect by Lieutenant-General Sir Henry Pownall: in naval matters by Commodore G. R. G. Allen: in presenting the Air aspect by Air Chief Marshal Sir Guy Garrod: and on European and general questions by Colonel F. W. Deakin, of Wadham College, Oxford, who has helped me with my work Marlborough: His Life and Times. *I have had much assistance from the late Sir Edward Marsh, Mr. Denis Kelly, and Mr. C. C. Marsh. I must in addition make my acknowledgments to the very large number of others who have kindly read these pages and commented upon them.*

Lord Ismay has also given me his invaluable aid, as have my other friends.

I record my obligations to Her Majesty's Government for the permission to reproduce the text of certain official documents of which the Crown Copyright is legally vested in the Controller of Her Majesty's Stationery Office. At the request of Her Majesty's Government, on security grounds, I have paraphrased some of the telegrams I have quoted. These changes have in no way altered the sense or substance of the telegrams.

I am indebted to the Roosevelt Trust for the use they have permitted me of the President's telegrams I have quoted: to Captain Samuel Eliot Morison, U.S.N.R., whose books on naval operations give a clear presentation of the actions of the United States Fleet: and also to others who have allowed their private letters to be published.

The publishers wish to thank the owners, named and unnamed, of the photographs used to illustrate this book.

Contents

Illustrations

Maps and Diagrams

Theme of the Book

HOW THE POWER OF THE GRAND ALLIANCE BECAME PREDOMINANT

The Eighth Army at Bay

General Auchinleck had issued instructions in February that whereas Tobruk was essential as a supply base for offensive operations, yet if we were forced to withdraw 'it is not my intention to continue to hold it once the enemy is in a position to invest it effectively. Should this appear inevitable, the place will be evacuated and the maximum amount of destruction carried out in it'. In consequence of these orders the defences had not been maintained in good shape. Many mines had been lifted for use elsewhere, gaps had been driven through the wire for the passage of vehicles, and the sand had silted up much of the anti-tank ditch so that in places it was hardly an obstacle. Only on the western and south-western faces of the perimeter were the defences strong; elsewhere, and especially to the east, they were in bad condition. At the same time masses of supplies, ammunition, and petrol were accumulated in the place.

General Ritchie proposed to make use of the Tobruk western defences by incorporating them as part of a general defensive line running south-eastwards to El Adem, supported by a mobile force farther south to prevent encirclement. He reported to Auchinleck that this arrangement might involve the investment of Tobruk by the enemy, if only for a short time. If this was not acceptable there was no option but to withdraw the entire garrison. Auchinleck would not at first countenance the plan. He telegraphed to Ritchie on June 14: 'Tobruk must be held and the enemy not allowed to invest it. This means that the Eighth Army must hold the line Acroma–El Adem and southwards'; and later: 'The defences of Tobruk and other strong places will be used as pivots of manœuvre, but on no account will any part of the Eighth Army be allowed to be surrounded in Tobruk and invested there.'

At home we had no inkling that the evacuation of Tobruk had ever entered into the plans or thoughts of the commanders. It was certainly the Cabinet view that if the Eighth Army were beaten back Tobruk should remain, as in the previous year, a thorn in the enemy's side. In order to confirm that this view was shared by Auchinleck, I had, as set forth in an earlier chapter,* telegraphed to him on June 14 before I left for Washington:

> Presume there is no question in any case of giving up Tobruk.

Auchinleck had replied next day that he did not intend that the Eighth Army should be besieged in Tobruk, but had no intention whatever of giving up Tobruk. His orders to General Ritchie were not to allow his forces to be invested in Tobruk.

As this seemed to us equivocal we put the point precisely: 'War Cabinet interpret your telegram to mean that if the need arises General Ritchie would have as many troops as are necessary to hold the place for certain.'

To this on June 16 Auchinleck had replied:

> War Cabinet interpretation is correct. General Ritchie is putting what he considers an adequate force to hold it, even should it become temporarily isolated.

At the same time he sent the following to General Ritchie:

> Although I have made it clear to you that Tobruk must not be invested, I realise that its garrison may be isolated for short periods until our counter-offensive can be launched.

Had I seen this order I should not have been content with it.

* * *

General Klopper, commanding the 2nd South African Division, was placed in charge of the fortress. Supplies and ammunition for the garrison were sufficient for ninety days, and

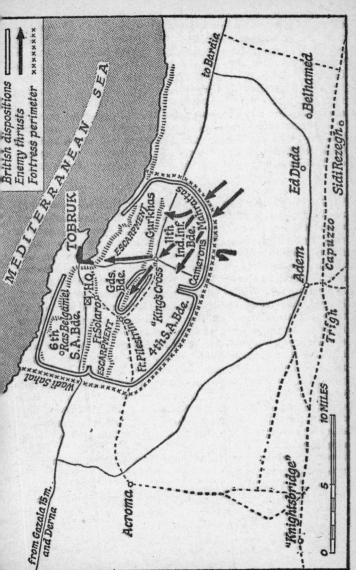

The Fall of Tobruk

General Klopper was confident that Tobruk could play its part in the plan, which included the retention by the Eighth Army of the strong points of El Adem and Belhamed outside the perimeter. The garrison included four infantry brigades (fourteen battalions), a tank brigade and sixty-one Infantry tanks, five regiments of field and medium artillery, and about seventy anti-tank guns.* In addition there were about 10,000 men in administrative and transport units centred round the port and its base installations. In all, a total of about 35,000 men were within the perimeter, a force about equal to that which had held Tobruk when it was first besieged a year before. The dispositions for the defence are shown in the attached sketch No. 1.

* * *

After a lull of only two days, on June 16 Rommel renewed his offensive. In a series of rapid blows he took El Adem, Belhamed, and Acroma. On June 17 he defeated our 4th Armoured Brigade at Sidi Rezegh, reducing them to a strength of only twenty tanks. By the 19th Tobruk was isolated and surrounded, and until tank replenishments came to hand there was no effective armoured force to support or relieve the garrison from outside. At 6 a.m. on June 20 the enemy opened a heavy bombardment with guns and dive-bombers on the south-eastern part of the Tobruk perimeter, held by the 11th Indian Infantry Brigade. Half an hour later the attack was launched, led by the 21st Panzer Division, supported by the 15th Panzer Division, together with the Italian armoured division and a motorised infantry division. With our own armour outside Tobruk temporarily disposed of, Rommel could afford to put his full weight into this single blow. It fell mainly on a battalion of the Indian Brigade, in a sector where the defences were at their weakest. They were soon deeply penetrated. No fighter protection could be given to our troops as our Air Force was withdrawn to distant landing-grounds.

General Klopper ordered a counter-attack by his tanks and

* Tobruk Order of Battle:
    H.Q. 2nd South African Division
    4th and 6th South African Infantry Brigades.
    Two composite South African battalions from 1st South African Division.
    7th South African Reconnaissance Battalion (armoured cars).
    11th Indian Infantry Brigade.
    201st Guards Brigade.
    32nd Army Tank Brigade (4th and 7th Battalions).
    2nd and 3rd South African Field Artillery Regiments.
    25th Field Artillery Regiment.
    67th and 68th Medium Artillery Regiments.

part of the Coldstream Guards. This effort, hastily organised
and delivered piecemeal, failed. All remaining British tanks
were thrown into the cauldron south-east of the road junction
called 'King's Cross', where the remnants of the Indians were
fighting it out. But it was of no avail. By noon only a handful
of our tanks survived and our supporting batteries were over-
run. Enemy tanks swung west and north, but the main body
drove straight for 'King's Cross'. At 2 p.m. Rommel himself
was there. He ordered one group directly on to Tobruk. It
suffered heavily from artillery fire, but reached the Solaro ridge
at 3.30 p.m., and by 6 p.m. was on the outskirts of Tobruk.
Another group was sent due west from 'King's Cross', along
the ridge towards Pilastrino, where they met the Guards Brigade
hastily forming front to meet attack from this unexpected
direction.

All that afternoon and evening the Guards Brigade, strongly
supported by our artillery, fought a stern battle, and suffered
heavy losses. Some ground was lost and the brigade headquarters was captured, but at nightfall the enemy had been
brought to a halt. The situation was parlous. The western and
southern sides of the perimeter were intact and the Gurkhas on
the extreme left were holding out, but the enemy were in possession of a great part of the Tobruk fortress. All our reserve
troops were pinned down. Demolition was ordered of the closely
threatened base installations. In Tobruk itself the reserve of
transport, necessary if the remnants of the garrison were to be
evacuated, was immobilised and soon to be destroyed.

*   *   *

At 8 p.m. on June 20 General Klopper reported to the
Eighth Army Headquarters: 'My H.Q. surrounded. Infantry on
perimeter still fighting hard. Am holding out, but I do not
know how long.' He asked for instructions, and was told: 'Come
out to-morrow night preferably ; if not, to-night.' He called his
senior officers to conference and asked their views. Some said
that effective resistance was no longer possible. With the main
supplies in enemy hands ammunition was running short ; to
continue fighting meant heavy casualties to no purpose. Let all
who could break out. But others were for fighting on. The transport, without which escape was not possible, had been captured.
There was hope that a relieving column might come from the
south. Let what remained be concentrated in the south-west

corner of the perimeter and fight on till relieved. At 2 a.m. the moon set and a break-out through the minefields, even if hitherto practicable, became impossible. General Klopper held a radio telephone conversation with General Ritchie and told him that the situation was a 'shambles'. If resistance were continued terrible casualties would result ; he was 'doing the worst'. General Ritchie instructed him: 'Every day and hour of resistance materially assists our cause. I cannot tell the tactical situation, and must therefore leave you to act on your own judgment regarding capitulation. ... The whole of the Eighth Army has watched with admiration your gallant fight.'

*   *   *

At dawn on the 21st General Klopper sent out a parlementaire with an offer to capitulate, and at 7.45 a.m. German officers came to his headquarters and accepted his surrender. His orders were received by many of his troops, some of whom had hardly been engaged, with incredulity and dismay. To some of his commanding officers he had to issue personal instructions, for they would accept them from no other source. According to German records 33,000 of our men were taken prisoners. Despite General Klopper's orders many attempts were made by small parties to escape, but without transport nearly all failed. Only one considerable group was successful. Defiant and undaunted, 199 officers and men of the Coldstream Guards and 188 South Africans, having collected some lorries, set out together, and, breaking through the perimeter, made a wide sweep that brought them at nightfall to the Egyptian frontier seventy miles away.

The hopes of the garrison of help from a relieving force had been vain. The 7th Armoured Division was re-forming in the desert to the south, and on the 20th received orders to dispatch a force in aid. But Rommel was too quick for them. Before it had even started all was over.

*   *   *

The Germans captured vast quantities of stores. Here is the account of General Westphal, later Rommel's Chief of Staff:

The booty was gigantic. It consisted of supplies for 30,000 men for three months and more than 10,000 cubic metres of petrol. *Without this booty adequate rations and clothing for the armoured divisions would not have been possible in the coming months.* Stores arriving by sea had only on one occasion—in April 1942—been enough to supply the army for one whole month.*

The news of the capture of Tobruk without the need of a long siege revolutionised the Axis plans. Hitherto it had been intended that after Tobruk was taken Rommel should stand on the Egyptian frontier and that the next major effort should be the capture of Malta by airborne and seaborne forces. As late as June 21 Mussolini reiterated these orders. The day after Tobruk fell Rommel reported that he proposed to destroy the small British forces left on the frontier, and thus open the way to Egypt. The condition and morale of his forces, the large captures of munitions and supplies, and the weakness of the British position prompted pursuit 'into the heart of Egypt'. He requested approval. A letter also arrived from Hitler pressing Rommel's proposals upon Mussolini.

> Destiny has offered us a chance which will never occur twice in the same theatre of war. ... The English Eighth Army has been practically destroyed. In Tobruk the port installations are almost intact. You now possess, Duce, an auxiliary base whose significance is all the greater because the English themselves have built from there a railway leading almost into Egypt. If at this moment the remains of this British Army are not pursued to the last breath of each man, the same thing will happen as when the British were deprived of success when they nearly reached Tripoli and suddenly stopped in order to send forces to Greece. ...†

The Duce needed no persuasion. Elated at the prospect of conquering Egypt, he postponed the assault on Malta till the beginning of September, and Rommel—now a Field-Marshal, rather to Italian surprise—was authorised to occupy the relatively narrow passage between Alamein and the Qattara Depression as the starting-point for future operations whose final objective was the Suez Canal. Kesselring held a different view. Believing that the Axis position in the Desert would never be secure until Malta was captured, he was alarmed at the change of plan. He pointed out to Rommel the dangers of this 'foolhardy enterprise.'

*   *   *

---

* Westphal, *Heer in Fesseln*, p. 180. General Westphal is incorrect in his statement regarding captured petrol. All bulk petrol stocks in Tobruk were destroyed before the town fell.
† Quoted in Cavallero, *Commando Supremo*, p. 277.

Hitler himself had not been confident of success against Malta, as he mistrusted the ability of the Italian troops who would have formed the major part of the expedition. The attack might well have failed. Nevertheless it now seems certain that the shattering and grievous loss of Tobruk spared the island from the supreme trial. This is a consolation of which no good soldier, whether involved or not, should avail himself. The burden falls upon the High Command rather than on General Klopper, and still less upon his troops.

General Ritchie proved himself both a competent Staff Officer and later a resolute Corps Commander. Nevertheless it was a bad arrangement by which he left his desk as General Auchinleck's Deputy Chief of Staff to become the commander of the Eighth Army. The *rôles* are different and should be divorced. The personal association of Auchinleck and Ritchie did not give Ritchie a chance of those independent conceptions on which the command of violent events depends. The lack of clear thought and the ill-defined responsibility between General Auchinleck and his recent Staff Officer, General Ritchie, had led to a mishandling of the forces which in its character and consequences constitutes an unfortunate page in British military history. It was not possible to judge the event at the time. The Tobruk commanders were prisoners of war. But now that the salient facts are known the truth should not be obscured.

*　　　*　　　*

What remained of the Eighth Army was now drawn back behind the frontier. In a telegram of June 21 the Middle East Defence Committee at Cairo described the alternative courses open to them:

> First, to fight the enemy on the frontier defences. Without adequate armoured forces this entails risking the loss of all our infantry holding the frontier position. Second course, to delay the enemy on the frontier with forces which are kept fully mobile, while withdrawing main body of Eighth Army to the Matruh defences. This, coupled with delaying action by our air forces, gives us the best chance of gaining time in which to reorganise and build up a striking force for an offensive. . . . We have decided on the second course.

I did not welcome this decision, and telegraphed from Washington as follows:

Prime Minister to General Auchinleck   22 June 42

C.I.G.S. Dill and I earnestly hope stern resistance will be made on the Sollum frontier line. Stresses which enemy has undergone are doubtless severe. Very important reinforcements are on their way. A week gained may be decisive. We do not know exact dates of the deployment of the New Zealand Division, but had expected it would be by the end of the month. 8th Armoured and 44th are approaching and near. We agree with General Smuts that you may draw freely upon Ninth and Tenth Armies, as the danger from north is more remote. Thus you can effect drastic roulement with the three divisions now east of the Canal.

2. I was naturally disconcerted by your news, which may well put us back to where we were eighteen months ago and leave all the work of that period to be done over again. However, I do not feel that the defence of the Delta cannot be effectively maintained, and I hope no one will be unduly impressed by the spectacular blows which the enemy has struck at us. I am sure that with your perseverance and resolution and continued readiness to run risks the situation can be restored, especially in view of the large reinforcements approaching.

3. Here in Washington the President is deeply moved by what has occurred, and he and other high United States authorities show themselves disposed to lend the utmost help. They authorise me to inform you that the 2nd United States Armoured Division, specially trained in desert warfare in California, will leave for Suez about July 5, and should be with you in August. You need not send the Indian Division and 288th Indian Armoured Brigade back to India as proposed. Measures are also being taken in addition to those described in the Chiefs of Staff's telegram to divert India-bound aircraft to the Libyan theatre. . . .

4. The main thing now is for you to inspire all your forces with an intense will to resist and strive and not to accept the freak decisions produced by Rommel's handful of heavy armour. Make sure that all your man-power plays a full part in these critical days. His Majesty's Government are quite ready to share your responsibilities in making the most active and daring defence.

However, Auchinleck adhered to his opinion.

*   *   *

Rommel swiftly organised his pursuit, and on June 24 crossed the frontier to Egypt, opposed only by our light mobile

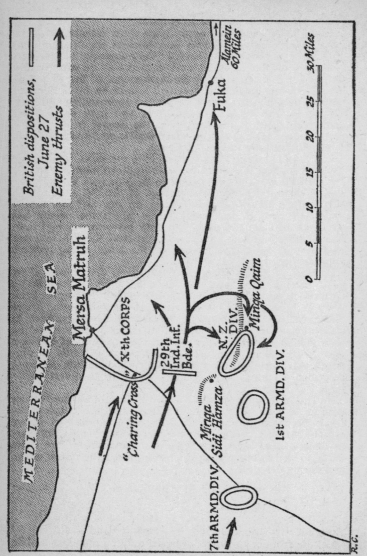

The New Zealanders at Minqa Qaim.

columns, and the stubborn and magnificent fighter squadrons of the Royal Air Force, who really covered the retreat of the Eighth Army to Mersa Matruh. Their position here was not strong. About the town itself there was an organised defensive system, but south of it were only some lines of unconnected minefields inadequately guarded. As in the case of the rejected frontier position, the Matruh line, if it were to be successfully held, needed a powerful armoured force to guard its southern flank. The 7th Armoured Division, though now rebuilt to nearly a hundred tanks, was not yet capable of such a task.

General Auchinleck himself came forward to Matruh on June 25, and decided to take over direct operational command of the Army from General Ritchie. He should have done this when I asked him to in May.

Prime Minister to General Auchinleck   28 June 42

I am very glad you have taken command. Do not vex yourself with anything except the battle. Fight it out wherever it flows. Nothing matters but destroying the enemy's armed and armoured force. A strong stream of reinforcements is approaching. We are sure you are going to win in the end.

General Auchinleck quickly concluded that it was not possible to make a final stand at Matruh. Arrangements were already in hand for the preparation and occupation of the Alamein position, a hundred and twenty miles farther back. To halt the enemy, if only for a time, the following dispositions were made: The Xth Corps, with the 10th Indian and 50th British Infantry Divisions, held the Matruh defences. Farther south, under command of the XIIIth Corps, were the 29th Indian Infantry Brigade, covering a six-mile gap in the minefields, and the New Zealand Division. The 1st Armoured Division and the 7th Armoured Division guarded the Desert Flank.

The New Zealand Division, which had arrived at Matruh from Syria on June 21, were at length moved on the 26th into action on the ridge about Minqa Qaim. That evening the enemy broke through the front of the 29th Indian Infantry Brigade, where the minefield was incomplete. The next morning they streamed through the gap, and then, passing behind the New Zealanders, encircled and attacked them from three sides. Desperate fighting continued all day, and at the end it seemed that the division was doomed. General Freyberg had been severely wounded. But he had a worthy successor. Brigadier Inglis was determined to break out. Shortly after midnight the 4th New

Zealand Brigade moved due east across country with all its
battalions deployed and bayonets fixed. For a thousand yards no
enemy were met. Then firing broke out. The whole brigade
charged in line. The Germans were taken completely by surprise, and were routed in hand-to-hand fighting under the
moon. The rest of the New Zealand Division struck south by
circuitous routes. This is how Rommel has described the episode:

> The wild flare-up which ensued involved my own battle
> headquarters. ... The exchanges of fire between my forces
> and the New Zealanders reached an extraordinary pitch of
> intensity. Soon my headquarters were surrounded by burn-
> ing vehicles, making them the target for continuous enemy
> fire at close range. I had enough of this after a while, and
> ordered the troops with the staff to move back south-east-
> wards. The confusion reigning on that night can scarcely be
> imagined.*

Thus the New Zealanders broke clear, and the whole division
was reunited in a high state of discipline and ardour near the
Alamein position, eighty miles away. So little were they disorganised that they were used forthwith to stiffen the defences
at Alamein.

Prime Minister to General Freyberg   4 July 42
> Deeply moved to hear of your new wound and new glory.
> Trust that your injury is not serious and that you will soon be
> back commanding your splendid division. All good wishes to
> you and to them.

*   *   *

The two divisions of the Xth Corps around Matruh were also
brought back to safety, though with difficulty. On June 27 they
had struck southwards at the enemy break-through, without
bringing it to a halt. The enemy pressed on and threatened the
coastal road. The Corps was ordered to retire eastwards. They
fought their way down the road until blocked by an enemy
force. Then they struck south across the desert to Alamein. The
XXXth Corps had been withdrawn earlier to Alamein. When
joined there by the Xth and XIIIth Corps the whole army, on
June 30, was ranged on or behind the new position. The troops
were amazed rather than depressed.

*   *   *

* Desmond Young, *Rommel*, p. 269.

Casey had been active and helpful in this convulsion. I requested him to grip the situation at the rear and in the Cairo stewpot.

Prime Minister to Minister of State   30 June 42
I wish to let you know how much I appreciate the part you have played not only in the main situation, but also in the change of command, which I have long desired and advocated. While Auchinleck fights at the front you should insist upon the mobilisation for battle of all the rearward services. Everybody in uniform must fight exactly as they would if Kent and Sussex were invaded. Tank hunting parties with sticky bombs and bombards, defence to the death of every fortified area or strong building, making every post a winning-post and every ditch a last ditch. This is the spirit you have got to inculcate. No general evacuation, no playing for safety. Egypt must be held at all costs.

I was also aware that the Army would never have escaped in good order without the devoted aid of the Air Force, who fought from the advanced airfields till these were actually over-run. Now they could work from well-established bases in Egypt against the advancing enemy.

Prime Minister to Air Chief Marshal Tedder   4 July 42
Here at home we are all watching with enthusiasm the brilliant, supreme exertions of the Royal Air Force in the battle now proceeding in Egypt. From every quarter the reports come in of the effect of the vital part which your officers and men are playing in this Homeric struggle for the Nile Valley. The days of the Battle of Britain are being repeated far from home. We are sure you will be to your glorious army the friend that endureth to the end.

*   *   *

The Alamein position runs from the railway station of that name to the impassable Qattara Depression, thirty-five miles to the southward. This was a long line for the forces available to hold. Much work had been done, but except for semi-permanent fortifications around Alamein itself the line consisted chiefly of disconnected works. The flanks however were secure and the Eighth Army had been strongly reinforced. The New Zealand Division was in perfect order after the fine action it had fought. The 9th Australian Division was also soon to arrive and win high distinction. With the advantage of short communications, and with Alexandria only forty miles away, the

The Western Desert

reorganisation of the Eighth Army did not take long. Auchinleck, once in direct command, seemed a different man from the thoughtful strategist with one eye on the decisive battle and the other on the vague and remote dangers in Syria and Persia. He sought at once to regain the tactical initiative. As early as July 2 he made the first of a series of counter-attacks which continued until the middle of the month. These challenged Rommel's precarious ascendancy. I sent my encouragement, on the morrow of the Vote of Censure debate, which had been an accompaniment to the cannonade.

Prime Minister to General Auchinleck 4 July 42
I cannot help liking very much the way things seem to be going. If fortune turns I am sure you will press your advantage, as you say, 'relentlessly'.

*   *   *

The surrender of the South African Division under a South African commander at Tobruk had been a dire stroke to General Smuts in the political as well as the military sphere.

Prime Minister to General Smuts 4 July 42
I have been so much harried by the weaker brethren in the House of Commons since my return from America last week that this is the first chance I have had of telling you how deeply I grieve for the cruel losses you have sustained in your gallant South African divisions, and how I admire the indomitable manner in which you have inspired South Africa to face this heavy blow.
2. We have been through so much together and are so often in harmony of thought that I do not need to say much now about the lamentable events of the last three weeks. I am still hopeful that all can be retrieved. The President gave me three hundred of their latest Sherman tanks, which are far superior to the Grants, and a hundred 105-mm. self-propelled gun howitzers as anti-tank weapons. These should reach Egypt by the beginning of September. The President is also sending Liberators up to about one hundred, which should arrive during July. Two heavy Halifax bombing squadrons from England will be in action during the next ten days. Another sixty American fighters are being rushed across the Atlantic via Takoradi. All this is additional to our regular reinforcement of the air. As you probably know, the 8th Armoured Division, with 350 tanks, mostly Valentines, is landing now. The 44th British Infantry Division should land July 23, and the 51st a month later. Whether these forces

will be able to play their part depends upon the battle now proceeding at Alamein.

General Smuts was imperturbable. His mind moved majestically amid the vagaries of Fortune. No one knew better than he how to

> meet with Triumph and Disaster,
> And treat those two impostors just the same.

General Smuts to Prime Minister   7 July 42

What with your most heartening message and news from Middle East foreshadowing that tide is turning at El Alamein, yesterday was one of my happiest recent days. I do believe Rommel has overstretched himself, and if Auchinleck remains in personal charge not only will Tobruk be avenged, but our counter-stroke may carry us right on to Tripoli and save both Egypt and Malta. The reinforcements you foreshadow will go far to assist in achieving this great object, and I hope it will not again be necessary to deflect them to some other theatre. Not only would Egypt be secured, but a base thus established for the coming offensive against the weakest Axis partner may have other important results. I believe possible German attempt to reach Iraq oil through Syria may also thus be thwarted. I am thus for fullest exploitation of victory, which I believe is in sight owing to Rommel's over-reaching audacity.

Auchinleck may meet with serious difficulties. His transport has suffered seriously in long retreat, and enemy will try to destroy pipeline and railways to delay his advance, while enemy reinforcements may be expected. Our air superiority and relentless bombing of enemy ports and communications will however have their effect.

As America is now our great strategic reserve for the final blows, much of your time will have to be devoted to wisely guiding Washington in its war effort and not letting vital war direction slip out of our hands. I think your service in this respect can now be at least as great as your Empire war service. Your contacts with Roosevelt are now a most valuable war asset, and I hope your weaker brethren with their purely domestic outlook will be made to realise this.

*   *   *

Prime Minister to Mr. Fraser and Mr. Curtin*   11 July 42

The division which you consented to leave in the Middle

---

* *To Mr Curtin only:* I am very glad that the 9th Australian Division is now in action in the Western Desert, and am very thankful to you for making it available for this vital key point of the war.

East is doing splendid work in the Western Desert, and has already brought fresh fame to New Zealand's arms at this vital key point of the war.

... The unforeseeable tide of disaster which drove us from Gazala to Alamein with the loss of Tobruk and fifty thousand men has now for the time being been stemmed. General Auchinleck has received strong reinforcements, raising his army to a hundred thousand men, with another twenty thousand well forward in the Delta behind them. He is thus about double Rommel in men. He has a fair equality in artillery, but is still somewhat weaker in armour. This imposes prudence upon him for two reasons. First, a retirement is much worse for him than for Rommel, who has nothing but deserts behind him, and, secondly, far more strength is coming to General Auchinleck than to the enemy.

It was very fortunate that four months ago I obtained from President Roosevelt the shipping to carry an additional forty thousand men to the East without deciding on their destination till they rounded the Cape. Without these the reinforcements now proved so needful by the hazards of war could not have been at hand.

When in Washington I obtained from the President three hundred of the latest and finest tanks [Shermans] in the American Army. They were taken from the very hands of the American troops, who eagerly awaited them, and were sent by special convoy direct to Suez. With them went one hundred 105-mm. self-propelled guns, which definitely outmatch the 88-mm., the whole being accompanied by a large number of American key men. These should arrive early September. Apart from the 8th Armoured Division, and in addition to the two armoured and one Army tank brigades now in action forward, we have in the Delta the personnel of four armoured brigades awaiting re-equipment. About half these men are desert-trained in tanks. We should therefore be able to bring into action incomparably the most powerful and best-trained armoured division yet seen in the Middle East, or indeed anywhere. But I hope the issue will be decided in our favour earlier. This is especially desirable because of dangers that may, though I do not say they will, develop on the northern approaches to Egypt.

Scarcely less important are the air reinforcements given me by the President on the morrow of Tobruk. As you know, we have not hitherto been able, for technical as well as military reasons, to provide heavy bomber squadrons for the Middle East, though they have often asked for them. But now the President has assigned to the defence of Egypt the group of twenty Liberators which was on its way to India, after bombing Roumanian oilfields, ten other Liberators which had already reached India, and a group of thirty-five Liberators from the United States. These with our own Liberators make up about eighty-five of these heavy bombers, which should all be available this month. At the same time our two Halifax squadrons will come into action, making up to 127 heavy bombers in all. It is this force I rely upon to beat up the ports of Tobruk and Benghazi, hampering Rommel's reinforcements, besides of course playing the part of a battle-fleet in preventing a seaborne invasion of Egypt. We have great enterprises in preparation for the revictualling of Malta, but as these deal with future operations you will not, I am sure, wish me to mention details.

Besides this, every preparation has been made to defend the Delta should the battles in the Desert go against us. Here we have very large numbers of men, all of whom have been ordered to take part in the defence of Egypt exactly as if it was England that was invaded. The cultivation and irrigation of the Delta make it literally the worst ground in the world for armoured vehicles, and armour as a factor would lose a great deal of its predominance. All ideas of evacuation have been repressed, the intention being to fight for every yard of ground to the end. As I have said however I do not think this situation will arise.

The House of Commons has proved a rock in these difficult days, as it did in the struggle against Napoleon, and I have also been greatly encouraged by the goodwill of your Government and people. I never felt more sure that complete ultimate victory will be ours. But the struggle will be long and we must not relax for an instant.

*   *   *

Rommel's communications were indeed strained to the utmost limit and his troops exhausted. Only a dozen German tanks were still fit for action, and the superiority of the British Air Force, especially in fighters, was again becoming dominant. Rommel reported on July 4 that he was suspending his attacks and going over to the defensive for a while in order to regroup and replenish his forces. He was still confident however of taking Egypt, and his opinion was shared by Mussolini and by Hitler. The Fuehrer indeed, without reference either to the Italians or to his own naval command, postponed the attack on Malta until the conquest of Egypt was complete.

Auchinleck's counter-attacks pressed Rommel very hard for the first fortnight of July. He then took up the challenge, and from July 15 to July 20 renewed his attempts to break the British line. On the 21st he had to report that he was checked: 'The crisis still exists.' On the 26th he was contemplating withdrawal to the frontier. He complained that he had received little in the way of replenishments; he was short of men, tanks, and artillery; the British Air Force was extremely active. And so the battle swayed back and forth until the end of the month, by which time both sides had fought themselves to a standstill. The Eighth Army under Auchinleck had weathered the storm, and in its stubborn stand had taken seven thousand prisoners. Egypt was still safe.

CHAPTER 2

Decision for 'Torch'

*Need to Reach Strategic Decisions with the United States – My
Telegram to the President, July 8 – Choice of Commanders –
We Suggest General Marshall for the Cross-Channel Task –
Clarification of Code-Names – I Ask General McNaughton,
Canadian Army, to Study 'Jupiter' – The President's Reply
about Code-Names – The Pith of My Thought, July 14 – Ten-
sions at Washington – The President's Decision to Send His
Principal Advisers to Confer with Us – Dill's Full Account of
the Washington Scene – The Delegation Arrives – The Presi-
dent's Massive Document of July 16 – 'Franklin D. Roosevelt,
Commander-in-Chief' – Chiefs of Staff's Meeting at Chequers,
July 18 – My Notes for the Conference of July 20 – The Discussion Resumed, July 22 – 'Gymnast' Rechristened 'Torch'**
– I Rejoice at the Decisions – The President's Satisfaction –
Telegram from Dill of July 30 – My Suggestions to the Presi-
dent about Commands – I Start on a Journey.*

During this month of July, when I was politically at my weakest
and without a gleam of military success, I had to procure from
the United States the decision which, for good or ill, dominated
the next two years of the war. This was the abandonment of
all plans for crossing the Channel in 1942 and the occupation
of French North Africa in the autumn or winter by a large
Anglo-American expedition. I had made a careful study of the
President's mind and its reactions for some time past, and I
was sure that he was powerfully attracted by the North African
plan. This had always been my aim, as was set forth in my papers
of December 1941. Everyone in our British circle was by now
convinced that a Channel crossing in 1942 would fail, and no
military man on either side of the ocean was prepared to recommend such a plan or to take responsibility for it. There was by

---

* The following shortly explain the code-names occurring in this chapter:
   ACROBAT: The advance into Tripolitania.
   BOLERO: Preparations for the main invasion of France, afterwards the foundation
     of 'Overlord'.
   GYMNAST: The landing in North-West Africa, later called 'Torch'.
   JUPITER: Operations in Northern Norway.
   ROUND-UP: The invasion of German-dominated Europe, afterwards called 'Over-
     lord'.
   SLEDGEHAMMER: The attack on Brest or Cherbourg in 1942.

now general agreement on the British side that no major cross-Channel operation could take place before 1943, but that all preparation for mounting it in the greatest strength should continue with the utmost zeal.

On June 11 the War Cabinet had agreed that preparations for 'Sledgehammer', the attack on Brest or Cherbourg, should be vigorously pressed forward, 'on the understanding that the operation would not be launched except in conditions which held out a good prospect of success.' The position was studied again by the Chiefs of Staff at the beginning of the following month. On July 2 they drafted a memorandum commenting on the earlier discussions in the War Cabinet. They stated that 'At the War Cabinet on June 11 the Prime Minister laid down, and the War Cabinet generally approved, that operations in 1942 should be governed by the following two principles: (1) no substantial landing in France in 1942 unless we are going to stay, and (2) no substantial landing in France unless the Germans are demoralised by failure against Russia. It seems to us that the above conditions are unlikely to be fulfilled, and that therefore the chances of launching Operation "Sledgehammer" this year are remote.'

It was therefore necessary to simplify our policy. The moment had come to bury 'Sledgehammer', which had been dead for some time. With the general agreement of all my colleagues and the Chiefs of Staff I stated the case with whatever force I could command and in the plainest terms in an important telegram to the President.

Former Naval Person to President   8 July 42
No responsible British general, admiral, or air marshal is prepared to recommend 'Sledgehammer' as a practicable operation in 1942. The Chiefs of Staff have reported, 'The conditions which would make "Sledgehammer" a sound, sensible enterprise are very unlikely to occur'. They are now sending their paper to your Chiefs of Staff.

2. The taking up of the shipping is being proceeded with by us for camouflage purposes, though it involves a loss in British imports of perhaps 250,000 tons. But far more serious is the fact that, according to Mountbatten, if we interrupt the training of the troops we should, apart from the loss of landing-craft, etc., delay 'Round-up' or 1943 'Bolero' for at least two or three months, even if the enterprise were unsuccessful and the troops had to be withdrawn after a short stay.

3. In the event of a lodgment being effected and maintained it would have to be nourished, and the bomber effort on Germany would have to be greatly curtailed. All our energies would be involved in defending the bridgehead. The possibility of mounting a large-scale operation in 1943 would be marred, if not ruined. All our resources would be absorbed piecemeal on the very narrow front which alone is open. It may therefore be said that premature action in 1942, while probably ending in disaster, would decisively injure the prospect of well-organised large-scale action in 1943.

4. I am sure myself that French North Africa ['Gymnast'] is by far the best chance for effecting relief to the Russian front in 1942. This has all along been in harmony with your ideas. In fact, it is your commanding idea. Here is the true Second Front of 1942. I have consulted the Cabinet and Defence Committee, and we all agree. Here is the safest and most fruitful stroke that can be delivered this autumn.

5. We of course can aid in every way, by transfer of either American or British landing forces from the United Kingdom to 'Gymnast', and with landing-craft, shipping, etc. You can, if you choose, put the punch in partly from here and the rest direct across the Atlantic.

6. It must be clearly understood that we cannot count upon an invitation or a guarantee from Vichy. But any resistance would not be comparable to that which would be offered by the German Army in the Pas de Calais. Indeed, it might be only token resistance. The stronger you are, the less resistance there would be and the more to overcome it. This is a political more than a military issue. It seems to me that we ought not to throw away the sole great strategic stroke open to us in the Western theatre during this cardinal year.

7. Besides the above we are studying very hard the possibility of an operation in Northern Norway, or, if this should prove impracticable, elsewhere in Norway. The difficulties are great owing to the danger of shore-based aircraft attack upon our ships. We are having frightful difficulties about the Russian convoys. All the more is it necessary to try to clear the way and maintain the contact with Russia.

*　　　*　　　*

All this involved the choosing of commanders, and I sent two further messages to the President.

Former Naval Person to President　　　　　　　　8 July 42
We have been deeply considering the question of command of maximum 'Bolero' [the main crossing of the English

Channel]. It would be agreeable to us if General Marshall would undertake this supreme task in 1943. We shall sustain him to the last inch.

2. The War Cabinet authorise me to convey the above to you.

8 July 42

I hope, Mr. President, you will make sure that the appointment of a United States commander over 'Bolero', 1943, does not prejudice operations of immediate consequence, such as 'Gymnast'.

Another thing was to clear up the nomenclature. Under the ever-changing pressure of events the labels describing the many and various plans had become sadly confused or obsolete. The mere process or re-writing the labels was salutary and helpful.

Former Naval Person to President   6 July 42

Our code-words need clarification. By 'Bolero' we British mean the vast arrangements necessary both in 1942 and 1943 for the operation against the Continent. The Joint Anglo-American Staffs committees are all working on this basis. They are not operational, but purely administrative. What you in conversation have called 'One-third Bolero' we have hitherto been calling 'Sledgehammer'. The name 'Round-up' has been given to the 1943 operation. I do not much like this name, as it might be thought over-confident or over-gloomy, but it has come into considerable use. Please let me know whether you have any wishes about this. The 'Gymnast' you and I have in view is, I think, the variant called by your Staffs 'Semi-Gymnast'. I also use the word 'Jupiter' to describe an operation in the Far North.

*   *   *

I still hoped for 'Jupiter'. Little or no progress had been made with its detailed planning. I thought that this operation would give a glorious opportunity to the Canadian Army, which had now for two years been eating its heart out in Britain, awaiting the invader. I therefore had a long talk on this subject in the garden at Chequers with General McNaughton, of whom I had a high opinion, and whose influence with the Canadian Government was powerful. I explained the whole position to him in all its bearings, and asked him whether he would conduct a personal inquiry into the scheme and make a plan, for which all aid would be given him by our technical departments. He agreed to do this, and promised to do his best.

Prime Minister to C.I.G.S. and C.O.S. Committee   8 July 42
General McNaughton should be entrusted with the preliminary study and planning of 'Jupiter', being given all the necessary assistance by the Chiefs of Staff organisation. Climate proclaims that the Canadian Army should undertake this task, if it is thought feasible. The decision whether or not to adopt the plan will be reserved.

I did not hear from the General for a long time.

*   *   *

The President replied about the labels in a manner which showed how clearly and deeply he comprehended the issues involved. He made three proposals:

1. That the term 'Bolero' be used to designate the preparation for and movement of United States forces into the European theatre, preparations for their reception therein, and the production, assembly, transport, reception, and storage of equipment and supplies necessary for support of the United States forces in operation against the European continent.
2. That the term 'Sledgehammer' to be used to designate an offensive operation of the British and American troops against the European continent in 1942, to be carried out in case of German internal collapse, or imminent Russian military collapse which necessitates an emergency attack in order to divert German forces from the Russian front.
3. That the term 'Round-up', or any other name which you may desire, be used to designate an offensive operation against German-dominated Europe, to be carried out by combined American and British forces in 1943 or later.

I therefore minuted to the Chiefs of Staff:

Prime Minister to Brigadier Hollis   15 July 42
I fear that to change the name 'Round-up' would make the Americans think there was some change of purpose. Therefore we must stick to this boastful, ill-chosen name, and hope it does not bring us bad luck.
I think we had better not alter the President's wording. We are not now dealing with policy, but only with nomenclature.
Draft accordingly, and promulgate after obtaining American agreement.

*   *   *

On the eve of grave decisions I sent to the President the pith of my thought.

Former Naval Person to President   14 July 42
    I am most anxious for you to know where I stand myself at the present time. I have found no one who regards 'Sledgehammer' as possible. I should like to see you do 'Gymnast' as soon as possible, and that we in concert with the Russians should try for 'Jupiter'. Meanwhile all preparations for 'Round-up' in 1943 should proceed at full blast, thus holding the maximum enemy forces opposite England. All this seems to me as clear as noonday.

*   *   *

But before the final decision for action could be obtained there was a pause. Strong tensions grew in the supreme American war direction. General Marshall was divided from Admiral King as between Europe and the Pacific. Neither was inclined to the North African venture. In this deadlock the President's liking for North Africa grew steadily stronger. Field-Marshal Dill's qualities had won him the confidence of all the rival schools of thought, and his tact preserved their goodwill. My correspondence with him throws an intimate light on the processes at work.

Prime Minister to Field-Marshal Dill (*Washington*) 12 July 42
    I have had the full text of the Staff paper sent to you by air. You should draw particular attention to Mountbatten's Note showing the mortal injury that would be done to 'Round-up' by 'Sledgehammer'. Apart altogether from this, no one is able to solve the problems of 'Sledgehammer' itself.
    2. 'Gymnast' affords the sole means by which United States forces can strike at Hitler in 1942. If 'Gymnast' were successful our resulting threat to Italy would draw important German air forces off Russia. 'Gymnast' does not interrupt the vast preparations and training for 'Round-up' now proceeding on this side. It only means that six United States divisions will be withdrawn intact from 'Round-up'. These might surely be replaced by new U.S. divisions, which would be ready before the transportation schedule is accomplished.
    3. However, if the President decides against 'Gymnast' the matter is settled. It can only be done by troops under the American flag. The opportunity will have been definitely rejected. Both countries will remain motionless in 1942, and will be concentrated on 'Round-up' in 1943.

4. There could be no excuse in these circumstances for the switch of United States effort [to the Pacific], and I cannot think that such an attitude would be adopted.

It was felt by all who met at the White House to decide these issues that a visit to England offered the only hope of reaching accord. I learned that the President proposed to send his most trusted friends and officers over to see us.

Field-Marshal Dill to Prime Minister   15 July 42
Marshall leaves for England with Harry Hopkins and King to-morrow evening.
Broadly, objections to 'Gymnast' are:
(*a*) It would necessitate drawing naval forces from Pacific, particularly carriers, which are urgently required for operations U.S. have in hand there, and of which you are aware.
(*b*) It would necessitate new line of sea communications, which they would have difficulty in maintaining together with other commitments.
(*c*) To strike only at Casablanca, where landings are difficult and facilities for maintenance poor, would withdraw nothing from Russian front, and to strike inside Mediterranean, at, say, Algiers, and even Bizerta, would be too hazardous, particularly in view of ease with which Axis could cut communication through Straits of Gibraltar.
(*d*) 'Gymnast' would build up into such a large commitment as to destroy any possibility of 'Round-up' in 1943.

Vague plans for action in Pacific have been put to President. . . .
All these activities would use up shipping at present earmarked for 'Bolero', and would reduce the U.S. air forces sent to Britain by some two-thirds. . . . It is quite clear that Pacific ventures can give no immediate relief to Russia, and will be slow to obtain anything decisive against Japan.
There is no doubt that Marshall is true to his first love, but he is convinced that there has been no real drive behind the European project. Meetings are held, discussions take place, and time slips by. Germany will never again be so occupied in the East as she is to-day, and if we do not take advantage of her present preoccupation we shall find ourselves faced with a Germany so strong in the West that no invasion of the Continent will be possible. We can then go on pummelling each other by air, but the possibility of a decision

will have gone. Marshall feels, I believe, that if a great business-man were faced with pulling off this *coup* or going bankrupt he would strain every nerve to pull off the *coup*, and would probably succeed.

King's war is against the Japanese.

I have a feeling (based on nothing more than the American thought that the Pacific could be a substitute for 'Bolero' and the strong American desire to build up an army of seven millions) that there are highly placed Americans who do not believe that anything better than a stalemate with Germany is possible.

May I suggest with all respect that you must convince your visitors that you are determined to beat the Germans, that you will strike them on the continent of Europe at the earliest possible moment even on a limited scale, and that anything which detracts from this main effort will receive no support from you at all? Marshall believes that your first love is 'Gymnast', just as his is 'Bolero', and that with the smallest provocation you always revert to your old love. Unless you can convince him of your unswerving devotion to 'Bolero' everything points to a complete reversal of our present agreed strategy and the withdrawal of America to a war of her own in the Pacific, leaving us with limited American assistance to make out as best we can against Germany.

* * *

The President was conscious of the strength of the arguments against 'Sledgehammer'. If he placed it in the forefront of his communications to us, it was to convince General Marshall that it would have every chance. But if no one would touch it, what then? There was the wave of American Staff opinion which argued, 'If nothing can be done this year in Europe let us concentrate on Japan, and thus bring the United States Army and Navy thought together and unite General Marshall with Admiral King.' July 15, when the Vote of Censure was being debated in the House of Commons, when Auchinleck's battle for the defence of Cairo hung in the balance, was also 'a very tense day in the White House'. We are told, 'The United States Chiefs of Staff were in a "fish or cut bait" mood', and that the President said this would amount to 'taking up your dishes'. The meaning of these homely expressions was of course 'If Britain won't or can't do "Sledgehammer" in 1942, let us leave the European theatre and concentrate on Japan.' This, said the President, in effect amounted to abandoning the

European side of the war. There is no evidence that either General Marshall or Admiral King harboured such ideas, But there was a strong surge of feeling in the powerful second rank of the American Staff. The President withstood and brushed aside this fatal trend of thought.

His second conviction was that the United States Army must fight against the Germans in 1942. Where then could this be but in French North Africa? 'This was,' says Mr. Stimson, 'his secret war baby.' The movement of the force of the argument and of the President's mind to this conclusion was remorseless. The purpose of my visit to Washington three weeks earlier had been to obtain this decision. The fall of Tobruk, the political clamour at home, and the undoubted loss of prestige which our country, and I as its representative, suffered from this disaster had rendered it impossible for me to obtain satisfaction. But the grim questions had to be answered none the less. I was certain that the clarity and unity of our views would earn their reward.

*   *   *

Our American visitors landed at Prestwick on Saturday, July 18, and travelled by train to London. Here they went into immediate conference with the American Service Chiefs now established in the capital, Eisenhower, Clark, Stark, and Spaatz. The debate on 'Sledgehammer' was renewed. Opinion among the American leaders was still strongly in favour of pressing on exclusively with this operation. Only the President himself seemed to have been impressed by my arguments. He had drafted for the delegation the most massive and masterly document on war policy that I ever saw from his hand.*

MEMORANDUM FOR HON. HARRY L. HOPKINS, GENERAL
MARSHALL, AND ADMIRAL KING

Subject: Instructions for London Conference, July 1942

16 July 42

1. You will proceed immediately to London as my personal representatives for the purpose of consultation with appropriate British authorities on the conduct of the war.

2. The military and naval strategic changes have been so great since Mr. Churchill's visit to Washington that it became necessary to reach immediate agreement on joint

* Robert Sherwood, *Roosevelt and Hopkins*, pp. 603–5.

operational plans between the British and ourselves along two lines:

(a) Definite plans for the balance of 1942.

(b) Tentative plans for the year 1943, which of course will be subject to change in the light of occurrences in 1942, but which should be initiated at this time in all cases involving preparation in 1942 for operations in 1943.

3. (a) The common aim of the United Nations must be the defeat of the Axis Powers. There cannot be compromise on this point.

(b) We should concentrate our efforts and avoid dispersion.

(c) Absolute co-ordinated use of British and American forces is essential.

(d) All available U.S. and British forces should be brought into action as quickly as they can be profitably used.

(e) It is of the highest importance that U.S. ground troops be brought into action against the enemy in 1942.

4. British and American material promises to Russia must be carried out in good faith. If the Persian route of delivery is used preference must be given to combat material. This aid must continue as long as delivery is possible, and Russia must be encouraged to continue resistance. Only complete collapse, which seems unthinkable, should alter this determination on our part.

5. In regard to 1942, you will carefully investigate the possibility of executing 'Sledgehammer'. Such an operation would definitely sustain Russia this year. 'Sledgehammer' is of such grave importance that every reason calls for accomplishment of it. You should strongly urge immediate all-out preparations for it, that it be pushed with utmost vigour, and that it be executed whether or not Russian collapse becomes imminent. In the event Russian collapse becomes probable, 'Sledgehammer' becomes not merely advisable but imperative. The principal objective of 'Sledgehammer' is the positive diversion of German air forces from the Russian front.

6. Only if you are completely convinced that 'Sledgehammer' is impossible of execution with reasonable chance of serving its intended purpose inform me.

7. *If 'Sledgehammer' is finally and definitely out of the picture I want you to consider the world situation as it exists at that time, and determine upon another place for U.S. troops to fight in 1942.**

It is my present view of the world picture that:

(a) If Russia contains a large German force against her

* Author's italics.

'Round-up' becomes possible in 1943, and plans for 'Round-up' should be immediately considered and preparations made for it.

(*b*) If Russia collapses and German air and ground forces are released 'Round-up' may be impossible of fulfilment in 1943.

8. The Middle East should be held as strongly as possible whether Russia collapses or not. I want you to take into consideration the effect of losing the Middle East. Such loss means in series:

(1) Loss of Egypt and the Suez Canal.

(2) Loss of Syria.

(3) Loss of Mosul oil-wells.

(4) Loss of the Persian Gulf through attacks from the north and west, together with access to all Persian Gulf oil.

(5) Joining hands between Germany and Japan and the probable loss of the Indian Ocean.

(6) The very important probability of German occupation of Tunis, Algiers, Morocco, Dakar, and the cutting of the ferry route through Freetown and Liberia.

(7) Serious danger to all shipping in the South Atlantic, and serious danger to Brazil and the whole of the east coast of South America. I include in the above possibilities the use by the Germans of Spain, Portugal, and their territories.

(8) You will determine the best methods of holding the Middle East. These methods include definitely either or both of the following:

(*a*) Sending aid and ground forces to the Persian Gulf, to Syria, and to Egypt.

(*b*) *A new operation in Morocco and Algeria intended to drive in against the back door of Rommel's armies. The attitude of French colonial troops is still in doubt.**

9. I am opposed to an American all-out effort in the Pacific against Japan with the view to her defeat as quickly as possible. It is of the utmost importance that we appreciate that defeat of Japan does not defeat Germany and that American concentration against Japan this year or in 1943 increases the chance of complete German domination of Europe and Africa. On the other hand, it is obvious that defeat of Germany or the holding of Germany in 1942 or in 1943 means probable eventual defeat of Germany in the European and African theatre and in the Near East. *Defeat of Germany means the defeat of Japan, probably without firing a shot or losing a life.**

* Author's italics.

10. Please remember three cardinal principles—speed of decision on plans, unity of plans, attack combined with defence but not defence alone. This affects the immediate objective of U.S. ground forces fighting against Germans in 1942.

11. I hope for total agreement within one week of your arrival.

FRANKLIN D. ROOSEVELT
Commander-in-Chief

That same evening I held a meeting of the Chiefs of Staff Committee at Chequers. The essential part of the record read as follows:

The discussion showed that there was complete agreement between the Prime Minister on the one hand and the Chiefs of Staff on the other.

In respect of action in 1942, the only feasible proposition appeared to be 'Gymnast'. It would be much to our advantage to get a footing in North Africa cheaply, in the same way as the Germans got Norway cheaply, by getting there first. 'Gymnast' would in effect be the right wing of our Second Front. An American occupation of Casablanca and district would not be sufficient. The operations would have to extend to Algiers, Oran, and possibly farther east. If the Americans could not supply the forces for all of these, we might undertake the more easterly operations with British troops accompanied by small American contingents. It was probable that the United States would be unable to supply all the naval forces necessary for 'Gymnast' in addition to those necessary for their 'Bolero' convoys. In that event we should have to help them out.

I was naturally aware that the American war leaders, now gathered in London, still had to be convinced that our view was the only practicable one. Hopkins came to Chequers over the week-end, and we went over informally the divergence between us.

On Monday morning, July 20, the first meeting with the American delegates was held in the Cabinet room.

My summary of the attitude of the British Government is on record.

PRIME MINISTER'S NOTES FOR MEETING ON JULY 20, 1942

I do not desire to discuss this morning the merits of the various grave major proposals which are before us, but rather to survey the general scene and suggest the most convenient method and sequence of our conferences. We must reach decisions, and though these affect the whole future of the war there is no reason why the process should be protracted.

The first question is 'Sledgehammer'. Should we do it or not? But here also arises immediately the question, in what form? Our visitors may be thinking of one thing, while we have been working mainly at another. If we have been unable to devise a satisfactory plan ourselves, we will give the most earnest, sympathetic attention to any American plan. It is most important that no one should come to these discussions with a closed mind, either for or against any particular project. It is of course necessary to consider not only whether a thing can be done, but whether on balance it would be a profitable use of our resources at the present time.

We must consider the effect of doing or not doing 'Sledgehammer' on the future of 'Round-Up', for which all the 'Bolero' preparations are proceeding. We are ardently in favour of 'Round-up'. But here again what is 'Round-up'? Is it necessarily confined to an attack upon the western seaboard of France? Is the idea of a second front necessarily confined within those limits? Might it not be extended even more widely, and with advantage? We have been inclined to think that 'Sledgehammer' might delay or even preclude 'Round-up'. On the other hand, it may be contended that the fortunes of 'Round-up' do not depend to any large extent on what we do, but on what happens in Russia.

We have hitherto discussed 'Sledgehammer' on the basis that Russia is either triumphant or crushed. It is more probable that an intermediate situation will confront us. The Russian battle may long hang in the balance ; or, again, the result may be indeterminate, and the Russian front will be maintained, though somewhat farther to the east.

If 'Sledgehammer' is excluded what are we to do pending 'Round-up'? Or, if it is held that the exclusion of 'Sledgehammer' destroys 'Round-up', what are we to do anyway?

Here I will come to the second chapter, the operation 'Gymnast'. This should certainly be examined in all its various forms and from every angle. The Germans will probably not wait indefinitely before occupying the 'Gymnast' area and drawing Spain and Portugal into their system. Even though not strong enough to invade Britain with Russia still on their hands, they might easily find enough for that. We have to face the prospect of a German occupation of the North African and West African coasts. How serious would be the disadvantages of this?

The case for or against 'Gymnast' is powerfully affected by the course of the battle now raging in Egypt. Should

General Auchinleck win his advance westward may be very rapid. 'Acrobat' might then again come into view, with possibilities of action against Sicily and Italy, and also of regaining the air control of the Southern Mediterranean, with all the saving of shipping that would result therefrom.

A wide gap now exists in our defences. The Levant–Caspian front is almost bare. If General Auchinleck wins the Battle of Egypt we could no doubt build up a force of perhaps eight divisions, which, with the four Polish divisions when trained, would play a strong part in delaying a German southward advance. But if General Auchinleck cannot drive the enemy to a safe distance away from Egypt, or if, having driven them, he pursues them into 'Acrobat', then the only shield for the vital region south of the Caspian is the Russian southern armies. We cannot yet say how they will fare. It is far too early to assume that they will break. Even at the worst they should retire in force through the Caucasus and hold the mountain range through the winter and retain, possibly with our air assistance, the naval command of the Caspian Sea. These are great bulwarks. At present they are our only bulwarks. . . .

There was also a brief discussion on 'Anakim' (operations in Burma) and on what steps we could take to help in the Pacific theatre.

*   *   *

The next meeting was held on the afternoon of July 22. General Marshall opened the discussion by saying that he and his colleagues had reached a deadlock in their talks with the British Chiefs of Staff, and therefore that they would have to report to the President for instructions.

I replied that I fully shared the ardent desire of the President and his Service advisers 'to engage the enemy in the greatest possible strength at the earliest possible moment', but that I felt sure that, with the limited forces at our disposal, we should not be justified in attempting 'Sledgehammer' in 1942. I pointed to the number of ugly possibilities looming in front of us. There might, for example, be a collapse in Russia, or the Germans might move into the Caucasus, or they might beat General Auchinleck and occupy the Nile Delta and the Suez Canal, or again they might establish themselves in North Africa and West Africa and thereby put an almost prohibitive strain on our shipping. Nevertheless, disagreement between Great Britain and America would have far greater consequences than all the above possibilities. It was therefore agreed that the American Chiefs of Staff should report to the President that the British were not prepared to go ahead with 'Sledgehammer' and ask for instructions.

President Roosevelt replied at once that he was not surprised at the disappointing outcome of the London talks. He agreed that it was no use continuing to press for 'Sledgehammer' in the face of British opposition, and instructed his delegation to reach a decision with us on some operation which would involve American land forces being brought into action against the enemy in 1942.

Thus 'Sledgehammer' fell by the wayside and 'Gymnast' came into its own. Marshall and King, though naturally disappointed, bowed to the decision of their Commander-in-Chief, and the greatest goodwill between us all again prevailed.

I now hastened to rechristen my favourite. 'Gymnast', 'Super-Gymnast', and 'Semi-Gymnast' vanished from our code-names. On July 24 in an instruction from me to the Chiefs of Staff 'Torch' became the new and master term. On July 25 the President cabled to Hopkins that plans for landing in North Africa to take place 'not later than October 30' should go ahead at once. That evening our friends set off on their journey back to Washington.

*   *   *

All was therefore agreed and settled in accordance with my long-conceived ideas and those of my colleagues, military and political. This was a great joy to me, especially as it came in what seemed to be the darkest hour. At every point except one the plans I cherished were adopted. 'Jupiter' alone (the Norway enterprise) I could not carry, although its merits were not disputed. I did not give up this plan yet, but in the end I failed to establish it. For months past I had sought 'No "Sledgehammer",' but instead the North African invasion *and* 'Jupiter'. 'Jupiter' fell by the way.

But I had enough to be thankful for.

*   *   *

Former Naval Person to President Roosevelt   27 July 42

I was sure you would be as pleased as I am, indeed as we all are here, at the results of this strenuous week. Besides reaching complete agreement on action, relations of cordial intimacy and comradeship have been cemented between our high officers. I doubt if success would have been achieved without Harry's invaluable aid.

2. We must establish a second front this year and attack at the earliest moment. As I see it this second front consists of a main body holding the enemy pinned opposite 'Sledgehammer' and a wide flanking movement called 'Torch' (hitherto called 'Gymnast'). Now that everything is decided we can, as you say, go full steam ahead. All depends on secrecy and speed and on having a regular schedule of political and military action. Every hour counts, and I agree with you that October 30 is the latest date which should be accepted.

3. Secrecy can only be maintained by deception. For this purpose I am running 'Jupiter', and we must also work up 'Sledgehammer' with the utmost vigour. These will cover all movements in the United Kingdom. When your troops start for 'Torch' everyone except the secret circles should believe that they are going to Suez or Basra, thus explaining tropical kit. The Canadian Army here will be fitted for Arctic service. Thus we shall be able to keep the enemy in doubt till the last moment.

4. Meanwhile I hope 'Bolero' processes will continue at full blast, subject only to any necessary impingement upon them made by 'Torch', which impingement eventuates only in a certain delay. Thus we shall be able to strike left-handed, right-handed, or both-handed.

The President was as pleased as I was to find such complete agreement between all the experts upon what we had both long cherished.

President to Prime Minister   28 July 42

The Three Musketeers arrived safely this afternoon, and the wedding is still scheduled. I am of course very happy in the result, and especially in the successful meeting of minds. I cannot help feeling that the past week represented a turning-point in the whole war and that now we are on our way shoulder to shoulder. I agree with you that secrecy and speed are vital, and I hope the October date can be advanced. I will talk with Marshall in regard to scale of supplies and equipment in terms of tonnage and in terms of the U.K. importations of food and raw materials. Also I will do my best to get the air squadrons on the Russian southern flank. I fully agree that this should be done.

The commanders had now to be settled.

Field-Marshal Dill to Prime Minister   30 July 42

I would urge that you should at once clear the question of command with the President. I feel myself that Marshall is the man for the job, and I believe he would accept. Equally clearly he cannot be spared from here at present; but Eisenhower could well act with his authority. President has not yet approached Marshall on this question. This may be due to President's fear of losing him, but the Eisenhower deputy idea may be welcome.

If this were agreed, then Eisenhower would be able to collect his Combined Staff and really function. In doing this it would be wise if Eisenhower were to delegate the planning and preparations for 'Sledgehammer' to someone else, obviously a Britisher, so that Eisenhower with his own staff could be free, apart from a general supervision of 'Sledgehammer' to concentrate entirely on 'Torch'. Surely 'Torch' is what matters now above all else, and 'Torch' requires much detailed planning, and the allotment of forces and tasks and training and what not. It will require furious work from now till its launching, and the sooner it can be launched clearly the better.

May I express my admiration for the way in which you have steered these difficult negotiations to so successful a conclusion. I hope to be in London early next week, when I would like, if I may, to come and see you.

About the commands I telegraphed to the President.

Former Naval Person to President   31 July 42

I should be grateful for a decision about the command of 'Bolero', 'Sledgehammer', 'Round-up', and 'Torch'. [This meant the 'Bolero', 'Sledgehammer', and 'Round-up' group and 'Torch'.] It would be agreeable to us if General Marshall were designated for the Supreme Command of 'Round-up', and that in the meanwhile General Eisenhower should act as his deputy here. We would appoint General Alexander as Task Force Commander in the first instance, to work with and under General Eisenhower. Both these men would work at 'Torch', and General Eisenhower would also for the time being supervise the 'Bolero'–'Sledgehammer' business. He will thus be able to draw for 'Torch' the necessary forces with the least injury to 'Bolero' and 'Round-up'. As soon as 'Torch' has taken shape he would command it, with Alexander and an American commander as Task Force Commanders of the two forces, starting from United Kingdom and United States. When this party starts out to do the job we should be glad if you would nominate either General Marshall or another

[as] *locum tenens* to carry forward the work of 'Bolero', 'Sledgehammer', and 'Round-up'. We will supply him also with a deputy.

2. It seems important to act quickly, as committtees are too numerous and too slow. If you prefer other arrangements pray let me know your wishes.

Field-Marshall Dill to Prime Minister   1 Aug 42

The President has gone Hyde Park for short rest, but before going he issued orders for full steam ahead 'Torch' at the earliest possible moment. He has asked Combined Chiefs of Staff to tell him on August 4 earliest date when landing could take place. Risk of whittling to Pacific may still exist, but President entirely sound on this point.

In the American mind 'Round-up' in 1943 is excluded by acceptance of 'Torch'. We need not argue about that. A one-track mind on 'Torch' is what we want at present, and I conclude you would accept Marshall for this command if the President so desired, and not stipulate that he should be reserved for 'Round-up', in spite of what you say in your telegram to President of July 31.

3. May what you are at have the success which courage and imagination deserve.

This message reached me at midnight on the Lyneham Airfield, where I was about to set forth upon a journey of which the next chapter will offer both explanation and account.

CHAPTER 3

My Journey to Cairo. Changes in Command

The doubts I had about the High Command in the Middle East were fed continually by the reports which I received from many quarters. It became urgently necessary for me to go there and settle the decisive questions on the spot. It was at first accepted that this journey would be by Gibraltar and Takoradi and thence across Central Africa to Cairo, involving five or even six days' flying. As this would carry me through tropical and malarious regions, a whole series of protective injections was prescribed. Some of these would take ten days to give their immunity, and involved considerable discomfort and even inactivity meanwhile. Several members of the War Cabinet also took a very close and friendly interest in my health, and became an opposing factor to be reasoned with.

However, at this juncture there arrived in England a young American pilot, Captain Vanderkloot, who had just flown from the United States in the aeroplane 'Commando', a Liberator plane from which the bomb-racks had been removed and some sort of passenger accommodation substituted. This machine was certainly capable of flying along the route prescribed with good margins in hand at all stages. Portal, the Chief of the Air Staff, saw this pilot and cross-examined him about 'Commando'. Vanderkloot, who had already flown about a million miles, asked why it was necessary to fly all round by Takoradi, Kano, Fort Lamy, El Obeid, etc. He said he could make one bound from Gibraltar to Cairo, flying from Gibraltar eastwards in the afternoon, turning sharply south across Spanish or Vichy territory as dusk fell, and then proceeding eastward till he struck the Nile about Assiout, when a turn to the northwards would bring us in another hour or so to the Cairo landing-ground north-west of the Pyramids. This altered the whole picture. I could be in Cairo in two days without any trouble about Central African bugs and the inoculations against them. Portal was convinced.

We were all anxious about the reaction of the Soviet Government to the unpleasant though inevitable news that there would be no crossing of the Channel in 1942. It happened that on the night of July 28 I had the honour of entertaining the King to dinner with the War Cabinet in the propped-up garden-room at Number 10, which we used for dining. I obtained His Majesty's approval privately for my journey, and immediately he had gone brought the Ministers, who were in a good frame of mind, into the Cabinet Room and clinched matters. It was settled that I should go to Cairo in any case, and should propose to Stalin that I should go on to see him. I therefore telegraphed to him as follows:

Prime Minister to Premier Stalin   30 July 42
We are making preliminary arrangements for another effort to run a large convoy through to Archangel in the first week of September.

2. I am willing, if you invite me, to come myself to meet you in Astrakhan, the Caucasus, or similar convenient meeting-place. We could then survey the war together and take decisions hand-in-hand. I could then tell you plans we have made with President Roosevelt for offensive action in 1942. I would bring the Chief of the Imperial General Staff with me.

3. I am starting for Cairo forthwith. I have serious business there, as you may imagine. From there I will, if you desire it, fix a convenient date for our meeting, which might, so far as I am concerned, be between August 10 and 13, all being well.

4. The War Cabinet have endorsed my proposals.

Premier Stalin to Premier Churchill   31 July 42

On behalf of the Soviet Government I invite you to the
U.S.S.R. to meet the members of the Government. I should
be very grateful if you could come to the U.S.S.R. to consider jointly the urgent questions of war against Hitler, as the
menace from these quarters to Great Britain, the United
States of America, and the U.S.S.R. has now reached a special
degree of intensity.

I think the most suitable meeting-place would be Moscow, as neither I nor the members of the Government and
the leading men of the General Staff could leave the capital
at the moment of such an intense struggle against the Germans.

The presence of the Chief of the Imperial General Staff
would be extremely desirable.

The date of the meeting please fix yourself in accordance
with the time necessary for completion of your business in
Cairo. You may be sure beforehand that any date will suit
me.

Let me express my gratitude for your consent to send the
next convoy with war materials for the U.S.S.R. at the beginning of September. In spite of the extreme difficulty of diverting aircraft from the battle-front we will take all possible
measures to increase the aerial protection of the convoy.

Prime Minister to Premier Stalin   1 Aug 42

I will certainly come to Moscow to meet you, and will fix
the date from Cairo.

*   *   *

Meanwhile the battle on the Alamein position centring on
the Ruweisat Ridge continued, and seemed to hang in the
balance, although in fact by this time the energy of Rommel's
thrust required replenishment and our defence was more than
holding its own. Plans were now made for me to fly to Cairo,
and I cabled to General Auchinleck accordingly:

31 July 42

I hope to arrive in Cairo on Monday, August 3. The
C.I.G.S. should arrive by a different route on the same day.
I have asked Field-Marshal Smuts and General Wavell to try
to come there during the same week. Let nothing take your
eye off the ball.

General Brooke, the Chief of the Imperial General Staff was
already at Gibraltar flying to Cairo via Malta. I cabled to him
as follows:

1 Aug 42

How necessary it is for us to get to the Middle East at once is shown by the following extract from Auchinleck's telegram received yesterday:

'An exhaustive conference on tactical situation held yesterday with Corps Commanders. Owing to lack of resources and enemy's effective consolidation of his positions we reluctantly concluded that in present circumstances it is not feasible to renew our efforts to break enemy front or turn his southern flank. It is unlikely that an opportunity will arise for resumption of offensive operations before mid-September. This depends on enemy's ability to build up his tank force. Temporarily therefore our policy will be defensive, including thorough preparations and consolidations in whole defensive area. In the meantime we shall seize at once any opportunity of taking the offensive suddenly and surprising the enemy. . . .'

It had been arranged that Sir Alexander Cadogan should come with me to represent the Foreign Office. We started after midnight on Sunday, August 2, from Lyneham in the bomber 'Commando'. This was a very different kind of travel from the comforts of the Boeing flying-boats. The bomber was at this time unheated, and razor-edged draughts cut in through many chinks. There were no beds, but two shelves in the after cabin enabled me and Sir Charles Wilson, my doctor, to lie down. There were plenty of blankets for all. We flew low over the South of England in order to be recognised by our batteries, who had been warned, but who were also under 'Alert' conditions. As we got out to sea I left the cockpit and retired to rest, fortified by a good sleeping cachet.

We reached Gibraltar uneventfully on the morning of August 3, spent the day looking round the fortress, and started at 6 p.m. for Cairo, a hop of 2,000 miles or more, as the détours necessary to avoid the hostile aircraft around the Desert battle were considerable. Vanderkloot, in order to have more petrol in hand, did not continue down the Mediterranean till darkness fell, but flew straight across the Spanish zone and the Vichy quasi-hostile territory. Therefore, as we had an armed escort till nightfall of four Beaufighters we in fact openly violated the neutrality of both these regions. No one molested us in the air, and we did not come within cannon-shot of any important town. All the same I was glad when darkness cast her shroud over the harsh landscape and we could retire to such sleeping

42

accommodation as 'Commando' could offer. It would have been very tiresome to make a forced landing on neutral territory, and even descent in the desert, though preferable, would have raised problems of its own. However, all 'Commando's' four engines purred happily, and I slept sound as we sailed through the starlit night.

It was my practice on these journeys to sit in the co-pilot's seat before sunrise, and when I reached it on this morning of August 4 there in the pale, glimmering dawn the endless winding silver ribbon of the Nile stretched joyously before us. Often had I seen the day break on the Nile. In war and peace I had traversed by land or water almost its whole length, except the 'Dongola Loop', from Lake Victoria to the sea. Never had the glint of daylight on its waters been so welcome to me.

Now for a short spell I became 'the man on the spot'. Instead of sitting at home waiting for the news from the front I could send it myself. This was exhilarating.

*   *   *

The following issues had to be settled in Cairo. Had General Auchinleck or his staff lost the confidence of the Desert Army? If so, should he be relieved, and who could succeed him? In dealing with a commander of the highest character and quality, of proved ability and resolution, such decisions are painful. In order to fortify my own judgment I had urged General Smuts to come from South Africa to the scene, and he was already at the Embassy when I arrived. We spent the morning together, and I told him all our troubles and the choices that were open. In the afternoon I had a long talk with Auchinleck, who explained the military position very clearly. The next morning at his request I saw General Corbett, of whom the Commander-in-Chief had a very high opinion. He told me that Auchinleck was anxious to lay down the command of the Eighth Army at the earliest moment and return to his wider sphere in Cairo. He then surprised me by saying, 'I am to succeed him in command of the Army. In fact I have been living with my kit packed for the last week.' This arrangement had certainly not been considered by us. After luncheon General Wavell arrived from India, and at six o'clock I held a meeting about the Middle East, attended by all the authorities—Smuts, Casey, the C.I.G.S., Wavell, Auchinleck, Admiral Harwood, and Tedder for the Air. We did a lot of business with a very great measure of agreement. But all the time my mind kept turning to the prime question of the command.

It is not possible to deal with changes of this character without reviewing the alternatives. In this part of the problem the Chief of the Imperial General Staff, whose duty it was to appraise the quality of our generals, was my adviser. I first offered the Middle East Command to him. General Brooke would of course have greatly liked this high operational appointment, and I knew that no man would fill it better. He thought it over, and had a long talk the next morning with General Smuts. Finally he replied that he had been C.I.G.S. for only eight months, he believed he had my full confidence, and the Staff machine was working very smoothly. Another change at this moment might cause a temporary dislocation at this critical time. It may well be also that out of motives of delicacy he did not wish to be responsible for advising General Auchinleck's supersession and then taking the post himself. His reputation stood too high for such imputations; but I had now to look elsewhere.

Alexander and Montgomery had both fought with him in the battle which enabled us to get back to Dunkirk in May 1940. We both greatly admired Alexander's magnificent conduct in the hopeless campaign to which he had been committed in Burma. Montgomery's reputation stood high. If it were decided to relieve Auchinleck we had no doubt that Alexander must be ordered to carry the load in the Middle East. But the feelings of the Eighth Army must not be overlooked. Might it not be taken as a reproach upon them and all their commanders of every grade if two men were sent from England to supersede all those who had fought in the desert? Here General Gott seemed in every way to meet the need. The troops were devoted to him and he had not earned the title 'Strafer' by nothing. But then there was the view which Brooke reported to me, that he was very tired and needed a rest. It was at this moment too early to take decisions. I had travelled all this way to have the chance of seeing and hearing what was possible in the short time which might be claimed and spared.

*   *   *

The hospitality of Sir Miles Lampson was princely. I slept in his air-cooled bedroom and worked in his air-cooled study. It was intensely hot, and those were the only two rooms in the

house where the temperature was comfortable. In these otherwise agreeable surroundings we dwelt for more than a week,
sensing the atmosphere, hearing opinions, and visiting the front
or the large camps to the east of Cairo in the Kassassin area,
where our powerful reinforcements were now steadily arriving.

On August 5 I visited the Alamein positions. I drove with
General Auchinleck in his car to the extreme right flank of the
line west of El Ruweisat, which was held by the Australian 9th
Division. Thence we proceeded along the front to his headquarters behind the Ruweisat Ridge, where we were given
breakfast in a wire-netted cube, full of flies and important
military personages. I had asked for various officers to be
brought, but above all General 'Strafer' Gott. It was said that
he was worn down with his hard service. This was what I wanted
to find out. Having made the acquaintance of the various Corps
and Divisional Commanders who were present, I therefore
asked that General Gott should drive with me to the airfield,
which was my next stop. Objection was raised by one of Auchinleck's staff officers that this would take him an hour out of
his way ; but I insisted he should come with me. And here was
my first and last meeting with Gott. As we rumbled and jolted
over the rough tracks I looked into his clear blue eyes and
questioned him about himself. Was he tired, and had he any
views to give? Gott said that no doubt he was tired, and that he
would like nothing better than three months' leave in England,
which he had not seen for several years, but he declared himself
quite capable of further immediate efforts and of taking any
responsibilities confided to him. We parted at the airfield at two
o'clock on this afternoon of August 5. By the same hour two
days later he had been killed by the enemy in almost the very
air spaces through which I now flew.

At the airfield I was handed over to Air Vice-Marshal Coningham, who, under Tedder, commanded all the air-power which
had worked with the Army, and without whose activity the
immense retreat of five hundred miles could never have been
accomplished without even greater disasters than we had suffered. We flew in a quarter of an hour to his headquarters,
where luncheon was provided, and where all the leading Air
officers, from Group Captains upwards, were gathered. I was
conscious of an air of nervousness in my hosts from the moment
of my arrival. The food had all been ordered from Shepheard's
Hotel. A special car was bringing down the dainties of Cairo.

But it had gone astray. Frantic efforts were being made to find it. At last it arrived.

This turned out to be a gay occasion in the midst of care—a real oasis in a very large desert. It was not difficult to perceive how critical the Air was of the Army, and how both Air and Army were astonished at the reverse which had befallen our superior forces. In the evening I flew back to Cairo, and sent the following:

Prime Minister to Deputy Prime Minister   5 Aug 42

Just returned from a long but invigorating day with Eighth Army, visiting Alamein and Ruweisat and seeing South African and Australian troops, interviewing Generals Morshead, Ramsden, and Gott, spending morning with Auchinleck and afternoon with Tedder, Coningham, and the Royal Air Force. Troops were very cheerful, and all seem confident and proud of themselves, but bewildered at having been baulked of victory on repeated occasions. I propose to visit all the formations, both forward and rear, while pondering on the recommendations I shall have to make to the Cabinet.

2. I am discussing the whole situation with Smuts, who is a fount of wisdom. Wherever the fault may lie for the serious situation which exists, it is certainly not with the troops, and only to a minor extent with their equipment.

3. I am purposely keeping my future movements vague. I am very glad the House was contented with the statement. This change and open air are doing me a great deal of good.

All the next day, the 6th, I spent with Brooke and Smuts, and in drafting the necessary telegrams to the Cabinet. The questions that had now to be settled not only affected the high personalities, but also the entire structure of command in this vast theatre. I had always felt that the name 'Middle East' for Egypt, the Levant, Syria, and Turkey was ill-chosen. This was the Near East. Persia and Iraq were the Middle East; India, Burma, and Malaya the East; and China and Japan the Far East. But, far more important than changing names, I felt it necessary to divide the existing Middle East Command, which was far too diverse and expansive. Now was the time to effect this change in organisation.

Prime Minister to Deputy Prime Minister   6 Aug 42, 8.15 p.m.

As a result of such inquiry as I have made here, and after prolonged consultations with Field-Marshal Smuts and C.I.G.S. and Minister of State, I have come to the conclusion that a drastic and immediate change is needed in the High Command.

2. I therefore propose that the Middle East Command shall be reorganised into two separate Commands, namely:

    (*a*) 'Near East Command', comprising Egypt, Palestine, and Syria, with its centre in Cairo, and

    (*b*) 'Middle East Command', comprising Persia and Iraq, with its centre in Basra or Baghdad.

The Eighth and Ninth Armies fall within the first and the Tenth Army in the second of these Commands.

3. General Auchinleck to be offered the post of C.-in-C. the new Middle East Command. The title remains the same, but its scope is reduced. It may however become more important later. It also preserves General Auchinleck's association with India. It must be remembered that General Wavell's appointment as C.-in-C. India was for the duration of the war, and that the India Office have always desired that Auchinleck should return there if possible. I know of nothing that should prevent the eventual realisation of this plan, though of course no promise can be made in respect of events which are unforeseeable.

4. General Alexander to be Commander-in-Chief the Near East.

5. General Montgomery to succeed Alexander in 'Torch'. I regret the need of moving Alexander from 'Torch', but Montgomery is in every way qualified to succeed [him in that].

6. General Gott to command the Eighth Army under Alexander.

7. General Corbett to be relieved as C.G.S. Near East.

8. General Ramsden to be relieved as G.O.C. XXXth Corps.

9. General Dorman-Smith to be relieved as Deputy C.G.S.*

10. It will be necessary to find two Corps Commanders for the Eighth Army in the place of Gott and Ramsden. We have ideas for both these posts, but it would be better for the C.I.G.S. to discuss these and a number of junior changes which require to be made with Gott and Alexander when the last-named arrives. . . .

---

* The references to the Officers whose names figure in this list are factual only. Neither they nor my later remarks are to be taken as imputing personal blame to any individual. These were the principal changes in Commands and Staff at the time when General Auchinleck was replaced by General Alexander.

Major-General Dorman-Smith only became Deputy Chief of Staff on June 16, 1942. He thus bears no responsibility for the fall of Tobruk or the defeats at Gazala. From June 25 to August 4 he acted as General Auchinleck's Principal Operations Officer at Headquarters Eighth Army during the operation described in Chapter 1. My appreciation in that Chapter of the handling of the Eighth Army is supported by Rommel's remarkable tribute.

12. The above constitute the major simultaneous changes which the gravity and urgency of the situation here require. I shall be grateful to my War Cabinet colleagues if they will approve them. Smuts and C.I.G.S. wish me to say they are in full agreement that amid many difficulties and alternatives this is the right course to pursue. The Minister of State is also in full agreement. I have no doubt the changes will impart a new and vigorous impulse to the Army and restore confidence in the Command, which I regret does not exist at the present time. Here I must emphasise the need of a new start and vehement action to animate the whole of this vast but baffled and somewhat unhinged organisation. The War Cabinet will not fail to realise that a victory over Rommel in August or September may have a decisive effect upon the attitude of the French in North Africa when 'Torch' begins.

13. I hope I may receive Cabinet approval at the earliest possible moment, and that Alexander will start forthwith. It is necessary that he should reach here before I and the C.I.G.S. start for Russia. This I hope to do Sunday or Monday. The changes should become effective from Monday, and public announcements must follow at the earliest moment compatible with the interests of the fighting front. Meanwhile the utmost secrecy must be observed.

The War Cabinet accepted my view about drastic and immediate changes in the High Command. They warmly approved the selection of General Alexander, and said that he would leave England at once. They did not however like the idea of reorganising the Middle East Command into two separate Commands. It seemed to them that the reasons which led to the setting up of the Unified Command were now stronger than they had been when the decision to do so was taken in December 1941. They agreed that Montgomery should take Alexander's place in 'Torch', and had summoned him to London at once. They were content to leave it to me to settle the other appointments.

Prime Minister to Deputy Prime Minister   6/7 Aug 42

Our proposal to divide the Command is made entirely on merits. I doubt if the disasters would have occurred in the Western Desert if General Auchinleck had not been distracted by the divergent considerations of a too widely extended front. ... He would have taken direct command of the battle which began at the end of May but for reluctance to become 'immersed in tactical problems in Libya'. This phrase in itself reveals the false proportion engendered by extraneous responsibilities. It is in fact the 'tactical problems of Libya' which dominate our immediate affairs.

The two Commands are separated by desert areas of three or four hundred miles, and the only lateral communications between them are by the railway through Turkey, which we cannot use for the passage of troops, by motor tracks across the desert, and by sea voyage round Arabia taking nearly fourteen days. Both Commands have entirely different bases of supply. . . . We are all convinced that the arrangement now proposed is sound on geographical, strategic, and administrative grounds. . . . Only the need of making an abrupt and decisive change in the command against Rommel and giving the Army the sense of a new start has induced me to propose the redistribution of Commands. I should be most reluctant to embarrass Alexander with remote cares at a moment when all our fortunes turn upon the speedy and decisive defeat of Rommel.

I earnestly hope that my colleagues will find themselves able on further consideration of this most difficult problem to authorise me to proceed as I propose. In all this I have the complete agreement of Smuts and C.I.G.S. A decision has now become most urgent, since Alexander has already started and Auchinleck has of course no inkling of what is in prospect. I must apprise him to-morrow.

I am most grateful for the agreement of the Cabinet to the other parts of my plan, grave though they be.

The War Cabinet replied that my telegram had not entirely removed their misgivings, but that as I was on the spot with Smuts and the C.I.G.S., who both agreed with the proposal, they were prepared to authorise the action proposed. They strongly represented however that the continuance of the title of Commander-in-Chief Middle East if General Auchinleck were appointed to command in Persia and Iraq would lead to confusion. I saw this was right and accepted their advice.

*   *   *

I spent all August 7 visiting the 51st Scottish Division, who had just landed. As I went up the stairs after dinner at the Embassy I met Colonel Jacob. 'This is bad about Gott,' he said. 'What has happened?' 'He was shot down this afternoon flying into Cairo.' I certainly felt grief and impoverishment at the loss of this splendid soldier, to whom I had resolved to confide the most direct fighting task in the impending battle. All my plans were dislocated. The removal of Auchinleck from the

Supreme Command was to have been balanced by the appointment to the Eighth Army of Gott, with all his Desert experience and prestige, and the whole covered by Alexander's assumption of the Middle East. What was to happen now?

Prime Minister to Deputy Prime Minister   7 Aug 42
    Deeply regret Gott has just been shot down in the air and killed.

There could be no doubt who his successor should be.

Prime Minister to Deputy Prime Minister
    C.I.G.S. decisively recommends Montgomery for Eighth Army. Smuts and I feel this post must be filled at once. Pray send him by special plane at earliest moment. Advise me when he will arrive.

It appeared that the War Cabinet had already assembled at 11.15 p.m. on August 7 to deal with my telegrams of that day, which had just been decoded. Discussion was still proceeding upon them when a secretary came in with my new messages, stating that Gott was dead, and secondly asking that General Montgomery should be sent out at once. I have been told this was an acute moment for our friends in Downing Street. However, as I have several times observed, they had been through much and took it doggedly. They sat till nearly dawn, agreed in all essentials to what I had proposed, and gave the necessary orders about Montgomery.

*   *   *

When sending my message to the Cabinet telling them of Gott's death I had asked that General Eisenhower should not be told that we had proposed to give him Montgomery in place of Alexander. But this was too late: he had been told already. The further change of plan involved a consequent dislocation of a vexatious kind in the preparation of 'Torch'. Alexander had been chosen to command the British First Army in that great enterprise. He had already started to work with General Eisenhower. They were getting on splendidly together, as they always did. Now Alexander had been taken from him for the Middle East. Ismay was sent to convey the news and my apologies to Eisenhower for this break in continuity and disturbance of contacts which the hard necessity of war compelled. Ismay dilated upon Montgomery's brilliant qualities as a commander in the field. Montgomery arrived at Eisenhower's headquarters almost immediately, and all the civilities of a meeting of this kind between the commanders of armies of different nations woven into a single enterprise had been discharged. The very next morning, the 8th, Eisenhower had to be informed that Montgomery must fly that day to Cairo to command the Eighth Army. This task also fell to Ismay. Eisenhower was a broad-minded man, practical, serviceable, dealing with events as they came in cool selflessness. He naturally however felt disconcerted by the two changes in two days in this vital post in the vast operation confided to him. He was now to welcome a third British Commander. Can we wonder that he asked Ismay, 'Are the British really taking "Torch" seriously?' Nevertheless the death of Gott was a war fact which a good soldier understood. General Anderson was appointed to fill the vacancy, and Montgomery started for the airfield with Ismay, who thus had an hour or more to give him the background of these sudden changes.

A story—alas, not authenticated—has been told of this conversation. Montgomery spoke of the trials and hazards of a soldier's career. He gave his whole life to his profession, and lived long years of study and self-restraint. Presently fortune smiled, there came a gleam of success, he gained advancement, opportunity presented itself, he had a great command. He won a victory, he became world-famous, his name was on every lip. Then the luck changed. At one stroke all his life's work flashed away, perhaps through no fault of his own, and he was flung into the endless catalogue of military failures. 'But,' expostulated Ismay, 'you ought not to take it so badly as all that. A very fine army is gathering in the Middle East. It may well be that you are not going to disaster.' 'What!' cried Montgomery, sitting up in the car. 'What do you mean? I was talking about Rommel!'

*   *   *

I spent the 8th with the Yeomanry Division. These fine troops, hitherto wasted and never yet effectively engaged with the enemy, were camped along the Kassassin road. For two years they had served in the Middle East, mainly in Palestine, and I had not been able to have them equipped and worked up to the high quality of which they were capable. At last they had reached the back of the front and were to go into action. Now, at this moment in their career, it had been necessary to take all their tanks from them in order to feed and rearm the fighting line. This was a staggering blow for these eager men. It was my task to go from brigade to brigade and explain to all the officers gathered together, two or three hundred at a time, why they must suffer this mutilation after all their zeal and toil. But I had good news as well. The 300 Shermans were already approaching through the Red Sea, and in a fortnight the division would begin to be armed with the most powerful armoured vehicles current at that time. I told them the story of my morning with the President and General Marshall on the morrow of Tobruk; how these Shermans had been longed and thirsted for by the 1st United States Armoured Division, and how they had been taken from them almost as soon as they had been issued in order to give us a chance—or perhaps I said the certainty—of saving Alexandria, Cairo, and Egypt from conquest. They would have the Shermans. They would become the leading armoured unit in the world. I think they were consoled by this.

I clattered back on the long road to Cairo, and reached the city before 5 p.m.

* * *

I now had to inform General Auchinleck that he was to be relieved of his command, and, having learned from past experience that that kind of unpleasant thing is better done by writing than orally, I sent Colonel Jacob by air to his headquarters with the following letter:

CAIRO
August 8, 1942

Dear General Auchinleck,
    On June 23 you raised in your telegram to the C.I.G.S. the question of your being relieved in this Command, and you mentioned the name of General Alexander as a possible successor. At that time of crisis for the Army His Majesty's Government did not wish to avail themselves of your high-minded offer. At the same time you had taken over the effective command of the battle, as I had long desired and had suggested to you in my telegram of May 20. You stemmed the adverse tide, and at the present time the front is stabilised.
    2. The War Cabinet have now decided, for the reasons which you yourself had used, that the moment has come for a change. It is proposed to detach Iraq and Persia from the present Middle Eastern Theatre. Alexander will be appointed to command the Middle East, Montgomery to command the Eighth Army, and I offer you the command of Iraq and Persia,

including the Tenth Army, with headquarters at Basra or Baghdad. It is true that this sphere is to-day smaller than the Middle East, but it may in a few months become the scene of decisive operations, and reinforcements for the Tenth Army are already on the way. In this theatre, of which you have special experience, you will preserve your associations with India. I hope therefore that you will comply with my wish and directions with the same disinterested public spirit that you have shown on all occasions. Alexander will arrive almost immediately, and I hope that early next week, subject of course to the movements of the enemy, it may be possible to effect the transfer of responsibility on the Western battlefront with the utmost smoothness and efficiency.

3. I shall be very glad to see you at any convenient time if you should so desire.

> Believe me,
> Yours sincerely,
> WINSTON S. CHURCHILL

PS. Colonel Jacob, who bears this letter, is also charged by me to express my sympathy in the sudden loss of General Gott.

I kept the President fully informed.

Former Naval Person to President Roosevelt   8 Aug 42
You will no doubt have seen the cables sent by the British Chiefs of Staff, London, to the combined Chiefs of Staff, Washington, about accelerating the date of 'Torch'. I am sure that nothing is more vital than this, and that superhuman efforts should be made. Every day counts. I have already telegraphed to London welcoming the appointment of General Eisenhower as Allied Commander-in-Chief for 'Torch', and the British Chiefs are co-operating with him to the full. . . .
I have been busy here with a reorganisation of the High Command which was necessary. I am detaching Iraq and Persia from the Middle East Command and transferring General Auchinleck there. Alexander will succeed him as Commander-in-Chief Middle East, General Gott, who was to have been appointed to command Eighth Army under Alexander, was killed yesterday. I propose to appoint General Montgomery in his place. This will promote the utmost concentration upon the battle. A victory here might have a decisive effect upon the attitude of the French towards 'Torch'.

In the evening Jacob returned. Auchinleck had received this stroke with soldierly dignity. He was unwilling to accept the new command, and would come to see me the next day.

Jacob's diary records:

The Prime Minister was asleep. He awoke at six o'clock, and I had to recount to him as best I could what had passed between me and General Auchinleck. C.I.G.S. joined us. . . . The Prime Minister's mind is entirely fixed on the defeat of Rommel, and on getting General Alexander into complete charge of the operations in the Western Desert. He does not understand how a man can remain in Cairo while great events are occurring in the Desert and leave the conduct of them to someone else. He strode up and down declaiming on this point, and he means to have his way. 'Rommel, Rommel, Rommel, Rommel!' he cried. 'What else matters but beating him?'

On the morning of August 9 General Alexander arrived, and breakfasted with the C.I.G.S. and me.

General Auchinleck reached Cairo just after midday, and we had an hour's conversation, which was at once bleak and impeccable.

I telegraphed accordingly:

Prime Minister to General Ismay   10 Aug 42
... General Auchinleck is disinclined to accept the command of the Iraq–Persia theatre. ... As however I am convinced that he is the best man for the job, I have given him a few more days to consider the matter further. I shall not press him unduly, but I am anxious that he should not take his decision while under the immediate effects of the blow, which he has accepted with dignity, but naturally not without distress.

Appropriate military authorities are studying the problem connected with the proposed institution of a separate command for Iraq and Persia and the administrative changes consequent thereupon. I should be glad if at the same time the Chiefs of Staff would also propose the best methods for giving effect to the policy. General Smuts has returned to South Africa, but C.I.G.S. and General Alexander share my conviction that this separation is desirable at the present time. . . .

I wrote further to General Auchinleck the same day:

On my return journey I propose to hold a conference at Baghdad on the 14th or 15th in order to discuss, *inter alia*, the machinery of an independent Command for Iraq and Persia. . . .

By then I should like to know whether you feel able to

undertake the very difficult and serious task which I proposed to you. If, as I trust will be the case, you feel whole-heartedly that you can take your station in the line I hope you will meet me in Baghdad, provided of course that the transference of Command has been effected here.

General Alexander came to see me that evening, and final arrangements for the changes in command were drafted. I reported the details to London:

Prime Minister to General Ismay, for those concerned
10 Aug 42

You should announce at once that General Gott has been killed in action.

2. On the 8th I informed General Auchinleck by letter of the decision which had been reached, and yesterday, 9th, he visited me here. The transfer of responsibility will be effected in three days from the 9th unless General Alexander asks for a few more days, which is unlikely. Alexander will inform you when the transfer is complete, and thereupon you should make an announcement in the following form.

(*a*) General Alexander has assumed command of His Majesty's forces in the Middle East, in succession to General Auchinleck.

(*b*) General Montgomery has been appointed to command the Eighth Army, in succession to General Ritchie.

(*c*) General McCreery has been appointed Chief of Staff to General Alexander.

(*d*) General Lumsden, who has recovered from his wound, has been appointed to the command of the XXXth Corps, vice General Gott, killed in action.

3. While strict secrecy must be observed till General Alexander's report that he has taken over is received, it would seem desirable that the Minister of Information should explain to the newspaper proprietors and/or editors in confidence beforehand what is intended, and impress upon them the importance of giving the Army of the Western Desert the utmost stimulus from these drastic changes in the High Command. Similar action will be taken here by the Minister of State. . . .

7. I have given General Alexander the following directive, which is most agreeable to him, and in which C.I.G.S. concurs:

'1. Your prime and main duty will be to take or destroy at the earliest opportunity the German–Italian Army commanded by Field-Marshal Rommel, together with all its supplies and establishments in Egypt and Libya.

'2. You will discharge or cause to be discharged such

other duties as pertain to your Command, without prejudice to the task described in paragraph 1, which must be
considered paramount in His Majesty's interests.'

It may no doubt be possible in a later phase of the war to alter
the emphasis of this directive, but I am sure that simplicity
of task and singleness of aim are imperative now.

Alexander's reply, sent six months later, will be recorded
in due course.

CHAPTER 4

Moscow

The First Meeting

*My Journey to Moscow – Mr. Harriman Comes with Me –
Over the Mountains to Teheran – The Shah's Summer Palace
– Conference about the Trans-Persian Railway – Teheran to
Moscow – The Caspian and the Volga – Arrival in Moscow –
State Villa Number Seven – Meeting with Stalin in the Kremlin
– A Bleak Opening – 'No Second Front in 1942' – Hard Words –
A Dark Background Created – I Unfold the 'Torch' Plan – I
Draw My Crocodile – 'May God Prosper this Undertaking' –
Stalin's Masterly Comprehension – The End of a Long Day.*

During my stay in Cairo preparations had gone forward for the
journey to Moscow.

On August 4 I had telegraphed to Stalin:

Prime Minister to Premier Stalin   4 Aug 42
 We plan to leave here one day, arriving Moscow the next,
with intermediate stop at Teheran.
 Details will have to be arranged in part by our R.A.F.
authorities in Teheran in consultation with yours. I hope you
may instruct latter to give the benefit of their assistance in
every way.
 I cannot yet give any indication regarding dates beyond
what I have already suggested to you.

I was also anxious that the Americans should play a close
part in the coming talks.

Former Naval Person to President Roosevelt 5 Aug 42
 I should greatly like to have your aid and countenance in
my talks with Joe. Would you be able to let Averell come
with me? I feel that things would be easier if we all seemed
to be together. I have a somewhat raw job. Kindly duplicate
your reply to London. Am keeping my immediate movements
vague.

President to Former Naval Person (Cairo) 5 Aug 42
 I am asking Harriman to leave at earliest possible moment
for Moscow. I think your idea is sound, and I am telling Stalin

Harriman will be at his and your disposal to help in any way. Harriman joined me in Cairo in time to come with us.

*   *   *

Late on the night of August 10, after a dinner of notables at the genial Cairo Embassy, we started for Moscow. My party, which filled three planes, now included the C.I.G.S., General Wavell, who spoke Russian, Air Marshal Tedder, and Sir Alexander Cadogan. Averell Harriman and I travelled together. By dawn we were approaching the mountains of Kurdistan. The weather was good and Vanderkloot in high spirits. As we drew near to these serrated uplands I asked him at what height he intended to fly them. He said nine thousand feet would do. However, looking at the map I found several peaks of eleven and twelve thousand feet, and there seemed one big one of eighteen or twenty thousand, though that was farther off. So long as you are not suddenly encompassed by clouds, you can wind your way through mountains with safety. Still, I asked for twelve thousand feet, and we began sucking our oxygen tubes. As we descended about 8.30 a.m. on the Teheran airfield and were already close to the ground I noticed the altimeter registered four thousand five hundred feet, and ignorantly remarked, 'You had better get that adjusted before we take off again.' But Vanderkloot said, 'The Teheran airfield is over four thousand feet above sea-level.'

Sir Reader Bullard, His Majesty's Minister in Teheran, met me on arrival. He was a tough Briton, with long experience of Persia and no illusions.

We were too late to leap the northern range of the Elburz Mountains before dark, and I found myself graciously bidden to lunch with the Shah in a palace with a lovely swimming pool amid great trees on an abrupt spur of the mountains. The mighty peak I had noticed in the morning gleamed brilliant pink and orange. In the afternoon in the garden of the British Legation there was a long conference with Averell Harriman and various high British and American railway authorities, and it was decided that the United States should take over the whole Trans-Persian railway from the Gulf to the Caspian. This railway, newly completed by a British firm, was a remarkable engineering achievement. There were 390 major bridges on its track through the mountain gorges. Harriman said the President was willing to undertake the entire responsibility for working it to full capacity, and could provide locomotives, rolling-stock, and skilled men in military units to an extent impossible for us. I therefore agreed to this transfer, subject to stipulations about priority for our essential military requirements. On account of the heat and noise of Teheran, where every Persian seems to have a motor-car and blows his horn continually, I slept amid tall trees at the summer residence of the British Legation about a thousand feet above the city.

At 6.30 next morning, Wednesday, August 12, we started, gaining height as we flew through the great valley which led to Tabriz, and then turned northwards to Enzeli, on the Caspian. We passed this second range of mountains at about eleven thousand feet, avoiding both clouds and peaks. Two Russian officers were now in the plane, and the Soviet Government assumed responsibility for our course and safe arrival. The snow-clad giant gleamed to the eastward. I noticed that we were flying alone, and a wireless message explained that our second plane, with the C.I.G.S., Wavell, Cadogan, and others, had had to turn back over Teheran because of engine trouble. In two hours the waters of the Caspian Sea shone ahead. Beneath was Enzeli. I had never seen the Caspian, but I remembered how a quarter of a century before I had, as Secretary of State for War, inherited a fleet upon it which for nearly a year ruled its pale, placid waters. We now came down to a height where oxygen was no longer needed. On the western shore, which we could dimly see, lay Baku and its oil-fields. The German armies were now so near the Caspian that our course was set for Kuibyshev, keeping well away from Stalingrad and the battle area. This took us near the delta of the Volga. As far as the eye could reach spread vast expanses of Russia, brown and flat and with hardly a sign of human habitation. Here and there sharp rectilineal patches of ploughed land revealed an occasional State farm. For a long way the mighty Volga gleamed in curves and stretches as it flowed between its wide, dark margins of marsh. Sometimes a road, straight as a ruler, ran from one wide horizon to the other. After an hour or so of this I clambered back along the bomb bay to the cabin and slept.

I pondered on my mission to this sullen, sinister Bolshevik State I had once tried so hard to strangle at its birth, and which, until Hitler appeared, I had regarded as the mortal foe of civilised freedom. What was it my duty to say to them now?

General Wavell, who had literary inclinations, summed it all up in a poem. There were several verses, and the last line of each was, 'No Second Front in nineteen forty-two.' It was like carrying a large lump of ice to the North Pole. Still, I was sure it was my duty to tell them the facts personally and have it all out face to face with Stalin, rather than trust to telegrams and intermediaries. At least it showed that one cared for their fortunes and understood what their struggle meant to the general war. We had always hated their wicked régime, and, till the German flail beat upon them, they would have watched us being swept out of existence with indifference and gleefully divided with Hitler our Empire in the East.

The weather being clear, the wind favourable, and my need to get to Moscow urgent, it was arranged to cut the corner of Kuibyshev and go on straight to the capital. I fear a splendid banquet and welcome in true Russian hospitality was thus left on one side. At about five o'clock the spires and domes of Moscow came in sight. We circled around the city by carefully prescribed courses along which all the batteries had been warned, and landed on the airfield, which I was to revisit during the struggle.

Here was Molotov at the head of a concourse of Russian generals and the entire Diplomatic Corps, with the very large outfit of photographers and reporters customary on these occasions. A strong guard of honour, faultless in attire and military punctilio, was inspected, and marched past after the band had played the National Anthems of the three Great Powers whose unity spelt Hitler's doom. I was taken to the microphone and made a short speech. Averell Harriman spoke on behalf of the United States. He was to stay at the American Embassy. M. Molotov drove me in his car to my appointed residence, eight miles out of Moscow, 'State Villa No. 7'. While going through the streets of Moscow, which seemed very empty, I lowered the window for a little more air, and to my surprise felt that the glass was over two inches thick. This surpassed all records in my experience. 'The Minister says it is more prudent,' said Interpreter Pavlov. In a little more than half an hour we reached the villa.

* * *

Everything was prepared with totalitarian lavishness. There was placed at my disposal, an aide-de-camp, an enormous, splendid-looking officer (I believe of a princely family under the Czarist régime), who also acted as our host and was a model of courtesy and attention. A number of veteran servants in white jackets and beaming smiles waited on every wish or movement of the guests. A long table in the dining-room and various sideboards were laden with every delicacy and stimulant that supreme power can command. I was conducted through a spacious reception room to a bedroom and bathroom of almost equal size. Blazing, almost dazzling, electric lights displayed the spotless cleanliness. The hot and cold water gushed. I longed for a hot bath after the length and the heat of the journey. All was instantly prepared. I noticed that the basins were not fed by separate hot and cold water taps and that they had no plugs. Hot and cold turned on at once through a single spout, mingled to exactly the temperature one desired. Moreover, one did not wash one's hands in the basins, but under the flowing current of the taps. In a modest way I have adopted this system at home. If there is no scarcity of water it is far the best.

After all necessary immersions and ablutions we were regaled in the dining-room with every form of choice food and liquor, including of course caviare and vodka, but with many other dishes and wines from France and Germany far beyond our mood or consuming powers. Besides, we had but little time before starting for Moscow. I had told Molotov that I should be ready to see Stalin that night, and he proposed seven o'clock.

I reached the Kremlin, and met for the first time the great Revolutionary Chief and profound Russian statesman and warrior with whom for the next three years I was to be in intimate, rigorous, but always exciting, and at times even genial, association. Our conference lasted nearly four hours. As our second aeroplane had not arrived with Brooke, Wavell, and Cadogan, there were present only Stalin, Molotov, Voroshilov, myself, Harriman, and our Ambassador, with interpreters. I have based this account upon the record which we kept, subject to my own memory, and to the telegrams I sent home at the time.

The first two hours were bleak and sombre. I began at once with the question of the Second Front, saying that I wished to speak frankly and would like to invite complete frankness from Stalin. I would not have come to Moscow unless he had felt sure that he would be able to discuss realities. When M.

Molotov had come to London I had told him that we were
trying to make plans for a diversion in France. I had also made
it clear to M. Molotov that I could make no promises about
1942, and had given M. Molotov a memorandum to this effect.
Since then an exhaustive Anglo-American examination of the
problem had been carried out. The British and American
Governments did not feel themselves able to undertake a major
operation in September, which was the latest month in which
the weather was to be counted upon. But, as M. Stalin knew,
they were preparing for a very great operation in 1943. For
this purpose a million American troops were now scheduled to
reach the United Kingdom as their point of assembly in the
spring of 1943, making an expeditionary force of 27 divisions,
to which the British Government were prepared to add 21 divisions. Nearly half of this force would be armoured. So far only
two and a half American divisions had reached the United
Kingdom, but the big transportation would take place in
October, November, and December.

I told Stalin that I was well aware that this plan offered no
help to Russia in 1942, but thought it possible that when the
1943 plan was ready it might well be that the Germans would
have a stronger army in the West than they now had. At this
point Stalin's face crumpled up into a frown, but he did not
interrupt. I then said I had good reasons against an attack on
the French coast in 1942. We had only enough landing-craft for
an assault landing on a fortified coast—enough to throw ashore
six divisions and maintain them. If it were successful, more
divisions might be sent, but the limiting factor was landing-craft,
which were now being built in very large numbers in the United
Kingdom, and especially in the United States. For one division
which could be carried this year it would be possible next year
to carry eight or ten times as many.

Stalin, who had begun to look very glum, seemed uncon-
vinced by my argument, and asked if it was impossible to
attack any part of the French coast. I showed him a map
which indicated the difficulties of making an air umbrella anywhere except actually across the Straits. He did not seem to
understand, and asked some questions about the range of fighter
planes. Could they not, for instance, come and go all the
time? I explained that they could indeed come and go, but at
this range they would have no time to fight, and I added that
an air umbrella to be of any use had to be kept open. He then

said that there was not a single German division in France of any value, a statement which I contested. There were in France twenty-five German divisions, nine of which were of the first line. He shook his head. I said that I had brought the Chief of the Imperial General Staff and General Sir Archibald Wavell with me in order that such points might be examined in detail with the Russian General Staff. There was a point beyond which statesmen could not carry discussions of this kind.

Stalin, whose glumness had by now much increased, said that, as he understood it, we were unable to create a second front with any large force and unwilling even to land six divisions. I said that this was so. We could land six divisions, but the landing of them would be more harmful than helpful, for it would greatly injure the big operation planned for next year. War was war but not folly, and it would be folly to invite a disaster which would help nobody. I said I feared the news I brought was not good news. If by throwing in 150,000 to 200,000 men we could render him aid by drawing away from the Russian front appreciable German forces, we would not shrink from this course on the grounds of loss. But if it drew no men away and spoiled the prospects for 1943 it would be a great error.

Stalin, who had become restless, said that his view about war was different. A man who was not prepared to take risks could not win a war. Why were we so afraid of the Germans? He could not understand. His experience showed that troops must be blooded in battle. If you did not blood your troops you had no idea what their value was. I inquired whether he had ever asked himself why Hitler did not come to England in 1940, when he was at the height of his power and we had only 20,000 trained troops, 200 guns, and 50 tanks. He did not come. The fact was that Hitler was afraid of the operation. It is not so easy to cross the Channel. Stalin replied that this was no analogy. The landing of Hitler in England would have been resisted by the people, whereas in the case of a British landing in France the people would be on the side of the British. I pointed out that it was all the more important therefore not to expose the people of France by a withdrawal to the vengeance of Hitler and to waste them when they would be needed in the big operation in 1943.

There was an oppressive silence. Stalin at length said that if we could not make a landing in France this year he was not entitled to demand it or to insist upon it, but he was bound to say that he did not agree with my arguments.

* * *

I then unfolded a map of Southern Europe, the Mediterranean, and North Africa. What was a 'Second Front'? Was it only a landing on a fortified coast opposite England? Or could it take the form of some other great enterprise which might be useful to the common cause? I thought it better to bring him southward by steps. If, for instance, we could hold the enemy in the Pas de Calais by our concentrations in Britain, and at the same time attack elsewhere—for instance, in the Loire, the Gironde, or alternatively the Scheldt—this was full of promise. There indeed was a general picture of next year's big operation. Stalin feared that it was not practicable. I said that it would indeed be difficult to land a million men, but that we should have to persevere and try.

We then passed on to the bombing of Germany, which gave general satisfaction. M. Stalin emphasised the importance of striking at the morale of the German population. He said he attached the greatest importance to bombing, and that he knew our raids were having a tremendous effect in Germany.

After this interlude, which relieved the tension, Stalin observed that from our long talk it seemed that all we were going to do was no 'Sledgehammer', no 'Round-up', and pay our way by bombing Germany. I decided to get the worst over first and to create a suitable background for the project I had come to unfold. I did not therefore try at once to relieve the gloom. Indeed, I asked specially that there should be the plainest speaking between friends and comrades in peril. However, courtesy and dignity prevailed.

* * *

The moment had now come to bring 'Torch' into action. I said that I wanted to revert to the question of a Second Front in 1942, which was what I had come for. I did not think France was the only place for such an operation. There were other places, and we and the Americans had decided upon another plan, which I was authorised by the American President to impart to Stalin secretly. I would now proceed to do so. I emphasised the vital need of secrecy. At this Stalin sat up and grinned and said that he hoped that nothing about it would appear in the British Press.

I then explained precisely Operation 'Torch'. As I told the whole story Stalin became intensely interested. His first question was what would happen in Spain and Vichy France. A little later on he remarked that the operation was militarily right, but he had political doubts about the effect on France. He asked particularly about the timing, and I said not later than October 30, but the President and all of us were trying to pull it forward to October 7. This seemed a great relief to the three Russians.

I then described the military advantages of freeing the Mediterranean, whence still another front could be opened. In September we must win in Egypt, and in October in North Africa, all the time holding the enemy in Northern France. If we could end the year in possession of North Africa we could threaten the belly of Hitler's Europe, and this operation should be considered in conjunction with the 1943 operation. That was what we and the Americans had decided to do.

To illustrate my point I had meanwhile drawn a picture of a crocodile, and explained to Stalin with the help of this picture how it was our intention to attack the soft belly of the crocodile as we attacked his hard snout. And Stalin, whose interest was now at high pitch, said, 'May God prosper this undertaking.'

I emphasised that we wanted to take the strain off the Russians. If we attempted that in Northern France we should meet with a rebuff. If we tried in North Africa we had a good chance of victory, and then we could help in Europe. If we could gain North Africa Hitler would have to bring his Air Force back, or otherwise we would destroy his allies, even, for instance, Italy, and make a landing. The operation would have an important influence on Turkey and on the whole of Southern Europe, and all I was afraid of was that we might be forestalled. If North Africa were won this year we could make a deadly attack upon Hitler next year. This marked the turning-point in our conversation.

Stalin then began to present various political difficulties. Would not an Anglo-American seizure of 'Torch' regions be misunderstood in France? What were we doing about de Gaulle? I said that at this stage we did not wish him to intervene in the operation. The [Vichy] French were likely to fire on de

Gaullists but unlikely to fire on Americans. Harriman backed this very strongly by referring to reports, on which the President relied, by American agents all over 'Torch' territories, and also to Admiral Leahy's opinion.

*   *   *

At this point Stalin seemed suddenly to grasp the strategic advantages of 'Torch'. He recounted four main reasons for it: first, it would hit Rommel in the back; second, it would over-awe Spain; third, it would produce fighting between Germans and Frenchmen in France; and, fourth, it would expose Italy to the whole brunt of the war.

I was deeply impressed with this remarkable statement. It showed the Russian Dictator's swift and complete mastery of a problem hitherto novel to him. Very few people alive could have comprehended in so few minutes the reasons which we had all so long been wrestling with for months. He saw it all in a flash.

I mentioned a fifth reason, namely, the shortening of the sea route through the Mediterranean. Stalin was concerned to know whether we were able to pass through the Straits of Gibraltar. I said it would be all right. I also told him about the change in the command in Egypt, and of our determination to fight a decisive battle there in late August or September. Finally, it was clear that they all liked 'Torch', though Molotov asked whether it could not be in September.

I then added, 'France is down and we want to cheer her up.' France had understood Madagascar and Syria. The arrival of the Americans would send the French nation over to our side. It would intimidate Franco. The Germans might well say at once to the French, 'Give us your Fleet and Toulon.' This would stir anew the antagonisms between Vichy and Hitler.

I then opened the prospect of our placing an Anglo-American Air Force on the southern flank of the Russian armies in order to defend the Caspian and the Caucasian mountains and generally to fight in this theatre. I did not however go into details, as of course we had to win our battle in Egypt first, and I had not the President's plans for the American contribution. If Stalin liked the idea we would set to work in detail upon it. He replied that they would be most grateful for this aid, but that the details of location, etc., would require study. I was very keen on this project, because it would bring about more hard fighting between the Anglo-American air-power and the Germans, all of which aided the gaining of mastery in the air under more fertile conditions than looking for trouble over the Pas de Calais.

We then gathered round a large globe, and I explained to Stalin the immense advantages of clearing the enemy out of the Mediterranean. I told Stalin I should be available should he wish to see me again. He replied that the Russian custom was that the visitor should state his wishes and that he was ready to receive me at any time. He now knew the worst, and yet we parted in an atmosphere of goodwill.

The meeting had now lasted nearly four hours. It took half an hour or more to reach State Villa No. 7. Tired as I was, I dictated my telegram to the War Cabinet and the President after midnight, and then, with the feeling that at least the ice was broken and a human contact established, I slept soundly and long.

Moscow

A Relationship Established

Late the next morning I awoke in my luxurious quarters. It was Thursday, August 13—to me always 'Blenheim Day'. I had arranged to visit M. Molotov in the Kremlin at noon in order to explain to him more clearly and fully the character of the various operations we had in mind. I pointed out how injurious to the common cause it would be if owing to recriminations about dropping 'Sledgehammer' we were forced to argue publicly against such enterprises. I also explained in more detail the political setting of 'Torch'. He listened affably, but contributed nothing. I proposed to him that I should see Stalin at 10 p.m. that night, and later in the day got word that eleven o'clock would be more convenient, and as the subjects to be dealt with would be the same as those of the night before would I wish to bring Harriman? I said 'Yes,' and also Cadogan, Brooke, Wavell, and Tedder, who had meanwhile arrived safely from Teheran in a Russian plane. They might have had a very dangerous fire in their Liberator.

Before leaving this urbane rigid diplomatist's room I turned to him and said, 'Stalin will make a great mistake to treat us roughly when we have come so far.' For the first time Molotov unbent. 'Stalin,' he said, 'is a very wise man. You may be sure that, however he argues, he understands all. I will tell him what you say.'

I returned in time for luncheon to State Villa Number Seven.

*   *   *

Out of doors the weather was beautiful. It was just like what we love most in England—when we get it. I thought we would explore the domain. State Villa Number Seven was a fine large, brand-new country house standing in its own extensive lawns and gardens in a fir wood of about twenty acres. There were agreeable walks, and it was pleasant in the beautiful August weather to lie on the grass or pine-needles. There were several fountains, and a large glass tank filled with many kinds of goldfish who were all so tame that they would eat out of your hand. I made a point of feeding them every day. Around the whole was a stockade, perhaps fifteen feet high, guarded on both sides by police and soldiers in considerable numbers. About a hundred yards from the house was an air-raid shelter. At the first opportunity we were conducted over it. It was of the latest and most luxurious type. Lifts at either end took you down eighty or ninety feet into the ground. Here were eight or ten large rooms inside a concrete box of massive thickness. The rooms were divided from each other by heavy sliding doors. The lights were brilliant. The furniture was stylish 'Utility', sumptuous and brightly coloured. I was more attracted by the goldfish.

*   *   *

We all repaired to the Kremlin at 11 p.m., and were received only by Stalin and Molotov, with their interpreter. Then began a most unpleasant discussion. Stalin handed me a document. When it was translated I said I would answer it in writing, and that he must understand we had made up our minds upon the course to be pursued and that reproaches were vain. Thereafter we argued for about two hours, during which he said a great many disagreeable things, especially about our being too much afraid of fighting the Germans, and if we tried it like the Russians we should find it not so bad ; that we had broken our promise about 'Sledgehammer'; that we had failed in delivering the supplies promised to Russia and only sent remnants after we had taken all we needed for ourselves. Apparently these complaints were addressed as much to the United States as to Britain.

I repulsed all his contentions squarely, but without taunts of any kind. I suppose he is not used to being contradicted repeatedly, but he did not become at all angry, or even animated. He reiterated his view that it should be possible for the British and Americans to land six or eight divisions on the Cherbourg peninsula, since they had domination of the air. He felt that if the British Army had been fighting the Germans as much as the Russian Army it would not be so frightened of them. The Russians, and indeed the R.A.F., had shown that it was possible to beat the Germans. The British infantry could do the same provided they acted at the same time as the Russians.

I interposed that I pardoned the remarks which Stalin had made on account of the bravery of the Russian Army. The proposal for a landing in Cherbourg overlooked the existence of the Channel. Finally Stalin said we could carry it no further. He must accept our decision. He then abruptly invited us to dinner at eight o'clock the next night.

Accepting the invitation, I said I would leave by plane at dawn the following morning—*i.e.*, the 15th. Joe seemed somewhat concerned at this, and asked could I not stay longer. I said certainly, if there was any good to be done, and that I would wait one more day anyhow. I then exclaimed that there was no ring of comradeship in his attitude. I had travelled far to establish good working relations. We had done our utmost to help Russia, and would continue to do so. We had been left entirely alone for a year against Germany and Italy. Now that the three great nations were allied, victory was certain, provided we did not fall apart, and so forth. I was somewhat animated in this passage, and before it could be translated he made the remark that he liked the tone of my utterance. Thereafter the talk began again in a somewhat less tense atmosphere.

He plunged into a long discussion of two Russian trench mortars firing rockets, which he declared were devastating in their effects, and which he offered to demonstrate to our experts if they could wait. He said he would let us have all information about them, but should there not be something in return? Should there not be an agreement to exchange information about inventions? I said that we would give them everything without any bargaining, except only those devices which, if carried in aeroplanes over the enemy lines and shot down, would make our bombing of Germany more difficult. He accepted this. He also agreed that his military authorities should meet our generals, and this was arranged for three o'clock in the afternoon. I said they would require at least four hours to go fully into the various technical questions involved in 'Sledgehammer', 'Round-up', and 'Torch'. He observed at one moment that 'Torch' was 'militarily correct', but that the political side required more delicacy—*i.e.*, more careful handling. From time to time he returned to 'Sledgehammer', grumbling about it. When he said our promise had not been kept I replied, 'I repudiate that statement. Every promise has been kept,' and I pointed to the *aide-mémoire* I gave Molotov. He made a sort of apology, saying that he was expressing his sincere and honest opinions, that there was no mistrust between us, but only a difference of view.

Finally I asked about the Caucasus. Was he going to defend the mountain chain, and with how many divisions? At this he sent for a relief model, and, with apparent frankness and evident knowledge, explained the strength of this barrier, for which he said twenty-five divisions were available. He pointed to the various passes and said they would be defended. I asked were they fortified, and he said, 'Yes, certainly.' The Russian front line, which the enemy had not yet reached, was north of the main range. He said they would have to hold out for two months, when the snow would make the mountains impassable. He declared himself quite confident of their ability to do this, and also recounted in detail the strength of the Black Sea Fleet, which was gathered at Batum.

All this part of the talk was easier, but when Harriman asked about the plans for bringing American aircraft across Siberia, to which the Russians had only recently consented after long American pressing, he replied, curtly, 'Wars are not won with plans.' Harriman backed me up throughout, and we neither of us yielded an inch nor spoke a bitter word.

Stalin made his salute and held out his hand to me on leaving, and I took it.

* * *

I reported to the War Cabinet on August 14:

We asked ourselves what was the explanation of this performance and transformation from the good ground we had reached the night before. I think the most probable is that his Council of Commissars did not take the news I brought as well as he did. They may have more power than we suppose, and less knowledge. Perhaps he was putting himself on the record for future purposes and for their benefit, and also letting off steam for his own. Cadogan says a similar hardening up followed the opening of the Eden interview at Christmas, and Harriman says that this technique was also used at the beginning of the Beaverbrook mission.

It is my considered opinion that in his heart, so far as he has one, Stalin knows we are right, and that six divisions on 'Sledgehammer' would do him no good this year. Moreover, I am certain that his surefooted and quick military judgment makes him a strong supporter of 'Torch'. I think it not impossible that he will make amends. In that hope I persevere. Anyhow, I am sure it was better to have it out this way than any other. There was never at any time the slightest suggestion of their not fighting on, and I think myself that Stalin has good confidence that he will win.

When I thanked Stalin for the forty Boston aircraft he made a half-disdainful gesture, saying, 'They are American planes. When I give you Russian planes then you may thank me.' By this he did not mean to disparage the American planes, but said that he counted on his own strength.

I make great allowances for the stresses through which they are passing. Finally, I think they want full publicity for the visit.

* * *

The following was the *aide-mémoire* which Stalin had handed me :

13 Aug 42

As a result of an exchange of views in Moscow which took place on August 12 of this year, I ascertained that the Prime Minister of Great Britain, Mr. Churchill, considered the organisation of a Second Front in Europe in 1942 to be impossible. As is well known, the organisation of a Second Front in Europe in 1942 was pre-decided during the sojourn of Molotov in London, and it found expression in the agreed Anglo-Soviet communiqué published on June 12 last. It is also known that the organisation of a Second Front in Europe has as its object the withdrawal of German forces from the Eastern Front to the West and the creation in the West of a serious base of resistance to the German-Fascist forces, and the affording of relief by this means to the situation of the

Soviet forces on the Soviet-German front in 1942. It is easy to grasp that the refusal of the Government of Great Britain to create a Second Front in 1942 in Europe inflicts a mortal blow to the whole of Soviet public opinion, which calculates on the creation of a Second Front, and that it complicates the situation of the Red Army at the front and prejudices the plan of the Soviet command. I am not referring to the fact that the difficulties arising for the Red Army as a result of the refusal to create a Second Front in 1942 will undoubtedly be detrimental to the military situation of England and all the remaining Allies. It appears to me *and my colleagues** that the most favourable conditions exist in 1942 for the creation of a Second Front in Europe, inasmuch as almost all the forces of the German Army, and the best forces to boot, have been withdrawn to the Eastern Front, leaving Europe an inconsiderable amount of forces, and these of inferior quality. It is unknown whether the year of 1943 will offer conditions for the creation of a Second Front as favourable as 1942.

We are of opinion therefore that it is particularly in 1942 that the creation of a Second Front in Europe is possible and should be effective. I was however unfortunately unsuccessful in convincing Mr. Prime Minister of Great Britain thereof, while Mr. Harriman, the representative of the President of the United States, fully supported Mr. Prime Minister in the negotiations held in Moscow.

The next morning, August 14, having rested well, I prepared, with the aid of the C.I.G.S. and Cadogan, the following reply, which seemed to me suitable and conclusive:

The best Second Front in 1942 and the only large-scale operation possible from the Atlantic is 'Torch'. If this can be effected in October it will give more aid to Russia than any other plan. It also prepares the way for 1943, and has the four advantages mentioned by Premier Stalin in the conversation of August 12. The British and United States Governments have made up their minds about this, and all preparations are proceeding with the utmost speed.

2. Compared with 'Torch', the attack with six or eight Anglo-American divisions on the Cherbourg peninsula and the Channel Islands would be a hazardous and futile operation. The Germans have enough troops in the West to block us in this narrow peninsula with fortified lines, and would concentrate all their air forces in the West upon us. In the opinion of all the British naval, military, and air authorities, the operation could only end in disaster. Even if the lodgment

* My italics.—W. S. C.

were made it would not bring a single division back from Russia. It would also be far more a running sore for us than for the enemy, and would use up wastefully and wantonly the key men and the landing-craft required for real action in 1943. This is our settled view. The C.I.G.S. will go into details with the Russian commanders to any extent that may be desired.

3. No promise has been broken by Great Britain or the United States. I point to paragraph 5 of my *aide-mémoire* given to Mr. Molotov on June 10, 1942, which distinctly says, 'We can therefore give no promise.' This *aide-mémoire* followed upon lengthy conversations, in which the very small chance of such a plan being adopted was made abundantly clear. Several of these conversations are on record.

4. However, all the talk about an Anglo-American invasion of France this year has misled the enemy, and has held large air forces and considerable military forces on the French Channel coast. It would be injurious to all common interests, especially Russian interests, if any public controversy arose in which it would be necessary for the British Government to unfold to the nation the crushing arguments which they conceive themselves to possess against 'Sledgehammer'. Widespread discouragement would be caused to the Russian armies, who have been buoyed up on this subject, and the enemy would be free to withdraw further forces from the West. The wisest course is to use 'Sledgehammer' as a blind for 'Torch', and proclaim 'Torch' when it begins as the Second Front. This is what we ourselves mean to do.

5. We cannot admit that the conversations with M. Molotov about the Second Front, safeguarded as they were by reservations both oral and written, formed any ground for altering the strategic plans of the Russian High Command.

6. We reaffirm our resolve to aid our Russian Allies by every practicable means.

*   *   *

That evening we attended the official dinner at the Kremlin, where about forty people, including several of the military commanders, members of the Politburo, and other high officials were present. Stalin and Molotov did the honours in cordial fashion. These dinners were lengthy, and from the beginning many toasts were proposed and responded to in very short speeches. Silly tales have been told of how these Soviet dinners became drinking-bouts. There is no truth whatever in this. The Marshal and his colleagues invariably drank their toasts from tiny glasses, taking only a sip on each occasion. I had been well brought up.

During the dinner Stalin talked to me in lively fashion through the interpreter Pavlov. 'Some years ago,' he said, 'we had a visit from Mr. George Bernard Shaw and Lady Astor.' Lady Astor suggested that Mr. Lloyd George should be invited to visit Moscow, to which Stalin had replied, 'Why should we ask him? He was the head of the intervention.' On this Lady Astor said, 'That is not true. It was Churchill who misled him.' 'Anyhow,' said Stalin, 'Lloyd George was head of the Government and belonged to the Left. He was responsible, and we like a downright enemy better than a pretending friend.' 'Well, Churchill is finished finally,' said Lady Astor. 'I am not so sure,' Stalin had answered. 'If a great crisis comes the English people might turn to the old war-horse.' At this point I interrupted, saying. 'There is much in what she said. I was very active in the intervention, and I do not wish you to think otherwise.' He smiled amicably, so I said, 'Have you forgiven me?' 'Premier Stalin, he say,' said Interpreter Pavlov, 'all that is in the past, and the past belongs to God.'

*   *   *

In the course of one of my later talks with Stalin I said, 'Lord Beaverbrook has told me that when he was on his mission to Moscow in October 1941 you asked him, "What did Churchill mean by saying in Parliament that he had given me warnings of the impending German attack?" I was of course,' said I, 'referring to the telegram I sent you in April '41,' and I produced the telegram which Sir Stafford Cripps had tardily delivered. When it was read and translated to him Stalin shrugged his shoulders. 'I remember it. I did not need any warnings. I knew war would come, but I thought I might gain another six months or so.' In the common cause I refrained from asking what would have happened to us all if we had gone down for ever while he was giving Hitler so much valuable material, time, and aid.

*   *   *

As soon as I could I gave a more formal account of the banquet to Mr. Attlee and the President.

Former Naval Person to Deputy Prime Minister and the President   17 Aug 42
The dinner passed off in a very friendly atmosphere and

the usual Russian ceremonies. Wavell made an excellent speech in Russian. I proposed Stalin's health, and Alexander Cadogan proposed death and damnation to the Nazis. Though I sat on Stalin's right I got no opportunity of talking about serious things. Stalin and I were photographed together, also with Harriman. Stalin made quite a long speech proposing the 'Intelligence Service', in the course of which he made a curious reference to the Dardanelles in 1915, saying that the British had won and the Germans and Turks were already retreating, but we did not know because the intelligence was faulty. This picture, though inaccurate, was evidently meant to be complimentary to me.

2. I left about 1.30 a.m., as I was afraid we should be drawn into a lengthy film and was fatigued. When I said good-bye to Stalin he said that any differences that existed were only of method. I said we would try to remove even those differences by deeds. After a cordial handshake I then took my departure, and got some way down the crowded room, but he hurried after me and accompanied me an immense distance through corridors and staircases to the front door, where we again shook hands.

3. Perhaps in my account to you of the Thursday night meeting I took too gloomy a view. I feel I must make full allowance for the really grievous disappointment which they feel here that we can do nothing more to help them in their immense struggle. In the upshot they have swallowed this bitter pill. Everything for us now turns on hastening 'Torch' and defeating Rommel.

*   *   *

It had been agreed between Stalin and me that there should also be meetings between the high military authorities on both sides. Two conferences were held on August 15.

I reported the results to Mr. Attlee and the President as follows:

At a conference in Moscow on Saturday [August 15] Voroshilov and Shaposhnikov* met Brooke, Wavell, and Tedder, who offered detailed reasons about no 'Sledge-hammer'. No impression was made, as the Russians, though entirely good-humoured, were acting under strict instructions. They did not even attempt to argue the matter in serious detail. After some time C.I.G.S. asked for details about the Caucasus position, to which Voroshilov replied he had no authority to speak on this point, but would ask for it.

* The Russian Chief of Staff.

Accordingly, in the afternoon a second meeting was held, at which the Russians repeated what Stalin had said to us, to the effect that twenty-five divisions would be assigned to the defence of the Caucasus mountain line and the passages at either end, and that they believed they could hold both Batum and Baku and the Caucasus range until the winter snows greatly improved their position. However, C.I.G.S. is by no means reassured. For instance, Voroshilov stated that all the passes were fortified, but when C.I.G.S. had flown at 150 feet all up the west bank of the Caspian he only saw the northern line of defence being begun with anti-tank obstacles, pill-boxes, etc. In my private conversation with Stalin he revealed to me other solid reasons for his confidence, including a counter-offensive on a great scale, but as he asked me to keep this specially secret I will not refer to it further here. My own feeling is that it is an even chance they will hold, but C.I.G.S. will not go so far as this.

*   *   *

I had been offended by many things which had been said at our conferences. I made every allowance for the strain under which the Soviet leaders lay, with their vast front flaming and bleeding along nearly 2,000 miles, and the Germans but fifty miles from Moscow and advancing towards the Caspian Sea. The technical military discussions had not gone well. Our generals had asked all sorts of questions to which their Soviet colleagues were not authorised to give answers. The only Soviet demand was for 'A Second Front NOW'. In the end Brooke was rather blunt, and the military conference came to a somewhat abrupt conclusion.

We were to start at dawn on the 16th. On the evening before I went at seven o'clock to say good-bye to Stalin. We had a useful and important talk. I asked particularly whether he would be able to hold the Caucasus mountain passes, and also prevent the Germans reaching the Caspian, taking the oilfields round Baku, with all that meant, and then driving southwards through Turkey or Persia. He spread out the map, and then said with quiet confidence, 'We shall stop them. They will not cross the mountains.' He added, 'There are rumours that the Turks will attack us in Turkestan. If they do I shall be able to deal with them as well.' I said there was no danger of this. The Turks meant to keep out, and would certainly not quarrel with England.

Our hour's conversation drew to its close and I got up to say good-bye. Stalin seemed suddenly embarrassed, and said in a more cordial tone than he had yet used with me, 'You are leaving at daybreak. Why should we not go to my house and have some drinks?' I said that I was in principle always in favour of such a policy. So he led the way through many passages and rooms till we came out into a roadway still within the Kremlin, and in a couple of hundred yards gained the apartment where he lived. He showed me his own rooms, which were of moderate size, simple, dignified, and four in number—a dining-room, working room, bedroom, and a large bathroom. Presently there appeared, first a very aged housekeeper and later a handsome red-haired girl, who kissed her father dutifully. He looked at me with a twinkle in his eye, as if, so I thought, to convey, 'You see, even we Bolsheviks have family life.' Stalin's daughter started laying the table, and in a short time the housekeeper appeared with a few dishes. Meanwhile Stalin had been uncorking various bottles, which began to make an imposing array. Then he said, 'Why should we not have Molotov? He is worrying about the communiqué. We could settle it here. There is one thing about Molotov—he can drink.' I then realised that there was to be a dinner. I had planned to dine at State Villa Number Seven, where General Anders, the Polish commander, was awaiting me, but I told my new and excellent interpreter, Major Birse, to telephone that I should not be back till after midnight. Presently Molotov arrived. We sat down, and, with two interpreters, were five in number. Major Birse has lived twenty years in Moscow, and got on very well with the Marshal, with whom he for some time kept up a running conversation, in which I could not share.

We actually sat at this table from 8.30 p.m. till 2.30 the next morning, which, with my previous interview, made a total of more than seven hours. The dinner was evidently improvised on the spur of the moment, but gradually more and more food arrived. We pecked and picked, as seemed to be the Russian fashion, at a long succession of choice dishes, and sipped a variety of excellent wines. Molotov assumed his most affable manner, and Stalin, to make things go, chaffed him unmercifully.

Presently we talked about the convoys to Russia. This led him to make a rough and rude remark about the almost total destruction of the Arctic convoy in June. I have recounted this incident in its place. I did not know so much about it then as I do now.

'Mr. Stalin asks,' said Pavlov, with some hesitation, 'has the British Navy no sense of glory?' I answered, 'You must take it from me that what was done was right. I really do know a lot about the Navy and sea-war.' 'Meaning,' said Stalin, 'that I know nothing.' 'Russia is a land animal,' I said; 'the British are sea animals.' He fell silent and recovered his good-humour. I turned the talk on to Molotov. 'Was the Marshal aware that his Foreign Secretary on his recent visit to Washington had said he was determined to pay a visit to New York entirely by himself, and that the delay in his return was not due to any defect in the aeroplane, but because he was off on his own?'

Although almost anything can be said in fun at a Russian dinner, Molotov looked rather serious at this. But Stalin's face lit with merriment as he said:

'It was not to New York he went. He went to Chicago, where the other gangsters live.'

Relations having thus been entirely restored, the talk ran on. I opened the question of a British landing in Norway with Russian support, and explained how, if we could take the North Cape in the winter and destroy the Germans there the path of the convoys would henceforward be open. This idea was always, as has been seen, one of my favourite plans. Stalin seemed much attracted by it, and, after talking of ways and means, we agreed we must do it if possible.

*　　*　　*

It was now past midnight, and Cadogan had not appeared with the draft of the communiqué.

'Tell me,' I asked, 'have the stresses of this war been as bad to you personally as carrying through the policy of the Collective Farms?'

This subject immediately roused the Marshal.

'Oh, no,' he said, 'the Collective Farm policy was a terrible struggle.'

'I thought you would have found it bad,' said I, 'because you were not dealing with a few score thousands of aristocrats or big landowners, but with millions of small men.'

'Ten millions,' he said, holding up his hands. 'It was fearful. Four years it lasted. It was absolutely necessary for Russia, if we were to avoid periodic famines, to plough the land with tractors. We must mechanise our agriculture. When we gave tractors to the peasants they were all spoiled in a few months. Only Collective Farms with workshops could handle tractors. We took the greatest trouble to explain it to the peasants. It was no use arguing with them. After you have said all you can to a peasant he says he must go home and consult his wife, and he must consult his herder.' This last was a new expression to me in this connection.

'After he has talked it over with them he always answers that he does not want the Collective Farm and he would rather do without the tractors.'

'These were what you call Kulaks?'

'Yes,' he said, but he did not repeat the word. After a pause, 'It was all very bad and difficult—but necessary.'

'What happened?' I asked.

'Oh, well,' he said, 'many of them agreed to come in with us. Some of them were given land of their own to cultivate in the province of Tomsk or the province of Irkutsk or farther north, but the great bulk were very unpopular and were wiped out by their labourers.'

There was a considerable pause. Then, 'Not only have we vastly increased the food supply, but we have improved the quality of the grain beyond all measure. All kinds of grain used to be grown. Now no one is allowed to sow any but the standard Soviet grain from one end of our country to the other. If they do they are severely dealt with. This means another large increase in the food supply.'

I record as they come back to me these memories, and the strong impression I sustained at the moment of millions of men and women being blotted out or displaced for ever. A generation would no doubt come to whom their miseries were unknown, but it would be sure of having more to eat and bless Stalin's name. I did not repeat Burke's dictum, 'If I cannot have reform without injustice, I will not have reform.' With the World War going on all round us it seemed vain to moralise aloud.

About 1 a.m. Cadogan arrived with the draft, and we set to work to put it into final form. A considerable sucking-pig was brought to the table. Hitherto Stalin had only tasted the dishes, but now it was half-past one in the morning and around his usual dinner hour. He invited Cadogan to join him in the conflict, and when my friend excused himself our host fell upon the victim single-handed. After this had been achieved he went abruptly into the next room to receive the reports from all sectors of the front, which were delivered to him from 2 a.m. onwards. It was about twenty minutes before he returned, and by that time we had the communiqué agreed. Finally, at 2.30 a.m. I said I must go. I had half an hour to drive to the villa, and as long to drive back to the airport. I had a splitting headache, which for me was very unusual. I still had General Anders to see. I begged Molotov not to come and see me off at dawn, for he was clearly tired out. He looked at me reproachfully, as if to say, 'Do you really think I would fail to be there?'

The following was the published text of the communiqué.

Prime Minister of Great Britain, Mr. Winston Churchill, with the President of the Council of the People's Commissars of U.S.S.R., J. V. Stalin

Negotiations have taken place in Moscow between President of the Council of the People's Commissars of U.S.S.R., J. V. Stalin, and Prime Minister of Great Britain, Mr. Winston Churchill, in which Mr. Harriman, representing the President of the United States of America, participated. There took part in the discussions the People's Commissars for Foreign Affairs, V. M. Molotov, Marshal K. E. Voroshilov, from the Soviet side ; the British Ambassador, Sir A. Clark Kerr, C.I.G.S. Sir A. Brooke, and other responsible representatives of the British armed forces, and the Permanent Under-Secretary of State for Foreign Affairs, Sir A. Cadogan, from the British side.

A number of decisions were reached covering the field of the war against Hitlerite Germany and her associates in Europe. This just war of liberation both Governments are determined to carry on with all their power and energy until the complete destruction of Hitlerism and any similar tyranny has been achieved. The discussions, which were carried on in an atmosphere of cordiality and complete sincerity, provided an opportunity of reaffirming the existence of the close friendship and understanding between the Soviet Union, Great Britain, and the United States of America, in entire accordance with the Allied relationships existing between them.

*   *   *

We took off at 5.30 a.m. I was very glad to sleep in the plane, and I remember nothing of the landscape or journey till we reached the foot of the Caspian and began to climb over the Elburz Mountains. At Teheran I did not go to the Legation, but to the cool, quiet glades of the summer residence, high above the city. Here a great press of telegrams awaited me. I had planned a conference for the next day at Baghdad with most of our high authorities in Persia and Iraq, but I did not feel I could face the heat of Baghdad in the August noonday, and it was quite easy to change the venue to Cairo. I dined with the Legation party that night in the agreeable woodland, and was content to forget all cares till morning.

From Teheran I sent a message to Stalin:

Prime Minister to Premier Stalin   16 Aug 42

On arriving at Teheran after a swift and smooth flight I take occasion to thank you for your comradeship and hospitality. I am very glad I came to Moscow, firstly because it was my duty to tell the tale, and secondly because I feel sure our contacts will play a helpful part in furthering our cause. Give my regards to Molotov.

I also reported to the War Cabinet and the President.

16/17 Aug 42

I went to wind up with M. Stalin at 7 p.m. yesterday, and we had an agreeable conversation, in the course of which he gave me a full account of the Russian position, which seemed very encouraging. He certainly speaks with great confidence of being able to hold out until the winter. At 8.30 p.m., when I got up to leave, he asked when was the next time he was going to see me. I said that I was leaving at dawn. He then said, 'Why do not you come over to my apartment in the Kremlin and have some drinks?' I went, and stayed to dinner, to which M. Molotov was also summoned. M. Stalin introduced me to his daughter, a nice girl, who kissed him shyly, but was not allowed to dine. The dinner and the communiqué lasted till 3 a.m. this morning. I had a very good interpreter and was able to talk much more easily. The greatest goodwill prevailed, and for the first time we got on to easy and friendly terms. I feel that I have established a personal relationship which will be helpful. We talked a great deal about 'Jupiter', which he thinks essential in November or December. Without it I really do not see how we are going to be able to get through the supplies which will be needed to keep this tremendous fighting army equipped. The Trans-Persian route is only working at half what we hoped. What he requires most of all are lorries. He would rather have lorries than tanks, of which he is making 2,000 a month. Also he wants aluminium.

'On the whole,' I ended, 'I am definitely encouraged by my

visit to Moscow. I am sure that the disappointing news I brought could not have been imparted except by me personally without leading to really serious drifting apart. It was my duty to go. Now they know the worst, and having made their protest are entirely friendly ; this in spite of the fact that this is their most anxious and agonising time. Moreover, Stalin is entirely convinced of the great advantages of "Torch", and I do trust that it is being driven forward with superhuman energy on both sides of the ocean.'

CHAPTER 6

Return to Cairo

A Message from the King – Operation 'Pedestal' to Save Malta – A Fierce Battle – A Hard-Bought but Decisive Victory – Malta Recovers Dominance in the Central Mediterranean – Gort Comes to Cairo – Crisis in India – Decision to Arrest Gandhi and Others – Chiang Kai-shek's Intrusion – Correspondence with the President – Order Easily Maintained – The Attack on Dieppe – Heroic Efforts and Heavy Losses – A Reconnaissance in Force – Valuable Lessons – Air Support for the Soviet Southern Flank – The Transference of the Persian Railway to United States Management – Gift to Australia to Replace the 'Canberra' – Another Visit to the Desert Front, August 19 – Alexander and Montgomery in Command – Impending Attack by Rommel – Importance of Preserving the Eighth Army's Manœuvring Independence – A Survey of the Prospective Battlefield – At Bernard Freyberg's New Zealand Division Headquarters – My Report to the War Cabinet of August 21 – Final Days in Cairo – Stern Measures to Defend the Line of the Nile – Home by Air.

On my return to Cairo I received congratulations from the King.

> *His Majesty the King to Prime Minister*   17 Aug 42
>
> I am delighted that your talks with Stalin ended on such a friendly note. As a bearer of unwelcome news your task was a very disagreeable one, but I congratulate you heartily on the skill with which you accomplished it. The personal relationship which you have established with Stalin should be valuable in the days to come ; and your long journey has, I am sure, been well worth while.
>
> I hope that you are not too tired, and that you will be able to take things more easily now.
>
> My best wishes for a safe and comfortable journey home when your business is completed.

I replied on the following day:

Prime Minister to the King   18 Aug 42

Mr. Churchill, with his humble duty to Your Majesty, has been much encouraged by Your Majesty's most gracious message.

2. Mr. Churchill hopes to deal with a number of important and urgent problems here during the present week. He is in the best of health and not at all tired. Your Majesty is always so kind, and these fresh marks of your confidence are most agreeable.

*   *   *

I also heard from General Smuts.

General Smuts to Prime Minister   19 Aug 42

I have read your Moscow messages with deepest interest, and congratulate you on a really great achievement. Your handling of a critical psychological situation was masterly, and final effect on my mind is that you have achieved even more than you appear to realise and have firmly and finally bound Russia to us for this war at least. The quarrelsome interlude was evidently a clumsy attempt by Stalin to save appearances for himself while really accepting 'Torch' as a better plan than 'Sledgehammer'. Your introduction of air assistance for Caucasus was a shrewd point, and well worth pursuing with Roosevelt. I must say after reading your account of talks I feel much happier about Russia than I had felt before. There appears now to be a good prospect of Hitler having to spend another winter in Russian mud, while we clear Mediterranean basin and establish a firm base for Second Front next year. For the moment all depends on Alexander's success, and on 'Torch' being undertaken as soon as possible consistent with firm prospect of success. We dare not fail with this venture, on which so much depends for our victory.

After your recent Herculean labours I implore you to relax. You cannot continue at the present pace. Please follow Charles Wilson's advice, as you expect nation to follow yours.

*   *   *

During my visit to Moscow several affairs of high importance in which I was deeply interested had reached their climax. The disappointments of the June convoys to Malta showed that only large-scale and speedy relief could save the fortress. The suspension of the North Russian convoys after the disaster in July enabled the Admiralty to draw heavily upon the Home Fleet.

Admiral Syfret in the *Nelson*, with the *Rodney*, three large carriers, seven cruisers, and thirty-two destroyers, entered the Mediterranean on August 9 for Operation 'Pedestal'. The *Furious* was added to fly aircraft into Malta. The enemy had meanwhile strengthened his air forces in Sardinia and Sicily.

On August 11 Admiral Syfret's fleet, escorting fourteen fast merchant ships loaded with supplies, was off Algiers. The carrier *Eagle* was sunk by a U-boat, but the *Furious* successfully flew off her Spitfires to Malta. The next day the expected air attacks began. One merchant ship and a destroyer were sunk, and the carrier *Indomitable* damaged. Thirty-nine enemy aircraft and an Italian U-boat were destroyed. On approaching the Narrows that evening Admiral Syfret with the battleships withdrew according to plan, leaving Rear-Admiral Burrough to continue with the convoy. The night that followed brought a crescendo of attacks by U-boats and E-boats, and by morning seven merchant ships had been lost, as well as the cruisers *Manchester* and *Cairo*. Two other cruisers and three of the merchant ships, including the American tanker *Ohio*, whose cargo was vital, were damaged.

Undaunted, the survivors held on for Malta. Daylight on the 13th brought a renewal of the air attacks. The *Ohio* was hit again and stopped, as well as another merchant ship. By now the remnants of the convoy were within supporting distance of the Malta defences, and that evening three ships, the *Port Chalmers, Melbourne Star,* and *Rochester Castle,* at last entered the Grand Harbour. Valiant efforts were now being made to bring in the three cripples still afloat. The *Brisbane Star* arrived successfully the next day, and on the 15th, the *Ohio*, in tow and growing ever more unmanageable under ceaseless air attack, was at last brought triumphantly into port. Thus in the end five gallant merchant ships out of fourteen got through with their precious cargoes. The loss of three hundred and fifty officers and men and of so many of the finest ships in the Merchant Navy and in the escorting fleet of the Royal Navy was grievous. The reward justified the price exacted. Revictualled and replenished with ammunition and vital stores, the strength of Malta revived. British submarines returned to the island, and, with the striking forces of the Royal Air Force, regained their dominating position in the Central Mediterranean.

It should have been within the enemy's power, as it was clearly his interest, to destroy this convoy utterly. Two Italian cruiser squadrons sailed to intercept it on the morning of the 13th south of Pantelleria, when it was already heavily damaged and dispersed. They needed strong air support to enable them to operate so close to Malta, and here the effects of Admiral Vian's earlier action in March against the Italian Fleet bore fruit. Unwilling again to co-operate with the Italian Navy, the German air forces insisted on attacking alone. A heated controversy arose at headquarters, and a German admiral records that an appeal was made to Mussolini, on whose intervention the cruisers were withdrawn before they got to the Sicilian Narrows. Two of them were torpedoed by British submarines while returning to harbour. The German continues: 'A more useless waste of fighting power cannot be imagined. The British operation, in spite of all the losses, was not a defeat, but a strategical failure of the first order by the Axis, the repercussions of which will one day be felt.'

On August 17 I telegraphed:

Prime Minister to First Lord and First Sea Lord   17 Aug 42
Please convey my compliments to Admirals Syfret, Burrough, and Lyster and all officers and men engaged in the magnificent crash through of supplies to Malta, which cannot fail to have an important influence on the immediate future of the war in the Mediterranean.

2. Papers here report thirteen enemy aircraft shot down, but this was only by the Malta force, and I have seen no mention of the thirty-nine additional shot down by the carriers, which puts a very different complexion on the air fighting.

The safe arrival of the convoy enabled me to invite Lord Gort to Cairo. I greatly desired to hear all about Malta from him. Gort and his aide-de-camp, Lord Munster (who was a Minister when the war began, but insisted on going to the front), arrived safely. They were both very thin and looked rather haggard. The General and his staff had made a point of sharing rigorously the starvation rations of the garrison and civil population. They were cautiously re-nourished at the Embassy. We had long talks, and when we parted I had the Malta picture clearly in my mind.

*   *   *

During my absence from London a crisis had arisen in India. The Congress Party committed themselves to an aggressive

policy taking the form of sabotage of railways and of fomenting riots and disorder. Mob violence became rampant over
large tracts of the countryside. This threatened to jeopardise
the whole war effort of India in face of the Japanese invasion
menace. The Viceroy's Council, upon which there was only one
Englishman, proposed unanimously to arrest and intern Gandhi,
Nehru, and the principal members of the Congress Party. The
War Cabinet, advised by their Committee on India, immediately
endorsed this drastic policy. When the news of the arrests was
published Generalissimo Chiang Kai-shek, at that time regarded
in the United States as the supreme champion of Asiatic freedom, sent voluminous protests to the President, which he forwarded to me. I resented this Chinese intervention. 'The
Government of India,' I wrote to the President, 'have no doubt
of their ability to maintain order and carry on government
with efficiency, and secure India's maximum contribution to the
war, whatever the Indian Congress may say or do, provided of
course that their authority is not undermined.' The President
responded helpfully.

President to Former Naval Person (Cairo)   9 Aug 42
   In view of the message you have sent me, I have replied to
Chiang Kai-shek that it does not seem to me to be wise or
expedient for the time being to consider taking any of the
steps which he suggested in his message to me. I have emphasised the fact that we would of course not wish to pursue any
course which would undermine the authority of the Indian
Government at this critical time. I have however told him
that I would be glad to have him keep in close touch with me
with regard to this and any other questions which affect the
vital interests of the United Nations because of my belief
that it is wiser to have him feel that his suggestions sent to
me receive friendly consideration. I fear that if I did not do
so he would be more inclined to take action on his own initiative, which I know you will agree might be very dangerous
at this moment. I have therefore left the door open for him
to make any further suggestions which he may have in mind
later on, and should he think the need exists.

To the Viceroy I sent the strongest assurances of support, to
which he replied:

Viceroy of India to Prime Minister   20 Aug 42
   I am much encouraged by your kind message. We are confronted by an awkward situation, and I am by no means confident that we have yet seen the worst. But I have good hope

we may clear up position before either Jap or German is well placed to put direct pressure upon us.

The fact that a number of crises break out at the same time does not necessarily add to the difficulty of coping with them. One set of adverse circumstances may counterbalance and even cancel out another. American opinion remained quiescent in view of the struggle with Japan. The measures proposed by the Viceroy and confirmed by the War Cabinet were soon effective. They proved the superficial character of the Congress party's influence upon the masses of the Indian peoples, among whom there was deep fear of being invaded by Japan, and who looked to the King-Emperor to protect them. During the whole of this direct trial of strength with the Congress leaders many thousands of fresh volunteers came forward to join the Indian Army. What was at one time feared would become the most serious rebellion in India since the Sepoy Mutiny of 1857 fizzled out in a few months with hardly any loss of life.

*   *   *

On the 17th I received news of the attack on Dieppe, plans for which had been started in April after the brilliant and audacious raid on St. Nazaire. On May 13 the outline plan (Operation 'Rutter') was approved by the Chiefs of Staff Committee as a basis for detailed planning by the Force Commanders. More than ten thousand men were to be employed by the three Services. This was of course the most considerable enterprise of its kind which we had attempted against the Occupied French coastline. From available intelligence it appeared that Dieppe was held only by German low-category troops amounting to one battalion, with supporting units making no more than 1,400 men in all. The assault was originally fixed for July 4, and the troops embarked at ports in the Isle of Wight. The weather was unfavourable and the date was postponed till July 8. Four German aircraft made an attack upon the shipping which had been concentrated. The weather continued bad and the troops disembarked. It was now decided to cancel the operation altogether. General Montgomery, who, as Commander-in-Chief of South-Eastern Command, had hitherto supervised the plans, was strongly of opinion that it should not be remounted, as the troops concerned had all been briefed and were now dispersed ashore.

However, I thought it most important that a large-scale operation should take place this summer, and military opinion seemed unanimous that until an operation on that scale was undertaken no responsible general would take the responsibility of planning for the main invasion.

In discussion with Admiral Mountbatten it became clear that time did not permit a new large-scale operation to be mounted during the summer, but that Dieppe could be remounted (the new code-name was 'Jubilee') within a month, provided extraordinary steps were taken to ensure secrecy.

For this reason no records were kept, but after the Canadian authorities and the Chiefs of Staff had given their approval I personally went through the plans with the C.I.G.S., Admiral Mountbatten, and the Naval Force Commander, Captain J. Hughes-Hallett. It was clear that no substantial change between 'Jubilee' and 'Rutter' was suggested, beyond substituting Commandos to silence the flank coastal batteries in place of airborne troops. This was now possible as two more infantry landing-ships had become available to carry the Commandos, and the chances of weather conditions causing 'Jubilee' once more to be abandoned were considerably reduced by omitting the airborne drop. In spite of an accidental encounter between the landing-craft carrying one of the Commandos and a German coastal convoy, one of the batteries was completely destroyed and the other prevented from seriously interfering with the operation; so that this change in no way affected the outcome of the operation.

Our post-war examination of their records shows that the Germans did not receive, through leakages of information, any special warning of our intention to attack. However, their general estimate of the threat to the Dieppe sector led to an intensification of defence measures along the whole front. Special precautions were ordered for periods like that between August 10 and August 19, when moon and tide were favourable for landings. The division responsible for the defence of the Dieppe sector had been reinforced during July and August, and was at full strength and on routine alert at the moment of the raid. The Canadian Army in Britain had long been eager and impatient for action, and the main part of the landing force was provided by them. The story is vividly told by the official historian of the Canadian Army* and in other official publications, and need not be repeated here. Although the utmost

* Colonel C. P. Stacey, *The Canadian Army, 1939–45.*

gallantry and devotion were shown by all the troops and by the British Commandos and by the landing-craft and their escorts, and many splendid deeds were done, the results were disappointing and our casualties were very heavy. In the Canadian 2nd Division 18 per cent. of the five thousand men embarked lost their lives and nearly two thousand of them were taken prisoners.

Looking back, the casualties of this memorable action may seem out of proportion to the results. It would be wrong to judge the episode solely by such a standard. Dieppe occupies a place of its own in the story of the war, and the grim casualty figures must not class it as a failure. It was a costly but not unfruitful reconnaissance in force. Tactically it was a mine of experience. It shed revealing light on many shortcomings in our outlook. It taught us to build in good time various new types of craft and appliances for later use. We learnt again the value of powerful support by heavy naval guns in an opposed landing, and our bombardment technique, both marine and aerial, was thereafter improved. Above all it was shown that individual skill and gallantry without thorough organisation and combined training would not prevail, and that team work was the secret of success. This could only be provided by trained and organised amphibious formations. All these lessons were taken to heart.

Strategically the raid served to make the Germans more conscious of danger along the whole coast of Occupied France. This helped to hold troops and resources in the West, which did something to take the weight off Russia. Honour to the brave who fell. Their sacrifice was not in vain.

*　　　*　　　*

While in Cairo I pressed the question of giving strong air support to the Soviet southern flank.

Prime Minister (Cairo) to Deputy Prime Minister,　19 Aug 42
Foreign Secretary, General Ismay, and C.A.S.

I agree that there is no possibility of influencing the situation in the next sixty days. I also agree that nothing can be moved before the decision here, which will certainly be reached in forty days, and may come much sooner.

2. Matter must be viewed as long-term policy ; namely, to place on the southern flank of the Russian armies a substantial British and, later on, American Air Force,

(*a*) in order to strengthen the Russian air-power generally ;

(*b*) in order to form the advance shield of all our interests in Persia and Abadan ;

(*c*) for moral effect of comradeship with the Russians, which will be out of all proportion to the forces employed. We must have the means to do them a friendly act, especially in view of the difficulties of P.Q. convoys after September ; and

(*d*) because this is no dispersion of forces, but a greater concentration on the supreme Air Force target, namely, wearing down the German Air Force by daily fighting contact. We can fight them at more advantage in the ordinary conditions of the battle-front than by looking for trouble over the Channel. It pays us to lose machine for machine.

3. I have committed H.M.G. to this policy in my talks with Stalin, and I must ask the Cabinet for support. See also, when it reaches you, the account of the military conversations in Moscow, and also my correspondence with the President on the matter, to which he attaches great importance.

4. C.A.S. should prepare a draft project for a movement of the kind outlined by Air Chief Marshal Tedder, which can be first sent to the President by me with a covering telegram. If his reply is satisfactory I will then make a firm offer to Stalin, which might not be operative till November, but which would enable immediate work to be started on surveying and preparing the landing-grounds and would give us access to the Russian sphere in Persia and the Caucasus. If things go well we will advance with the Russians' southern wing ; if ill, we shall anyhow have to put forces of this order in North Persia. I wish to telegraph to the President before I leave here. Final decision can be taken at home when we hear what he says.

5. Everybody always finds it convenient to ease themselves at the expense of Russia, but grave issues depend upon preserving a good relationship with this tremendous army, now under dire distress. It will take a lot to convince me that action within the limits mentioned by Tedder will interfere with 'Torch'.

* * *

I was also able to complete the important business about transferring the Persian railway to American management which we had discussed at Teheran.

Prime Minister to Deputy Prime Minister,   21 Aug 42
General Ismay, and others concerned

As a result of conferences which we held in Teheran and Cairo with Mr. Harriman and his American railway experts we are all agreed that I should accept the President's offer to take over the working of the Trans-Persian railway and the port of Khorramshahr. We cannot run it unless they provide 60 per cent. of the total personnel required. Their offer is to take it over as a task, becoming our servants so far as all movement is concerned, but managing everything on American lines, with American personnel, military and civil. Transference would be gradual and spread over a good many months. When completed it will release about 2,000 British railway personnel, who will be urgently required on other parts of our military railway system. You will see my telegram to the President as it passes through.

Former Naval Person to President Roosevelt   22 Aug 42

I have delayed my reply until I could study the Trans-Persian situation on the spot. This I have now done, both at Teheran and here, and have conferred with Averell, General Maxwell, General Spalding, and their railway experts. The traffic on the Trans-Persian railway is expected to reach 3,000 tons a day for all purposes by the end of the year. We are all convinced that it ought to be raised to 6,000 tons. Only in this way can we ensure an expanding flow of supplies to Russia while building up the military forces which we must move into Northern Persia to meet a possible German advance.

2. To reach the higher figure it will be necessary to increase largely the railway personnel and to provide additional quantities of rolling-stock and technical equipment. Furthermore the target will only be attained in reasonable time if enthusiasm and energy are devoted to the task and a high priority accorded to its requirements.

3. I therefore welcome and accept your most helpful proposal contained in your telegram, that the railway should be taken over, developed, and operated by the United States Army. With the railway should be included the ports of Khorramshahr and Bandarshahpur. Your people would thus undertake the great task of opening up the Persian corridor, which will carry primarily your supplies to Russia. All our people here agree on the benefits which would follow your approval of this suggestion. We should be unable to find the resources without your help, and our burden in the Middle East would be eased by the release for use elsewhere of the British units now operating the railway. The railway and ports would be managed entirely by your people, though the

allocation of traffic would have to be retained in the hands of the British military authorities, for whom the railway is an essential channel of communication for operational purposes. I see no obstacle in this to harmonious working. . . .

*   *   *

The Australian cruiser *Canberra* had been sunk on the night of August 9 by the Japanese near Guadalcanal, in the Solomons.

Prime Minister to First Lord and First Sea Lord   23 Aug 42
  Australia have lost their 8-inch cruiser *Canberra*. It might have lasting effect on Australian sentiment if we gave freely and outright to Royal Australian Navy one of our similar ships. Please give your most sympathetic consideration to the project and be ready to tell me about it when I return. Meanwhile I am not mentioning it to anyone.

This suggestion was adopted, and the cruiser *Shropshire* was presented to the Australian Government.

*   *   *

On August 19 I paid another visit to the Desert Front, I drove with Alexander in his car out from Cairo past the Pyramids, about 130 miles through the desert to the sea at Abusir. I was cheered by all he told me. As the shadows lengthened we reached Montgomery's headquarters, at Burg-el-Arab. Here the afterwards famous caravan was drawn up amid the sand-dunes by the sparkling waves. The General gave me his own wagon, divided between office and bedroom. After our long drive we all had a delicious bathe. 'All the armies are bathing now at this hour all along the coast,' said Montgomery as we stood in our towels. He waved his arm to the westward. Three hundred yards away about a thousand of our men were disporting themselves on the beach. Although I knew the answer, I asked, Why do the War Office go to the expense of sending out white bathing drawers for the troops? Surely this economy should be made.' They were in fact tanned and burnt to the darkest brown everywhere except where they wore their short pants.

How fashions change! When I marched to Omdurman forty-four years before the theory was that the African sun must at all costs be kept away from the skin. The rules were strict. Special spine-pads were buttoned on to the back of all our khaki coats. It was a military offence to appear without a pith helmet. We were advised to wear thick underclothing, following Arab custom enjoined by a thousand years of experience. Yet now half-way through the twentieth century many of the white soldiers went about their daily toil hatless and naked except for the equal of a loin cloth. Apparently it did them no harm. Though the process of changing from white to bronze took several weeks and gradual application, sunstroke and heatstroke were rare. I wonder how the doctors explain all this.

After we had dressed for dinner—my zip hardly takes a minute to put on—we gathered in Montgomery's map wagon. There he gave us a masterly exposition of the situation, showing that in a few days he had firmly gripped the whole problem. He accurately predicted Rommel's next attack, and explained his plans to meet it. All of which proved true and sound. He then described his plans for taking the offensive himself. He must however have six weeks to get the Eighth Army into order. He would re-form the divisions as integral tactical units. We must wait till the new divisions had taken their place at the front and until the Sherman tanks were broken in. Then there would be three Army Corps, each under an experienced officer, whom he and Alexander knew well. Above all the artillery would be used as had never been possible before in the Desert. He spoke of the end of September. I was disappointed at the date, but even this was dependent upon Rommel. Our information showed that a blow from him was imminent. I was myself already fully informed, and was well content that he should try a wide turning movement round our Desert Flank in order to reach Cairo, and that a manœuvre battle should be fought on his communications.

At this time I thought much of Napoleon's defeat in 1814. He too was poised to strike at the communications, but the Allies marched straight on into an almost open Paris. I thought it of the highest importance that Cairo should be defended by every able-bodied man in uniform not required for the Eighth Army. Thus alone would the field army have full manœuvring freedom and be able to take risks in letting its flank be turned before striking. It was with great pleasure that I found we were all in agreement. Although I was always impatient for offensive action on our part at the earliest moment, I welcomed the prospect of Rommel breaking his teeth upon us before our main attack was launched. But should we have time to organise the defence of Cairo? Many signs pointed to the audacious commander who faced us only a dozen miles away striking his supreme blow before the end of August. Any day indeed, my friends said, he might make his bid for continued mastery. A fortnight or three weeks' delay would be all to our good.

* * *

On August 20 we sallied forth early to see the prospective battlefield and the gallant troops who were to hold it. I was taken to the key point south-east of the Ruweisat Ridge. Here, amid the hard, rolling curves and creases of the desert, lay the mass of our armour, camouflaged, concealed, and dispersed, yet tactically concentrated. Here I met the young Brigadier Roberts, who at that time commanded the whole of our armoured force in this vital position. All our best tanks were under him. Montgomery explained to me the disposition of our artillery of all natures. Every crevice of the desert was packed with camouflaged concealed batteries. Three or four hundred guns would fire at the German armour before we hurled in our own.

Although of course no gatherings of troops could be allowed under the enemy's continuous air reconnaissance, I saw a great many soldiers that day, who greeted me with grins and cheers. I inspected my own regiment, the 4th Hussars, or as many of them as they dared to bring together—perhaps fifty or sixty—near the field cemetery, in which a number of their comrades had been newly buried. All this was moving, but with it all there grew a sense of the reviving ardour of the Army. Everybody said what a change there was since Montgomery had taken command. I could feel the truth of this with joy and comfort.

* * *

We were to lunch with Bernard Freyberg. My mind went back to a similar visit I had paid him in Flanders, at his battle-post in the valley of the Scarpe, a quarter of a century before, when he already commanded a brigade. Then he had blithely offered to take me for a walk along his outposts. But knowing him and knowing the line as I did I declined. Now it was the other way round. I certainly hoped to see at least a forward observation post of these splendid New Zealanders, who were in contact about five miles away. Alexander's attitude showed he would not forbid but rather accompany the excursion. But Bernard Freyberg flatly refused to take the responsibility, and this was not a matter about which orders are usually given, even by the highest authority.

Instead we went into his sweltering mess tent, and were offered a luncheon, far more magnificent than the one I had eaten on the Scarpe. This was an August noonday in the desert. The set piece of the meal was a scalding broth of tinned New Zealand oysters, to which I could do no more than was civil. Presently Montgomery, who had left us some time before, drove up. Freyberg went out to salute him, and told him his place had been kept and that he was expected to luncheon. But 'Monty', as he was already called, had, it appeared, made it a rule not to accept hospitality from any of his subordinate commanders. So he sat outside in his car eating an austere sandwich and drinking his lemonade with all formalities. Napoleon also might have stood aloof in the interests of discipline. *Dur aux grands* was one of his maxims. But he would certainly have had an excellent roast chicken, served him from his own *fourgon*. Marlborough would have entered and quaffed the good wine with his officers—Cromwell, I think, too. The technique varies, and the results seem to have been good in all these cases.

We spent all the afternoon among the Army, and it was past seven when we got back to the caravan and the pleasant waves of its beach. I was so uplifted by all I had seen that I was not at all tired and sat up late talking. Before Montgomery went to bed at ten o'clock, in accordance with his routine, he asked me to write something in his personal diary. I did so now and on several other occasions during the long war. Here is what I wrote this time:

'May the anniversary of Blenheim, which marks the opening of the new Command, bring to the Commander-in-Chief of the Eighth Army and his troops the fame and fortune they will surely deserve.'*

* * *

I sent the following report home:

Prime Minister to Deputy Prime Minister, for   21 Aug 42
War Cabinet, General Ismay, and others concerned
    Have just spent two days in the Western Desert visiting H.Q. Eighth Army. Brooke, Alexander, Montgomery, and I went round together, seeing 44th Division, 7th Armoured Division, and 22nd Armoured Brigade, and representatives of the New

---

* See facsimile reproduction opposite.

Note August 13 Gen. Montgomery assumed command of the Desert army. (Sept. 4. 1943)

May the anniversary of Blenheim which marks the opening of this new command bring to the Commander in Chief of the Eighth Army & his troops the fame & fortune they will surely deserve.

Aug. 20. 1942   Winston S. Churchill.

Zealand Division. I saw a great number of men and all the principal commanders in the XIIIth Corps area, also again Air Marshal Coningham, who shares headquarters with General Montgomery.

2. I am sure we were heading for disaster under the former régime. The Army was reduced to bits and pieces and oppressed by a sense of bafflement and uncertainty. Apparently it was intended in face of heavy attack to retire eastwards to the Delta. Many were looking over their shoulders to make sure of their seat in the lorry, and no plain plan of battle or dominating will-power had reached the units.

3. So serious did this appear that General Montgomery insisted on taking command of the Eighth Army as soon as he had visited the front, and by Alexander's decision the whole command in the Middle East was transferred on the 13th.

4. Since then, from what I could see myself of the troops and hear from their commanders, a complete change of atmosphere has taken place. Alexander ordered Montgomery

to prepare to take the offensive and meanwhile to hold all positions, and Montgomery issued an invigorating directive to his commanders, of which I will circulate the text on my return. The highest alacrity and activity prevails. Positions are everywhere being strengthened, and extended forces are being sorted out and regrouped in solid units. The 44th and the 10th Armoured Divisions have already arrived in the forward zone. The roads are busy with the forward movement of troops, tanks, and guns. General Horrocks commands the XIIIth Corps. Ramsden remains with the XXXth Corps. General Lumsden is forming the Xth Corps for a mass of manœuvre for the offensive battle towards the end of September. For this a bold and comprehensive plan has been made.

5. However, it seems probable that Rommel will attack during the moon period before the end of August. He has lost valuable shipments, on which he counted, and underrates our strength, but we must not underrate his. We must expect a very wide turning movement by perhaps 20,000 Germans and 15,000 Italians, comprising formations of two Panzer and four or five Axis motorised divisions. The ensuing battle will be hard and critical, but I have the greatest confidence in Alexander and Montgomery, and I feel sure the Army will fight at its best. If Rommel does not attack in August he will be attacked himself at greater relative disadvantage in September. This would fit in well with 'Torch'.

6. For an August battle we should have at the front about 700 tanks, with 100 replacements, about 700 serviceable aircraft, 500 field guns, nearly 400 6-pounder and 440 2-pounder anti-tank guns; but as we have only 24 medium guns we are definitely weaker in medium artillery. As parachute descents must be expected on a large scale and Rommel will no doubt bid high for victory, the Army will be extended to the full.

7. To give the fullest manœuvring power to the Eighth Army in the event of its being attacked next week, a strong line of defence is being developed along the Delta from Alexandria to Cairo. The 51st [Highland] Division is taking station there. I shall visit it to-morrow. I drew General Alexander's attention to the inundation plans which we made two years ago, and action has been taken at various points.

8. To sum up, while I and others would prefer the September to the August battle, because of our growing strength, I am satisfied that we have lively, confident, resolute men in command, working together as an admirable team under leaders of the highest military quality. Everything has been done and is being done that is possible, and it is now my duty to return home, as I have no part to play in the battle, which

must be left to those in whom we place our trust. I have still a good deal of business to settle. As you will see from other telegrams, Gort is here and Platt arrives to-morrow. C.I.G.S. and I plan to start Sunday night by a route which you will learn in a separate telegram. I hope to be available for my weekly luncheon with the King on Tuesday if that should be His Majesty's wish.

9. My general impression of 'Jubilee' [Dieppe] is that the results fully justified the heavy cost. The large-scale air battle alone justified the raid.

10. I thank you all most warmly for the support you have given me while engaged in these anxious and none too pleasant tasks.

*   *   *

On August 22 I visited the Tura caves, near Cairo, where vital repair work was being done. Out of these caves the stones of the Pyramids had been cut some time before. They came in very handy now. The reader will have seen my perpetual complaints of the bad servicing and slowness of repairs of our aircraft and tanks. Everything looked very smart and efficient on the spot, and an immense amount of work was being done day and night by masses of skilled men. But I had my tables of facts and figures and remained dissatisfied. The scale was far too small. The original fault lay with the Pharaohs for not having built more and larger Pyramids. Other responsibilities were more difficult to assign. We spent the rest of the day flying from one airfield to another, inspecting the installations and addressing the ground staffs. At one point two or three thousand airmen were assembled. I also visited, brigade by brigade, the Highland Division, just landed. It was late when we got back to the Embassy.

*   *   *

During these last days of my visit all my thought rested upon the impending battle. At any moment Rommel might attack with a devastating surge of armour. He could come in by the Pyramids with hardly a check except a single canal till he reached the Nile, which flowed serenely by at the bottom of the Residency lawn. Lady Lampson's baby son smiled from his pram amid the palm-trees. I looked out across the river at the flat expanses beyond. All was calm and peaceful, but I suggested to the mother that it was very hot and sultry in Cairo and could not be good for children. 'Why not send the baby away to be braced by the cool breezes of the Lebanon?' But she did not take my advice, and none can say she did not judge the military situation rightly.

In the fullest accord with General Alexander and the C.I.G.S. I set on foot a series of extreme measures for the defence of Cairo and the water-lines running northward to the sea. Rifle-pits and machine-gun posts were constructed, bridges mined and their approaches wired, and inundations loosed over the whole wide front. All the office population of Cairo, numbering thousands of staff officers and uniformed clerks, were armed with rifles and ordered to take their stations, if need be, along the fortified water line. The 51st Highland Division was not yet regarded as 'desert-worthy', but these magnificent troops were now ordered to man the new Nile front. The position was one of great strength because of the comparatively few causeways which cross the canalised flooded or floodable area of the Delta. It seemed quite practicable to arrest an armoured rush along the causeways. The defence of Cairo would normally have belonged to the British general who commanded the Egyptian Army, all of whose forces were also arrayed. I thought it better however to place the responsibility, should an emergency occur, upon General Maitland-Wilson— 'Jumbo'—who had been appointed to the Persia–Iraq Command, but whose headquarters during these critical weeks were forming in Cairo. To him I issued a directive to inform himself fully of the whole defence plan, and to take responsibility from the moment when General Alexander told him that Cairo was in danger.

I had now to go home on the eve of battle and return to far wider but by no means less decisive affairs. I had already obtained the Cabinet's approval of the directive to be given to General Alexander. He was the supreme authority with whom I now dealt in the Middle East. Montgomery and the Eighth Army were under him. So also, if it became necessary, was Maitland-Wilson and the defence of Cairo. 'Alex', as I had long called him, had already moved himself and his personal headquarters into the desert by the Pyramids. Cool, gay, comprehending all, he inspired quiet, deep confidence in every quarter.

*　　　*　　　*

We sailed off from the Desert airfield at 7.5 p.m. on August

23, and I slept the sleep of the just till long after daylight. When I clambered along the bomb-bay to the cockpit of the 'Commando' we were already approaching Gibraltar. I must say it looked very dangerous. All was swathed in morning mist. One could not see a hundred yards ahead, and we were not flying more than thirty feet above the sea. I asked Vanderkloot if it was all right, and said I hoped he would not hit the Rock of Gibraltar. His answers were not particularly reassuring, but he felt sufficiently sure of his course not to go up high and stand out to sea, which personally I should have been glad to see him do. We held on for another four or five minutes. Then suddenly we flew into clear air, and up towered the great precipice of Gibraltar, gleaming on the isthmus and strip of neutral ground which joins it to Spain and the mountain called the Queen of Spain's Chair. After three or four hours' flying in mist Vanderkloot had been exact. We passed the grim rock-face a few hundred yards away without having to alter our course, and made a perfect landing. I still think it would have been better to go aloft and circle round for an hour or two. We had the petrol and were not pressed for time. But it was a fine performance.

We spent the morning with the Governor, and flew home in the afternoon, taking a wide sweep across the Bay of Biscay when darkness fell.

CHAPTER 7

The Final Shaping of 'Torch'

*General Eisenhower to Command – Agreeable Contacts with
the United States Generals – Need for a Simple Directive – A
Bombshell from Washington – American Apprehension of
Going Inside the Mediterranean – My Telegram to the President
of August 27 – The President's Reply of August 30 – Ameri-
can Belief that the French Would Not Fire on Their Troops –
My Telegram to the President of September 1 – The President's
Reply of September 3 – My Proposal that Eisenhower Should
Fly to Washington to Explain – An Unsent Letter from Me to
Harry Hopkins – A Survey of the Deadlock and its Causes –
Better News from the President, September 4 – We Agree: Hurrah! – O.K., Full Blast – Planning and Timing – Further Discussion with Generals Eisenhower and Clark – My Telegram
to the President, September 15 – 'An American Enterprise, in
which We are Your Helpmeets' – Date of 'Torch' Fixed for
November 8 – Rommel's Last Thrust for Cairo – The Combat
of Alam Halfa.*

When I left London on my missions to Cairo and Moscow the
commander for 'Torch' had not been chosen. I had suggested
on July 31 that if General Marshall were designated for the
Supreme Command of the cross-Channel operation in 1943 General Eisenhower should act as his deputy and forerunner in
London and work at 'Torch', which he would himself command, with General Alexander as his second. Opinion moved
forward on these lines, and before I started from Cairo for
Moscow the President sent me the two following telegrams:

President to Former Naval Person (Cairo)   6 Aug 42
     The proposal of the British Chiefs of Staff dated August 6
that General Eisenhower be designated as Commander-in-
Chief for the 'Torch' operation is acceptable to me and to
the United States Chiefs of Staff. The formal directive for
General Eisenhower's guidance submitted by the British Chiefs
of Staff is being studied, and will be reported upon shortly.

And on the 8th:

I wholly agree date for 'Torch' should be advanced, and I am asking three weeks' advance over the selected date.

Announcement of Eisenhower command I leave to discretion of Chiefs of Staff in London and Washington.

*   *   *

When on August 24 I returned from Cairo to London much remained to be decided about the final shaping of our plans, and on the following day Generals Eisenhower and Clark came to dine with me to discuss the state of the operation.

I was at this time in very close and agreeable contact with these American officers. From the moment they arrived in June I had arranged a weekly dinner at Number 10 on Tuesdays. These meetings seemed to be a success. I was nearly always alone with them, and we talked all our affairs over, back and forth, as if we were all of one country. I set great value on these personal contacts. Irish stew turned out to be very popular with my American guests, and especially with General Eisenhower. My wife was nearly always able to get this. I soon began to call him 'Ike'. For Mark Clark and Bedell Smith, the latter of whom arrived early in September as Chief of Staff to Eisenhower, I coined the titles 'the American Eagle' and 'the American Bulldog'. You have to look at their photographs to see why. We also had a number of informal conferences in our downstairs dining-room, beginning at about ten o'clock at night and sometimes running late. Several times the American generals came for a night or a week-end to Chequers. Nothing but shop was ever talked on any of these occasions.

One of General Eisenhower's aides-de-camp, a friend from civil life, has suggested in his book that all these meetings were a great burden upon the already overworked American officers. If this be true they showed great politeness and address in concealing their feelings. Anyhow, I am sure these close relationships were necessary for the conduct of the war, and I could not have grasped the whole position without them. At one of our meetings, on September 28, I certainly rendered a service to Bedell Smith and his chief. It was not very late at night, but I noticed that 'the Beetle', as he was also called, looked frightfully tired and ill. I suggested that he should go to bed, but he insisted on remaining. There was a moment when I thought he was going to faint and fall off his chair. I therefore closed the discussion. On the way upstairs I asked Eisenhower to come alone with me into the Cabinet room. I closed the door and said, 'If you want Bedell in this battle you should send him to hospital this very night, no matter what he says. Otherwise you will lose him altogether.' Eisenhower acted with his customary decision. Next day Bedell Smith was in hospital. He had to have two blood transfusions in the next two days, and was kept a fortnight from all work and mostly in bed. Thus he was able to play his important part in the design which dominated our minds.

*　　*　　*

After my talk with the American generals I telegraphed to the President:

Former Naval Person to President Roosevelt　　26 Aug 42

I am concentrating my main thought upon 'Torch' from now on, and you may trust me to do my utmost to make your great strategic conception a decisive success. It seems to me from talks I have had with Eisenhower, Clark, and our own people here that the best, and indeed the only, way to put this job through is to fix a date for the party and make everything conform to that, rather than saying it will start when everything is ready. It would be an immense help if you and I were to give Eisenhower a directive something like this: 'You will start "Torch" on October 14, attacking with such troops as are available and at such places as you deem fit.' This will alter the whole character of the preparations. Eisenhower will really have the power he should have as the Allied Commander-in-Chief. Endless objections, misgivings, and well-meant improvements will fall back into their proper places, and action will emerge from what will otherwise be almost unending hummings and hawings. I think Eisenhower would like this, and it would anyhow give him a chance which he has not now got.

2. As I see this operation, it is primarily political in its foundations. The first victory we have to win is to avoid a battle; the second, if we cannot avoid it, to win it. In order to give us the best chances of the first victory, we must (a) present the maximum appearance of overwhelming strength at the moment of the first attack, and (b) attack at as many places as possible. This is an absolutely different kind of operation from the Dieppe business or any variants of 'Sledgehammer'. There we were up against German efficiency and the steel-bound, fortified coasts of France. In 'Torch' we have to face at the worst weak, divided opposition and an enormous choice of striking-points at which to land. Risks and difficulties will

be doubled by delay and will far outstrip any increase of our forces. Careful planning in every detail, safety first in every calculation, far-seeing provisions for a long-term campaign, to meet every conceivable adverse contingency, however admirable in theory, will ruin the enterprise in fact. Anything later than the date I have mentioned enormously increases the danger of leakage and forestalment.

3. In order to lighten the burden of responsibility on the military commanders, I am of opinion that you and I should lay down the political data and take this risk upon ourselves. In my view, it would be reasonable to assume (a) that Spain will not go to war with Britain and the United States on account of 'Torch'; (b) that it will be at least two months before the Germans can force their way through Spain or procure some accommodation from her (c) that the French resistance in North Africa will be largely token resistance, capable of being overcome by the suddenness and scale of the attack, and that thereafter the North African French may actively help us under their own commanders; (b) that Vichy will not declare war on the United States and Great Britain; (e) that Hitler will put extreme pressure on Vichy, but that in October he will not have the forces available to overrun Unoccupied France while at the same time we keep him pinned in the Pas de Calais, etc. All these data may prove erroneous, in which case we shall have to settle down to hard slogging. For this we have already been prepared, but a bold, audacious bid for a bloodless victory at the outset may win a very great prize. Personally, I am prepared to take any amount of responsibility for running the political risks and being proved wrong about the political assumptions.

4. It is evident that these assumptions would be greatly helped by a battle won in the Western Desert. Either Rommel attacks us by the August moon, or we shall attack him by the end of September. Either way there will be a decision, and I feel very confident that the decision will be helpful.

5. I have refrained, as you know, from going into any details here because I feel that a note must be struck now of irrevocable decision and superhuman energy to execute it.

*   *   *

But at this moment a bombshell arrived from Washington. Serious divergences had opened between the British and American Staffs on the character and scope of our plan to invade and occupy French North Africa. The United States Chiefs of Staff disliked very much the idea of committing themselves to large operations beyond the Straits of Gibraltar. They seemed to have the feeling that in some sort of way their armies would be cut off in the inland sea. General Eisenhower, on the other hand, fully shared the British view that powerful action inside the Mediterranean, above all including Algeria, was vital to success. His views, so far as he may have pressed them, did not seem to influence his military superiors. He was also hampered in his planning by the insistence of various American departments concerned that all must be delayed until their respective consignments of men or store ships had definitely started. In so vast an operation there were bound to be laggard items, and to wait for the last of these would impose an indefinite delay in fixing zero day.

The American Chiefs of Staff now pressed their view, which I and my advisers resisted.

Former Naval Person to President Roosevelt   27 Aug 42
We are all profoundly disconcerted by the memorandum sent us by the United States Joint Chiefs of Staff on the 25th instant about 'Torch'. It seems to me that the whole pith of the operation will be lost if we do not take Algiers as well as Oran on the first day. In Algiers we have the best chance of a friendly reception, and even if we got nothing except Algeria a most important strategic success would have been gained. General Eisenhower, with our cordial support, was in fact planning landings at Philippeville and Bone for Day 3. We cannot of course be sure of getting to Tunis before the Germans, but neither is it certain that the Germans would be well received by the French in Tunis even if Vichy gave them permission.

2. Strongly established in Algeria, with Oran making good the communications, we could fight the Germans for Tunis even if they got there. But not to go east of Oran is making the enemy a present not only of Tunis but of Algiers. An operation limited to Oran and Casablanca would not give the impression of strength and of widespread simultaneous attack on which we rely for the favourable effect on the French in North Africa. We are all convinced that Algiers is the key to the whole operation. General Anderson, to whom this task has been assigned by Eisenhower, is confident of his ability to occupy Algiers. The occupation of Algeria and the movement towards Tunis and Bizerta is an indispensable part of the attack on Italy, which is the best chance of enlisting French co-operation and one of the main objects of our future campaign.

3. We are all agreed about Oran, and of course we should

like to see Casablanca occupied as well, but if it came to choosing between Algiers and Casablanca it cannot be doubted that the former is incomparably the more hopeful and fruitful objective. Inside the Mediterranean landings can be made in October on four days out of five. On the Atlantic shores of Morocco the proportion is exactly reversed, only one day in five being favourable.

4. Nevertheless, if the operations at Oran and Algiers yield good reactions and results, entry might easily be granted to a force appearing off Casablanca, and a feint would certainly be justified. It is however by far the most difficult point of attack, and the one most remote from the vital objectives in the Mediterranean. Casablanca might easily become an isolated failure and let loose upon us for a small reward all the perils which have anyway to be faced in this great design. So far as Algiers is concerned, all we ask from you is an American contact team to show the [American] flag. We [ourselves] cannot however do Algiers and Oran at the same time. If therefore you wish to do Casablanca on a large scale, with all its risks, it is indispensable that United States forces should continue to be directed on Oran as now planned by the Allied Commander-in-Chief.

5. A complete change in the plans such as the memorandum suggests would of course be fatal to the date, and thus possibly to the whole plan. In October Hitler will not have the power to move into Spain or into Unoccupied France. In November and with every week that passes his power to bring pressure upon the Vichy and Madrid Governments increases rapidly.

6. I hope, Mr. President, you will bear in mind the language I have held to Stalin, supported by Harriman with your full approval. If 'Torch' collapses or is cut down as is now proposed I should feel my position painfully affected. For all these reasons I most earnestly beg that the memorandum may be reconsidered, and that the American Allied Commander-in-Chief may be permitted to go forward with the plans he has made, upon which we are all now working night and day. The Staffs are communicating similar views to their American colleagues.

On August 30 I received the President's reply.

President Roosevelt to Former Naval Person   30 Aug 42
I have considered carefully your telegram in reference to the 'Torch' operation. It is my earnest desire to start the attack at the earliest possible moment. Time is of the essence, and we are speeding up preparations vigorously.

I feel very strongly that the initial attacks must be made by an exclusively American ground force, supported by your naval, transport, and air units. The operation should be undertaken on the assumption that the French will offer less resistance to us than they will to the British. I would even go so far as to say I am reasonably sure a simultaneous landing by British and Americans would result in full resistance by all French in Africa, whereas an initial American landing without British ground forces offers a real chance that there would be no French resistance, or only a token resistance. I need a week, if possible, after we land to consolidate the position for both of us by securing the non-resistance of the French. I sincerely hope I can get this.

Then your force can come in to the eastward. I realise full well that your landing must be made before the enemy can get there. It is our belief that German air and parachute troops cannot get to Algiers or Tunis in any large force for at least two weeks after the initial attack. Meanwhile your troops would be ashore, we hope, without much opposition, and would be moving eastward. As to the place of the landings, it seems to me that we must have a sure and permanent base on the north-west coast of Africa, because a single line of communications through the Straits is far too hazardous in the light of our limited joint resources.

I propose therefore that (a) American troops land simultaneously near Casablanca and near Oran ; (b) that they seek to establish road and rail communication with each other back of the mountains. The distance is little more than 300 miles. This gives to the enterprise a supply base in Morocco, which is outside the Straits and can be used to reinforce and supply the operations in Algiers and Tunis. The real problem seems to be that there is not enough cover and combat loadings for more than two landings. I realise it would be far better to have three, with you handling the one to the eastward a week after we get it. To this end I think we should re-examine our resources and strip everything to the bone to make the third landing possible. We can give up the Russian convoy temporarily at that time and risk or hold up other merchant shipping.

It is essential of course that all ships now assigned to Eisenhower for his two landings remain intact. Hence the eastward landing must be made on ships not now available to 'Torch'. I will explore this at our end. Can we not get an answer on this within forty-eight hours or less?

I want to emphasise however that under any circumstances one of our landings must be on the Atlantic.

The directive to the Commander-in-Chief of the operation should prescribe that the attack should be launched at the earliest practicable date. The date should be consistent with the preparation necessary for an operation with a fair chance of success, and accordingly it should be determined by the Commander-in-Chief ; but in no event later than October 30. I still would hope for October 14.

* * *

As can be seen from this telegram, another series of difficulties arose from the strength of the American view that while United States forces would probably be admitted by the French without fighting, or perhaps even welcomed, any appearance of the British would entail fierce and obstinate resistance. Certainly memories of Oran, Dakar, Syria, Madagascar, and our blockade were grave causes of antagonism between Britain and Vichy. The American Ambassador, Admiral Leahy, on the other hand, was intimate and friendly with Pétain. We were always anxious to preserve the American character of the expedition, and I was so anxious for them to agree to it that from the outset I had welcomed President Roosevelt's assuming the leadership. However, when it came to working out the plan it was found necessary that very large numbers of the troops, the bulk of the transportation, at least an equal contribution in the air, and two-thirds of the naval force engaged would have to be British. I did not wholly share the American view that either they were so beloved by Vichy or we so hated as to make the difference between fighting and submission, but I was very willing that, provided the necessary forces were set in motion and the operation was not fatally restricted in its scope, we should keep as much in the background as was physically possible. I would even have agreed to such British troops as had to be used in the first assaults wearing American uniform. Nothing mattered but success. But that must not be compromised for lack of the necessary force, or by unsound restrictions on its employment. As all agreement between the Staffs had failed the issue had to be settled personally between the President and me.

* * *

Former Naval Person to President Roosevelt   1 Sept 42
We have carefully considered your last. The Chiefs of Staff have also talked things over with Eisenhower.

2. We could not contest your wish, if you so desire it, to take upon the United States the whole burden, political and military, of the landings. Like you I assign immense importance to the political aspect. I do not know what information you have of the mood and temper of Vichy and North Africa, but of course if you can get ashore at the necessary points without fighting or only token resistance that is the best of all. We cannot tell what are the chances of this.

3. I hope however that you have considered the following points:

(a) Will not British participation be disclosed by the assembly of British small craft and aircraft at Gibraltar for some time beforehand?

(b) Would it not be disclosed at the time of landing whatever flag we wear?

(c) Would not initial fighting necessarily be between French and British aircraft and French batteries and British ships?

(d) If the approach and landing take place in the dark, as is indispensable to surprise, how will the Americans be distinguished from British? In the night all cats are grey.

(e) What happens if, as I am assured is 4–1 probable, surf prevents disembarkation on Atlantic beaches?

4. Moreover, if, contrary to your hopes, the landings are stubbornly opposed and even held up, we shall not be able to give you the follow-up help for some considerable time, because all our assault vessels would have been used for your troops, and our reinforcements would be embarked in vessels which can only enter by captured harbours. Thus, if the political bloodless victory, for which I agree with you there is a good chance, should go amiss, a military disaster of very great consequence will supervene. We could have stormed Dakar in September 1940 if we had not been cluttered up with preliminary conciliatory processes. It is that hard experience that makes our military experts rely so much upon the simplicity of force. Will you have enough American trained and equipped forces to do this all by yourselves, or at any rate to impress the enemy by the appearance of ample strength?

5. This sudden abandonment of the plan on which we have hitherto been working will certainly cause grievous delay. General Eisenhower says that October 30 will be the very earliest date. I myself think that it may well mean the middle of November. Orders were given to suspend loadings yesterday in order that, if necessary, all should be recast. I fear the substitution of November for October will open up a

whole new set of dangers far greater than those which must anyhow be faced.

6. Finally, in spite of the difficulties it seems to us vital that Algiers should be occupied simultaneously with Casablanca and Oran. Here is the most friendly and hopeful spot where the political reaction would be most decisive throughout North Africa. To give up Algiers for the sake of the doubtfully practicable landing at Casablanca seems to us a very serious decision. If it led to the Germans forestalling us not only in Tunis but in Algeria the results on balance would be lamentable throughout the Mediterranean.

7. Mr. President, to sum up, 'Torch', like 'Gymnast' before it, has always been viewed as primarily a United States enterprise. We have accepted an American command and your leadership, and we will do our utmost to make a success of any plan on which you decide. We must however say quite plainly that we are sure that the best course is to persevere along the general lines so clearly set out in the agreed directive handed to General Eisenhower on August 14. I am sure that if we both strip ourselves to the bone, as you say, we could find sufficient naval cover and combat loadings for simultaneous attempts at Casablanca, Oran, and Algiers.

President Roosevelt to Prime Minister   3 Sept 42

Your message of September 1 has been received and given careful consideration.

2. Your willingness to co-operate by agreeing that all initial landings will be made by United States ground forces is appreciated. It is true that British participation in the form of naval and air support will be disclosed to the defenders early in the operation. However, I do not believe that this will have quite the same effect that British forces making the first beach landing would have.

3. Bad surf conditions on the Atlantic beaches is a calculated risk. The use of numerous small lightly defended ports may be necessary.

4. It will be necessary to use all available combat loaders in the first assault. The assaulting troops, regardless of whether they are British or American, must seize a port before follow-up forces can be landed. Regardless of what troops arrive subsequent to the initial landing, the situation will be the same.

5. In view of your urgent desire that Algiers should be occupied simultaneously with Casablanca and Oran, we offer the following solution:

(1) Simultaneous landings at Casablanca, Oran, and

Algiers, with assault and immediate follow-up troops generally as follows:

(a) Casablanca (United States troops): 34,000 in the assault and 24,000 in the immediate follow-up, to land at a port.

(b) Oran (United States troops): 25,000 in the assault and 20,000 in the immediate follow-up, to land at a port.

(c) Algiers (United States and British troops): in the beach landing 10,000 United States troops, followed within the hour by British troops, to make the landing secure, the follow-up to be determined by the Commander-in-Chief. This follow-up to land at a port in non-combat-loaded ships.

(2) *Troops*. For the above landings the United States can furnish:

(a) from the United States, the Casablanca force, and

(b) from the United Kingdom, the Oran force and 10,000 men for the Algiers force.

As immediate follow-up forces we have one armoured division in the United States and one armoured division in the United Kingdom (both less elements included in the assault echelons), with supporting and service troops, including ground echelons of air units. Later, additional infantry and armoured divisions can be furnished from the United States and the remaining United States troops in the United Kingdom can be made available.

(3) *Shipping*. The following shipping can be made available by the United States, to sail from United States ports October 20:

(a) Combat loaders with a lift of 34,000 men.

(b) Transports, other than combat loaders, with a lift of 52,000 men, with sufficient cargo vessels to support this personnel. In addition to this shipping there will be available in the United Kingdom United States transports with personnel lift of 15,000 and nine cargo vessels which have been previously set aside by agreement to transport United States troops from the United Kingdom for this operation. In round numbers, the shipping shown as available in the United States is estimated to be sufficient to move the first, second, and third convoys of the Casablanca force.

(4) *Naval*. The United States cannot provide forces for escort and support in this operation in excess of those now available in the Atlantic, plus all ships which can be expedited in readiness for service, as is now being done.

6. The above shows the total ground, naval, and shipping

effort which the United States can put into this operation. If the operation is to be executed along the lines indicated, namely, simultaneous landings at Casablanca, Oran, and Algiers, all the remaining requirements must be furnished from British sources. As we see it, this would mean, in general, that it will be necessary for you to furnish:

(*a*) all shipping (including combat loaders) required for the Oran and Algiers forces, except the United States shipping now in the United Kingdom earmarked for 'Torch';

(*b*) the additional troops required for the Algiers assault and follow-up forces; and

(*c*) the naval forces required for the entire operation, less the United States naval force indicated above.

7. In order that I may continue with vigorous preparations for the execution of 'Torch' at the earliest practicable date, please confirm by cable that the United Kingdom will provide the troop-lift, troops, naval forces, and shipping noted herein as necessary.

8. I reiterate the belief expressed in my telegram of August 30, that the Commander-in-Chief should be directed to execute the operation at the earliest practicable date, and that this date should be fixed by him. I am convinced of the absolute necessity for an early decision. I feel that the operation as outlined herein is as far as I can go towards meeting your views, and it seems to me to be a practical solution which retains the Algiers operation and is sufficiently strong to be a good risk throughout.

9. Our latest and best information from North Africa is as follows:

An American expedition led in all three phases by American officers will meet little resistance from the French Army in Africa. On the other hand, a British-commanded attack in any phase or with the de Gaullist co-operation would meet with determined resistance....

Because of this information I consider it vital that some responsibility be placed [on] high Americans for relations with French military and civil authorities in Africa.

As you and I decided long ago, *we* were to handle the French in North Africa, while you were to handle the situation in Spain.

Former Naval Person to President Roosevelt   3 Sept 42

We have spent the day looking into physical possibilities. Accepting your general outlines, we think that a working plan can be made on the basis that the emphasis is shifted somewhat, namely, reducing Casablanca by ten or twelve thousand (making up deficiency in the follow-ups). These troops, with their combat-loaded ships, would give sufficient strength inside, while making the entire assault American. This evens up the three landings and gives the essential appearance of strength at all vital points. Without such a transference there is no hope of Algiers, on account of shortage of combat loaders and landing-craft. We all think this would be a great blemish on the plan.

2. To-morrow we suggest that either General Clark or General Eisenhower should come with Admiral Ramsay, who knows the whole transportation escort story and the naval aspect from our end, and Mountbatten on the landing details, which are crucial, party reaching you Sunday morning. We do not here know what naval forces you are able to supply. Please let these be imparted to Admiral Cunningham, to whom, in view of the importance of the operation, we propose to give the naval command, under the Allied Commander-in-Chief.

3. Delay due to change already extends three weeks. Free French have got inkling and are leaky. Every day saved is precious. We have therefore already ordered work to go forward on these lines, but of course the decision rests with you.

At this time, when all hung in the balance, I thought it right to give Harry Hopkins the whole of my thought, and leave to his discretion how he would press the matter upon the President.

Prime Minister to Mr. Harry Hopkins   4 Sept 42

I send you by hand of Dickie Mountbatten this letter, because I know how wholly your heart is centred in the cause and the peerless services you have rendered it. You should use your own discretion about showing it to our great friend, and if you think it would vex him in any way do not do so. I leave it to your judgment, it being entirely an 'off the record' document.

1. I am deeply perturbed by the way 'Torch' is being knocked about, and above all at the needless delays, which add so much to our joint troubles. It had been a long and slow business getting rid of 'Sledgehammer', but when you left here on July 25 all was set for full steam ahead, and I certainly thought that Marshall had reconciled himself to the President's final decision. We gladly accepted General Eisenhower as the Allied Commander-in-Chief, and he and Clark, these two very fine officers, set to work at once. It was

not however until the 14th of August that a definite directive was received from the Combined Staffs in Washington. Upon this all thoughts were concentrated. An amphibious operation like this has to fit together like a jewelled bracelet; for each particular landing-place the right ships must be chosen, and these ships must be loaded in accordance with the needs of the particular work each landing party has to do. This does not affect all the ships, as many can work common service, but quite a proportion have to be fitted to their *rôle* and to the slope of the beaches and depth of the water off the coasts they are to strike. I do not wish to exaggerate this, because naturally one has to take a chance in a good many things, but the more careful the arrangements the better the results.

2. At any rate, all was going forward, and until a week ago there was no reason why we should not have made the date October 15. Then suddenly out of the blue arrived the shattering memorandum of the United States Chiefs of Staff, which altered the whole character and emphasis of the operation— discarding Algiers, the softest and most paying spot, and throwing all the major weight upon Casablanca and the Atlantic shore, which after prolonged study we think may be quite impossible on account of the surf for a sea landing, and which is certainly four to one against, even in October. It seemed so easy, no doubt, to say, 'Abandon Algiers; switch around to Casablanca; find other troops for Oran', but look at the effect this had on all the work which had been done. I have been a witness of the distresses into which your two brilliant officers have been thrown by the delays and by the changes in policy coming from the United States Chiefs of Staff. Indeed, Eisenhower's position has been a very painful one. On the one hand, below him British and American Staff Officers clamouring for decisions on a whole host of points of detail; on the other, the restriction of the rigid and at the same time changeable control from across the ocean. What is the use of putting up an Allied Commander-in-Chief or Supreme Commander if he cannot have the slightest freedom in making his plan or deciding how, when, and where to apply his forces? We are prepared to take his decisions and to obey. Even if we do not agree we will obey, after having put the facts before you. We are only out to help him in every way to give effect to the President's great strategic conception. Now the whole matter has to go back across the Atlantic and completely new schemes are set us. I do not see how a united command is possible if the Supreme Commander is not allowed to act.

3. Frankly, I do not understand what is at the back of all this. I thought there was agreement with Marshall and that

King had been paid off with what he needed for his Pacific war. But now it seems there is a bad come-back from the professional circles in the American Army, and I have a deep and growing fear that the whole of the President's enterprise may be wrecked bit by bit. With it will fall the brightest hope of the Allies and the only hope this year. One change of plan after another will produce delays; the enormous numbers of people in our two countries who will get wind of what is going on will make it sure that the enemy will be informed. With every day's delay the Germans have a better chance of forestalling us. Now the earliest that can be hoped for is the first week of November, but I should be very much surprised if it was not the last week. What will have happened by then in other quarters no one can predict.

4. What particularly puzzles me is that I do not know what are the reasons which make the United States Staffs so reluctant to go inside the Mediterranean, and especially to Algiers, and so eager to concentrate all the weight on Casablanca. Let us take first the resistance of the French. Generally speaking, I agree with the President's views and hopes about this. I think there is at least a fifty-fifty chance that the French will not shed American blood and have a massacre of American youth on the beaches of North Africa. The past and still more the future of France would forbid such an episode. At any rate, I think the risk is not disproportionate, and should be run because the prize is so great. But if this assumption is correct and the French make no resistance or only token resistance and thereafter come over to our side, as follows inevitably from their not resisting, this would apply simultaneously at Casablanca and Oran, and above all at Algiers, where the atmosphere is most favourable. If then you succeed in getting these ports easily and swiftly, as it must be, on the first day, the world is confronted with a new fact and we need not anticipate any trouble from Spain. There will be a peaceful occupation for liberation purposes of French North Africa, and the next step will be to build up the attack on Sicily and Italy, as well as on Rommel's back at Tripoli.

5. But take the other alternative. Let us assume that there is fighting, that the batteries fire, that the ports are denied and that French aircraft bombard Gibraltar harbour, as they did when the Dakar show was on. Then indeed the Spaniards may be tempted by the bribes and the threats of the Germans to take a hand in rendering Gibraltar untenable. I think myself they would wait until they were quite sure things had gone wrong before exposing themselves to our vengeance. Our hope in this case is surely to make the landings inside

the Mediterranean in as great a force and at as great a speed as possible, and overcome the French resistance, and get on shore and get some ports. This is why we do not understand the Casablanca emphasis, because it will be made at the expense of the landings inside, and if there is resistance inside *a fortiori* there will be resistance on the Atlantic shore, with this difference—that you can overcome the resistance inside and cannot overcome it outside unless the surf is favourable, which is four to one against. In short, the place to determine French action is inside, and if it is determined there in a favourable sense there will be no difficulty in occupying Casablanca by agreement later. On the other hand, what happens if there is a rebuff at Casablanca? What are all the troops to do that cannot land on the beaches through the surf and cannot go up the creeks and small harbours in the big ships by which they have crossed the Atlantic, and will have to face the shore batteries and the machine-gun defences of the harbour if they try a frontal attack on Casablanca port?

This letter was never sent to Hopkins, nor did Mountbatten have to cross the Atlantic. Before I had need to send it I received the following most helpful and hopeful telegram from the President:

President Roosevelt to Former Naval Person   4 Sept 42
. . . We are getting very close together. I am willing to reduce the Casablanca force by the number of combat loaders capable of carrying a force of one regimental combat team. Approximately 5,000 men. Since a similar reduction was made in original Oran assault force, this releases a total of British and United States combat loaders for some 10,000 men for use at Algiers. The combat-loaded force of American troops can be used as the nucleus on which to complete that force. I am sure that the additional troops can be found in the United Kingdom.

I do not see advantage of Eisenhower or Clark coming over at this time. I know they have heavy and pressing responsibilities in organising slowly arriving American forces, and I am sure we have a full understanding of their view-point. Furthermore, I do want to see Eisenhower later on before final take-off, and two trips appear out of the question. We would be glad to see Ramsay and Mountbatten if you wish to send them, but I do not desire that their visit shall cause any delay. I am directing all preparations to proceed. We should settle this whole thing with finality at once.

I hope to cable you to-day a list of United States naval craft which can be made available for the operation.

118

Former Naval Person to President Roosevelt   5 Sept 42

We agree to the military lay-out as you propose it. We
have plenty of troops highly trained for landing. If convenient, they can wear your uniform. They will be proud to do
so. Shipping will be all right.

2. I have just had your telegram,* and it is evident that
you too have skinned yourselves to the bone. Unless we
suffer serious losses in P.Q., we consider that naval forces now
jointly to be provided justify us in going full speed ahead
with staging the operations.

3. I am sending Admiral Ramsay,† with the agreement of
General Eisenhower, over at once to furnish Admiral Cunningham with the means of going into naval details with you.
It is imperative now to drive straight ahead and save every
hour. In this way alone shall we realise your strategical design
and the only hope of doing anything that really counts this
year.

4. We strongly endorse the request which we understand
Eisenhower has already made to Marshall that the force you
are releasing from Casablanca may be sent over here complete with its regimental combat team.

Kindest regards.

President Roosevelt to Prime Minister   5 Sept 42

Hurrah!

Former Naval Person to President Roosevelt   6 Sept 42

O.K., full blast.

*   *   *

It now remained to press forward the planning and timing
of the operation.

Prime Minister to Brigadier Hollis   6 Sept 42

There is no need for anyone to get excited for fear 'Torch'
should happen too early. Intense efforts must be made to
strike on October 31. To ensure this it would be well to aim
at October 29. I propose to telegraph to the President in this
sense. Surely if the Americans can be ready at their end we
can conform at ours?

* *President Roosevelt to Former Naval Person*   5 Sept 42
[Admiral] King reports maximum number of American naval vessels that can be made
available for 'Torch' operation: one modern battleship, two old battleships, one aircraft
carrier, two small converted aircraft-carriers (tentative planes carried total seventy-eight
fighters, thirty dive-bombers), two 8-inch cruisers, three large 6-inch cruisers, forty
destroyers, six fast mine-sweepers; total, fifty-seven vessels.
† Admiral Ramsay, who had commanded at Dover with conspicuous ability since the
beginning of the war, had been selected to undertake the naval planning of 'Torch'.

We must beware lest we give orders which lead to a general slacking off. If you announce October 31 as the earliest date it will certainly be ten days later.

On September 8 Eisenhower and Clark dined with me. It was our regular Tuesday meeting. I had come back from speaking in the House of Commons upon the results of my recent journey. The main purpose of our talk that evening was to discuss the final date of attack in North Africa. The planners were still aiming at November 4. I asked 'Ike' for his view. 'November 8—sixty days from to-day,' was his answer.* The new delay was apparently due to the need for equipping the American regimental combat teams. I offered, as before, to place our highly trained Commandos in American uniform in order to avoid further delay. 'Ike' however was anxious to keep to the all-American character of the operation.

On September 15 I telegraphed to the President :

Former Naval Person to President Roosevelt   15 Sept 42
I entirely agree with your political outlook on 'Torch'. It is sound unless we are forestalled. There is no sign that the enemy is aware, and the mood of France is now at its very best. I count the days.

In the whole of 'Torch', military and political, I consider myself your lieutenant, asking only to put my view-point plainly before you. We shall have a wireless station of overriding power available by zero, so that if you dictate your appeals to France and other propaganda material to gramophone records beforehand these can be blared out over everything during the performance. We British will come in only as and when you judge expedient. This is an American enterprise, in which we are your helpmeets.

I had however my own anxieties about Spain.

Prime Minister to Secretary of State for Foreign   16 Sept 42
Affairs, and to Brigadier Hollis, for C.O.S. Committee
We shall have to watch very carefully Spanish reactions to preparations for 'Torch' which will become evident at Gibraltar. I should like to have a short report on what we shall be putting into Gibraltar in preparation for 'Torch', with a time-table. How much of these preparations would exceed the normal for a big Malta convoy?

2. The arrival of large numbers of aircraft will be the crux of the problem, and the use of the neutral ground will be involved.

* Harry C. Butcher, *Three Years with Eisenhower* (English edition), p. 82.

3. What will happen if, about a fortnight before zero 'Torch', the Germans put pressure on Spain for an explanation of these preparations and demand either that the neutral ground is cleared or that they are allowed to install their own aircraft in the Valencia airfields? What are the likely Spanish reactions to this pressure, and what should be our attitude? We might be faced with a show-down with Franco over this at an awkward moment. I think we should have our plans prepared.

The final decision was taken on September 22 at a Chiefs of Staff meeting at which I presided and Eisenhower was present. The date of 'Torch' was fixed for November 8.

*   *   *

In the midst of all the tense correspondence with the President about our major operation Rommel made his determined but, as it proved, his last thrust towards Cairo. Until this was over my thoughts lay in the Desert and the trial of strength impending there. I had full confidence in our new commanders, and was sure that our numerical superiority in troops, armour, and air-power was higher than it had ever been before. But after the unpleasant surprises of the past two years it was difficult to banish anxiety. As I had been so lately over the very ground where the battle was to be fought, and had the picture of the creased and curving rocky desert, with its hidden batteries and tanks and our Army crouched for a counter-spring, so vividly in my mind's eyes, the whole scene was fiercely lighted. Another reverse would not only be disastrous in itself, but would damage British prestige and influence in the discussions we were having with our American Allies. On the other hand, if Rommel were repulsed growing confidence and the feeling that the tide was about to turn in our favour would help carry all our other affairs to agreement.

General Alexander had promised to send me the word 'Zip' (which I took from the clothes I so often wore) when it actually began. 'What do you now think' I asked him on August 28, 'of the probabilities of "Zip" coming this moon? Military Intelligence opinion now does not regard it as imminent. All good wishes.' ' "Zip" now equal money every day,' he replied, 'from now onwards. Odds against [it are] increasing till September 2, when it can be considered unlikely.' On the 30th I received the monosyllabic signal 'Zip', and telegraphed to Roosevelt and Stalin: 'Rommel has begun the attack for which we have been preparing. An important battle may now be fought.'

Rommel's plan, correctly deduced by Montgomery, was to pass his armour through the weakly defended mine-belt in the southern part of the British front and then swing north to roll up our position from flank and rear. The critical ground for the success of this manœuvre was the Alam Halfa ridge, and Montgomery's dispositions were made principally to ensure that this did not fall into enemy hands.

During the night of August 30 the two armoured divisions of the German Afrika Korps penetrated the mine-belt, and next morning moved to the Ragil Depression. Our 7th Armoured Division, withdrawing steadily before them, took station on the eastward flank. To the north of the German armour two Italian armoured divisions and one motorised also attempted to cross the minefield. They had little success. It was deeper than they had expected, and they found themselves under severe harassing fire from the enfilading artillery of the New Zealand Division. The German 90th Light Division however successfully penetrated, to form a hinge for the armour's northern swing. At the other end of the line simultaneous holding attacks were made on the 5th Indian and 9th Australian Divisions; these were repulsed after some stiff fighting. From the Ragil Depression the German–Italian armour had the option of striking north against the Alam Halfa ridge or north-east towards Hammam. Montgomery hoped that they would not take the latter course. He preferred to fight on his chosen battle-ground, the ridge. A map which showed easy going for tanks in that direction and bad going farther east had been planted upon Rommel. General von Thoma, captured two months later, stated that this false information had its intended effect. Certainly the battle now took the precise form that Montgomery desired.

On the evening of the 31st a northward thrust was repulsed and the enemy's armoured mass went into laager for a night, uncomfortably spent under continuous artillery fire and violent air bombardment. Next morning they advanced against the centre of the British line, where the 10th Armoured Division were now concentrated to meet them. The sand was much heavier than they had been led to believe and the resistance far stronger than they had hoped. The attack, though renewed in the afternoon, failed. Rommel was now deeply committed. The Italians had foundered. He had no hope of reinforcing his

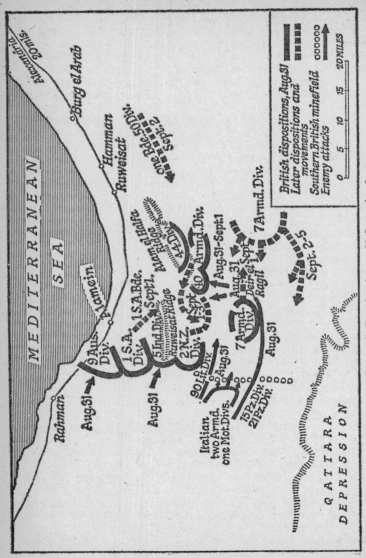

Rommel's Repulse, August 31–September 5.

forward armour and the heavy going had consumed much of his scanty fuel. He had probably heard also of the sinking of three more tankers in the Mediterranean. So on September 2 his armour took up a defensive posture and awaited attack.

Montgomery did not accept the invitation, and Rommel had no alternative but to withdraw. On the 3rd the movement began, harassed in flank by the 7th British Armoured Division, which took a heavy toll of unarmoured transport vehicles. That night the British counter-attack began, not on the enemy armour, but on the 90th Light and the Trieste Motorised Divisions. If these could be broken, then the gaps in the minefield might be blocked before the German armour could return through them. The New Zealand Division made strong attacks, but they were fiercely resisted and the Afrika Korps escaped. Montgomery now stopped the pursuit. He planned to seize the initiative when the time was ripe, but not yet. He was content to have repulsed Rommel's final thrust for Egypt with such heavy loss. At relatively little cost to themselves the Eighth Army and the Desert Air Force had inflicted a heavy stroke upon the enemy and caused another crisis in his supply. From documents captured later we know that Rommel was in dire straits and of his insistent demands for help. We know too that he was a wearied, ailing man at the time. The consequences of Alam Halfa, as the engagement was called, were effective two months later.

Our losses were 110 officers and 1,640 men. Of these the British lost 984, the Australians 257, the New Zealanders 405, the South Africans 65, and the Indians 39. It was indeed an Empire battle, in which the Mother Country bore the brunt.

CHAPTER 8

Suspense and Strain

A Trying Interlude – An Unbroken Catalogue of Misfortunes – The top of the Pass – Unity and Strength of the War Cabinet – Lord Trenchard Advocates Concentration on the Air – My Reply of September 4 – Sir Stafford Cripps Criticises Our War Methods – My Discussion with Him – He Wishes to Resign from the Government – My Letter to Him of September 22 – My Colleagues Urge Him to Delay His Resignation – He Decides to Remain till After the Battle – He Becomes Minister of Aircraft Production – Consequential Changes in the Government – The Four-Power Plan – My Minute to the Foreign Secretary, October 21 – I Look Forward to the United States of Europe.

Although our two great operations at both ends of the Mediterranean were now settled and all preparations for them were moving forward, the period of waiting was one of suppressed but extreme tension. The inner circle who knew were anxious about what would happen. All those who did not know were disquieted that nothing was happening.

I had now been twenty-eight months at the head of affairs, during which we had sustained an almost unbroken series of military defeats. We had survived the collapse of France and the air attack on Britain. We had not been invaded. We still held Egypt. We were alive and at bay ; but that was all. On the other hand, what a cataract of disasters had fallen upon us! The fiasco of Dakar, the loss of all our Desert conquests from the Italians, the tragedy of Greece, the loss of Crete, the unrelieved reverses of the Japanese war, the loss of Hong Kong, the overrunning of the A.B.D.A. Command and all its territories, the catastrophe of Singapore, the Japanese conquest of Burma, Auchinleck's defeat in the Desert, the surrender of Tobruk, the failure, as it was judged, at Dieppe—all these were galling links in a chain of misfortune and frustration to which no parallel could be found in our history. The fact that we were no longer alone, but instead had the two most mighty nations in the world in alliance fighting desperately at our side, gave indeed assurances of ultimate victory. But this, by removing the sense of mortal peril, only made criticism more free. Was it strange that the whole character and system of the war direction, for which I was responsible, should have been brought into question and challenge?

It is indeed remarkable that I was not in this bleak lull dismissed from power, or confronted with demands for changes in my methods, which it was known I would never accept. I should then have vanished from the scene with a load of calamity on my shoulders, and the harvest, at last to be reaped, would have been ascribed to my belated disappearance. For indeed the whole aspect of the war was about to be transformed. Henceforward increasing success, marred hardly by a mishap, was to be our lot. Although the struggle would be long and hard, requiring the most strenuous effort from all, we had reached the top of the pass, and our road to victory was not only sure and certain, but accompanied by constant cheering events. I was not denied the right to share in this new phase of the war because of the unity and strength of the War Cabinet, the confidence which I preserved of my political and professional colleagues, the steadfast loyalty of Parliament, and the persisting goodwill of the nation. All this shows how much luck there is in human affairs, and how little we should worry about anything except doing our best.

A number of eminent people with whom I was in various degrees of intimacy felt the stress of these two months acutely. One of the ablest and most important of the Dominion High Commissioners wrote a weighty letter which reached me, and was also circulated in our select circle. This document began: 'The emotional value of Mr. Churchill is no doubt very great, but . . .' There followed a long catalogue of my failures and a wealth of proposals for lightening my burdens by taking power out of my hands.

* * *

My friend Lord Trenchard, whom I had known and often worked with over a quarter of a century, wrote a powerful paper, of which he sent me a copy, advocating a concentration on bombing *in exelsis*.

29 Aug 42

We and the Americans are in course of organising huge armies (maybe as much as six to eight millions for the United States alone). These armies will need enormous quantities of material and industrial man-power to maintain them, of merchant shipping to convey that material, and other ships (and aircraft) to protect it in convoy. It is doubtful if the sources of raw material available to the Allies will be sufficient to equip these forces, and on a scale which will enable them to sustain heavy operations in the face of setbacks and wastage. . . .

Time is short and we are at a parting of the ways. The risk is that we shall try to go down two roads, and that our air-power will be inextricably entangled in large schemes and protracted operations of two-dimensional warfare. . . .

For the country to get mixed up this year or next in land warfare on the continent of Europe is to play Germany's game—it is to revert to 1914–18. It is to bring in against us the one enormously powerful military asset remaining to the enemy—namely, the German Army. Our strength and advantage over Germany is in the air—the British and the American Air Force. . . .

The strategy of warfare to-day is undergoing a greater change than that caused by the invention of gunpowder or the coming of the modern battleship. The power of the air grows every day. It has progressed enormously since 1939. The bombs and the bomber to-day are vastly different from those in use when war broke out. . . .

Britain and America are growing stronger in the air every day. There is no realisable limit to the power we can achieve in this arm *if we concentrate our efforts on a policy which realises what we can do—and do quickly*. . . .

The policy of victory by land forces entails stupendous drains on material and man-power. Air, the new dimension, the power in military science, has given the Allied nations the great alternative. If we decide to use it with determination and concentration we can not only save millions of lives, but we can shorten the war by months, perhaps by years. . . .

As the enemy conquered Poland and France by their 'tank blitz', so can we smash the German machine by the 'bomber blitz'. . . .

Finally, the carrying out of this policy requires that there should be one brain responsible for the purely military (in its widest sense) strategical conception of the war in Europe, supported of course by a staff representative of all three Services. It would be essential that this commander should be one who believes in his weapon, the power of the air, and should have had experience of command in this war. There are many such.

*   *   *

Making all allowances for the shoemaker who said there is nothing like leather, I considered this paper, coming from a high authority like Lord Trenchard, so important that I had it printed and circulated, together with a similar document by Air Marshal Harris, to the War Cabinet and Chiefs of Staff, with the following note:

I do not myself adopt or endorse the views expressed. ... Nevertheless, as these papers are written with force and vigour I thought they might be of interest to my colleagues. They also serve as a considerable answer to those who attack the usefulness of our bombing policy.

To Lord Trenchard I wrote:

Prime Minister to Viscount Trenchard　　　　　　　4 Sept 42
Many thanks for your interesting paper. As you may have heard, I am a champion of Bomber Command, and I do my utmost to strengthen it in every way and to prevent it from being wrongfully inroaded upon.

While admitting and admiring the force of your arguments, I think you spoil a good case by overstating it. You certainly push it to lengths where very few people here or in the United States would agree with you. However, as I am most anxious to combat the attacks made upon what is called 'the luxury bombing of Germany' and the campaign of disparagement which has been pressed upon bombing from so many quarters, I am circulating your paper to the War Cabinet, as I did a recent document by Air Marshal Harris.

With regard to your last paragraph, it is very difficult to divorce the head of the executive in any country from the chief responsibility for the conduct of the war. In the United States and Russia the head of the executive is also Commander-in-Chief, although neither Mr. Roosevelt nor Premier Stalin has any military experience or training. In this country it would be even more difficult to separate the chief constitutional authority from all control over the war sphere, which is identical with the whole life and fortunes of the nation. To pick an airman, give him plenary powers, and tell him to win the war is certainly a policy, but I wonder whether you have thought it out in all its implications. He would certainly have great difficulty with the other two Services. He would also have difficulty with the Allies, who adopt quite different systems, and particularly with the United States, who hold rigidly to a subordinate Air Force. There might also be trouble with the House of Commons, the Cabinet, and all that sort of thing. Should the right man be found however many of these difficulties could be overcome by his becoming at the same time Prime Minister. If I were convinced that this solution would bring about a speedy victory I should be very glad to make way for him. Would it be too much to inquire whom you have in mind? You say there are many. I was not aware that our Services were so rich in talent as to have a number of officers who have already commanded in this war who take your view about the air, and who are capable of being the 'one brain responsible for the purely military (in its widest sense) strategical conception of the war in Europe'.

With good wishes. . . .

Trenchard replied on September 8:

. . . My paper was not written for you, as I know too well that you are keen on hitting our chief enemy in Germany. It was written for a certain number of people who I thought might be influenced by the views of a complete outsider like myself. . . .

My last paragraph was not intended in any shape or form to have the meaning you have attached to it. I was not suggesting that the head of the executive should be divorced from the chief responsibility for the war. I have never expressed or held such a view. What I was trying to say was this. In many newspapers and discussions it has been suggested that there should be one Commander-in-Chief appointed for Europe—a man like Marshall or Wavell—and I wanted to combat the idea that it must necessarily be an Army man. If air is the dominant force, the force that can give us victory, why *must* the commander be a military man? Why is our strategy to be based on the 'ground' view when we know now that it is the air which decides? . . .

*   *   *

But the most serious comment on our war methods came from Sir Stafford Cripps, the Lord Privy Seal. As Leader of the House of Commons his position was one of prime importance. On him fell the burden of explaining our successive defeats and disappointments to the House of Commons, and he certainly discharged this task with skill and loyalty. Severance between him and me during this period of oppressive pause would have created a political crisis. I was therefore very gravely concerned to find, on my return from abroad at the end of August, that he had developed serious doubts about the state of the national morale and the effectiveness of our machinery for the central direction of the war. In the mood of public opinion at home he detected a widespread sense of frustration and discontent. Workers, he believed were suffering a demoralising sense of futility when they heard that the weapons which they had strained every nerve to produce had been found wanting in Libya. Scientists and technicians with ideas for operational devices were receiving no encouragement. Business men were exasperated at official delays and indecisions and at the wasteful proliferation of committees. In the Services officers and men were baffled and disturbed by evidence of inadequate military leadership. There was, he thought, an urgent need to infuse a new spirit of vigour and enthusiasm into the nation's war effort. For this purpose he proposed a series of reforms in our machinery of government. With some of these I found myself in full sympathy, and initiated action to give effect to them. But on the main question of the technical direction of the war I was profoundly at variance with the views expressed by the Lord Privy Seal. He did not, it is true, suggest that I should be superseded or displaced from my position: he proposed instead that as Minister of Defence I should have associated with me, as advisers, three persons of the calibre of the Chiefs of Staff who would supervise the Joint Planning Staffs and would be free to devote the whole of their time to military planning in its broadest sense. These three were to form an independent War Planning Directorate, which would keep under review the whole strategy of the war and consider all future operations; and for these purposes they were to supersede the Chiefs of Staff Committee. In each theatre of war there would be a single Commander with full power over all the naval, land, and air forces. These Commanders, advised by a small joint staff, would be responsible directly to the War Planning Directorate. The conception was, in brief, that the Minister of Defence should turn himself into a Supreme Commander-in-Chief directly commanding all three Services all over the world, so that from the Minister downwards there would be an unbroken chain of foresight, planning, and action.

This was in truth a planner's dream. The new Directorate, concerned solely with planning and armed with full powers of direction and control, would be free to go its way without distraction by the daily cares which beset the Chiefs of Staff in controlling the forces over which they exercised command. These manifold cares would continue to be left to the Chiefs of Staff and the staffs which served them in their individual and collective capacities, while the Supreme Command elaborated its strategy and plans in splendid isolation. I did not believe that such a dualism could succeed, and I addressed myself with zeal and vigour to the Lord Privy Seal's proposals. I judged them to be misconceived in theory and unworkable in practice. The guiding principle of war direction is, in my opinon, that war plans should be formulated by those who have the power and the responsibility for executing them. Under the system which we had evolved in the hard school of experience the need for inter-Service planning was fully met by the Chiefs of Staff Committee and its subordinate bodies, in which those carrying the responsibility for execution came together to make jointly the plans which they were to carry out. The establishment of a War Planning Directorate divorced from the Service staffs responsible for action would have been vicious in principle, for it would have created two rival bodies, one responsible and one irresponsible, yet both nominally of equal status. It would have confronted Ministers with the constant need to disregard the advice of one or other of these bodies. It would have led at once to immediate and violent friction. Was an admiral to be appointed to the War Planning Directorate with power to tell the First Lord how to move the Fleet, or an air marshal 'of equal calibre' to criticise by implication the Chief of the Air Staff? It was easy to see the dangers and antagonisms inherent in such a system. Any clever person can make plans for winning a war if he has no responsibility for carrying them out. Such ingenuity and resource is to be encouraged in the members of Planning Staffs, so long as they are definitely and effectively subordinated in status to the Service chiefs who carry the executive responsibility. I was not however prepared to invite a disembodied Brains Trust to browse about among our secrets and add to the already immense volume of committees and reports. My long experience in these matters had taught me that a Minister of Defence must work with and through responsible advisers—that is to say, war chiefs who can give effect to the decisions taken and are accountable for the results. There had never been a period, in this war or the last, when the relations between the Prime Minister and the three Service chiefs were so good and smooth, or when there was such complete identity of view upon all the measures to be taken. Why then should I withdraw my confidence from those professional advisers whom I considered to be the best that the Services had at this time, in order to bestow it in part at least upon officers who would be not only less responsible but less capable? It was a delusion to suppose that there was a large supply of officers 'of equal calibre' to those whom I had chosen to discharge the heavy responsibilities of the Chiefs of Staff.

With these and similar arguments I wrestled with the Lord Privy Seal and strove to win him over to my point of view. This stern discussion occupied the larger part of September. But I did not succeed in convincing him, and on September 21 he intimated to me that he felt it his duty to resign his position in the Government, in which he held so commanding an office. Since his return from India, he said, he no longer felt that I relied upon his help, and found himself increasingly out of touch with my mind on a wide range of subjects on which, as Leader of the House of Commons, he ought to have an intimate knowledge. He was deeply anxious about the war situation, and, in the light of the developments of recent months and the heavy responsibilities weighing upon all members of the War Cabinet, he was anxious to know how I viewed the future. To this I replied:

My dear Cripps,   22 Sept 42
I am surprised and somewhat pained to receive your letter. I was certainly not aware of any change in our relationship since you first took office seven months ago. I thought we were on the most cordial terms when I set out on my journey at the beginning of August. In the seven weeks that have passed since then I have been away for nearly a month, and you later for more than a week. Apart from Cabinets (of which we have had three, aggregating six hours and a half, in the last twenty-four hours) I always do my best to see my principal colleagues. I have always found our conversations agreeable and stimulating. I hope you will not fail to come and see me whenever you wish.

With regard to the further memorandum which you have been good enough to send me on the whole system and method by which, for good or for ill, I endeavour to discharge my task of presiding over the Government and the conduct of the war, no one knows better than you the controversial significance of all that you write. I also have convictions on these matters, which are the result of long experience and heavy responsibility. Another would no doubt do differently.

I do not intend to argue here, as it would be endless, but I am sure you would not underrate the wisdom, knowledge, and precision of mind of the First Sea Lord if you had worked with him as closely as I have under the hard stresses of this war. Indeed, I cannot help saying that I feel you are less than generous to the Admiralty achievement by which we have lived.

You ask me how I view the future. I view it with hope, and, I trust, with undiminished firmness of spirit. Great operations impend which are in full accordance with your own conceptions and on which we are all agreed. We must have the fibre and fortitude to endure the delays and await the outcome. As I myself find waiting more trying than action, I can fully understand the uneasiness you say you feel.

Yours very sincerely,
WINSTON S. CHURCHILL

I realised, none the less, that he would not again give me his full confidence and that he could not for long take his full share of responsibility as a colleague in the War Cabinet. It was clear to me that if he resigned from the Government on this account keen political controversy must follow ; and, although I was resolved to face this, I hoped that it would not take place while all hung in the balance in Africa. Several of my colleagues in the War Cabinet urged him to consider whether his resignation at this juncture would not be injurious to the public interest, having regard to the great operations which were now drawing ever nearer to their decisive moment. Although it was evident that if we won the impending battles in North Africa my position would be overwhelmingly strengthened and his proportionately reduced, his patriotism ruled his conduct.

My dear Prime Minister   3 Oct 42
In accordance with my promise when I saw you yesterday, I am writing to you about my position in the War Cabinet, which we have been discussing during the last few days.

You have not convinced me that the changes which I have suggested in the central direction of the war are unnecessary. I firmly believe that alterations of that nature are essential if we are to make the most of our war potential.

Such a conviction would have led me to ask you to place my resignation in the hands of H.M. the King, were it not for the special circumstances to which you and my other colleagues have drawn my attention.

I fully realise however, as you have impressed upon me, that this precise moment is one of great anxiety for the country and for the Government. In such circumstances it is clear that nothing avoidable should be done during these particular critical days by the suggestion of disunity or of differences as to the central direction of the war, which might disturb the morale of our fighting men or increase our international difficulties.

These temporary considerations seem to me to override even the necessity for the changes that I have suggested, and I have therefore decided that it is my duty, in the interests of the successful prosecution of the coming operations, to delay taking any further action as regards my position in the War Cabinet until the operations are at least well launched.

When the time arrives I will revert to this matter.

It is, I am sure, unnecessary for me to add that in the meantime I shall do my utmost to assist you in every possible way and that I shall give you my most energetic support wherever and whenever I can.

PS. I have shown this letter to Anthony Eden and Clem Attlee, and have told the other members of the War Cabinet of the general line of my action.

My dear Stafford Cripps,   3 Oct 42

I am sure that you are right to withhold your resignation until the great operations upon which we have all agreed have been, as you say, at least well launched. The discussions attending your departure from the Government could not fail at the present time to be harmful to the public interest and to the safety of British and American troops. It would be very difficult for me to take part in them without saying something from which the enemy might draw conclusions. On the other hand, you are fully entitled to bring our differences to an issue at a later stage. Meanwhile I thank you for your assurance that you will give me all possible help in the interval, and I shall certainly reciprocate your aid and courtesy to the full.

*   *   *

In the event Sir Stafford Cripps did not withdraw entirely from the Government. Although he was no longer willing to accept the full responsibilities entailed by membership of the War Cabinet itself, I was anxious to find some other field of service within the Government in which his talents and energies could continue to be used. In November, when the battle in Africa was fairly launched, I prevailed upon him to take Ministerial charge of the Ministry of Aircraft Production, an office which he held with increasing skill and effectiveness until the end of the war. I am glad to be able to acknowledge my sense of obligation to him for the loyal and efficient service which he rendered as a Production Minister during those three difficult years. Elsewhere in this book I have said that an exalted brooding over the work of others is only too often the lot of a Minister without departmental duties. For a man of his keen intellect, as yet untempered by administrative experience, his exalted ideals, and his skill in theoretical exposition, this form of activity held a strong though dangerous appeal. His great intellectual energy needed to be harnessed to a more practical task ; and the success which he achieved as Minister of Aircraft Production, no less than the sense of frustration which he suffered as Lord Privy Seal, only deepens my regret that he should have declined my original proposal that he should join the Government in the first instance as Minister of Supply.

*   *   *

It will be convenient if at this point, in defiance of chronology, I complete this part of my story by recording the other Cabinet changes which became necessary at the end of November. I had long felt the need to have a Minister resident in Washington to handle the numerous supply problems which arose with the United States Administration and could best be settled at a Ministerial level. Colonel J. J. Llewellin readily agreed to make way for Sir Stafford Cripps at the Ministry of Aircraft Production and to assume instead this responsible rôle in Washington. Viscount Cranborne, who had a heavy task as Leader of the House of Lords, accepted the office of Lord Privy Seal and surrendered his departmental duties at the Colonial Office to Colonel Oliver Stanley, who was willing at this time to abandon his military work and to resume Ministerial office. Mr. Anthony Eden agreed to add to his duties as Foreign Secretary the task of leading the House of Commons.

Sir Stafford Cripps's transfer to the Ministry of Aircraft Production left a vacancy in the War Cabinet, which was filled by Mr. Herbert Morrison. As Home Secretary and Minister of Home Security he had used his great administrative ability to advantage in adapting our Civil Defence organisation to meet the varying challenges of 1940 and 1941 ; now he had rather more time in which to deploy his political agility. My War Cabinet colleagues were glad to have his assistance in their councils.

*   *   *

Amid these internal political stresses I found some relief in examining the proposals which the Foreign Office were elaborating, in consultation with the State Department in Washington, on the future of world government after the war. The

Foreign Secretary circulated to the War Cabinet in October an important document on this subject entitled 'The Four-Power Plan', under which the supreme direction would have come from a council composed of Great Britain, the United States, Russia, and China. I am glad that I found strength to put my own opinions on record in the following minute.

Prime Minister to Foreign Secretary   21 Oct 42
   In spite of the pressure of events, I will endeavour to write a reply. It sounds very simple to pick out these four Big Powers. We cannot however tell what sort of a Russia and what kind of Russian demands we shall have to face. A little later on it may be possible. As to China, I cannot regard the Chungking Government as representing a great world-Power. Certainly there would be a faggot vote on the side of the United States in any attempt to liquidate the British overseas Empire.
   2. I must admit that my thoughts rest primarily in Europe —the revival of the glory of Europe, the parent continent of the modern nations and of civilisation. It would be a measureless disaster if Russian barbarism overlaid the culture and independence of the ancient States of Europe. Hard as it is to say now, I trust that the European family may act unitedly as one under a council of Europe. I look forward to a United States of Europe in which the barriers between the nations will be greatly minimised and unrestricted travel will be possible. I hope to see the economy of Europe studied as a whole. I hope to see a Council consisting of perhaps ten units, including the former Great Powers, with several con- federations—Scandinavian, Danubian, Balkan, etc.—which would possess an international police and be charged with keeping Prussia disarmed. Of course we shall have to work with the Americans in many ways, and in the greatest ways, but Europe is our prime care, and we certainly do not wish to be shut up with the Russians and the Chinese when Swedes, Norwegians, Danes, Dutch, Belgians, Frenchmen, Spaniards, Poles, Czechs, and Turks will have their burning questions, their desire for our aid, and their very great power of making their voices heard. It would be easy to dilate upon these themes. Unhappily the war has prior claims on your atten- tion and on mine.

*   *   *

Thus we approached the great military climax upon which all was to be staked.

CHAPTER 9

Soviet 'Thank You'

Vehement Resolves to Help Russia – Anglo-American Air Support on Their Southern Flank: Operation 'Velvet' – The President Agrees – Hopes of Renewing the Arctic Convoys after 'Torch' – My Telegram to Stalin, September 6 – My Further Efforts for Operation 'Jupiter' – Need to Inform Stalin of the Suspension of the Arctic Convoys – Correspondence with the President – The Peril in the Caucasus: My Confidence – The Treatment of Our Merchant Seamen at Archangel and Murmansk – Molotov at His Worst – The President's Telegram to Me of October 5 About Helping Russia – Stalin's Telegram of October 5 – My Comments to the President, October 7 – I Outline the 'Velvet' Plan to Stalin – His 'Thank You' – Soviet Suspicions and Propaganda – The Magnificent Struggle of the Russian Armies – German Failure to Reach the Oilfields – The Lure of Stalingrad – Hitler Dismisses Halder – The Vast Russian Counter-stroke – The Pincers Meet, November 23 – Doom of the Sixth German Army.

I returned from Moscow with new resolve to aid Russia to the very limits of our power. It was clear that the coming winter campaign would be the supreme crisis of the struggle in the East, that the Russian southern flank in the Don and the Caucasus regions were to be the theatre, and the oilfields of Baku and the domination of the Caspian area the immediate German goal. I had been impressed by Stalin's solid confidence that he would win, and knew from what he had told me at the Kremlin that he planned some tremendous counter-stroke. There was little enough that we could do to sway this gigantic conflict. We must send supplies at all costs by every route to the Russian armies. We must maintain the Arctic convoys and develop the Trans-Persian railway. The only direct military help we could give was to place a strong Anglo-American Air Force in the Caspian area. Even this must wait for its fulfilment till victory was gained in the Western Desert. Meanwhile all preparations for it would go forward, under the name of Operation 'Velvet'.

As soon as I got home I presented the project formally to the President.

Former Naval Person to President Roosevelt   30 Aug 42

The project of placing on the southern flank of Russian armies a British and presently American Air Force must be viewed as a long-term policy in our co-operation with Russia and for the defence of the Persian oilfields. The main reasons appear to be:

(*a*) to strengthen the Russian air-power generally;

(*b*) to form the advance shield of all our interests in Persia and Abadan;

(*c*) for moral effect of comradeship with the Russians, which will be out of all proportion to the forces employed; and

(*d*) because this is no dispersion of forces, but a greater concentration on the supreme Allied Air Force target, namely, wearing down the German Air Force by daily fighting contact.

2. Following on the various references to this subject which occur in our correspondence, and to the favour with which you have viewed it in principle, I have committed His Majesty's Government in my talks with Stalin to the general policy and have stated that you also took a great interest in the matter. I now submit, Mr. President, a formal draft, on which you may feel disposed to give me your decision:

(i) The proposal is to establish in Trans-Caucasia an Anglo-American Air Force to assist the Russian land and air forces in holding the line of the Caucasus mountains and the Black Sea coast. The necessary air forces would be withdrawn from Egypt as soon as the situation in the Western Desert is such that they can be spared from that front, and could be concentrated in the Baku-Batum area in about two months from that time.

(ii) This proposal has already been offered in general terms to Premier Stalin, who accepted it gratefully and indicated that the details of the plan should receive further study. In discussion between the C.I.G.S., Air Marshal Tedder, and Marshal Voroshilov it was agreed that combined planning and preparation should start at once, and the suggestion put that Allied air representatives should go to Moscow for this purpose.

3. Subject to American agreement, the force envisaged would comprise the following units: eight short-range fighter squadrons, one long-range fighter squadron, three light bomber squadrons, two medium bomber squadrons, one

United States heavy bombardment group, and possibly, later, one general reconnaissance squadron.

4. Owing to the extreme difficulties which the lack of good ground communications will impose on the maintenance of this force, ample air transport will be essential for its maintenance. One United States transport group of approximately fifty aircraft is considered the minimum necessary for this purpose.

5. Thus the American contribution suggested is one heavy bombardment group now in Egypt and one transport group, which is not at present available in the Middle East. The former will require an adequate flow of aircraft and trained crews to meet attrition. In addition it is of the utmost importance that every effort should be made to ensure that at least the aircraft and air crews, both first-line and replacements, together with minimum maintenance parties of the United States Pursuit and Medium Bomber groups scheduled for the Middle East, should be operationally fit in Egypt by the dates agreed. Even if Rommel is driven out of Cyrenaica the air defence of Egypt and our long line of communications in the Western Desert will be a heavy commitment. It is also vitally important that the R.A.F. allocations of American fighters for Egypt be fully and promptly supplied, since we must expect a high rate of attrition in the Caucasus area, not only in air fighting, but on account of the poor communications and lack of adequate repair facilities in that area.

6. The force will have to rely for the protection of its bases and line of communications mainly on the Russian forces, but we should be prepared to send light anti-aircraft units for the defence of aerodromes. We might also have to send some engineer units for work on aerodromes.

7. It is important that the ground echelon of the force should be kept as small as possible consistent with the effective operation of the aircraft, since it can only be concentrated and maintained at the expense of Russian supplies through the Persian Gulf route. The interference with these supplies should not be serious. The concentration of the force will involve a movement on the rail and sea communications between Iraq and the Caucasus of the order of 12,000 personnel, 2,000 vehicles, and 4,000 tons of stores. Its subsequent maintenance, on the assumption that petrol and lubricants can be supplied by the Russians, should not exceed 200 tons a day, of which a substantial proportion should be lifted by air.

8. The force will operate under the strategic control of the Russian High Command, but will remain a homogeneous

Allied force under a British air officer, with the right of appeal to his own Government.

9. The foregoing should constitute the basis of instructions to a mission consisting of British and American Air Force officers, who should be dispatched forthwith to Russia to undertake the necessary planning reconnaissance and practical preparations in combination with the Russians. It is urgently important that this be put in hand without delay.

The President, who was at this time engaged in the Congressional elections, replied briefly.

President to Prime Minister　　　　　　　　　　31 Aug 42
I will let you know by Tuesday in regard to your telegram. I am in full accord with desirability of it, and will make every effort to dovetail it into the other operations.

Also we are working on the Persian railway problem, and I will advise you.

*　　　*　　　*

I was most anxious that everything in our power should be done to send convoys to Stalin.

Prime Minister to First Sea Lord　　　　　　　26 Aug 42
It is true that no one can tell how far an enterprise like 'Torch', once begun, will carry us. Nevertheless we should now make plans to resume the P.Q. convoys late in October or the beginning of November. It may be that losses in 'Torch', or great and hopeful developments there, will force or induce us to concentrate all our efforts in the Mediterranean. But the results of battle explain themselves and we have to accept them.

2. Although I indicated in my conversations with Stalin, and it is upon the record that 'Torch' would affect the P.Q.s, I think it would be a great mistake at this crisis to send him news which amounts to the fact that he will get nothing more after the September convoy this year. We should therefore get the utmost help we can from the President, and push ahead with plans for the P.Q.s until or unless we are made to give them up by main force. I still think means may be found to run them. If not, there will be overwhelming reasons for not doing so.

At the beginning of September a further Arctic convoy sailed. Its adventures have been described in an earlier chapter.* I informed Stalin of this movement.

* Book 7, Chapter 15

Prime Minister to Premier Stalin   6 Sept 42

Convoy P.Q.18, with forty ships, has started. As we cannot send our heavy ships within range of enemy shore-based aircraft, we are providing a powerful destroyer striking force, which will be used against the enemy's surface ships should they attack us east of Bear Island. We are also including in the convoy escort, to assist in protecting it against air attack, an auxiliary aircraft-carrier just completed. Further, we are placing a strong line of submarine patrols between the convoy and the German bases. The risk of an attack by German surface ships still however remains serious. This danger can only be effectively warded off by providing in the Barents Sea air striking forces of such strength that the Germans will not risk their heavy ships any more than we will risk ours in that area. For reconnaissance we are providing eight Catalina flying-boats and three Photographic Reconnaissance Unit Spitfires to operate from North Russia. To increase the scale of air attack we have sent thirty-two torpedo-carrying aircraft, which have suffered loss on the way, though we hope that at least twenty-four will be available for operation. These, with the nineteen bombers, the ten torpedo-carrying aircraft, the forty-two short-range and forty-three long-range fighters which we understand you are providing, will almost certainly not be enough to act as a final deterrent. What is needed is more long-range bombers. We quite understand that the immense pressure put upon you on the main line of battle makes it difficult to supply any more Russian Army long-range bombers ; but we must stress the great importance of this convoy, in which we are using seventy-seven warships, requiring to take in 15,000 tons of fuel during the operation. If you can transfer more long-range bombers to the north temporarily, please do so. It is most needful for our common interests.

2. Rommel's attack in Egypt has been sharply rebuffed, and I have good hopes we may reach a favourable decision there during the present month.

3. The operation 'Torch', though set back about three weeks beyond the earliest date I mentioned to you, is on, full blast.

4. I am awaiting the President's answer to definite proposals I have made him for bringing a British-American air contingent into action during the winter on your southern flank. He agrees in principle, and I am expecting to receive his plans in detail. I will then cable you again. Meanwhile I hope that planning with regard to airfields and communications may proceed as was agreed, subject to your approval, by your officers while I was in Moscow. For this purpose we are anxious

to send Staff officers from Egypt to Moscow, in the first instance, as soon as you are ready for us to do so.

5. We are watching with lively admiration the continued magnificent resistance of the Russian armies. The German losses are certainly heavy and winter is drawing nearer. I shall give, when I address the House of Commons on Tuesday, an account of my visit to Moscow, of which I retain most pleasing memories, in what I hope you will regard as agreeable terms.

6. Please give my good wishes to Molotov and thank him for his congratulations on my safe return. May God prosper all our undertakings.

Premier Stalin to Premier Churchill   8 Sept 42

I received your message on September 7. I understand all-importance of safe arrival of convoy P.Q.18 in Soviet Union and necessity of taking measures for its defence. Difficult as it is for us to transfer at the present moment an additional number of long-range bombers for this task, we have decided to do so. To-day orders have been given to send additional long-range bombers for the purpose mentioned by you.

I wish you success in the outcome of operations against Rommel in Egypt, and also full success in Operation 'Torch'.

The heavy losses suffered by the Arctic convoys, including twelve ships in P.Q.18, the deteriorating position in the Atlantic, and the increased demands upon our shipping for 'Torch' forced us to consider whether or not we could keep up these sailings on the Northern route to Russia. I had already warned the President of this.

President to Former Naval Person   16 Sept 42

We are prepared to take over the Persian railway, and all plans are now being developed. We are examining closely the Anglo-American Air Force in Southern Russia, and I hope to have word for you very soon in regard to this. I fully appreciate the importance of Stalin knowing that we mean business. . . . If the decision is against sending further convoys I will of course do everything I can with Stalin.

The urgency of this question of convoys lay behind the increased attention which I now gave to the 'Jupiter' project. The reader will remember that I had asked General McNaughton, the Canadian Commander-in-Chief in England, to report on this plan. On September 16 I commented upon his paper to the Chiefs of Staff.

Prime Minister to General Ismay, for C.O.S. Committee
16 Sept 42

OPERATION 'JUPITER'*

To keep contact with Russia and to keep the Russian armies equipped and in the field by a continued stream of supplies must be considered one of the three or four most important vital objects before us. For this the greatest sacrifices and exertions must be made by the Allies. The total defeat of Russia or the reduction of that country to a minor military factor would let the whole mass of the German armies loose upon us. The President has stated that he regards the maintenance of the P.Q. convoys as an operation of equal magnitude with 'Torch', although he is ready to skip one or perhaps two for the sake of 'Torch'.

2. The alternative before us is therefore:

(*a*) to go on with the P.Q. convoys (perhaps missing one or two) in addition to 'Torch' and all it implies, all through 1943. Indeed, the scale of the convoys must be increased. The Russians have been solemnly promised larger quotas, and they will become more dependent on imported arms as their own territory is reduced by enemy invasion; or

(*b*) to clear the Germans out of the north of Norway by some form of the operation 'Jupiter'.

When we consider the losses attendant on the sending of these convoys, that they have to take place at least three times in every two months, and the grievous consequences of our announcing, on the other hand, that we can send no more, it may well be that 'Jupiter', with all its cost and risk, will be found not only necessary but cheapest in the long run.

3. I have now read the McNaughton report, which certainly does not err on the side of underrating the difficulties before us. Making allowances for this, the McNaughton report can be taken as a basis for further discussions.

4. When the winter comes the Russians must take the offensive against the German lines. Here in the North is as good a place as any, and, having regard to their vital need of Allied munitions, I have no doubt, after my conversations with Premier Stalin, that they not only will resist attacks upon the Murmansk and Archangel railways, but also would be willing to set on foot a heavy offensive towards Petsamo. At any rate, before dogmatising about it we must find out what they would be prepared to do. I am assuming however that they would not only bring enough forces to the North to attack the enemy, as proposed by General McNaughton, but also would if necessary undertake part of the landings themselves.

* See Book 7, p. Chapter 20.

5. The fitting of Operation 'Jupiter' into our war plans can only be considered in relation to 'Torch'. We cannot yet judge what 'Torch' will involve. If the French come over to us the whole of the 'Torch' area may be formed up against Germany in a week, or even a night. If this were so, we should have harbours with proper defences, airfields, eight or nine French divisions, a certain amount of air, and perhaps the French fleet in Toulon. In this case the British troops could be railed rapidly through to attack Tripoli from the west. There is no question of the Germans being able in the time mentioned—a fortnight, or even a month—to mount and launch a heavy attack. They have not got, above all, the air force to spare. We must expect that very heavy operations in Egypt and Libya will have been already in progress. Therefore, I think, if things go well for us on the North African shore, it may be that a large number of assault ships and tank-landing craft will be free to go north for 'Jupiter'. To these would be added all the additions to our tank-landing force and assault ships, over and above those assigned to 'Torch', which were coming into Britain under 'Bolero' for the purposes of 'Round-up'. It is no use saying the Americans have cancelled all this, because we have not yet given them the reasons against such improvident action. I am sure I can claim from the United States for the purposes of 'Jupiter' all the craft which were being prepared under 'Bolero' for an April 'Round-up', or at any rate enough of them. I admit the escorts are the pinch.

6. On the other hand, if the French fight the Americans in 'Torch' and ask the Germans to come and help them, and the Germans come, or the Spaniards turn against us and we have to fight neck or nothing in the 'Torch' area, naturally in that case 'Jupiter' does not have to be argued about.

7. I have no doubt we could have a couple of Arctic-trained American divisions, and with the Canadian Corps, and also several Russian divisions, apart from the Russian offensive, we could get together quite enough forces to conquer the 'Jupiter' area. But if we don't make preparations, not mere paper plans, now (which, anyhow, may come in for 1943–4), order the equipment, train the troops, etc., we are not even going to have the option.

8. It follows that if 'Jupiter' as well as 'Torch' should get going there could be no 'Round-up' till 1944. This is already the United States view. But 'Torch' by itself is no substitute for 'Round-up'.

I thought it wise to present this plan to Stalin, and proposed sending McNaughton himself to explain it to the Russian High

Command. It was also necessary to make clear to Stalin that whereas we were prepared to consider an operation on the lines of 'Jupiter', the commitments of 'Torch' would inevitably lead to a temporary reduction in the scale of supplies to Russia, and that another convoy on the scale of P.Q.18 was out of the question. On September 22 I telegraphed to the President as follows:

Former Naval Person to President Roosevelt   22 Sept 42
Following is text of telegram which I wish to send to Stalin:
'1. As I told you in Moscow, we are convinced that the most effective contribution that we and the United States can make in 1942 to the defeat of Germany is to launch 'Torch' at the earliest possible date.
'2. The date which has now been finally fixed with the President is early in November.
'3. The effect of 'Torch' must be either (*a*) to oblige the Germans to divert air and land forces to counter our move, or (*b*) to compel them to accept the new position created by the success of "Torch", which would then create a further diversion by the threat of attack against Sicily and the South of Europe.
'4. The considerable success of the last convoy operation was achieved only because no less than seventy-seven warships were employed in the operation. Protection on anything like this scale will be impossible until the end of the year, when the naval escorts which must now assemble for "Torch" can again be made available in Northern waters.
'5. In the meanwhile we are trying to find means of sending you supplies on a reduced scale by the Northern route during the rest of 1942.
'6. We intend to resume the full flow of supplies from January 1943.
'7. In order to reduce losses of merchant ships by enemy action, and thus make the convoys in 1943 as effective as possible, we are anxious to examine with you the possibility of carrying out Operation 'Jupiter' during this winter.
'8. I therefore suggest to you that I send to Moscow General McNaughton, Commander-in-Chief of the Canadian Army, arriving in the early days of October, so that he may discuss the matter fully with your Staff. He has already made a preliminary examination of this question.'

It was a disagreeable issue to face, and the President had not yet returned to Washington. On September 27 I received the following reply:

President to Prime Minister   27 Sept 42

I agree with you that the realities of the situation require us to give up P.Q.19. While I think that is a tough blow for the Russians, I nevertheless think that the purposes for which the escorts are to be used both as to time and place make that decision inevitable. P.Q.19 however would not have sailed under any circumstances for another ten days, and I feel very strongly that we should not notify the Russians until that time arrives and we know with finality that the convoy will not go. I can see nothing to be gained by notifying Stalin sooner than is necessary, and indeed much to be lost. Furthermore, I believe that within ten days we could come to a final conclusion regarding the Air Force in Trans-Caucasia, regarding which Stalin should be notified at the same time.

For security reasons I think it would be unwise to unload any of the ships at Iceland. While it is true that we are short of shipping, we probably do not need those particular ships for 'Torch', and I think we had better make the sacrifice of letting the ships remain idle in Iceland rather than risk giving the enemy the information that we are not running the next convoy. I believe that 'Torch' should not be delayed a single day. We are going to put everything into that enterprise, and I have great hopes for it.

I will be back in Washington Thursday, and will cable you then regarding the Air Force in the Caucasus and other matters. I am having a great trip. The training of our forces is far advanced and their morale excellent. Production is good, but must be better.

Former Naval Person to President   28 Sept 42

Earliest date P.Q.19 could have sailed is October 2—*i.e.,* five days from date of your message of September 27. However, if you think well we can keep it, as if it really was sailing, till 7th or even later. Bulk of the ships are in Scottish ports. Agree it is most important to make a firm offer about Caucasus air support.

*   *   *

The situation in the Caucasus still caused anxiety, though I did not believe the Germans would reach Baku. I had a standing bet on this with the C.I.G.S., on which I used to chaff him weekly at Cabinet: 'How is our bet going this week?' On the view taken of this depended whether General Wilson's Tenth Army in Persia should move forward.

All turned on timing.

Prime Minister to General Ismay, for C.O.S. Committee
28 Sept 42

General Wilson's proposals for taking up advanced positions in Persia are sound in principle and seem to be well worked out.

The price to be paid in cutting down Russian supplies is heavy, and the moment when P.Q.19 is cancelled is by no means the best for notifying the Russians. The question is therefore one of timing, and the answer depends upon the view taken of the German advance into the Caucasus. In the six weeks that have passed since the C.I.G.S. and I were in Moscow the Caucasus situation has improved markedly. More than forty of the sixty days for which Premier Stalin told me he would have to hold out have passed. The Russian resistance has been most vigorous. Their artillery still commands the borders of Novorossisk. The intruders over the high passes made no headway. Snow is falling on the Caucasian mountains. The Grozny oilfield has not yet been taken. The fortifications which the C.I.G.S. saw just beginning on the Caspian shore must now be much further advanced. Personally I have always felt that the Russians would hold the line of the Caucasus mountains until the spring, and that Baku would not be taken this year. I must admit that this view is temperamental rather than scientific. Nevertheless we must all feel that things have turned out better than many people expected.

2. In the light of the above, it would certainly seem that we could afford to wait for another fortnight before embarking on the forward move of the Tenth Army. By the middle of October it should be possible to see more clearly over the whole scene, and I suggest we wait until then before addressing the Russians and the Americans on the subject of trans-Persian tonnages.

3. The President has now promised to give an answer, presumably favourable, about 'Velvet' by October 7. A draft time-table should be prepared on the assumption that the answer is favourable. I am not clear whether the twenty squadrons of 'Velvet' involve all the aircraft, including the Army components, at the disposal of our Tenth Army. They will certainly be in advance of it and a shield to it, and if things go badly they will fall back on it. It would be convenient to have all the air units set out on a table even before the President's message is received.

4. It is not yet necessary or possible to make up our minds what to do with the Tenth Army if the German attack on Russia in 1942 should present itself as a definite failure. But this question will assume a greater precision when we

see how 'Lightfoot' [the Desert offensive] and 'Torch' go.

* * *

The Russians showed neither appreciation of our efforts nor understanding of our difficulties, and the following minor incident was a gloomy example of the state of our relations.

Prime Minister to M. Molotov   27 Sept 42
    The Foreign Secretary tells me that he has sent you a message about the British Naval Hospital at Vaenga being ordered to close and go home. I should be glad if you would look into the matter personally yourself. Terrible cases of mutilation through frost-bite are now arriving back here, and I have to consider constantly the morale of the merchant seamen, who have hitherto gone so willingly to man the merchant ships to Russia. The British hospital unit was sent simply to help, and implied no reflection on Russian arrangements under the pressure of air bombardment, etc. It is hard on men in hospital not to have nurses who speak their own language. At any rate, I hope you will give me some solid reason which I can give should the matter be raised in Parliament, as it very likely will be.

This was all I got:

M. Molotov to Prime Minister   2 Oct 42
    In my letter to Mr. Eden I asked him to acquaint you, Mr. Prime Minister, with the contents of my reply on the question of the British medical personnel in Archangel and Vaenga [Murmansk]. I think that if you glance at the memorandum of the Soviet Foreign Office of August 27 and my letter of September 12 addressed to the British Ambassador you will have the full information on the matter and will be in a position to draw the necessary conclusions as to the real state of affairs, particularly in regard to certain irregularities in the actions of the respective British naval authorities.

This grimace is a good example of how official jargon can be used to destroy any kind of human contact, or even thought itself.

* * *

On October 5 I received the President's comments upon my proposed message of September 22 to Stalin.

President to Prime Minister   2 Oct 42
    I have gone over carefully your proposed message to Stalin of September 22.

T—s.w.w.—8—F

I feel very strongly that we should make a firm commitment to put an Air Force in the Caucasus, and that that operation should not be contingent on any other.

The Russian front is to-day our greatest reliance, and we simply must find a direct manner in which to help them other than our diminishing supplies. We shall on our part undertake to replace in the Middle East all of our own planes which are transferred, and assist you in every way possible with your own air problems in the Middle East.

So far as P.Q.19 is concerned, I feel most strongly that we should not tell Stalin that the convoy will not sail. After talk with Admiral King I would like to urge that a different technique be employed, in which evasion and dispersion are the guiding factors. Thus let P.Q.19 sail in successive groups, comprising the fastest ships now loaded and loading for Russia. These groups would comprise two or three ships each, supported by two or three escorts, and sail at twenty-four- to forty-eight-hour intervals. They might have to go without the full naval covering support that would protect the convoy from the *Tirpitz* or heavy cruisers, but that must simply be a risk that we have to take. We know that so far as air attack is concerned the weather would in all probability not be against us every day and that the longer nights will be of help.

I believe we would stand a good chance of getting as high a proportion of the ships through as we did with P.Q.18. Under any circumstances I think it is better that we take this risk than endanger our whole relations with Russia at this time. I know that you and Pound will give this proposal of mine every consideration. I should tell you that our Ambassador [Admiral Standley] has asked to come home to deliver in person a very important message, and I have some fears as to what that message might be.

About 'Velvet' the President proposed that I should send the following to Stalin:

You will recall our conversation about putting a British-American Air Force in the Caucasus. I have examined this matter with the President, and we have determined to move to accomplish this without delay. I will let you know the extent of the Air Force that we can make available, and our plans for building the force up during succeeding months.

He ended:

Please let me know when you send [your] message to Stalin, and I will immediately send him a similar message, but I am certain both our messages should be so phrased as to leave a good taste in his mouth.

* * *

Throughout the following weeks discussions continued between myself and the President upon the possibilities of Operation 'Velvet' and ways and means of maintaining the Arctic convoys. On October 5, after nearly a month's silence, I received through M. Maisky the following telegram from Stalin:

5 Oct 42

I have to inform you that the situation in the Stalingrad area has deteriorated since the beginning of September. The Germans were able to concentrate in this area great reserves of aviation, and in this way managed to secure superiority in the air in the ratio of two to one. We have not enough fighters for the protection of our forces from the air. Even the bravest troops are helpless if they lack air protection. We more particularly require Spitfires and Air-Cobras. I told about all that in great detail to Mr. Wendell Willkie.

2. The ships with arms arrived at Archangel and are being unloaded. This is a great help. In view however of the scarcity of tonnage we would be prepared temporarily to forgo some forms of assistance, and in this way secure the increased number of the fighter aircraft.

3. The information of your Intelligence to the effect that Germany manufactures not more than 1,300 combat machines a month is not confirmed by our sources. According to our information, the German aircraft works, together with the works in the occupied countries engaged in the making of aircraft parts, are producing not less than 2,500 combat machines a month.

I passed this to the President, with the following comments:

Former Naval Person to President Roosevelt   7 Oct 42

There is no possibility of letting P.Q.19 sail in successive groups with reduced escorts as you suggest. Neither can the fact that the convoy is not sailing be concealed from the Russians any longer. Maisky is already aware of the position, though not officially informed, and I expect he has let Stalin know the general prospect. We are preparing ten ships to sail individually during the October dark.* They are all British ships for which the crews will have to volunteer, the dangers being terrible, and their sole hope if sunk far from help being Arctic clothing and such heating arrangements as

---

* Thirteen merchant ships sailed independently to Russia at this time. Five arrived.

can be placed in the lifeboats. Absolutely nothing else is possible unless you are able to help by providing some American ships for independent sailing after November 9, should experience have proved that the chances are sufficiently good.

2. I believe that the blunt truth is best with Stalin, but that there has been advantage in the delay of a fortnight in telling him, which you proposed. I feel strongly that he should be told now.

3. With regard to 'Velvet', nothing can move before the battle in Egypt. There is the danger that the Germans will pull their Air Force off Russia and turn it on to Egypt. There is also the probability that they will be forced anyway to turn a large proportion on to 'Torch'.

But, although we cannot be definite about an early date, it seems to me that we could be more definite as to the composition of the force. We have for weeks had the exact composition of the twenty squadrons planned out, subject to your concurrence and help. I should like to state the actual detail of the force and the time required for it to move and come into action.

4. I am puzzled to know what message Admiral Standley is bringing home to you, but I cannot believe it threatens a separate peace. So far the Russian campaign has been very adverse to Hitler, and though they are angry with us both they are by no means in despair.

5. If therefore we offer 'Velvet' as now defined, plus increased aircraft deliveries and the individual ships on the P.Q. route, I trust this will be sufficient to bridge the gap before 'Torch' opens.

*   *   *

On October 9 I telegraphed Stalin, outlining the 'Velvet' plan.

Prime Minister to Premier Stalin   9 Oct 42

We shall attack in Egypt towards the end of this month, and 'Torch' will begin early in November. The effect of these operations must be either:

(*a*) to oblige the Germans to send air and land forces to counter our move ; or

(*b*) to compel them to accept the new position created by our success, which would then create a diversion by the threat of attack against Sicily and the South of Europe.

2. Our attack in Egypt will be in good force. 'Torch' will be a heavy operation, in which, in addition to the United States Navy, 240 British warships and more than half a mil-

lion men will be engaged. This is all rolling forward irrevocably.

3. The President and I are anxious to put an Anglo-American Air Force on your southern flank and operate it under the strategic control of the Soviet High Command. Orders have been issued by us to assemble this force and take their station so that they would be available for combat early in the New Year. Most of this force will come from Egypt as soon as they can be disengaged from the battle there—which we believe will be successful on our part.

4. In the letter which M. Maisky delivered to me on October 5 you asked for a great increase in fighter aircraft supplied to Russia by this country and the United States. We will send you as soon as possible, by the Persian Gulf route, 150 Spitfires, with the equivalent of fifty more in the form of spares, to be sent as they become available, as a special reinforcement, which we cannot repeat. This special reinforcement is over and above the protocol supplies by the Northern route so far as it can be used. President Roosevelt will cable separately about the United States contribution.

5. I was greatly relieved that so large a proportion of the last convoy reached Archangel safely. This success was achieved only because no less than seventy-seven warships were employed on the operation. Naval protection will be impossible until our impending operations are completed. As the necessary escorts are withdrawn from 'Torch' they can again be made available in Northern waters.

6. Nevertheless we intend in the meanwhile to do our best to send you supplies by the Northern route by means of ships sailed independently instead of in escorted convoys. Arrangements have been made to sail ships from Iceland during the moonless period October 28–November 8. Ten of ours are preparing in addition to what the Americans will do. The ships will sail singly, at about 200-mile intervals, with occasional larger gaps, and rely on evasion and dispersion.

7. We hope to resume the flow of supplies in strongly escorted convoys from January 1943.

8. It would of course greatly help both you and us if the Germans could be denied the use of airfields in Northern Norway. If your staffs could make a good plan the President and I would at once examine the possibility of co-operating up to the limit of our ability.

The President took similar steps.

President to Prime Minister   9 Oct 42
I am sending the following message to Premier Stalin to-day:

'The Prime Minister has sent me copy of his message to you. We are going to move as rapidly as possible to place an Air Force under your strategic command in the Caucasus. I am now trying to find additional planes for you immediately, and will advise you soon. I am also trying to arrange to have some of our merchant ships transferred to your flag to increase your flow of materials in the Pacific. I have just ordered an automobile tyre plant to be made available to you. We are sending very substantial reinforcements to the Persian Gulf to increase the flow of supplies over the route, and are confident that this can be done. We are sending a large number of engines and other equipment as well as personnel. I am confident that our contemplated operation will be successful. Everyone in America is thrilled by the gallant defence of Stalingrad, and we are confident that it will succeed. Roosevelt.'

On October 13 I received a communication from Stalin. It was neither informative nor helpful.

Premier Stalin to Prime Minister   13 Oct 42
I received your message of October 9. Thank you.

*   *   *

The atmosphere was heavily charged with suspicion. The Moscow Press made great and belated play with the Hess episode. On October 15 Molotov made a public speech demanding the immediate trial of Hess as a war criminal by an international tribunal. On October 27 a leading Soviet publicist in a lecture denounced 'the machinations of Lady Astor and the "Cliveden Set"', who were alleged to be working for a separate peace.

None of this stuff affected in any way the views or feelings of the President or myself. We were doing our best. On October 27 I minuted to the Foreign Secretary:

I am sure it would be a great mistake to run after the Russians in their present mood; and still more to run around with them chasing a chimera. By all means let the Lord Privy Seal [Sir Stafford Cripps] focus and refresh in our minds the Hess story. When it is ready the Cabinet can consider whether the facts should be imparted to the Russian Government. I assure you the only thing that will do any good is fighting hard and winning victories. A great deal of fighting is now going on, and more is to come. Should success crown our efforts you will find we shall be in a very different position. Meanwhile I should treat the Russians coolly, not getting excited about the lies they tell, but going steadily on with our task. You must remember the Bolsheviks have undermined so many powerful Governments by lying, machine-made propaganda, and they probably think they make some impression on us by these methods.

2. I am awaiting the President's answer to my query about whether he has heard from Stalin in reply to his and my telegrams. As soon as I hear I will draft a telegram to Stalin myself. It will be quite short, asking if his 'Thank you' was in reply to my long telegram, and if so what steps does he propose to take about the twenty squadrons on the southern flank, anything additional about the Spitfires which we are sending, and the ships which are to slip through, one by one, in the dark period. Now that *Tirpitz* has gone south to Trondheim it may be possible after the first part of 'Torch' is over to reconsider the convoy question, but the problem will still be escort craft.

At the same time the President sent me the following telegram:

President to Prime Minister   28 Oct 42

I am not unduly disturbed about our respective responses or lack of responses from Moscow. I have decided they do not use speech for the same purposes as we do.

I had not heard of any difficulty at our end about arrangements for landing-fields on the Russian southern flank, but I shall explore that from my end at once.

I feel very sure the Russians are going to hold this winter, and that we should proceed vigorously with our plans both to supply them and to set up an Air Force to fight with them. I want us to be able to say to Mr. Stalin that we have carried out our obligations one hundred per cent.

*   *   *

The strains and stresses of the winter months were to be relieved by Alamein and 'Torch' and the great Russian victory at Stalingrad. In the Arctic a brilliant operation was, before the end of the year, to carry a convoy safely through. In retrospect it seems as if Soviet behaviour was in part due to the feeling that if they could survive the winter they could reject any direct military aid from the West, which they regarded as an infecting contact and as a blow to their prestige. I feel we at least deserve credit for our patience in the face of ceaseless affront from a Government which had been hoping to work with

Hitler, until it was assaulted and almost destroyed by him.

* * *

This is however the point at which to tell, all too briefly, the tale of the magnificent struggle and decisive victory of the Russian armies.

In order to free the way for the south-easterly drive to the Caucasus Rostov had to be taken and the Russians cleared from within the bend of the Lower Don. The first thrusts, on May 28, were from north of Kursk and Byelgorod. By July 7 the former had reached the outskirts of Rostov, but could not capture it. The long defensive flank from Orel to Voronezh was left to be guarded largely by Hungarians, while the German 4th Panzer Army drove down the western bank of the Don. A later thrust broke through the Russian defences before Izyum and joined the southerly drive. Finally, a third attack from Stalino swept round to reach the Lower Don above Rostov. All this went very much according to plan, though not quite so swiftly as had been hoped. Russian resistance was strong, but the several penetrations of their line by armoured and motorised troops enforced a general withdrawal, much harassed by the enemy, to behind the river Don.

After three weeks the first phase was virtually over and Hitler issued his orders for the next. The Southern Army Group was now divided into Army Group A, commanded by List, and Army Group B, under Bock. Hitler's directive of July 23 gave them their tasks. Army Group A was to capture the entire eastern shore of the Black Sea. After the capture of the Maikop oilfields a mobile force was to take Grozny. 'Subsequently the Baku area is to be captured by an advance along the Caspian Sea.' Army Group B, having established a defensive flank along the river Don, was to advance on Stalingrad, 'smash the enemy forces being assembled there, and occupy the city'. Mobile forces were to proceed down the Volga to Astrakhan.

Local operations by the Central Army Group were to take place in order to prevent the Russians withdrawing troops from that front, and in the north Leningrad was to be captured in early September. For this purpose Hitler ordered five divisions of the Eleventh Army, released by the capture of Sebastopol, to join the Northern Army Group, an improvident weakening of his major attack. They arrived in time not to attack, but to defend a German line sagging under Russian assault.

The German Campaign in Russia, 1942

The drive of the German Army Group A to reach the Caucasus had been led by Kleist's First Panzer Army of fifteen divisions. Once across the Don they made much headway against little opposition. They reached Maikop on August 9, to find the oilfields thoroughly destroyed. Another column took Mozdok on August 25, but was held on the river Terek and failed to reach the Grozny oilfields. Those of Baku, the greatest of them all, were still three hundred miles away. On the shore of the Black Sea Novorossisk was taken on September 10, and the Russian Black Sea Fleet, which had sheltered there when Sebastopol fell, sailed to Tuapse, where they remained. Hitler's orders to seize the whole of the Black Sea littoral could not be carried out. In the centre the Germans reached the foothills of the Caucasus, but no farther. Russian resistance, reinforced by fresh troops sent down by railway along the western shore of the Caspian, was everywhere firm. Kleist, weakened by diversions for the Stalingrad effort, struggled on till November. He took Nalchik on November 2. Winter conditions then intervened. His bolt was shot.

On the front of German Army Group B worse than failure befell. The lure of Stalingrad fascinated Hitler ; its very name was a challenge. The city was important as a centre of industry, and also a strong point on the defensive flank protecting his main thrust to the Caucasus. It became a magnet drawing to itself the supreme effort of the German Army and Air Force.

The deflection southward of the Fourth Panzer Army to help Army Group A to cross the Don also had serious consequences. It delayed the drive on Stalingrad, and by the time this army turned east again the Russian forces that had withdrawn across the river were reorganising. Resistance grew daily stiffer. It was not till September 15 that, after heavy fighting between the Don and the Volga, the outskirts of Stalingrad were reached. The battering-ram attacks of the next month made some progress at the cost of terrible slaughter. Nothing could overcome the Russians, fighting with passionate devotion amid the ruins of their city.

The German generals, long uneasy, had good cause for their anxiety. After three months of fighting the main objectives of the campaign, the Caucasus, Stalingrad, and Leningrad, were still in Russian hands. Casualties had been very heavy and replacements insufficient. Hitler, instead of sending fresh contingents forward to replace losses, was forming them into new and untrained divisions. In military opinion it was high time to call a halt, but 'the Carpet-eater' would not listen. At the end of September Halder, Hitler's Chief of Staff, finally resisted his master, and was dismissed. Hitler scourged his armies on.

By the middle of October the German position had markedly worsened. The frontage of Army Group B stretched over seven hundred miles. General Paulus's Sixth Army had expended its efforts at Stalingrad, and now lay exhausted with its flanks thinly protected by allies of dubious quality. Winter was near, when the Russians would surely make their counter-stroke. If the Don front could not be held the safety of the armies on the Caucasus front would be undermined. But Hitler would not countenance any suggestion of withdrawal. On November 19 the Russians delivered their long and valiantly prepared encircling assault, striking both north and south of Stalingrad upon the weakly defended German flanks. Four days later the Russian pincers met and the Sixth German Army was trapped between the Don and the Volga. Paulus proposed to break out. Hitler ordered him to hold his ground. As the days passed his army was compressed into an ever-lessening space. On December 12, in bitter weather, the Germans made a desperate effort to break through the Russian cordon and relieve their besieged Sixth Army. They failed. Thereafter, though Paulus and his army held out for seven more terrible weeks, their doom was certain.

CHAPTER 10

The Battle of Alamein

Preparations for the Desert Offensive – An Unwelcome Delay – General Alexander's Justification – The Battle Date Draws Near – 'Zip', October 23, 1942 – Montgomery's Dispositions – Bombardment by a Thousand Guns – General Assault – The Struggle Ebbs and Flows – Fruitful Thrust by the 9th Australian Division – Fierce Fighting of October 27 and 28 – Report to the Dominions Prime Ministers – My Congratulations to the Commanders – British Casualties – Montgomery's Final Plan: Operation 'Supercharge' – Forward Drive of the Australians – Rommel's Front Pierced – Our Armour Pursues – Alexander's Telegram of November 4 – Defeat and Destruction of the Enemy – 'Ring Out the Bells!' – Old-fashioned Tactics – The Hinge Turns.

In the weeks which followed the changes in command planning preparations and training went forward ceaselessly in Cairo and at the front. The Eighth Army was strengthened to an extent never before possible. The 51st and 44th Divisions had arrived from home and become 'desert-worthy'. Our strength in armour rose to seven brigades of over a thousand tanks, nearly half of them Grants and Shermans from the United States ; we now had a two-to-one superiority in numbers and at least a balance of quality. A powerful and highly trained artillery was for the first time in the Western Desert massed to support the impending attack.

The Air Force in the Middle East was, in accordance with the directive of October 7, 1941, subordinated to the military conceptions and requirements of the Commander-in-Chief. However, under Air Marshal Tedder there was no need for hard-and-fast precedents. The relations between the Air Command and the new generals were in every way agreeable. The Western Desert Air Force, under Air Marshal Coningham, had now attained a fighting strength of 550 aircraft. There were two other groups, in addition to the aircraft based on Malta, numbering 650 planes, whose task it was to harry enemy ports and supply routes across both the Mediterranean and the desert. Together with a hundred United States fighters and medium bombers, our total strength amounted to about 1,200 serviceable aircraft.

While all this was going forward it was necessary that I should have the earliest possible information of Alexander's intentions. Accordingly, on September 17:

Prime Minister to General Alexander   17 Sept 42
I am anxiously awaiting some account of your intentions. My understanding with you was the fourth week in September. Since then you have stated that the recent battle, which greatly weakened the enemy, has caused delay in regrouping, etc. I do not wish to know either your plan or the exact date, but I must know which week it falls in, otherwise I cannot form the necessary judgments affecting the general war.

Alexander told us in various telegrams that about October 24 had been chosen for 'Lightfoot', as the operation was to be called. 'Since there is no open flank, the battle,' he said, 'must be so stage-managed that a hole is blown in the enemy's front.' Through this the Xth Corps, comprising the main armour, which was to be the spearhead of our attack, would advance in daylight. This corps would not have all its weapons and equipment before October 1. It would then require nearly a month's training for its rôle. 'In my view it is essential that the initial break-in attack should be launched in the full moon period. This will be a major operation, which will take some time, and an adequate gap in the enemy's lines must be made if our armoured forces are to have a whole day in which to make their operation decisive. A full moon is in fact essential to my whole plan. I have carefully considered the timing in relation to "Torch", and have come to the conclusion that the best date for us to start would be minus 13 of "Torch"' (then fixed for November 4).

Prime Minister to Commander-in-Chief Middle East
             23 Sept 42
We are in your hands, and of course a victorious battle makes amends for much delay. Whatever happens we shall back you up and see you through.
There is a point about the fortifications which the enemy will make in the interval which I should like to put to you. Instead of a crust through which a way can be cleared in a night, may you not find twenty-five miles of fortifications, with blasted rock, gun-pits, and machine-gun posts. The tank was orginally invented to clear a way for the infantry in the

teeth of machine-gun fire. Now it is the infantry who will have to clear a way for the tanks, and it seems to me their task will be a very hard one now that fire-power is so greatly increased. No doubt you are thinking about all this and how so to broaden your front of attack as to make your superior numbers felt.

*   *   *

Nearly a month passed, and the battle date drew near.

Prime Minister to General Alexander　　　　20 Oct 42
　　Events are moving in our favour both in North Africa and Vichy France, and 'Torch' goes forward steadily and punctually. But all our hopes are centred upon the battle you and Montgomery are going to fight. It may well be the key to the future. Give my warmest regards to Montgomery and also Coningham. Let me have the word 'Zip' when you start.

The Air Force had already begun their battle, attacking enemy troops, airfields, and communications. Special attention was paid to their convoys. In September 30 per cent. of Axis shipping supplying North Africa was sunk, largely by air action. In October the figure rose to 40 per cent. The loss of petrol was 66 per cent. In the four autumn months over 200,000 tons of Axis shipping was destroyed. This was a severe injury to Rommel's army.
　　At last the word came:

C.-in-C. to Prime Minister and C.I.G.S.　　　　23 Oct 42
'Zip!'

I duly informed the President.

Former Naval Person to President Roosevelt　　　　23 Oct 42
　　The battle in Egypt began to-night at 8 p.m. London time. The whole force of the Army will be engaged. I will keep you informed. A victory there will be most fruitful to our main enterprise. All the Shermans and self-propelled guns which you gave me on that dark Tobruk morning will play their part.

*   *   *

General Montgomery had at his immediate disposal three armoured and the equivalent of seven infantry divisions. The concentration of so large a force demanded a number of ingenious deceptive measures and precautions. It was especially necessary that enemy aircraft should be prevented from overlooking

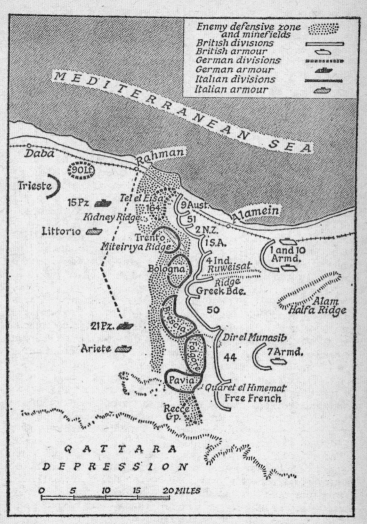

Legend:

	Enemy defensive zone and minefields
	British divisions
	British armour
	German divisions
	German armour
	Italian divisions
	Italian armour

M E D I T E R R A N E A N   S E A

Daba
Rahman
90Lt.
Trieste
15 Pz
Tel el Eisa
164
9 Aust.
Alamein
Kidney Ridge
51
Littorio
2 N.Z.
1 and 10 Armd.
Trento
1 S.A.
Miteiriya Ridge
4 Ind.
Bologna
Ruweisat
Ridge
Greek Bde.
Alam Halfa Ridge
50
Brescia
21 Pz.
Dir el Munasib
Ariete
Folgore
44
7 Armd.
Pavia
Quaret el Himemat
Free French
Recce Gp.

Q A T T A R A
D E P R E S S I O N

0   5   10   15   20 MILES

The Alamein Front, October 23, 1942

the preparations. All this was attended by great success and the attack came as a complete surprise.

In the full moon of October 23 nearly a thousand guns opened upon the enemy batteries for twenty minutes, and then turned on to their infantry positions. Under this concentration of fire, deepened by bombing from the air, the XXXth (General Leese) and XIIIth Corps (General Horrocks) advanced. Attacking on a front of four divisions, the whole XXXth Corps sought to cut two corridors through the enemy's fortifications. Behind them the two armoured divisions of the Xth Corps (General Lumsden) followed to exploit success. Strong advances were made under heavy fire, and by dawn deep inroads had been made. The engineers had cleared the mines behind the leading troops. But the minefield system had not been pierced in its depth, and there was no early prospect of our armour breaking through. Farther south the 1st South African Division fought their way forward to protect the southern flank of the bulge, and the 4th Indian Division launched raids from the Ruweisat Ridge, while the 7th Armoured and 44th Divisions of the XIIIth Corps broke into the enemy defences opposite to them. This achieved its object of inducing the enemy to retain his two armoured divisions for three days behind this part of the front while the main battle developed in the north.

So far however no hole had been blown in the enemy's deep system of minefields and defences. In the small hours of the 25th Montgomery held a conference of his senior commanders, at which he ordered the armour to press forward again before dawn in accordance with his original instructions. During the day more ground was indeed gained, after hard fighting; but the feature known as Kidney Ridge became the focus of an intense struggle with the enemy's 15th Panzer and Ariete armoured divisions, which made a series of violent counterattacks. On the front of the XIIIth Corps the attack was pressed no farther, in order to keep the 7th Armoured Division intact for the climax.

There had been serious derangements in the enemy's command. Rommel had gone to hospital in Germany at the end of September, and his place was taken by General Stumme. Within twenty-four hours of the start of the battle Stumme died of a heart attack. Rommel, at Hitler's request, left hospital and resumed his command late on the 25th.

Hard fighting continued on October 26 all along the deep

bulge so far forced into the enemy line, and especially again at Kidney Ridge. The enemy Air Force, which had been quiescent on the previous two days, now made its definite challenge to our air superiority. There were many combats, ending mostly in our favour. The efforts of the XIIIth Corps had delayed but could not prevent the movement of the German armour to what they now knew was the decisive sector of their front. This movement however was severely smitten by our Air Force.

At this moment a new and fruitful thrust was made by the 9th Australian Division, under General Morshead. They struck northwards from the bulge towards the sea. Montgomery was prompt to exploit this notable success. He held back the New Zealanders from their westward drive and ordered the Australians to continue their advance towards the north. This threatened the retreat of part of the German infantry division on the northern flank. At the same time he now felt the momentum of his main attack was beginning to falter in the midst of the minefields and strongly posted anti-tank guns. He therefore regathered his forces and reserves for a renewed and revived assault.

All through the 27th and the 28th a fierce conflict raged for Kidney Ridge against the repeated attacks of the 15th and 21st Panzer Divisions, now arrived from the southern sector. General Alexander has described the struggle in these words: *

On October 27 came a big armoured counter-attack in the old style. Five times they attacked with all available tanks, both German and Italian, but gained no ground and suffered heavy and, worse still, disproportionate casualties, for our tanks, fighting on the defensive, suffered but lightly. On October 28 [the enemy] came again, [after] prolonged and careful reconnaissance all the morning, to find the weak spots and locate our anti-tank guns, followed by a smashing concentrated attack in the afternoon with the setting sun behind him. The reconnaissance was less successful than in the old days, since both our tanks and anti-tank guns could engage him with longer range. When the enemy attempted to concentrate for the final attack the R.A.F. once more intervened on a devastating scale. In two and a half hours bomber sorties dropped eighty tons of bombs in his concentration area, measuring three miles by two, and the enemy's attack was defeated before he could even complete his forming up. This was the last occasion on which the enemy attempted to take the initiative.

* In a telegram dated November 9, sent to me after the battle.

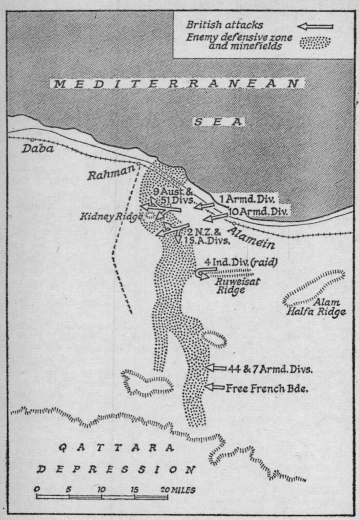

British attacks ←

Enemy defensive zone and minefields ⬝⬝⬝

M E D I T E R R A N E A N

S E A

Daba

Rahman

9 Aust. &
51 Divs.

1 Armd. Div.

10 Armd. Div.

Kidney Ridge

Alamein

2 N.Z. &
1 S.A. Divs.

4 Ind. Div. (raid)

Ruweisat
Ridge

Alam
Halfa Ridge

44 & 7 Armd. Divs.

Free French Bde.

Q A T T A R A

D E P R E S S I O N

0   5   10   15   20 MILES

Alamein: The Attack.

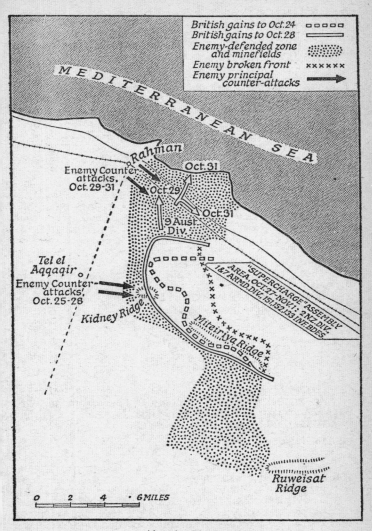

Legend:
- British gains to Oct. 24 □□□□□
- British gains to Oct. 28 ——————
- Enemy-defended zone and minefields ∴∴∴∴
- Enemy broken front ××××××
- Enemy principal counter-attacks ➤

MEDITERRANEAN SEA

Rahman

Oct. 31

Enemy Counter attacks. Oct. 29-31

Oct. 29

Oct. 31

9 Aust. Div.

Tel el Aqqaqir

Enemy Counter-attacks. Oct. 25-28

Kidney Ridge

"SUPERCHARGE" ASSEMBLY AREA. OCT. 27-NOV. 1: 2 N.Z. DIV. 1 & 7 ARMD. DIV. 151, 152, 133 INF. BDES.

Miteiriya Ridge

Ruweisat Ridge

0   2   4   6 MILES

Alamein: The Break-in.

In these days of October 26 and 28 three enemy tankers of vital importance were sunk by air attack, thus rewarding the long series of air operations which were an integral part of the land battle.

* * *

Although the issue still hung in suspense I thought the time had come to report the situation to the Dominions Prime Ministers.

Prime Minister to Prime Ministers of Canada, New Zealand, and Australia   28 Oct 42

The great battle in Egypt has opened well, although one cannot yet forecast its result. The enemy are short of ammunition and fuel, and we have just destroyed a most important tanker on which they must have been counting. Our forces are substantially superior in the air, in armour, including best armour, in artillery fire, and in numbers, and they have far easier lines of communication. Rommel is seriously ill, and has only been brought back as an extreme measure. In Alexander and Montgomery we have generals determined to fight the battle out to the very end. Should they succeed it will be very difficult for the enemy army to make a good retreat on account of his shortage of transport and fuel. It is therefore much better for us to fight him to a finish on this ground than farther west.

To Mr. Fraser:

You will have seen with pride and pleasure all that your valiant New Zealanders are doing and the part they are playing in what may well be a memorable event.

To Mr. Curtin:

You will have observed with pride and pleasure the distinguished part which the 9th Australian Division are playing in what may be an event of first magnitude.

And to General Alexander:

     29 Oct 42

The Defence Committee of the War Cabinet congratulate you on the resolute and successful manner in which the decisive battle which is now proceeding has been launched by you and General Montgomery. The Defence Committee feel that the general situation justifies all the risks and sacrifices involved in the relentless prosecution of this battle, and we assure you that whatever the cost you will be supported in all the measures which you take to shake the life out of Rommel's army and to make this a fight to the finish.

2. The brilliant success of the Air in sinking the tankers so vitally needed, the conditions of intense anxiety and strain behind the enemy's front, provide solid grounds for confidence in your final success. We should be glad to receive any general outline over and above what is contained in the reports which you may care to give of your immediate intentions.

3. In the meantime 'Torch' moves forward with complete secrecy and good fortune, so far, and we shall keep the date punctually.

4. *The following for you and Montgomery alone.* Clark has visited 'Torch' area and held long conference with friendly French generals. We have reason to believe that not only will little opposition be encountered, but that powerful assistance will be forthcoming. Events may therefore move more quickly, perhaps considerably more quickly, than had been planned. Decisive reactions may well be expected in France ; nothing sinister has yet cropped up in Spain. So far as we know the enemy have no idea of what is in store for them, and certainly no idea of its scale or imminence. Every good wish to you and Montgomery. Your battle continuing at full blast will play a memorable part.

General Alexander to Prime Minister and C.I.G.S.   30 Oct 42
   Montgomery and I [are] fully agreed utmost pressure of our offensive must be maintained. Enemy minefields and anti-tank guns have caused a lot of trouble and delay. We are now however about to put in a large-scale attack with infantry and tanks to break a way through for the Xth Corps. If this is successful it will have far-reaching results.

Prime Minister to Air Chief Marshal Tedder   30 Oct 42
   Many congratulations on the magnificent way in which you are cutting into the enemy in the air, on the ground, and on the sea. Pray give my compliments to Coningham, and also to all the officers and men who welcomed me so cordially in the Desert. I was sure then that great days lay ahead. Those days have come, and you are all playing a glorious part in them.

Air Chief Marshal Tedder to Prime Minister   31 Oct 42
   On behalf of all of us I wish to thank you most sincerely for your inspiring message of encouragement. We are all at full throttle and determined to make a job of it.

General Alexander to Prime Minister   31 Oct 42
    Thank you for your encouraging message. Enemy is fight-
ing desperately, but we are hitting him hard and continuously,
and boring into him without mercy. Have high hopes he will
crack soon.

General Alexander to Prime Minister and C.I.G.S.   1 Nov 42
    Best estimate of casualties up to 6 a.m., October 31: killed,
wounded, and missing—officers, 695; other ranks, 9,435.
    Formations with most casualties are 51st Highland Division
and 9th Australian Division, each about 2,000. 10th Armoured
Division, 1,350.
    Recovery of wounded tanks is getting on well. During first
six days 213 tanks were recovered. Of these only sixteen were
condemned as unrepairable.

*   *   *

Montgomery now made his plans and dispositions for the
decisive break-through (Operation 'Supercharge'). He took out
of the line the 2nd New Zealand and the 1st British Armoured
Divisions, the latter being in special need of reorganisation after
its notable share in the repulse of the German armour at Kidney
Ridge. The British 7th Armoured and 51st Divisions and a
brigade of the 44th were brought together and the whole welded
into a new reserve. The break-through was to be led by the 2nd
New Zealand Division, the 151st and 152nd British Infantry
Brigades, and the 9th British Armoured Brigade.
    Meanwhile, in Alexander's words,

    On the night of October 28 and again on October 30 the
Australians attacked northwards towards the coast, succeeding finally in isolating in the pocket thus formed the four
[German] battalions remaining there. The enemy appear to
have been firmly convinced that we intended to strike up the
road and railway, and he reacted to our thrust most vigorously. He moved up his 21st Armoured Division from its
position west of our salient, added to it his 90th Light Division, which was guarding the northern flank of the salient,
and used both in furious attacks to relieve his encircled
troops. Into the position vacated by the 21st Armoured Division he put the Trieste Division, his last uncommitted reserve
formation. While he was thus fully extended and was eking
out his remaining fresh formations in an attempt to extricate
one regiment, we were able to carry out, undisturbed, the
reorganisation of our forces for Operation 'Supercharge'.

The magnificent forward drive of the Australians, achieved by ceaseless bitter fighting, had swung the whole battle in our favour. At 1 a.m. on November 2 'Supercharge' began. Under a barrage of 300 guns the British brigades attached to the New Zealand Division broke through the defended zone, and the 9th British Armoured Brigade drove on ahead. They found however that a new line of defence strong in anti-tank weapons was facing them along the Rahman track. In a long engagement the brigade suffered severely, but the corridor behind was held open and the 1st British Armoured Division moved forward through it. Then came the last clash of armour in the battle. All the remaining enemy tanks attacked our salient on each flank, and were repulsed. Here was the final decision ; but even next day, the 3rd, when our air reports indicated that the enemy's retirement had begun, his covering rearguard on the Rahman track still held the main body of our armour at bay. An order came from Hitler forbidding any retreat, but the issue was no longer in German hands. Only one more hole had to be punched. Very early on November 4, five miles south of Tel el Aggagir, the 5th Indian Brigade launched a quickly mounted attack which was completely successful. The battle was now won, and the way finally cleared for our armour to pursue across the open desert.

General Alexander to Prime Minister   4 Nov 42
 After twelve days of heavy and violent fighting the Eighth Army has inflicted a severe defeat on the German and Italian forces under Rommel's command. The enemy's front has broken, and British armoured formations in strength have passed through and are operating in the enemy's rear areas. Such portions of the enemy's forces as can get away are in full retreat, and are being harassed by our armoured and mobile forces and by our air forces. Other enemy divisions are still in position, endeavouring to stave off defeat, and these are likely to be surrounded and cut off.
 The R.A.F. have throughout given superb support to the land battle, and are bombing the enemy's retreating columns incessantly.
 Fighting continues.

Prime Minister to General Alexander   4 Nov 42
 I send you my heartfelt congratulations on the splendid feat of arms achieved by the Eighth Army under the command of your brilliant lieutenant, Montgomery, in the Battle of Egypt. Although the fruits may take some days or even

weeks to gather it is evident that an event of the first magnitude has occurred which will play its part in the whole future course of the World War.

If the reasonable hopes of your telegram are maintained, and wholesale captures of the enemy and a general retreat are apparent, I propose to ring the bells all over Britain for the first time this war. Try to give me the moment to do this in the next few days. At least 20,000 prisoners would be necessary. You will realise that such a demonstration would be timely in the immediate advent of 'Torch', both in encouraging our friends in the 'Torch' area and in taking the enemy's eye off what is coming to him next quite soon.

'Torch' movements are proceeding with precision and so far amazing secrecy. We shall all have to take a new view of the general position before very long.

*   *   *

Rommel was now in full retreat, but there was transport and petrol for only part of his force, and the Germans, though they had fought valiantly, gave themselves priority in vehicles. Many thousands of men from six Italian divisions were left stranded in the desert, with little food or water, and no future but to be rounded up into prison camps. The battlefield was strewn with masses of destroyed or useless tanks, guns, and vehicles. According to their own records, the German armoured divisions, which had started the battle with 240 serviceable tanks, on November 5 mustered only thirty-eight. The German Air Force had given up the hopeless task of combating our superior Air, which now operated almost unhindered, attacking with all its resources the great columns of men and vehicles struggling westward. Rommel has himself paid notable tribute to the great part played by the Royal Air Force.* His army had been decisively beaten ; his lieutenant, General von Thoma, was in our hands, with nine Italian generals.

There seemed good hopes of turning the enemy's disaster into annihilation. The New Zealand Division was directed on Fuka, but when they reached it on November 5 the enemy had already passed. There was still a chance that they might be cut off at Mersa Matruh, upon which the 1st and 7th British Armoured Divisions had been thrust. By nightfall on the 6th they were nearing their objective, while the enemy were still trying to escape from the closing trap. But then rain came and for-

* Desmond Young, *Rommel*, p. 258.

ward petrol was scarce. Throughout the 7th our pursuit was halted. The twenty-four-hour respite prevented complete encirclement. Nevertheless four German divisions and eight Italian divisions had ceased to exist as fighting formations. Thirty thousand prisoners were taken, with enormous masses of material of all kinds. Rommel has left on record his opinion of the part played by our gunners in his defeat: 'The British artillery demonstrated once again its well-known excellence. Especially noteworthy was its great mobility and speed of reaction to the requirements of the assault troops.'*

The account of this rout may end with an extract from General Alexander's telegram of November 9:

> This great battle can be divided into four stages: The grouping and concentration of our forces for battle and deception methods employed, which gained for us surprise, that battle-winning factor. The break-in attack—that great concentration of force of all arms which punched a hole deep into his defences, and by its disruption created artificial flanks which gave us further opportunities for exploitation. The thrust now here, now there, which drew off his forces and made him use up his reserves in stopping holes and in repeated counter-attacks. The final thrust, which disrupted his last remaining line of defence and broke a way through —through which poured armoured and mobile formations.

General Alexander to Prime Minister   6 Nov 42
Ring out the bells! Prisoners estimated now 20,000, tanks 350, guns 400, M.T. several thousand. Our advanced mobile forces are south of Mersa Matruh. Eighth Army is advancing.

Recalling what happened after Cambrai in 1917, I decided on second thoughts not to ring the bells till after 'Torch', now on the verge, had begun successfully. I hoped however to do so within the week, and I so informed General Alexander.

* * *

The Battle of Alamein differed from all previous fighting in the Desert. The front was limited, heavily fortified, and held in strength. There was no flank to turn. A break-through must be made by whoever was the stronger and wished to take the offensive. In this way we are led back to the battles of the First World War on the Western Front. We see repeated here in Egypt the same kind of trial of strength as was presented at Cambrai

* Desmond Young, *Rommel*, p. 279.

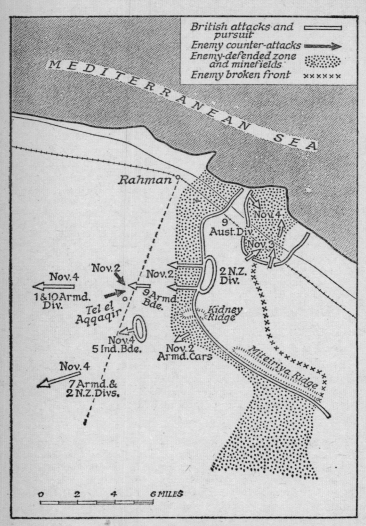

MEDITERRANEAN SEA

Rahman

Nov. 4

9
Aust. Div.

Nov. 3

2 N.Z.
Div.

Nov. 2   Nov. 2

Nov. 4   Nov. 2

1 & 10 Armd.   9 Armd.
Div.   Bde.

Tel el
Aqqaqir

Kidney
Ridge

Nov. 4
5 Ind. Bde.   Nov. 2
                   Armd. Cars

Miteiriya Ridge

Nov. 4

7 Armd. &
2 N.Z. Divs.

0   2   4   6 MILES

Alamein: The Break-through.

at the end of 1917, and in many of the battles of 1918, namely, short and good communication for the assailants, the use of artillery in its heaviest concentration, the 'drum-fire barrage', and the forward inrush of tanks.

In all this General Montgomery and his chief, Alexander, were deeply versed by experience, study, and thought. Montgomery was a great artillerist. He believed, as Bernard Shaw said of Napoleon, that cannons kill men. Always we shall see him trying to bring three or four hundred guns into action under one concerted command, instead of the skirmishing of batteries which was the inevitable accompaniment of swoops of armour in wide desert spaces. Of course everything was on a far smaller scale than in France and Flanders. We lost more than 13,500 men at Alamein in twelve days, but nearly 60,000 on the first day of the Somme. On the other hand, the fire-power of the defensive had fearfully increased since the previous war, and in those days it was always considered that a concentration of two or three to one was required, not only in artillery but men, to pierce and break a carefully fortified line. We had nothing like this superiority at Alamein. The enemy's front consisted not only of successive lines of strong-points and machine-gun posts, but of a whole deep area of such a defensive system. And in front of all there lay the tremendous shield of minefields of a quality and density never known before. For these reasons the Battle of Alamein will ever make a glorious page in British military annals.

There is another reason why it will survive. It marked in fact the turning of 'the Hinge of Fate'. It may almost be said, 'Before Alamein we never had a victory. After Alamein we never had a defeat.'

CHAPTER 11

The Torch is Lit

*General de Gaulle's Position – General Giraud, 'King-pin',
Arrives at Gibraltar – The Armadas Approach the Scene –
The President's Message to Pétain and Others – Eisenhower
Flies to Gibraltar, November 5 – The Rock in the War – Gen-
eral Giraud's Illusions – Explosion Hour! – A Curious Complica-
tion – Admiral Darlan in Algiers – Mr. Murphy and General
Juin Appeal to Him – His Hideous Plight – The British and
American Landings Begin – The American Attack on Oran,
November 8 – French Resistance Ceases at Oran and Algiers –
The All-American Landing in Morocco – General Béthouart's
Loyalty – Resident-General Noguès Regains Control – He
Orders Resistance – The 'Western Task Force' Lands – Fierce
Action Between the French Ships and the United States Fleet –
Noguès Surrenders, November 11 – Generals Giraud and Clark
Fly to Algiers – Icy Reception of Giraud by the French Com-
manders – The Germans Invade Unoccupied France – Darlan
Orders a General 'Cease Fire' Throughout North Africa –
Laval Learns the News – He Dominates Marshal Pétain – And
is Summoned to Berchtesgaden – General Clark Finally Rallies
Admiral Darlan – General Anderson Assumes Command in
Algeria – Rapid Progress Eastward – The Germans Reinforce
Tunis by Air – The Fate of the French Fleet in Toulon.*

The President's prejudices against General de Gaulle, the contacts he possessed through Admiral Leahy with Vichy, and our
memories of the leakage about Dakar two years before led
to a decision to withhold all information about 'Torch' from
the Free French. I did not contest these resolves. I was none the
less conscious of our British relationships with de Gaulle, and
of the gravity of the affront which he would have to suffer by
being deliberately excluded from all share in the design. I
planned to tell him just before the blow fell. As some means of
softening this slight to him and his Movement, I arranged to
confide the trusteeship of Madagascar to his hands. All the facts
before us in the months of preparation and everything we have
learnt since justify the view that bringing de Gaulle into the

business would have been deeply injurious to French reactions in North Africa.

Former Naval Person to President Roosevelt   5 Nov 42

It will be necessary for me to explain 'Torch' to de Gaulle some time during D minus 1, when it is certain the weather is all right. You will remember that I have exchanged letters with him of a solemn kind in 1940 recognising him as the leader of Free Frenchmen. I am confident his military honour can be trusted.

2. I shall explain to him that the reason I have not mentioned 'Torch' to him is that it is a United States enterprise and a United States secret, and that the reason he and his friends are not in on it is not any want of goodwill on our joint part towards him and his Movement, but because of the local complications in the 'Torch' area and the need to have as little fighting as possible. I am arranging to let him announce General Le Gentilhomme as Governor-General of Madagascar some time Friday. This we have been keeping for his consolation prize. It will be a proof that we do not think of throwing over the Free French. As for his relations with Giraud, I should think myself they will join forces politically, though under what conditions I cannot foresee. I hope you will approve of the course I propose.

President to Prime Minister   5 Nov 42

I am very apprehensive in regard to the adverse effect that any introduction of de Gaulle into the 'Torch' situation would have on our promising efforts to attach a large part of the French African forces to our expedition.

Therefore I consider it inadvisable for you to give de Gaulle any information in regard to 'Torch' until subsequent to a successful landing. You would then inform him that the American commander of an American expedition with my approval insisted on complete secrecy as a necessary safety precaution.

De Gaulle's announcement on Friday of Governor-General of Madagascar will not be of any assistance to 'Torch', and it should be sufficient at the present time to maintain his prestige with his followers.

Admiral Leahy agrees wholly with the thoughts expressed above.

The need to find some outstanding French figure was obvious, and to British and American eyes none seemed more appropriate than General Giraud, the fighting General of high rank whose dramatic, audacious escape from his prison in

Germany was a famous tale. I have mentioned my meeting with Giraud at Metz in 1937,* when I visited the Maginot Line, of which he commanded the principal sector. He told me about his adventures in the First World War as an escaped prisoner behind the German lines. As fellow escapees this gave us something in common. Now he had as an Army Commander repeated his youthful exploits in an even more sensational fashion. It is curious that I had telegraphed to the President in April, while 'Torch', the President's 'secret war baby', still lay in the womb of the future:

29 Apr 42

I am highly interested in the escape of General Giraud and his arrival at Vichy. This man might play a decisive part in bringing about things of which you had hopes. Please tell me anything you know.

Now after six months all this had become vital. The Americans entered into secret parleys with the General, and plans were made to bring him from the Riviera to Gibraltar at the decisive moment. Many hopes were based on 'King-pin', as he was called in our code. On November 3 I had telegraphed to the President:

'King-pin' has wirelessed us saying that he has decided to come over at once, and asking for an aeroplane to fetch him to Gibraltar. Eisenhower has replied advising that he use the British submarine under a United States captain which is already off the coast.

Not without danger from the sea, Giraud and his two sons were safely transported.

*   *   *

Meanwhile our great armadas were approaching the scene. We were determined to spare nothing to safeguard their passage. Most of the convoys which sailed from British ports had to cross the Bay of Biscay, traversing all the U-boat routes. Heavy escorts were needed, and we had somehow to conceal not only the concentration of shipping which from the beginning of October began to crowd the Clyde and other western ports, but also the actual sailing of the convoys. We were completely successful. The Germans were led by their own Intelligence to believe that Dakar was again our aim. By the end of October about forty German and Italian U-boats were stationed

* See Book 2, Chapter 5.

to the south and east of the Azores. They were successful in severely mauling a large convoy homeward bound for Sierra Leone, and sank thirteen ships. In the circumstances this could be borne. The first of the 'Torch' convoys left the Clyde on October 22. By the 26th all the fast troopships were under way and American forces were sailing for Casablanca direct from the United States. The whole expedition of about 650 ships was now launched upon the enterprise. They traversed the Bay of Biscay or the Atlantic unseen by the U-boats or by the Luftwaffe.

All our resources were at full strain. Far to the north our cruisers watched the Denmark Strait and the exits from the North Sea to guard against intervention by enemy surface ships. Others covered the American approach near the Azores, and Anglo-American bombers attacked the U-boat bases along the French Atlantic seaboard. Despite apparent U-boat concentrations towards the Gibraltar Straits, the leading ships began to enter the Mediterranean on the night of November 5–6 still undetected. It was not until the 7th, when the Algiers convoy was less than twenty-four hours from its destination, that it was sighted, and even then only one ship was attacked.

The time had come to launch the President's manifesto. I was concerned at the first draft he sent me, in which he addressed Marshal Pétain as 'My dear old friend' and revived the somewhat outdated glories of Verdun in 1916. I thought this would be the final touch with the de Gaullists.

Former Naval Person to President   3 Nov 42
Will you allow me to say that your proposed message to Pétain seems to me too kind? His stock must be very low now. He has used his reputation to do our cause injuries no lesser man could have done. I beg you to think of the effect on the de Gaullists, to whom we have serious obligations, and who have now to go through the great trial of being kept outside. I am advised that unfavourable reactions would be produced in various other quarters. Of course it is absolutely right to send him a friendly message, but will you consider toning it down a bit.

President to Prime Minister   4 Nov 42
I agree that message to Pétain should be toned down, and I have rewritten it so that I am sure it will not offend the friends of France.

The alterations which the President made were satisfactory, and may be studied in the published Hopkins papers.*

* * *

On November 5 Eisenhower by a hazardous flight reached Gibraltar. I had placed the fortress within his command as the temporary headquarters of the leader of this first large-scale American and British enterprise.

Gibraltar's climax in the war had now come. Military measures of defence were of course put into effect from September 1939 to prepare for a possible siege. Facing the Spanish frontier, a strong defensive system was gradually built up, overlooked by the Rock itself, out of which galleries were blasted for guns commanding the isthmus. Measures had to be taken also against attack from the sea and air, as well as by airborne forces. The vital need was water, and by the middle of 1940 distillation plants were completed in the solid rock affording ample supplies and storage. This was a prodigious work.

Gibraltar's greatest positive contribution to the war was the development of its new airfield and the use that was made of it. Starting from a mere landing-strip on the racecourse, this was developed from 1942 onwards into a broad runway over a mile long, its western end built out into Gibraltar Bay with the rubble from the tunnelling. Here the great concentration of aircraft for 'Torch' was made. The whole isthmus was crowded with machines, and fourteen squadrons of fighters were assembled for zero hour. All this activity necessarily took place in full view of German observers, and we could only hope they would think it was for the reinforcement of Malta. We did all we could to make them think so. Apparently they did.

Well may General Eisenhower write, 'Britain's Gibraltar made possible the invasion of North-West Africa.'†

General Eisenhower to Prime Minister   7 Nov 42
    Arrived here safely yesterday.

I have hopes of getting 'King-pin' to North Africa before [we land], but the arrangements are dependent upon good weather to enable him to transfer from submarine to aeroplane. I will report on this officially.

I should like once again to express to you personally my grateful thanks for your constant support and encouragement during the last few months. We are of good heart, and

---

* *The White House Papers of Harry L. Hopkins*, p. 643.
† Eisenhower, *Crusade in Europe*, p. 106.

have every confidence that good fortune will continue to be ours.

Giraud duly arrived at the rendezvous, and to help make things go well I sent him the following message:

> As a fellow escapee I am delighted that we are at work together. I remember all our talks at Metz. For thirty-five years I have had faith in France, and I rejoice that our two nations and the United States are now going to strike the first great blow together for the recovery of Alsace-Lorraine.

General Eisenhower to Prime Minister   8 Nov 42
> 'King-pin' was manifestly pleased to receive your message, and has asked me to transmit to you following reply:
> 'Thank you for your kind telegram. I too remember our frank talks at Metz. Like you, through difficulties and trials, I have never had any doubts of the final victory. I am certain to-day that, thanks to the effort of all, Alsace and Lorraine will remain French.'

Giraud had come with the idea that he would be appointed Supreme Commander in North Africa, and that the American and British armies, of whose strength he had no prior knowledge, would be placed under his authority. He himself strongly urged a landing in France instead of or in addition to Africa, and for some time seemed to imagine that this picture possessed reality. Argument, protracted over forty-eight hours, proceeded between him and General Eisenhower before this brave Frenchman could be convinced of the proportion of affairs. We had all counted overmuch upon 'King-pin', but no one was to be more undeceived than he about the influence he had with the French governors, generals, and indeed the Officer Corps, in North Africa.

*   *   *

The moment of the explosion had at last come. General Eisenhower, in his memoirs, has given a vivid account of his anxious experiences during the night of November 7–8, and all through the next few days. He was always very good at bearing stresses of this kind. The immensity of the stake that was being played, the uncertainty of the weather, by which all might be wrecked, the fragmentary news which arrived, the extraordinary complications of the French attitude, the danger from Spain—all, apart from the actual fighting, must have made this a very hard trial to the Commander, whose responsibilities were enormous and direct.

*   *   *

A curious but in the upshot highly fortunate complication now descended upon us. Admiral Darlan, having completed his tour of inspection in North Africa, returned to France. His son was stricken by infantile paralysis and taken into hospital at Algiers. The news of his dangerous condition led the Admiral to fly back on November 5. He thus happened to be in Algiers on the eve of the Anglo-American descent. This was an odd and formidable coincidence. Mr. Robert Murphy (American political representative in North Africa) hoped he would depart before the assault struck the shores. But Darlan, absorbed in his son's illness, tarried for a day, staying in the villa of a French official, Admiral Fénard.

Our leading hope in Algiers in recent weeks had been General Juin, the French Military Commander. His relations with Mr. Murphy had been intimate, although the actual date had not been imparted to him. A little after midnight on the 7th Murphy visited Juin to tell him that the hour had struck. A mighty Anglo-American army, sustained by overwhelming naval and air forces, was approaching, and would begin landing in Africa in a few hours. General Juin, although deeply engaged and loyal to the enterprise, was staggered by the news. He had conceived himself to possess full command of the situation in Algiers. But he knew that Darlan's presence completely overrode his authority. At his disposal were a few hundred ardent young Frenchmen. He knew only too well that all control of the military and political government had passed from his hands into those of the Minister-Admiral. Now he would certainly not be obeyed. Why, he asked, had he not been told earlier of zero hour? The reasons were obvious, and the fact would have made no difference to his authority. Darlan was on the spot and Darlan was master of all Vichy-French loyalties. Murphy and Juin decided to ask Darlan by telephone to come to them at once. Before two in the morning Darlan, roused from slumber by the urgent message from General Juin, came. On being told of the imminent stroke he turned purple and said, 'I have known for a long time that the British were stupid, but I always believed that the Americans were more intelligent. I begin to believe that you make as many mistakes as they do.'

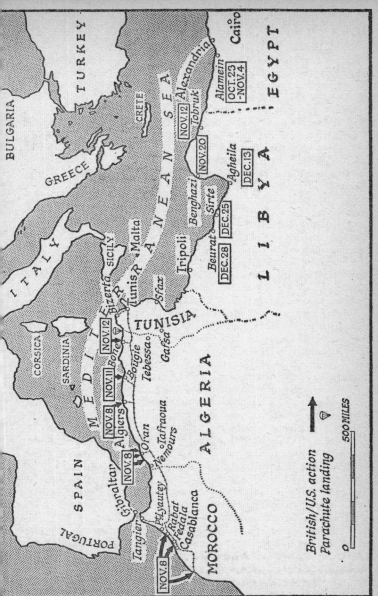

The North Coast of Africa.

Darlan, whose aversion to Britain was notorious, had for a long time been committed to the Axis. In May 1941 he had agreed to grant facilities to the Germans both at Dakar and for the passage of supplies to Rommel's armies through Tunisia. At the time this treacherous move had been stopped by General Weygand, who commanded in North Africa, and who succeeded in persuading Pétain to refuse this German demand. Hitler, at that time fully preoccupied with the impending Russian campaign, did not press the matter, despite contrary advice from his naval staff. In November of the same year Weygand, deemed unreliable by the Germans, was relieved of his command. Although nothing more was heard of the Axis plans to use Dakar against us, the Tunisian ports were later opened to Axis shipping, and played a part in feeding Rommel's armies during the summer of 1942. Now circumstances had changed, and with them Darlan's attitude, but whatever thoughts he might have nourished of aiding an Anglo-American occupation of North-West Africa he was still bound to Pétain in form and in fact. He knew that if he went over to the Allies he would become personally responsible for the inevitable invasion and occupation by Germany of Unoccupied France. The most he could be prevailed upon to do therefore was to ask Pétain by telegram for liberty of action. In the hideous plight in which he had become involved by the remorseless chain of events this was his only course.

Meanwhile the design unfolded. Very soon bands of young anti-Vichy Frenchmen, armed with rifles, surrounded the villa, resolved to make sure how its inmates intended to act. Ingress and exit were barred. Before daybreak fifty *gardes mobiles*, sent as a matter of routine by the police authority, arrived at the villa and dispersed the law-breaking band. They in their turn took charge of the party and placed Juin, Murphy, and his assistant, Mr. Kenneth Pendar, the American Vice-Consul at Marrakesh, who was with him, under arrest. They looked to Darlan for further instructions. He authorised Mr. Pendar to take his telegram to Pétain to the French naval headquarters in Algiers. The French admiral on duty, after making sure the message was genuine, dispatched it, but detained the messenger. The hour had struck, and the landings at Algiers and Oran were now in progress. When morning came and much news had arrived, Darlan and Juin, watching each other vigilantly, leaving Mr. Murphy under polite arrest, went to the Algiers headquarters in Fort l'Empereur, from which, timed 7.40 a.m., Darlan sent the following further telegram to Pétain:

At 7.30 the situation was as follows: Landings have been carried out by American troops and British ships at Algiers and in the neighbourhood. The defences have repulsed the attacks in several places, in particular in the port and at the naval headquarters. In other places landings have been effected by surprise and with success. The situation is getting worse and the defences will soon be overwhelmed. Reports indicate that massive unloadings are in preparation.

Soon after 1 a.m. on November 8 British and American landings began at many points east and west of Algiers under the direction of Rear-Admiral Burrough, R.N. Most careful preparations had been made for guiding the landing-craft to the chosen beaches. In the west leading units of the British 11th Brigade were completely successful, but farther east the ships and craft carrying the Americans were driven some miles from their planned positions by an unexpected tidal set, and in the darkness there was some confusion and delay. Fortunately we gained surprise and opposition along the coast was nowhere serious. After daylight, with the arrival of reinforcements, mastery was soon complete. An aircraft of the Fleet Air Arm, observing friendly signals from the ground, landed at Blida Airfield, and with the co-operation of the local French commander held it until Allied troops from the beaches arrived in support.

The most severe fighting was in the port of Algiers itself. Here the British destroyers *Broke* and *Malcolm* tried to force an entrance and land American Rangers on the mole in order to take over the harbour, occupy the batteries, and prevent the scuttling of ships. This bold action brought the two British ships under the point-blank fire of the defending batteries, and ended in disaster. The *Malcolm* was soon crippled, but the *Broke* entered the harbour at the fourth attempt and landed her troops. Later she was heavily damaged while withdrawing, and eventually sank. Many of the troops were trapped ashore and had to surrender.

At 11.30 a.m. Darlan sent a further telegram to his chief, saying, 'Algiers will probably be taken this evening.' And at 5 p.m., 'American troops having entered into the city, in spite of our delaying action, I have authorised General Juin, the Commander-in-Chief, to negotiate the surrender of the city of Algiers only.' Mr. Pendar, released from arrest, was given a safe-conduct to the American commander, and the surrender of Algiers took effect from 7 p.m. From that moment Admiral Darlan was in American power, and General Juin resumed control of his command under Allied direction.

*   *   *

At Oran the attack was made by the United States 'Centre Task Force', which had been trained and had embarked in Britain. The main assault, supported by the British Navy, was made in the Bay of Arzeu, to the east of the town, about 1 a.m. on November 8, while two secondary landings took place to the westward. There was stronger French opposition here than at Algiers. Various regular French units who had fought the British in Syria, and those forces under naval command whose memories of the British attack on Mers-el-Kebir in 1940 were bitter, resisted. Because of these earlier events the Americans had expected greater opposition here than anywhere else, but the landings were effected as planned. Meanwhile misfortune befell two subsidiary operations. The first was the audacious airborne descent which had been planned to seize the airfields behind Oran. A battalion of American parachute infantry set out from England on this daring adventure, but the formation became scattered over Spain in stormy weather. The leading elements pressed on, but their navigation was faulty and they landed some miles from their target. Later they joined their comrades, already ashore, and played their part in capturing the airfield at Tafaroui.

The second misfortune attended the gallant attempt by two small British warships to land a party of American troops in Oran harbour. Their object, as at Algiers, was to seize the port installations and so prevent the French from sabotaging them or scuttling shipping. The party therefore included many skilled technicians. The importance of this venture lay in the fact that it was imperative to bring the port of Oran into use as an Allied base at the earliest moment. Led by Captain F. T. Peters, R.N., the *Walney* entered the harbour, followed by the *Hartland*, soon after the main landings had been launched. Both were ex-American coastguard cutters transferred to us under Lend-Lease. They encountered murderous fire at point-blank range, and both ships were destroyed, with most of those on board. Captain Peters miraculously survived, only to meet his death a few days later in an aircraft disaster while returning to England. He was posthumously awarded the Victoria Cross and the American Distinguished Service Cross.

By dawn the French destroyers and submarines were active in Oran Bay, but were met with overwhelming force and either sunk or dispersed. Coastal batteries continued to oppose the landings, but were bombarded and bombed effectively by British naval forces, including the *Rodney*. Fighting continued until the morning of the 10th, when the American forces ashore launched their final attack on the city, and by noon the French capitulated.

Although French resistance had ceased at Oran and Algiers German reactions along the North African coast now rapidly increased, and our vital supply route by sea was soon threatened by a swarm of U-boats. They had some successes, including the sinking of three large liners returning empty from the landing beaches; but our counter-measures were vigorous, and by the end of November nine U-boats were destroyed in these waters.

* * *

For the all-American landing in Morocco there was hope of active local support. General Béthouart, the French Divisional Commander at Casablanca, had fought at Narvik. He was zealous against the Germans. He was in charge of the land defences of the greater part of the Moroccan coast. At a late stage he had been brought into the secret, and was prepared to accept Giraud as Supreme French Commander. He hoped that when the moment came both the Resident-General, Noguès, and Admiral Michelier would rally to the cause. The Allied agents had wished him to take no chances and arrest the Resident-General. This Béthouart was not prepared to do. He did not want to be accused of supplanting his chief. At 11 p.m. on November 7 he assembled at his headquarters those officers whom he had made privy to the design. He told them. 'The Americans are landing to-morrow morning at five o'clock.' At midnight the party left Casablanca in three cars, and two hours later took over the headquarters in Rabat, the capital, together with the telephone exchanges of the General Staff and the post office. Unluckily General Noguès' secret line was overlooked, and during the next fateful hours the Resident-General was able to communicate freely with the commanders of the main bases throughout Morocco.

On arrival at Rabat Béthouart sent his aide-de-camp to Noguès with written details of the discussions between Giraud and Murphy and of the imminent Allied landings. On Béthouart's orders Noguès was surrounded in his residence by a company of colonial infantry. He was enraged. He arrested the aide-de-camp, who was his own nephew, and at once rang up Admiral Michelier at the naval base at Casablanca. He was told that there was no evidence of any Allied approach to the coast. This negative news determined Noguès' action. He ordered the 'Alert', and told Michelier to supersede Béthouart, now in Rabat. At that moment the American fleet of more than a hundred ships, carrying General Patton's landing force, was in fact but thirty miles away ; but no word had yet reached Noguès even about the landings which were already in progress in Algeria. In this tense situation General Béthouart had every reason for anxiety. He alone had direct knowledge of the impending attack, but his *coup* in Rabat with his small band of supporters had merely placed all Morocco in a stage of siege behind Noguès.

At 5 a.m. Noguès received from the American Vice-Consul in Rabat a personal letter from President Roosevelt calling on him to aid the Allies. Two hours later, after the landings had begun, he informed Darlan in Algiers that he had rejected this United States ultimatum. Béthouart and his few adherents were surrounded. Noguès himself telephoned threatening to shoot the officers of the colonial regiment involved. All were arrested forthwith. Béthouart was tried by court-martial two days later, and was not finally released till November 17.

*   *   *

The assault on the exposed Atlantic coast of Morocco had given more anxiety during the planning than those within the Mediterranean. Not only had the whole expedition to be brought direct from American ports to their landing beaches over the North Atlantic, and in conformity with a fixed time-table, but grave concern was felt lest the weather along the coast should render landing impossible on the selected day, particularly so late in the season. On November 7 the weather forecasts received in Admiral Hewitt's flagship from London and Washington boded no good, and the Admiral had then to decide at once whether to adhere to his original plan or adopt the alternative, which entailed taking his whole force through the Gibraltar Straits and landing General Patton near Nemours on little-known beaches close to the frontiers of Spanish Morocco. Apart from other considerations, this plan involved serious and possibly fatal delay. Fortunately his staff confidently predicted a temporary local improvement in the weather, and the Admiral boldly, and as it turned out correctly, backed their judgment. The die was cast, and the fleet dispersed before dark to their several destinations.

The 'Western Task Force' reached the Moroccan coast before dawn on November 8. To allow for a longer approach in darkness the time chosen for this assault was three hours later than the landings in Algeria. This had been criticised beforehand by General Patton, as he believed, not without reason, that the broadcast appeal by the President to the French people of North Africa, which was timed for the Algerian landings at 1 a.m., would serve merely to warn the defences in Morocco. In the event the broadcast to Morocco was of no importance, but, as we have seen, the defences had none the less been 'Alerted'. The operations comprised three landings. In the centre the main attack was made at Fedala, close to Casablanca. Flanking attacks took place at Port Lyautey in the north and at Safi in the south. The weather in the morning was fair but hazy, and the surf on the beaches less severe than had been feared. Later the surf got worse, but by then a firm foothold had been gained in all areas. In some places the first troops landed unopposed, but resistance soon stiffened, and for a time there was severe fighting, particularly near Port Lyautey.

At sea a fierce action took place. In Casablanca lay the unfinished new battleship *Jean Bart*, incapable of movement but able to use her four 15-inch guns. She was soon engaged in a gun duel with the American battleship *Massachusetts,* while the French flotilla, supported by the cruiser *Primauguet*, put to sea to oppose the landing. They met the whole strength of the American fleet, and when operations ceased seven French ships and three submarines had been destroyed, with a thousand casualties. The *Jean Bart* had been gutted by fire and beached.

During the 9th the Americans consolidated their lodgment and thrust inland. It was not until the morning of November 11 that Noguès, under Darlan's orders, surrendered. 'I have lost,' he reported, 'all our fighting ships and aircraft after three days of violent combat.' Captain Mercier, of the *Primauguet*, longed for the Allied victory, but he died on her bridge in the execution of his orders. We may all be thankful if our lives have not been rent by such dire problems and conflicting loyalties.

* * *

Fragmentary news of these events and of official French resistance to the Allied landings began to come in to General Eisenhower's headquarters at Gibraltar. The Allied Supreme Commander was now faced with a grave political situation. He had agreed with Giraud to put him in command of those French forces who might rally to the Allied cause. Now there had suddenly and accidentally appeared in the centre of the scene a man who could in fact decide whether any French forces at all in North Africa would come over in an orderly fashion and join the Allies. The calculations that Giraud would provide a rallying-point had not yet been put to the test, and first reactions from the landing areas were not encouraging. On the morning of November 9 therefore General Giraud, and a little later General Clark, acting as General Eisenhower's personal deputy, flew to Algiers to arrange with the French authorities the immediate ending of all hostilities.

The reception of Giraud by the leading French commanders was icy. The local Resistance organisation, so long fostered by both American and British agents, had already collapsed. The first conference held by Clark that evening with Darlan produced no agreement. It was obvious that Giraud would not be accepted by any one of importance as Supreme French Commander. On the morning of November 10 General Clark arranged a second meeting with the Admiral. He told Eisenhower by radio that a deal with Darlan was the only solution. There was no time to engage in telegraphic discussions with London and Washington. Giraud was not present at this meeting. Darlan hesitated on the grounds of lack of instructions from Vichy. Clark gave him half an hour in which to make up his mind. The Admiral at length agreed to order a general 'Cease fire' throughout North Africa. 'In the name of the Marshal' he assumed complete authority throughout the French North African territories, and ordered all officials to remain on duty.

Later that day came the important news that the Germans had begun to invade Unoccupied France. This simplified Darlan's position. He could now maintain, and his word would be accepted by local officials and commanders, that Marshal Pétain

Algiers–Tunis.

Map labels:
C. Bon
Bizerta
Sousse
Sfax
Hamma Gabes
Médenine
Menzel Temime
Djedeida Tunis Dec. 3
Mateur
Pont du Fahs
Enfidaville
Kairouan
Fondouk
Hadjez
Teboursouk
Sbeitla
Kasserine
Le Kef
Thala
Souk el Arba
Nov. 16
Tebessa
Nov. 15
U.S. Bn.
Youks-les-Bains
Gafsa Nov. 17
Tabarka Nov. 18
Nov. 28
Nov. 25
Abiod
Bone Nov. 12
Philippeville
Guelma
Constantine
Djidjelli Nov. 13
Setif
Bougie Nov. 11
Algiers Nov. 8
Biskra

ALGERIA

TUNISIA

British / U.S. action
Parachute landings
French concentrations,
November

0 20 40 60 80 100 120 140 Miles

was no longer a free agent. The German move also struck Darlan's vital nerve. Very soon advanced German elements would be entering the great French naval base at Toulon. As in 1940, the fate of the French Fleet was now again in the balance. The only man whose prestige would be sufficient to get the French battle fleet to sea under these circumstances would be Darlan. He now acted decisively and telegraphed on the afternoon of November 11 to Metropolitan France that the Toulon fleet was to put to sea if in danger of imminent capture by the Germans. Allied naval and air dispositions were taken to protect the sortie of the French ships in such an event.

* * *

In the event the German High Command did not know where the great Allied convoys steaming towards North Africa were going until almost the last moment. The wide arc of U-boat patrols had been traversed at many points. But once the main armada had passed the Straits of Gibraltar their destination was more definite. Even then the Germans seem to have thought that the Allied expedition might be aiming at Italy or reinforcing Malta. In his diary the chief of the Italian General Staff, Marshal Cavallero, records a telephone conversation overheard between Goering and Kesselring.*

Goering: According to our calculations the convoy will be within the next forty to fifty hours in range of our Air Force, and therefore everything must be held in readiness.
Kesselring: Herr Reichsmarshal, and supposing a convoy attempts a landing in Africa?
Goering: To my mind a landing will be attempted in Corsica, in Sardinia, or at Derna or Tripoli.
Kesselring: It is more probable at a North African port.
Goering: Yes, but not in a French one.
Kesselring: If the convoy has to pass through the Sicily channel I shall have time.
Goering: If it doesn't aim at Sardinia it will certainly pass through the channel, where the Italians have not mined the waters, and this should be pointed out to them.

Not until midnight on November 7 was there official contact between the German authorities and Vichy. The head of the German Armistice Commission at Wiesbaden then summoned one of the French officers attached to that body and informed

* Cavallero, *Commando Supremo*, p. 371.

him that the objective of the large Allied convoys now in the Mediterranean would probably be Algeria and Tunisia. An offer of German military aid was sent to Vichy.

*　　　*　　　*

During the early hours of November 8 reports began to flow into Vichy of the Allied approach. Laval, sleeping at his house hard by, was rung up by the German political representative at Vichy, who repeated the offer of German support should the landings develop in force in North Africa. Laval hastened to the centre of government. At 4 a.m. the American Chargé d'Affaires, Mr. Pinckney Tuck, arrived at Marshal Pétain's private office with the letter from the President. Laval took control. He collected his close supporters and drafted a negative and hostile reply for the Marshal to sign in the morning. An hour later the Vichy Admiralty informed Darlan in Algiers of the German offer to give air support against the Allied landings. The reply from Darlan suggested that the German air forces based on Sicily and Sardinia should attack the Allied transports at sea.

It was not until 7 a.m. that the Marshal was awakened to hear the news. He showed little visible emotion or even interest in Laval's draft reply to the American President. He accepted it without demur, whistling a little hunting tune to himself. At nine he received Mr. Pinckney Tuck to hand him his reply. There are several accounts of the climate of this meeting. It is said that when Pétain handed the document to the American he gave him a knowing tap on the shoulder. The aged Marshal acted throughout these days like a man in a dream.

But any illusions of Vichy that a double game could still be played by them between the Allies and the Germans were soon dispelled. Nazi pressure hardened, and at 11.30 a.m. the Vichy Cabinet accepted the German offer of air support from Sicily and Sardinia. This caitiff decision enabled the Germans to take the quick, decisive action of occupying airfields in Tunisia, with all its costly consequences upon our campaign.

Later in the day a second Cabinet meeting accepted a formal rupture of diplomatic relations with the United States.

*　　　*　　　*

That evening Hitler summoned Laval to Berchtesgaden. Laval set out by car in the morning, but only reached Munich in thick fog early on the 10th. He was therefore on the road during the hours when Darlan was negotiating with the Allies in Algiers, and while the news of these parleys was injecting a little hope into those few men at Vichy who still wanted the Marshal to come out on the Allied side. Both Weygand, who had come to Vichy on purpose to dissuade the Marshal from giving in, and Admiral Auphan, Minister of Marine, tried their best. They even got him to agree to a draft telegram to Darlan approving his move. When Laval at Munich learnt of these moves, both at Algiers and at Vichy, he was enraged, and under threat of resignation extorted the Marshal's withdrawal of his telegram to Darlan.

Laval met Hitler late that afternoon. The Fuehrer, with his theatrical sense of history, treated the Frenchman to a discourse on past Franco-German relations, going back a long way. He also confronted him with a joint German-Italian note demanding French consent to Axis landings in Tunisia. Ciano, who was present, says Laval cut a pitiable figure. This may well be believed. Early in the morning of November 11 Laval was woken up by Abetz to be told that the Fuehrer had ordered the German Army to occupy the free zone of France. The same day the Italians occupied Nice and Corsica. So much for Vichy.

*　　　*　　　*

The Germans had intercepted Darlan's message to Vichy, and Laval under their pressure forced Pétain to send a message to Algiers disowning Darlan's actions. General Clark, when confronted with Darlan's apparent readiness to withdraw the orders he had issued, put the Admiral under arrest. The arrival of a secret message from Pétain however in a special naval code and the news of further German advances into Unoccupied France restored both the situation and the tempers of those concerned in Algiers. On the following day, November 11, it was agreed that Darlan should send categorical instructions to the Toulon fleet to put to sea, and further messages were sent to the French Resident-General in Tunisia, Admiral Esteva, to join the Allies.

*　　　*　　　*

Admiral Esteva was a faithful servant of Vichy. He followed the cataract of events with mounting confusion and alarm. As he was closer to the enemy in Sicily and on his eastern frontier, his position was worse than that of either Darlan or Noguès.

His high subordinates matched him in equal indecision. Already on November 9 units of the German Air Force occupied the important airfield at El Aouina. On the same day German and Italian troops arrived in Tunisia. Depressed and wavering, Esteva clung to a formal allegiance to Vichy, while the Axis forces in Tripolitania were coming from the east, and the Allies hastened from the west. The French General Barré, at first baffled by a problem the like of which, gentle reader, you have not yet been asked to solve, finally moved the bulk of the French garrison westwards and placed himself under the orders of General Giraud. At Bizerta however three torpedo-boats and nine submarines surrendered to the Axis.

In Alexandria, where the French naval squadron had been immobilised since 1940, parleys took place without effect. Admiral Godefroy, its commander, persisted in his loyalty to Vichy and refused to recognise the authority of Admiral Darlan. In his view, until the Allies had conquered Tunisia they could not claim that it was in their power to liberate France. Thus the ships continued in idleness until in the fullness of time we conquered Tunis.

At Dakar the Vichy Governor-General Boisson accepted Darlan's order to cease resistance on November 23, but the units of the French Navy there refused to join the Allies. Only after the completion of our conquest of all North Africa did the battleship *Richelieu* and the three cruisers with her rally to our cause.

*   *   *

As soon as the Algiers landing was well established General Anderson, as previously arranged, took over command from the United States General Ryder. He dispatched his 36th Infantry Brigade by sea to Bougie, which they took unopposed on November 11 ; one of its battalions reached Djidjelli Airfield next day. Two British parachute companies dropped on Bone on the 12th, and were supported by Commandos from the sea ; others on Souk-el-Arba Airfield on the 16th, whence they advanced to Beja, and farther on met Germans in position. The 36th Brigade, pressing on rapidly by road, crossed into Tunisia, and at Djebel Abiod on November 17 met German troops. Meanwhile United States parachutists had dropped at Youksles-Bains on the 15th, and reached Gafsa also two days later.

These rapid and unopposed movements had secured the

eastern airfields of Algeria necessary for the support of ground forces which could no longer be covered from Gibraltar, now 800 miles behind. Great dash and enterprise had been shown in gaining ground so fast, but now that the enemy were met the pace must slacken. The Germans had taken prompt measures. Their first contingents arrived by air on November 9, and soon two parachute regiments and four battalions of reinforcements originally destined to reinforce Rommel sought to bar the way. These were followed by advanced elements of the 10th Panzer Division, two Bersaglieri battalions, and six battalions of the Italian Superga Infantry Division. By the end of the month the Axis forces in Tunisia amounted to 15,000 fighting troops, with 100 tanks, 60 field guns, and 30 anti-tank guns. Their dive-bombers, based on the good airfields of Tunisia, were beginning to prove troublesome. But already we had brought a relief to the Russian armies. During November the Germans withdrew 400 operational aircraft, mostly long-range bombers, from the Eastern front for use in the Mediterranean. In this latter theatre a quarter of the whole German Air Force was now deployed, as compared with only a twelfth eighteen months before.

* * *

The Anglo-American descent in North Africa brought an immediate sequel in France. Since 1940 the Germans had drawn up detailed plans for the occupation of the free zone of France. The code-name was 'Attila', and the directive was issued by Hitler on December 10 of that year. The original purpose was to counteract any move of Weygand in North Africa. Each time that there was a tension in Franco-German relations the question of putting 'Attila' into force arose. The main objective of such an operation would be the capture intact of the principal units of the French Fleet, which lay at Toulon. But both Hitler and Raeder were consistent in working for collaboration with Vichy, wishing to avoid the commitments which would follow the total occupation of Metropolitan France.

The Allied landings in North Africa however revolutionised the position. It may well be that Laval's description to the Germans at Berchtesgaden of Darlan's talks with the Allies at Algiers was decisive. General Eisenhower was as anxious to lay his hands on the French Fleet as were the Germans. The main justification for negotiating with Darlan at all was his authority

Top: Winston Churchill, dressed in his famous 'zip suit', with Field-Marshal Smuts in Cairo. *Bottom:* In the garden of the British Embassy in Cairo. Sitting, from left to right: Field-Marshal J. Smuts; Winston S. Churchill; General Sir Claude Auchinleck; General Sir Archibald Wavell. Standing are: Air Marshal Sir Arthur Tedder; General Sir Alan Brooke, the C.I.G.S.; Admiral Sir H. Harwood; Mr. R. G. Casey

An American transport aircraft flying over the Pyramids (*Panorama*)

Top: A German machine-gun post in the Caucasus at 14,000 ft. (*Panorama*). *Bottom:* General von Paulus looks at the operational area before Stalingrad, where his 6th Army finally suffered the terrible defeat that was to mark the battle as one of the main turning points of the war

General Sir Bernard Montgomery, now Field-Marshal Viscount
Montgomery of Alamein

Operation 'Torch' has started. The Anglo-American troops participating wore a yellow arm-band. Here, American troops land at Surcouf—November 8, 1942

The Conference at Casablanca, January 1943, where the Allied war strategy for the period after the conquest of North Africa was decided. *Sitting left to right:* Admiral E. J. King, Mr. Churchill and President Roosevelt. *Standing:* Major-General Sir Hastings Ismay (*2nd from left*), Vice-Admiral Lord Louis Mountbatten and Field-Marshal Sir John Dill (*Panorama*)

Algiers Conference, June 1943. Around Churchill are, from left to right: Anthony Eden; General Sir Alan Brooke; Air Marshal Tedder; Admiral Cunningham; General Alexander; General Marshall; General Eisenhower; General Montgomery

R.A.F. photograph of Toulon harbour, where many French warships were sunk

with the Vichy admirals and officers. The Germans clearly could not afford to take any risks, and while Darlan was sending messages to Vichy and to Toulon urging the French Fleet to put to sea in the direction of Allied controlled ports the Germans were marching rapidly towards the Mediterranean coast.

Admiral Auphan, the Minister of Marine at Vichy, wished to stand by Darlan, but he was powerless in the face of Laval and of the attitude of the French commanders at Toulon. Admiral de Laborde, the Commander of the French Mediterranean Fleet, was fanatically anti-British. On hearing the news of the landings he wished to put to sea and attack the Allied convoys. He rejected Darlan's appeals to come over, and when the Germans arrived at the perimeter of the French naval base an agreement was made whereby a free zone round the harbour was to be garrisoned by French troops. Auphan reluctantly endorsed this arrangement, and attempts were made to put the port in a serious state of defence. But on November 18 the Germans demanded the withdrawal of all French troops from the zone, which could only be garrisoned by naval units. The following day Auphan resigned.

The Germans now planned a *coup de main* against the Fleet. The operation took place on November 27. The courage and resource of a few officers, including Laborde, who rallied at last, made possible the wholesale scuttling of the Fleet. One battleship, two battle-cruisers, seven cruisers, twenty-nine destroyers and torpedo-boats, and sixteen submarines were among the seventy-three ships which sank in the port.

* * *

The assault phase of 'Torch' had been a brilliant success, and was in itself a remarkable operation. The fall of Algiers and Casablanca had been obtained cheaply, partly through the intervention of Admiral Darlan. Through the vacillation of the French commanders in Tunisia we were robbed of complete success. In his report on these events Admiral Cunningham said: 'It is a matter for lasting regret to me that the bolder conception for the initial assault on Bone was not implemented. The enemy were surprised and off their balance. We failed to give the final push which would have tipped the scales.'

CHAPTER 12

The Darlan Episode

The Position of General de Gaulle and the Free French – My Telegram to the President of November 11 – His Reply, November 12 – Eisenhower Flies to Algiers – Darlan's Authority Prevails with the French in North and West Africa – Widespread Disquiet in England – I Warn the President, November 17 – His Public Statement – General Smuts's View from the Spot – Passion Mounts in England – 'The Darlan Deal' – The Secret Session, December 10 – French Military and Official Mentality – 'In the Name of the Marshal' – The House of Commons Convinced – Assassination of Admiral Darlan, December 24 – A Tragic Career.

The facts of the story told in the last chapter show briefly what happened on the spot and in what order. Although these events were political they were as much a part of the battle as the movement of troops or ships. General Clark dealt with Darlan in the only way which would accord with the prime theme of the enterprise, namely, the procuring of the utmost French support and the avoidance of bloodshed between the French and the Allies. He showed daring, sagacity, and power of decision. On Eisenhower fell the responsibility of accepting and sustaining what had been done. The conduct of both these American officers, who only a year before had been Brigadier-Generals, reached a high level of courage and good sense. Nevertheless their action raised issues of a moral and sentimental character of cardinal importance to the peoples of the United States and Great Britain, and reverberated through the Allied world. Hoping always that I understood the soul of France, I was at this time anxious about the President's vehement hostility to de Gaulle and his Movement. After all, this was the core of French resistance and the flame of French honour.

Former Naval Person to President Roosevelt   11 Nov 42
    It is surely of the highest importance to unify in every possible way all Frenchmen who regard Germany as the foe. The invasion of Unoccupied France by Hitler should give the opportunity for this. You will, I am sure, realise that His

Majesty's Government are under quite definite and solemn obligations to de Gaulle and his Movement. We must see they have a fair deal. It seems to me that you and I ought to avoid at all costs the creation of rival French *émigré* Governments, each favoured by one of us. We must try to fuse all anti-German French forces together and make a united Government. This may take some time, and nothing must prejudice the military operations, but we ought to make it clear to all parties what we want and what we are going to work for.

Meanwhile it became apparent that a decisive victory had been gained at Alamein.

President to Prime Minister   12 Nov 42

I am very happy with the latest news of your splendid campaign in Egypt, and of the success that has attended our joint landing in West and North Africa. This brings up the additional steps that should be taken when and if the south shore of the Mediterranean is cleared and under our control. It is hoped that you with your Chiefs of Staff in London and I with the Combined Staff here may make a survey of the possibilities, including a forward movement directed against Sardinia, Sicily, Italy, Greece, and other Balkan areas, and including the possibility of obtaining Turkish support for an attack through the Black Sea against Germany's flank.

In regard to de Gaulle, I have hitherto enjoyed a quiet satisfaction in leaving him in your hands. Apparently I have now acquired a similar problem in brother Giraud. I wholly agree that we must prevent rivalry between the French *émigré* factions, and I have no objection to a de Gaulle emissary visiting Giraud in Algiers. We must remember that there is also a cat-fight in progress between Giraud and Darlan, each claiming full military command of French forces in North and West Africa.

The principal thought to be driven home to all three of these prima donnas is that the situation is to-day solely in the military field, and that any decision by any one of them, or by all of them, is subject to review and approval by Eisenhower.

Also I think it would be well to find out before de Gaulle's man leaves for Africa just what his instructions are.

*   *   *

On November 13 General Eisenhower flew from Gibraltar to Algiers to take the responsibility for the bargain which Clark had just made with Darlan and assume direct control. The

Allied commanders and officials on the spot were unanimous that Darlan was the only Frenchman who could rally North-West Africa to the Allies. Giraud, whose power to command French allegiance was already exposed as a myth, had offered to work with Darlan when he heard of the German invasion of Unoccupied France. Darlan's authority was proved by the obedience to his 'Cease fire' orders at Oran, in Morocco, and throughout Algeria. A final and formal agreement was therefore signed between Darlan and Eisenhower on the same day. In London I thought that Eisenhower's action was overwhelmingly justified on military grounds. On November 14 I sent him the following message: 'Anything for the battle, but the politics will have to be sorted out later on.'

To the President I cabled:

Former Naval Person to President Roosevelt   15 Nov 42

We cannot say that our doubts or anxieties are removed by what is proposed or that the solution will be permanent or healthy. Nevertheless, in view of the dominating importance of speed and of the fact that the Allied Commander-in-Chief's opinion is so strongly and ably expressed and that it is endorsed by our officers, including Admiral Cunningham, who were with him on the spot, we feel we have no choice but to accept General Eisenhower's arrangements for maintaining local and interim equilibrium and for securing the vital positions in Tunis.

2. We feel sure you will consult us on the long-term steps, pursuing always the aim of uniting all Frenchmen who will fight Hitler.

*   *   *

As the facts of the Darlan agreement became known they caused widespread disquiet at home. I was conscious of the rising tide of opinion around me. I was grieved to find the success of our immense operation, and the victory of Alamein, overshadowed in the minds of many of my best friends by what seemed to them a base and squalid deal with one of our most bitter enemies. I considered their attitude unreasonable and not sufficiently considerate of the severities of the struggle and the lives of the troops. As their criticisms became sharper I grew resentful, and also somewhat contemptuous of their sense of proportion; but I understood what was troubling them and felt it myself. The reaction in the United States was not so violent as in England, but many were agog. I did not think that President Roosevelt was sufficiently impressed with the surge of feeling, and certainly not of British feeling.

Former Naval Person to President Roosevelt   17 Nov 42

I ought to let you know that very deep currents of feeling are stirred by the arrangement with Darlan. The more I reflect upon it the more convinced I become that it can only be a temporary expedient, justifiable solely by the stress of battle. We must not overlook the serious political injury which may be done to our cause, not only in France but throughout Europe, by the feeling that we are ready to make terms with the local Quislings. Darlan has an odious record. It is he who has inculcated in the French Navy its malignant disposition by promoting his creatures to command. It is but yesterday that French sailors were sent to their death against your line of battle off Casablanca, and now, for the sake of power and office, Darlan plays the turncoat. A permanent arrangement with Darlan or the formation of a Darlan Government in French North Africa would not be understood by the great masses of ordinary people, whose simple loyalties are our strength.

2. My own feeling is that we should get on with the fighting and let that overtake the parleys, and we are all very glad to hear that General Eisenhower expects to be able to order the leading elements of our First Army, to attack the Germans in Tunis and Bizerta in the course of the next dew days.

The President replied:

President to Prime Minister   18 Nov 42

I too have encountered the deep currents of feeling about Darlan. I felt I should act fast, so I have just given out a statement at my Press conference which I hope you will like, and I trust it will be accepted at face value.

I was relieved by his public statement,* which he had cabled me:

I have accepted General Eisenhower's political arrangements made for the time being in Northern and Western Africa. I thoroughly understand and approve the feeling in the United States and Great Britain and among all the other United Nations that in view of the history of the past two years no permanent arrangement should be made with Admiral Darlan. People in the United Nations likewise would never understand the recognition of a reconstitution of

* Abridged.

the Vichy Government in France or in any French territory. We are opposed to Frenchmen who support Hitler and the Axis.

No one in our Army has any authority to discuss the future Government of France and the French Empire. The future French Government will be established, not by any individual in Metropolitan France or overseas, but by the French people themselves after they have been set free by the victory of the United Nations. The present arrangement in North and West Africa is only a temporary expedient, justified solely by the stress of battle.

His statement proceeded:

Our first military objective was to save American and British lives on the one hand, and French lives on the other hand. The second was the vital factor of time. ... Every day of delay in the current operation would have enabled the Germans and Italians to build up a strong resistance, to dig in, and make a huge operation on our part essential before we could win. Here again many more lives will be saved under the present speedy offensive than if we had had to delay it for a month or more. ... Reports indicate that the French of North Africa are subordinating all political questions to the formation of a common front against the common enemy.

This met my view and the public need.

Former Naval Person to President Roosevelt   19 Nov 42
Your public statement about Darlan has settled the matter in the best possible way. I am as anxious however as you and Eisenhower that we should profit to the full in the actions which are impending by French co-operation. Also, I fully recognise that if Darlan and Company render real services during the operations these would naturally count in their favour. I feel pretty sure we are looking at it from exactly the same point of view. Every good wish.

*   *   *

General Smuts was with us at home in these days, and it was a comfort to find how close was our agreement. He now flew off, after a long talk, to the scene of action on his way back to South Africa. After a full discussion in Algiers he expressed himself in the following practical manner:

Field-Marshal Smuts to Prime Minister   20 Nov 42
After arrival this morning I had a long talk with Eisenhower and Cunningham, which I summarise for your in-

formation. As regards coming operation next Sunday or Monday, it is doubtful whether Anderson is strong enough to take Bizerta, but Tunis appears more hopeful. In any case, every effort will be made to press the enemy into as small an area or bridgehead as possible, so that air and other attack may finish him later. Farther south attempt will be made to clean up small pockets of enemy at Sfax and elsewhere, but no large forces will be employed in the Tripoli direction at present. Sea losses so far have been made good. Loss of personnel ships have been compensated by equal number of French ships acquired, and for every merchant vessel lost a U-boat has been sunk.

As regards Darlan, statements published have had unsettling effect on local French leaders, and it would be dangerous to go farther on those lines. Noguès has threatened to resign, and as he controls the Morocco population the results of such a step might be far-reaching. From the point of view of securing French co-operation and stabilising the situation nothing could be worse than impression that we were merely using leaders to discard them as soon as they have served our purpose. There can be no doubt that Darlan and his friends have burnt their boats and are doing their best to fight the Axis and consolidate French behind us in this fight. French are co-operating in non-combatant tasks, and even in fighting on small scale, but their fighting value is at present low for want of proper arms. Darlan was not Eisenhower's choice, but that of other French leaders, some of whom were his enemies and our strong supporters, and who all agreed that his leadership in co-operation was essential for our operations. It would be great mistake to create impression that he is to be discarded at early date. Military situation may call for his retention for fairly long period, and meanwhile an impression to contrary should not be publicly created.

I explained to Eisenhower that I do not think there was any intention to repeat or go beyond statements already made, which were only intended to correct impression that political accord with Vichy elements had been come to. Future political arrangements should be left to Governments concerned and agreement of French among themselves. I think it would be wise to pass on to President Roosevelt my strong impression that further anti-Darlan statements might be harmful to our cause, and indeed are not called for. We leave late this afternoon, and I shall signal you again from Cairo. Your company and talks last night were a great honour, and most deeply enjoyed. Thanks very much.

The President kept me in touch with his own mood.

President to Prime Minister   20 Nov 42
I told the Press yesterday in confidence an old Orthodox
Church proverb used in the Balkans that appears applicable
to our present Darlan–de Gaulle problem: 'My children, it is
permitted you in time of grave danger to walk with the devil
until you have crossed the bridge.'

In regard to North Africa and possibly additional future
areas, I think you and I might give some consideration to the
idea of appointing one Britisher and one American to whom
would be given authority not to administer civil functions
but to hold a veto power over French civil administrators,
and to direct them in rare instances to follow out certain
policies. For example, I sent word to Eisenhower that all political prisoners in North and West Africa must be released.
If Darlan fails to carry out this directive Eisenhower must at
once exercise his authority as Supreme Commander and take
independent action in the matter.

On December 5 General Eisenhower telegraphed to me:

. . . I assure you again that we are not entering a cabal designed to place Darlan at the head of anything except the local
organisation. Here he is entirely necessary, for he and he alone
is the source of every bit of practical help we have received.
If you will contemplate the situation existing along our lines
of communication, which extend 500 miles from here through
mountainous country to Tunisia, you will understand that
the local French could, without fear of detection, so damage
us that we would have to retreat hurriedly back to ports
from which we could supply ourselves by sea. Giraud quickly
gave up trying to help us, and it was only through Darlan's
help that we are now fighting the Boche in Tunisia instead of
somewhere in the vicinity of Bone or even west of that. It
appears to us that both Boisson and Darlan are committed
irrevocably to an Allied victory. . . .

Darlan had been smitten by the President's reference to a
'temporary expedient', and was beginning to feel his growing
isolation. At this time he wrote to General Clark:

Monsieur le Général,
Information from various sources tends to substantiate the
view that I am 'only a lemon which the Americans will drop
after they have squeezed it dry.'
In the line of conduct which I have adopted out of pure
French patriotic feeling, in spite of the serious disadvantages
which it entails for me, at the moment when it was extremely

easy for me to let events take their course without my intervention, my own personal position does not come into consideration.

I acted only because the American Government has solemnly undertaken to restore the integrity of French sovereignty as it existed in 1939, and because the armistice between the Axis and France was broken by the total occupation of Metropolitan France, against which the Marshal has solemnly protested.

I did not act through pride, ambition, or calculation, but because the position which I occupied in my country made it my duty to act.

When the integrity of France's sovereignty is an accomplished fact—and I hope that it will be in the least possible time—it is my firm intention to return to private life and to end my days, in the course of which I have ardently served my country, in retirement.

*   *   *

The Admiral held on only because he felt that for the moment he was indispensable to the Allied Command in North Africa and held the key of power. On November 22 the so-called Clark–Darlan Agreements were signed, setting up provisional machinery for administering the region. Two days later Governor-General Boisson, under persuasion from Darlan's emissaries, brought over French West Africa, with the great base of Dakar, to the Allies.

But passion ran high in England about the Darlan deal. It affected poignantly some of my friends who had been most affronted by Munich, with whose impulses I had moved at crucial moments before the war. 'Is this then what we are fighting for?' they asked. Many of those with whom I was in closest mental and moral harmony were in extreme distress. All these emotions were fanned by the de Gaulle Committee and organisation in our midst. The Press gave full expression to this mood. Certainly there was a real and vivid case to be made and to be met. Not only Parliament but the nation found it hard to swallow. 'De Gaulle banned; Darlan uplifted.' At the same time the facts could not be stated nor the arguments deployed in public. While in my own mind, rightly or wrongly, I never had the slightest doubt that it was my duty to support General Eisenhower and to save the lives of the soldiers committed to the enterprise, I was acutely sensitive to the opposite argument, and understood, if only to override, the discarded alternative conviction.

* * *

On December 9 I voiced my disquiet to the President:

Former Naval Person to President Roosevelt   9 Dec 42

I have been disturbed by reports received during the last few days from North Africa about conditions in French Morocco and Algeria. These reports, which come from independent and reliable sources, all paint the same picture of the results which follow from our inability in existing circumstances to exercise a proper control over the local French authorities in internal administrative matters. You are, I am sure, fully aware of this state of affairs, but I think it my duty to let you know the position as it appears in the light of our own reports.

2. These reports show that the S.O.L. [Service d'Ordre Légionnaire, a Vichy organisation of ex-Servicemen] and kindred Fascist organisations continue their activities and victimise our former French sympathisers, some of whom have not yet been released from prison. The first reaction of these organisations to the Allied landing was, rightly, one of fear, but it seems that they have now taken courage to regroup themselves and continue their activities. Well-known German sympathisers who had been ousted have been reinstated. Not only have our enemies been thus encouraged, but our friends have been correspondingly confused and cast down. There have been cases of French soldiers being punished for desertion because they tried to support the Allied forces during their landing. . . .

The next day, December 10, a month after the landing, the mounting pressures in the circles of which I was conscious led me to seek refuge in Secret Session of the House of Commons. The speech which I then made was conceived with the sole purpose of changing the prevailing opinion, and I chose with the greatest care the points to make. I began with some severe understatements.

The question which we must ask ourselves is not whether we like or do not like what is going on, but what are we going to do about it. In war it is not always possible to have everything go exactly as one likes. In working with allies it sometimes happens that they develop opinions of their own. Since 1776 we have not been in the position of being able to decide the policy of the United States. This is an American expedition in which they will ultimately have perhaps two or three times as large ground forces as we have, and three times the Air Force.

This was true at the time, but, as we shall see, was soon to be contradicted by events.

On sea the proportion is overwhelmingly in our favour, and we have of course given a vast amount of organisation and assistance in every way. Nevertheless the United States regards this as an American expedition under the ultimate command of the President of the United States, and they regard North-West Africa as a war sphere which is in their keeping, just as we regard the Eastern Mediterranean as a theatre for which we are responsible. We have accepted this position from the outset and are serving under their command. That does not mean we have not got a great power of representation, and I am of course in the closest touch with the President. It does however mean that neither militarily nor politically we are directly controlling the course of events. It is because it would be highly detrimental to have a debate upon American policy or Anglo-American relations in public that His Majesty's Government have invited the House to come into Secret Session. In Secret Session alone can the matter be discussed without the risk of giving offence to our great Ally, and also of complicating the relationships of Frenchmen, who, whatever their past, are now firing upon the Germans.

I hold no brief for Admiral Darlan. Like myself, he is the object of the animosities of Herr Hitler and of Monsieur Laval. Otherwise I have nothing in common with him. But it is necessary for the House to realise that the Government and to a large extent the people of the United States do not feel the same way about Darlan as we do. He has not betrayed them. He has not broken any treaty with them. He has not vilified them. He has not maltreated any of their citizens. They do not think much of him, but they do not hate him and despise him as we do over here. Many of them think more of the lives of their own soldiers than they do about the past records of French political figures. Moreover, the Americans have cultivated up to the last moment relations with Vichy which were of a fairly intimate character and which in my opinion have conduced to our general advantage. At any rate, the position of the Americans at Vichy gave us a window on that courtyard which otherwise would not have existed. . . .

Admiral Leahy has been Ambassador to Vichy until quite recently. He lived on terms of close intimacy with Marshal Pétain. He has at all times used his influence to prevent Vichy France becoming the ally of Germany or declaring war upon us when we have had to fire on Vichy troops at Oran or Dakar, in Syria or in Madagascar. On all these occasions I have believed, and have recorded my opinion beforehand, that France would not declare war; but a factor in forming that opinion was the immense American influence upon all Frenchmen, which influence of course increased enormously after the United States entered the war. Admiral Leahy is a close friend of President Roosevelt and was recently appointed his personal Chief of the Staff. The attitude of the United States executive and State Department towards Vichy and all its works must be viewed against this background. . . .

I now turn to examine a peculiar form of French mentality, or rather of the mentality of a large proportion of Frenchmen in the terrible defeat and ruin which has overtaken their country. I am not at all defending, still less eulogising, this French mentality. But it would be very foolish not to try to understand what is passing in other people's minds, and what are the secret springs of action to which they respond. The Almighty in His infinite wisdom did not see fit to create Frenchmen in the image of Englishmen. In a State like France, which has experienced so many convulsions—Monarchy, Convention, Directory, Consulate, Empire, Monarchy, Empire, and finally Republic—there has grown up a principle founded on the *droit administratif* which undoubtedly governs the action of many French officers and officials in times of revolution and change. It is a highly legalistic habit of mind, and it arises from a subconscious sense of national self-preservation against the dangers of sheer anarchy. For instance, any officer who obeys the command of his lawful superior or of one whom he believes to be his lawful superior is absolutely immune from subsequent punishment. Much therefore turns in the minds of French officers upon whether there is a direct, unbroken chain of lawful command, and this is held by many Frenchmen to be more important than moral, national, or international considerations. From this point of view many Frenchmen who admire General de Gaulle and envy him in his rôle nevertheless regard him as a man who has rebelled against the authority of the French State, which in their prostration they conceive to be vested in the person of the antique defeatist who to them is the illustrious and venerable Marshal Pétain, the hero of Verdun and the sole hope of France.

Now all this may seem very absurd to our minds. But there

is one point about it which is important to us. It is in accordance with orders and authority transmitted or declared to be transmitted by Marshal Pétain that the French troops in North-West Africa have pointed and fired their rifles against the Germans and Italians instead of continuing to point and fire their rifles against the British and Americans. I am sorry to have to mention a point like that, but it makes a lot of difference to a soldier whether a man fires his gun at him or at his enemy ; and even the soldier's wife or father might have a feeling about it too. . . .

All this is done in the sacred name of the Marshal, and when the Marshal bleats over the telephone orders to the contrary and deprives Darlan of his nationality the Admiral rests comfortably upon the fact or fiction—it does not much matter which—that the Marshal is acting under the duress of the invading Hun, and that he, Darlan, is still carrying out his true wishes. In fact, if Admiral Darlan had to shoot Marshal Pétain he would no doubt do it in Marshal Pétain's name. . . .

I must however say that personally I consider that in the circumstances prevailing General Eisenhower was right ; and even if he was not quite right I should have been very reluctant to hamper or impede his action when so many lives and such vitally important issues hung in the balance. I do not want to shelter myself in any way behind the Americans or anyone else.

I ended with some bitterness, the outcome of the stresses which I felt.

I must say I think he is a poor creature with a jaundiced outlook and disorganised loyalties who in all this tremendous African episode, West and East alike, can find no point to excite his interest except the arrangements made between General Eisenhower and Admiral Darlan. The struggle for the Tunisian tip is now rising to its climax and the main battle impends. Another trial of strength is very near on the frontiers of Cyrenaica. Both these battles will be fought almost entirely by soldiers from this Island. The First and Eighth British Armies will be engaged to the full. I cannot take my thoughts away from them and their fortunes, and I expect that will be the feeling of the House of Commons. . . .

I ask them to treat with proper reprobation that small, busy, and venomous band who harbour and endeavour to propagate unworthy and unfounded suspicions, and so to come forward unitedly with us in all the difficulties through which we are steadfastly and successfully making our way.

208

I do not remember any speech out of hundreds which I made where I felt opinion change so palpably and decisively. This was no case for applause, but only for results. The Commons were convinced, and the fact that all further Parliamentary opposition stopped after the Secret Session quenched the hostile Press and reassured the country. There was also the growing exhilaration of victory after so many hard months of disappointment or defeat.

General Eisenhower in his post-war book contributes from his own angle a practical and soldierly confirmation:

> It is possible to understand why de Gaulle was disliked within the ranks of the French Army. At the time of France's surrender in 1940 the officers who remained in the Army had accepted the position and orders of their Government and had given up the fight. From their view-point, if the course chosen by de Gaulle was correct, then every French officer who obeyed the orders of his Government was a poltroon. If de Gaulle was a loyal Frenchman they had to regard themselves as cowards. Naturally the officers did not choose to think of themselves in this light ; rather they considered themselves as loyal Frenchmen carrying out the orders of constituted civilian authority, and it followed that they officially and personally regarded de Gaulle as a deserter.*

*   *   *

Political affairs in North Africa deteriorated rapidly during the last days of 1942. Not only was there a desperate struggle against Giraud for power and recognition among the recent adherents to the Allied cause, Darlan, Noguès, Boisson, and others, but also active discontent among those men who had helped the Allied landings on November 8, and among the small but active group which was ardent for de Gaulle. In addition there was growing support for a movement to place the Comte de Paris, at this time living quietly near Tangier, at the head of a provisional war-time administration in North Africa in opposition to Vichy. The patchwork arrangement whereby Darlan was at the head of civil affairs and Giraud was in command of the French armed forces in North Africa came under increasing strain.

On December 19 the first emissary of de Gaulle, General Françoise d'Astier de la Vigerie, arrived unofficially in Algiers to explore the ground on behalf of his leader. He was the

* Eisenhower, *Crusade in Europe*, p. 84.

brother of Henri, who had played a leading part in the rising in the town of Algiers on November 8, and who was now implicated in the Royalist conspiracy which aimed at bringing the Comte de Paris to power. The de Gaullist visit was exploratory. The military co-operation of the Free French forces was formally offered both to Giraud and Eisenhower in discussions on December 20, but no decisions were taken. The practical result of General d'Astier de la Vigerie's visit was to stimulate the de Gaullist opposition to Darlan. Simultaneously with these talks the Monarchist elements in Algiers decided to press Darlan to abdicate and hand over to an all-party administration. It is not even now clear how much support they had.

On the afternoon of December 24 Darlan drove down from his villa to his offices in the Palais d'Été. At the door of his bureau he was shot down by a young man of twenty named Bonnier de la Chapelle. The Admiral died within the hour on the operating table of a near-by hospital. The youthful assassin had, according to some stories, been connected with Henri d'Astier, and under much persuasion had worked himself into an exalted state of mind as the saviour of France from wicked leadership. Apart from a small circle of personal friends grouped round d'Astier, there was no open support in Algiers for his act. He was tried by court-martial under Giraud's orders, and, much to his surprise, was executed by a firing squad shortly after dawn on December 26.

On receiving the news of Darlan's assassination General Eisenhower hurried back from the Tunisian front. In the circumstances the only thing to do was to nominate Giraud to fill the vacant place. We could not run the risk of civil disorder behind the front, and indirect though decisive pressure was exerted by the American authorities to achieve the appointment of Giraud to supreme though transitory political power in North Africa.

Darlan's murder, however criminal, relieved the Allies of their embarrassment at working with him, and at the same time left them with all the advantages he had been able to bestow during the vital hours of the Allied landings. His authority had passed smoothly to the organisation created in agreement with the American authorities during the months of November and December. Giraud filled the gap. The path was cleared for the French forces now rallied in North and North-West Africa to unite with the Free French Movement round de Gaulle, and comprising all Frenchmen throughout the world outside German control. On learning of Darlan's fate de Gaulle made the first approach. He was about to leave for Washington for a long-delayed first meeting with the President when the news reached London. He at once drafted and dispatched through Allied channels a message to Giraud. It seemed to me wise to put off the Washington visit in the hopes of uniting French Resistance. I explained the position in a telegram to the President, and sent him a copy of de Gaulle's message to Giraud.

Former Naval Person to President Roosevelt 27 Dec 42
As I told Harry, I had already asked United States Head-quarters, London, to delay for forty-eight hours the plane which was to carry de Gaulle, to see how the 'Torch' situation develops. It seems to me that we ought to try above anything to bring them all together and have some French nucleus, solid and united, to work with. I am seeing de Gaulle to-day, and will cable your further.

2. I am sure that North African settlement cannot be held up for 'Symbol' [our conference at Casablanca]. We have received news that 'King-pin' has been unanimously elected High Commissioner and Commander-in-Chief by the French group of notabilities. I have already informed Eisenhower that so far as we are concerned we entirely agree with this solution.

3. The War Cabinet attach much importance to Mac-millan's appointment and arrival [at Algiers]. We feel quite unrepresented there, yet our fortunes are deeply involved, and we are trying to make a solid contribution to your enterprise. Murphy's appointment has already been announced, and I hope you will agree to my publishing Macmillan's. He will be, I am sure, a help. He is animated by the friendliest feelings towards the United States, and his mother hails from Kentucky.

Here followed de Gaulle's message to Giraud, sent through the American Embassy in London:

27 Dec 42
The assassination at Algiers is an indication and a warning: an indication of the exasperation into which the tragedy of France has thrown the mind and soul of Frenchmen; a warning of the consequences of every kind which necessarily result from the absence of a national authority in the midst of the greatest national crisis of our history. It is more than ever necessary that this national authority should be established. I propose, my General, that you should meet me as soon as possible on French soil, either in Algeria or in

Chad, in order to study the means of grouping under a provisional central authority all French forces inside and outside the country and all the French territories which are in a position to struggle for the liberation and the salvation of France.

*   *   *

Few men have paid more heavily for errors of judgment and failure of character than Admiral Darlan. He was a professional figure, and a strong personality. His life's work had been to re-create the French Navy, and he had raised it to a position it had never held since the days of the French kings. He commanded the allegiance not only of the Naval Officer Corps, but of the whole Naval Service. In accordance with his repeated promises, he ought in 1940 to have ordered the fleets to Britain, to the United States, the African ports, anywhere out of German power. He was under no treaty or obligation to do so except assurances which he had voluntarily given. But this was his resolve until on that deadly June 20, 1940, he accepted from Marshal Pétain's hands the office of Minister of Marine. Then, perhaps influenced by motives of a departmental character, he gave his allegiance to Marshal Pétain's Government. Ceasing to be a sailor and becoming a politician, he exchanged a sphere in which he had profound knowledge for one where his chief guide was his anti-British prejudices, dating, as I have mentioned, from the Battle of Trafalgar, where his great-grandfather had fallen.

In this new situation he showed himself a man of force and decision who did not wholly comprehend the moral significance of much that he did. Ambition stimulated his errors. His vision as an Admiral had not gone beyond his Navy, nor as a Minister beyond immediate local or personal advantages. For a year and a half he had been a great power in shattered France. At the time when we descended upon North Africa he was the undoubted heir of the aged Marshal. Now suddenly a cataract of amazing events fell upon him. By a strange chance the illness of his son had drawn him to Algiers, where he fell into Anglo-American power.

We have recounted the stresses which he underwent. All French North and West Africa looked to him. The invasion of Vichy France by Hitler gave him the power, and it may be the right, to make a new decision. He brought to the Anglo-American Allies exactly what they needed, namely, a French voice which all French officers and officials in this vast theatre, now plunged in the war, would obey. He struck his final blow for us, and it is not for those who benefited enormously from his accession to our side to revile his memory. A stern, impartial judge may say that he should have refused all parley with the Allies he had injured, and defied them to do their worst with him. We may all be glad he took the opposite course. It cost him his life, but there was not much left in life for him. It seemed obvious at the time that he was wrong in not sailing the French Fleet to Allied or neutral ports in June 1940 ; but he was right in this second fearful decision. Probably his sharpest pang was his failure to bring over the Toulon fleet. Always he had declared it should never fall into German hands. In this undertaking before history he did not fail. Let him rest in peace, and let us all be thankful we have never had to face the trials under which he broke.

Problems of Victory

American military opinion, not only in the highest circles, was convinced that the decision for 'Torch' ruled out all prospect of a major crossing of the Channel into Occupied France in 1943. I had not yet brought myself to accept this view. I still hoped that French North-West Africa, including the Tunisian tip, might fall into our hands after a few months' fighting. In this case the main invasion of Occupied France from England would still be possible in July or August 1943. I was therefore most anxious that the strongest build-up of American power in Britain which our shipping would allow should proceed at the same time as 'Torch'. This idea of being able to use our left as well as our right hand, and the fact that the enemy must prepare himself against blows from either, seemed wholly in accordance with the highest economy of war. Events would decide whether we should thrust across the Channel or follow our luck in the Mediterranean, or do both. It seemed imperative, in the interests of the war as a whole and especially of aiding Russia, that the Anglo-American armies should enter Europe either from the west or from the east in the coming year.

There was however a danger that we might do neither. Even if our campaign in Algeria and Tunisia prospered swiftly, we should content ourselves with capturing Sardinia or Sicily or both, and put off crossing the Channel till 1944. This would mean a wasted year for the Western Allies, with results which might be fatal, not indeed to our survival, but to a decisive victory. We could not go on losing five or six hundred thousand tons of shipping a month indefinitely. A stalemate was Germany's last hope.

Before we knew what was going to happen at Alamein or to 'Torch', and while the teriffic struggle in the Caucasus seemed undecided, the British Chiefs of Staff were weighing all these issues. The Planners under them were also busy. Their reports were in my opinion unduly negative, and I commented on them to the Chiefs of Staff on November 9, while the landings in Africa were still proceeding:

It would be most regrettable to make no more use of the success of 'Torch' and Alamein in 1943 than the occupation of Sicily and Sardinia. We have already committed ourselves with the Americans to 'Round-up' in 1943, an operation on the greatest scale. The interposition of 'Torch' is no excuse for lying down during 1943, content with descents on Sicily and Sardinia and a few more operations like Dieppe (which can hardly be taken as a pattern).

The effort for the campaign of 1943 should clearly be a strong pinning down of the enemy in Northern France and the Low Countries by continuous preparations to invade, and a decisive attack on Italy, or, better still, Southern France; together with operations not involving serious shipping expense, and other forms of pressure to bring in Turkey and operate overland with the Russians into the Balkans.

If French North Africa is going to be made an excuse for locking up great forces on the defensive and calling it a 'commitment', it would be better not to have gone there at all. Is it really to be supposed that the Russians will be content with our lying down like this during the whole of 1943, while Hitler has a third crack at them? However alarming the prospect may seem, we must make an attempt to get on to the mainland of Europe and fight in the line against the enemy in 1943.

And further, on the 18th:

... Under the agreements made about 'Round-up' and 'Bolero' with General Marshall we were to have by April 1, 1943, twenty-seven American and twenty-one British divisions ready for the Continent, together with all the necessary landing-craft, etc. This task was solemnly undertaken and an immense amount of work has been done. ... We then went off to 'Torch', which is now in progress. But 'Torch' is only thirteen divisions, whereas we had been prepared to move forty-eight divisions against the enemy in 1943. We have therefore reduced our striking intent against the enemy by thirty-five divisions. Allowance should no doubt be made for the larger distances from here to 'Torch' compared with those across the Channel. But we have given Stalin to understand that the great attack on the Continent will come in 1943, and we are now working on a basis of thirty-five divisions short of what was purposed in the period April–July, or, in other words, little more than a quarter.

It is no use blinking at this or imagining that the discrepancy will not be perceived. I have no doubt myself that we and General Marshall over-estimated our capacity as measured by shipping, and also by the rate at which United States forces as well as special landing-craft, etc., could be ready. But there is a frightful gap between what the Chiefs of Staff contemplated as reasonable in the summer of 1942 for the campaign of 1943 and what they now say we can do in that campaign. I am not making criticisms, because I am in this myself to the full ; but I feel we have got to get much closer to grips with this whole business. I fear I shall have to go to the United States in the near future. No doubt we were planning too much for 1943 in the summer, but we are certainly planning too little now. I must repeat that 'Torch' is no substitute for 'Round-up'. It must also be remembered that we had proposed to continue the campaign in the Middle East while 'Round-up' was going forward, and now we have an easement there through the virtual destruction of Rommel. We have, in fact, pulled in our horns to an almost extraordinary extent, and I cannot imagine what the Russians will say or do when they realise it. My own position is that I am still aiming at a 'Round-up' retarded till August. I cannot give this up without a massive presentation of facts and figures which prove physical impossibility. These figures will however if they prove the case stultify our ambitions and judgment of this summer, and that of the Americans. . . .

I never meant the Anglo-American Army to be stuck in North Africa. It is a springboard and not a sofa. . . .

It may be that we should close down the Mediterranean activities by the end of June with a view to 'Round-up' in August. The issues will have to be settled on the highest levels after we have reached agreement among ourselves.

We were thus reaching from both sides of the Atlantic a sort of combined deadlock. The British Staffs favoured the Mediterranean and an attack upon Sardinia and Sicily, with Italy as the goal. The United States experts had given up all hopes of crossing the Channel in 1943, but were most anxious not to be entangled in the Mediterranean in such a way as to prevent their great design in 1944, 'It would seem,' as I wrote, 'that the sum of all American fears is to be multiplied by the sum of all British fears, faithfully contributed by each Service.'

* * *

The American Staffs, swayed by that undue liking for logical, clear-cut decisions, however desirable they may be, which I have ventured to note in earlier chapters, had in fact slowed down with a sweeping gesture the build-up of 'Bolero' in Great Britain after the 'Torch' decision had been taken. Late in November a written notification reached us from the administrative side of the United States machine which caused general astonishment. The following message which I sent to the President should incidentally, but I trust finally, dispose of the many American legends that I was inveterately hostile to the plan of a large-scale Channel crossing in 1943, and still more, of the post-war Soviet assertions that I used the operation 'Torch' with the deliberate intention of preventing a Second Front in 1943.

Former Naval Person to President Roosevelt   24 Nov 42
    We have had a letter from General Hartle stating that under directive from the United States War Department 'any construction in excess of the requirements for a force of 427,000 must be accomplished entirely by your own labour and with your own materials', and that 'Lend-Lease materials cannot be furnished in these instances'. This has caused us very great concern, not so much from the standpoint of Lend-Lease, but on grounds of grand strategy. We have been preparing under 'Bolero' for 1,100,000 men, and this is the first intimation we have had that this target is to be abandoned. We had no knowledge that you had decided to abandon for ever 'Round-up', and all our preparations were proceeding on a broad front under 'Bolero'.
    2. It seems to me that it would be a most grievous decision to abandon 'Round-up'. 'Torch' is no substitute for 'Round-up', and only engages thirteen divisions as against the forty-eight contemplated for 'Round-up'. All my talks with Stalin, in Averell's presence, were on the basis of a postponed 'Round-up', but never was it suggested that we should attempt no Second Front in Europe in 1943, or even 1944.
    3. Surely, Mr. President, this matter requires most profound consideration. I was deeply impressed with all General

Marshall's arguments that only by 'Round-up' could the main forces be thrown into France and the Low Countries, and only in this area could the main strength of the British Metropolitan and United States Overseas Air Forces be brought into action. One of the arguments we used against 'Sledgehammer' was that it would eat up in 1942 the seed-corn needed for the much larger 'Round-up' in 1943. No doubt we have all been sanguine of our shipping resources, but that is a matter which time can correct. Only by the building up of a 'Round-up' force here as rapidly and regularly as other urgent demands on shipping allow can we have the means of coming to grips with the main strength of the enemy and liberating the European nations. It may well be that, try as we will, our strength will not reach the necessary levels in 1943. But if so it becomes all the more important to make sure we do not miss 1944.

4. Even in 1943 a chance may come. Should Stalin's offensive reach Rostov-on-the-Don, which is his aim, a first-class disaster may overtake the German southern armies. Our Mediterranean operations following on 'Torch' may drive Italy out of the war. Widespread demoralisation may set in among the Germans, and we must be ready to profit by any opportunity which offers.

5. I do beg of you, Mr. President, to let me know what has happened. At present we are completely puzzled by this information and the manner in which it has reached us. It seems to me absolutely necessary either that General Marshall and Admiral King with Harry should come over here or that I should come with my people to you.

The President lost no time in correcting this misunderstanding, which had arisen at a lower level.

President to Prime Minister   26 Nov 42

We of course have no intention of abandoning 'Round-up'. No one can possibly know now whether or not we may have the opportunity to strike across the Channel in 1943, and if the opportunity comes we must obviously grasp it. However, the determination as to the size of the force which we should have in 'Bolero' in 1943 is a matter which should require our joint strategic consideration. It is my present thought that we should build up as rapidly as present active operations permit a growing striking force in the United Kingdom to be used quickly in the event of a German collapse, or a very large force later if Germany remains intact and assumes a defensive position.

The conclusions of the Combined Chiefs of Staff at the

meeting last summer in London indicated that the mounting of 'Torch' necessarily postponed the assembling of the required forces in the United Kingdom. In view of our requirements for the initiation and maintenance of 'Torch' our studies indicated that we could not send forces and material to the United Kingdom at this time in excess of that stated by General Hartle. Until we have provided adequately against the possible reactions from Spanish Morocco and are clear as to the situation in Tunisia, North Africa must naturally take precedence. We are far more heavily engaged in the South-West Pacific than I anticipated a few months ago. Nevertheless we shall continue with 'Bolero' as rapidly as our shipping and other resources permit. . . .

* * *

I now tried to survey the Mediterranean scene.

NOTE BY THE MINISTER OF DEFENCE
November 25, 1942

In settling what to do in a vast war situation like this it may sometimes be found better to take a particular major operation to which one is committed and follow that through vigorously to the end, making other things subordinate to it, rather than to assemble all the data from the whole world scene in a baffling array. After the needs of the major operation have been satisfied so far as possible, other aspects of the war will fall into their proper places. Moreover, it is by the continued stressing of the major operation that our will may be imposed upon the enemy and the initiative regained.

2. The paramount task before us is, first, to conquer the African shores of the Mediterranean and set up there the naval and air installations which are necessary to open an effective passage through it for military traffic ; and, secondly, using the bases on the African shore, to strike at the underbelly of the Axis in effective strength and in the shortest time.

3. There are therefore two phases—consolidation and exploitation. Dealing with consolidation first, we may hope that General Alexander will become master of the whole of Cyrenaica during the present month, and that he will be pressing the enemy in the Agheila position, or even at Sirte. We may also assume that in the same period or not long after the American and British forces will become masters of the whole of French North Africa, including Tunis, provided they press forward with their present energy and violence.

4. It will be necessary to set up air stations at suitable intervals along all the African shore in our power, but particularly and urgently in the Tunisian tip. The largest

installations for American bombers ought to be set up here, so that long-range bombers sent by the United States to North Africa, together with American bombers already based on the Middle East, can operate against Italian targets. The United States form of daylight attack would have its best chance in the better weather of the Mediterranean.

5. The bombing weight of the British night attack should be brought to bear on Italy whenever the weather is more favourable than for bombing Germany.

6. It will no doubt be necessary also to act against the Catania and Cagliari airfields, so as to keep down the attack on Tunis in the period of consolidation.

7. As soon as we are sure of ourselves, and consolidated, in French North Africa, including especially Tunis, two successive operations present themselves. The first is the advance to Tripoli. It is possible that General Alexander may be able to take this important prize from the east, and I have asked him how he feels about it, and how long he thinks he would require ; but we must also be prepared for a rapid advance from the west. Would General Anderson's two British divisions be sufficient, assuming that Tunis itself can be held by American and French Allied troops? I should like the best possible estimate of the time that this will take.

8. The second immediate objective is obviously either Sardinia or Sicily. The possession of one of these islands and of the airfields in the south would create an air triangle, in which we should fight for and secure air mastery. Moreover, from either of them continuous intensified short-range attacks on Naples, Rome and the Italian Fleet bases would raise the war against Italy to an intense degree. Let an immediate report be prepared in order that a decision may be taken. Whichever it may be, the fight for air control in the Central Mediterranean should be undertaken as a great air battle with extreme priority, the fullest advantage being taken of the Axis shortage of aircraft. ... Note that the preparations to attack Sardinia may take as long as those to attack Sicily, and that Sicily is by far the greater prize.

The rest of this paper deals with the need for drawing Turkey into the war. These arguments will find their own place later in the story.

*   *   *

I now turned back to the supreme project of crossing the Channel in 1943.

NOTE BY THE MINISTER OF DEFENCE

December 3, 1942

In April last General Marshall unfolded to us the plan subsequently called 'Round-up', of which 'Bolero' is the administrative counterpart. A massive argument was that 'Round-up' is the only way in which large American and British forces can be brought into direct contact with the enemy, and the British Metropolitan and United States Overseas Air Forces exercise their maximum power. American military opinion was solidly ranged behind this enterprise, and since then preparations under 'Bolero' have gone forward steadily, subject only to 'Torch'. As an addition to 'Round-up', 'Sledgehammer' was proposed in July. It was agreed by the combined Staffs that 'Torch' should be executed instead of 'Sledgehammer'. Meanwhile 'Bolero' was to continue, with preparations for a retarded or opportunist 'Round-up'.

2. However, the opinion was held by the American Staffs that the abandonment of 'Sledgehammer' and the adoption of 'Torch' in fact rendered 'Round-up' impossible in 1943, even though retarded. One reason for this was the probability of Russia being so seriously weakened that Hitler could bring back very large armies from the East, thus making the forces available for 'Round-up' in 1943 altogether insufficient. They also founded their opinion on the fact that the assembly of forces for 'Round-up' would be so delayed by the diversion of shipping to 'Torch' that we should not be strong enough during the 1943 season to effect an entry into the Continent, even against comparatively weak forces. The American military staff thus foresaw their troops being held idle in the United Kingdom, a situation which the President and General Marshall were anxious to avoid.

3. Besides the above, the shipping stringency has become pronounced. The progress of constructing landing-craft and training crews has been slowed down, if not largely arrested. 'Torch' is in full progress, with its serious demands on shipping, and we have in prospect the variants of 'Brimstone' [Sardinia], which, though secondary, are substantial operations.

4. On the other hand, the Russians have been led to believe that we were going to open a Second Front in 1943. 'Round-up' was explained to them by me in the presence of the United States representative, Mr. Harriman. These conversations at Moscow were duly reported to the President. I feel that Premier Stalin would have grave reasons to complain if our land offensive against Germany and Italy in 1943

were reduced to the scale of about thirteen divisions instead of nearly fifty, which have been mentioned to him. Moreover, apart from any Russian obligations, I feel that our offensive war plans for 1943 are on altogether too small a scale compared with the resources and power of Britain and the United States.

5. Recent most important events have altered, and are altering, the data on which thought on both sides of the Atlantic has hitherto proceeded. The Russians have not been defeated or weakened in the campaign of 1942. On the contrary, it is Hitler who has been defeated and the German Army which has been very grievously reduced. General von Thoma* was heard to say that the 180 German divisions on the Russian front are in many cases little more than brigades. The demoralisation among the Hungarian, Roumanian, and Italian troops on the Eastern front is marked. The Finns are no longer fighting, except for a few mountain troops.

6. The great battles now in progress at Stalingrad and in the central sector of the Russian front have not yet been decided. It may well be that the Russian offensives will produce far-reaching effects upon the German power. If the Sixth Army, which is now encircled before Stalingrad, is destroyed the Russian southern offensive may reach its objective at Rostov-on-the-Don. In this case the position of the three remaining German armies in the Northern Caucasus, already closely engaged by the Russians, may be seriously and perhaps even mortally compromised, again with measureless results. The Russian offensive in the central sector and the counter-attacks they are making at many points along the front may lead to a withdrawal of the German line to winter positions. The winter will impose formidable privations and ordeals upon the weakened German armies, in spite of the better railway system they now have. Before the end of 1942 it may be possible for us to draw with certainty at least the conclusion *that no important transfers of German troops can be made in 1943 from the Eastern to the Western theatre*. This would be a new fact of the first magnitude. . . .

9. The events which have taken place in France have compelled the Germans, in order to defend the southern coasts of France, to withdraw eleven divisions from the forty which stood opposite Britain in France and the Low Countries. Their task of maintaining internal security in France has been rendered more onerous. They will probably be compelled to find another four or even six divisions to protect and

* Taken prisoner at Alamein.

hold down Italy against the menace of 'Torch', and to garrison Sicily and perhaps Sardinia. The Yugoslav resistance continues, and no relief can be expected by the Axis in any part of the Balkan peninsula. On the contrary, they have the need to reinforce Greece, Roumania, and Bulgaria, on account of the general situation, as well as of the possible entry of Turkey against them, for which we are to work. None of these facts were present when 'Round-up' and 'Sledgehammer' were considered at the London conferences of July.

10. I am therefore of opinion that the whole position must be completely re-surveyed, with the object of finding means for engaging United States and British armies directly upon the Continent. For this purpose the assumptions set forth in the preceding paragraphs should be accepted as data. Besides these, it should be assumed that the North African shore is adequately equipped with air forces, and that the Mediterranean is open for military traffic by the end of March, thus securing a substantial relief in shipping; that any Sardinian operations are concluded by the beginning of June; that all landing-craft, etc., needed for 'Round-up' should be back in Great Britain by the end of June; that July should be devoted to preparation and rehearsal; and that August, or, if the weather is adverse, September, should be taken as the striking target.

I was very glad to find that my argument was welcomed by General Marshall, whom I had kept fully informed through Dill.

Field Marshal Dill to Prime Minister   14 Dec 42
I have had a private talk with Marshall. He is very encouraged to know that your thoughts and his are running on the same lines, but he has made it clear to me that until he sees the full development of operations in North Africa and has the views of Eisenhower his opinion as to our future strategy cannot be firm.

2. He is however getting more and more convinced that we should be in a position to undertake a modified 'Round-up' before the summer [of 1943] if, as soon as North Africa is cleared of Axis forces, we start pouring American forces into England instead of sending them to Africa for the exploitation of 'Torch'. Such an operation would, he feels, be much more effective than either 'Brimstone' or 'Husky', less costly in shipping, more satisfying to the Russians, engage many more German air forces, and be the most effective answer to any German attack through Spain.

3. Marshall would of course have liked to discuss these

questions with you and the Chiefs of Staff, but as American and British ideas now appear to be so close there is, he considers, less need for such personal discussions.

*　　*　　*

I have thus laid before the reader the position as I saw it at the close of 1942. It will no doubt be said that the course of events proved that I took too sanguine a view about the prospects in North-West Africa and the United States Staff were right in believing that the decision for 'Torch' which we had taken in July closed the possibility of 'Round-up' in 1943. Certainly that was what happened. No one could foresee at this time that Hitler would make his immense effort to reinforce the Tunisian tip by sending thither by air and sea, in spite of heavy losses, nearly a hundred thousand of his best troops. This was on his part a grave strategic error. It certainly delayed for several months our victory in Africa. If he had held the forces which were captured or destroyed there in May he might either have reinforced his retreating front against Russia, or have gathered the strength in Normandy which would have deterred us, even if we were so resolved, from trying 'Round-up' in 1943. Hardly anyone now disputes the wisdom of the decision to wait till 1944. My conscience is clear that I did not deceive or mislead Stalin. I tried my best. On the other hand, provided we invaded the mainland of Europe from the Mediterranean in the coming campaign and that the Anglo-American armies were in full contact with the enemy, I was not ill-content with the decision which Fate and facts were to impose.

CHAPTER 14

Our Need to Meet

Setback in Tunis – General Eisenhower's Christmas Eve Decision – Rapid Advance of the Eighth Army – Need for a Conference on the Highest Level – My Telegram to the President of November 26 – His Reply of December 3 – I Deprecate Purely Military Discussions, Especially in Moscow – Stalin Cannot Leave Russia – Further Correspondence with the President – An Anglo-American Meeting Imperative – The President's Letter of December 14 – He Proposes Casablanca for Our Meeting – All Preparations are Made – 'Admiral Q' – British and American Divergencies on Strategy – We Do Not Go to Casablanca Empty-handed – Alexander Reports Montgomery's Further Advance – Hope of Taking Tripoli.

There now came a definite check and setback in North Africa. Although we had the initiative and the advantage of surprise our build-up was inevitably slow. Shipping imposed its harsh limits. Unloading was hampered by air attacks on Algiers and Bone. Road transport was lacking. The single-line coastal railway, five hundred miles long, was in poor condition, with hundreds of bridges and culverts, any one of which might be sabotaged. With the arrival of German troops in large numbers by air in Tunis a high-class, stubborn, and violent resistance began. The French forces who had now joined our cause were over a hundred thousand strong. The majority were native troops of good quality, but as yet ill-equipped and unorganised. General Eisenhower thrust forward to Anderson's command every American unit on which he could lay his hands. We put in all we could. A British infantry brigade, with part of the United States 1st Armoured Division, attacked and captured Medjez, and on November 28 nearly reached Djedeida, only twelve miles from Tunis. This was the climax of the winter fighting.

Now came the rainy season. It poured. Our improvised airfields became quagmires. The German Air Force, though not yet strong in numbers, worked from good all-weather airfields. On December 1 they counter-attacked, frustrating the advance we had planned, and in a few days the British brigade was forced back to Medjez. Supplies could only reach the forward troops by sea on a small scale. Indeed, it was barely possible to nourish them, far less to make any accumulations. It was not till the night of December 22 that a renewed attack could be launched. This met with some initial success, but at dawn began three days of torrential rain. Our airfields became useless and vehicles could only move along the indifferent roads.

At a conference on Christmas Eve General Eisenhower decided to give up the plan for the immediate capture of Tunis and, until campaigning could begin again, to guard his forward airfields on the general line already gained. Although the Germans suffered important losses at sea, their strength in Tunisia continually grew. By the end of December their numbers approached fifty thousand.

*　　*　　*

While these operations were in progress the Eighth Army had covered immense distances. Rommel succeeded in withdrawing his shattered forces from Alamein to Agheila, watched by a patrol of the Long Range Desert Group, which had long been hidden near the latter place, counting and reporting all movements along the road. His rearguards were heavily pressed, but an attempt to head him off south of Benghazi failed. He paused at Agheila, while Montgomery, after his long advance, contended with the same difficulties of transport and supply on which his predecessors had foundered. On December 13 Rommel was dislodged and nearly cut off by a wide turning movement of the 2nd New Zealand Division. He suffered severely, and the Desert Air Force took heavy toll of his transport on the coast road. Montgomery could follow at first only with light forces. The Eighth Army had advanced twelve hundred miles since Alamein. After occupying Sirte and its landing-grounds on Christmas Day our troops closed with Rommel's next main position near Buerat at the end of the year.

*　　*　　*

The President's telegram to me of November 26, partly quoted in the preceding chapter, had also contained his proposal for a triple conference between representatives of the three Staffs.

I believe that as soon as we have knocked the Germans out of Tunisia we should proceed with a military strategical conference between Great Britain, Russia, and the United States. I am hoping that our military position in Africa will be such that a conference might be held in a month or six weeks. Our own Combined Chiefs of Staff will, I believe, have a recommendation for us within a few days as to what the next steps should be, but I feel very strongly that we have got to sit down at the table with the Russians. My notion would be a conference in Cairo or Moscow; that each of us would be represented by a small group, meeting very secretly. The conclusions of the conference would of course be approved by the three of us. I would probably send Marshall to head up our group but I presume that all services should be represented. I think it would be wise to keep the numbers down to three from each of us.

Will you let me know as soon as you can what you think of my proposal.

I replied the same day, saying that I did not believe a conference of experts would meet our need.

Former Naval Person to President Roosevelt   26 Nov 42

I entirely agree in principle that there should be a conference with the Russians, but I doubt very much whether a conference between officers on general war policy, apart from some special point, would be of much value. Certainly if a Russian delegation went to Cairo, which I deem unlikely, they would be so tied up that they would have to refer every point of substance back to Stalin at Moscow. If the conference were held in Moscow there would be less delay, but I trust that before British and United States missions went to Moscow they would have a joint and agreed view, to serve at least as a basis for discussion. I hope also that if General Marshall were sent by you he would not by-pass this country.

I think I can tell you in advance what the Soviet view will be. They will say to us both, 'How many German divisions will you be engaging in the summer of 1943? How many have you engaged in 1942?' They will certainly demand a strong Second Front in 1943 by the heavy invasion of the Continent either from the west or from the south or from both. This sort of argument, of which I had plenty in Moscow, requires to be met either by principals or by naval and shipping authorities, who would certainly have to be present. It would be very difficult to spare all our chiefs for so long at this time.

Stalin talked to me in Moscow in the sense of being willing to come to meet you and me somewhere this winter, and he mentioned Iceland. I pointed out that England was no farther and more convenient. He neither accepted nor rejected the idea. At the same time, apart from the climate, there is a lot to be said for a new triple Atlantic Conference in Iceland. Our ships might lie together in Halfjord, and we would place a suitable ship at Stalin's disposal wearing the Soviet flag *pro tem*. He talked with some zest of his desire to fly and of his confidence in the Russian machines. Only at a meeting between principals will real results be achieved. What about proposing it for January? By that time Africa should be cleared and the great battle in South Russia decided.

I may add that if ever I can persuade you to come to Iceland I shall never be satisfied unless you look in on this small place before returning.

On December 3 the President cabled me again.

President Roosevelt to Former Naval Person   3 Dec 42

I have been giving a good deal of thought to our proposed joint conference with the Russians, and I agree with you that the only satisfactory way of coming to the vital strategic conclusions the military situation requires is for you and me to meet personally with Stalin. My thought would be that each of us could be accompanied by a very small staff made up of our top Army, Air, and Naval Chiefs of Staff. I could bring Harry and Averell, but no State Department representative, although I believe we should arrive at tentative procedures to be adopted in event of a German collapse. I should like to see the conference held about January 15, or soon thereafter. Tunis and Bizerta should have been cleared up and Rommel's army liquidated before the conference. As to the place, Iceland or Alaska are impossible for me at this time of year, and I believe equally so for Stalin. I should prefer a secure place south of Algiers or in or near Khartoum. I don't like mosquitoes. I think the conference should be very secret and that the Press should be excluded. I would question the advisability of Marshall and the others going to England prior to the conference, because I do not want to give Stalin the impression that we are settling everything between ourselves before we meet him.

I think that you and I understand each other so well that prior conferences between us are unnecessary and when the time comes we can work things out from day to day. Our military people will also be in close co-operation at all times from now on.

I think that this conference may well result in knocking out Germany sooner than we anticipated. As you know, Stalin has already agreed to a purely military conference to be held in Moscow, and I have today sent him a message urging him to meet you and me. I believe he will accept.

I prefer a comfortable oasis to the raft at Tilsit.

I replied at once:

Former Naval Person to President Roosevelt   3 Dec 42

I am delighted at your proposal, which is the only way of making a good plan for 1943. At present we have no plan for 1943 which is on the scale or up to the level of events. It is grand of you to come, and I will meet you anywhere. I am telegraphing Stalin to reinforce your invitation.

2. Meanwhile I deprecate sending our military representatives to Moscow. It will only lead to a deadlock and queer the pitch. We still think that Marshall, King, and Arnold should come here in advance so that at least we have some definite plans as a basis for discussion when we all meet in January 'somewhere in Africa'. Otherwise Stalin will greet us with the question, 'Have you then no plan for the Second Front in Europe you promised me for 1943?'

3. Khartoum is at your disposal, and would be most satisfactory as regards weather, security, and communications. I will report on accommodation to-morrow. We should be honoured to be the hosts. I am not informed, though quite ready to learn, about the oases south of Algiers. Marrakesh I can personally vouch for as regards accommodation, climate, and, barring any extraordinary lapse, weather.

4. A supreme war conference, as this would be, ought to have the necessary staffs. For ourselves, I should like to bring Eden from the War Cabinet with me and three Chiefs or Vice-Chiefs of Staff, supported by a powerful secretariat, cipher staff, map room, etc.—say about twenty-five.

5. As to timing, the sooner the better. Every day counts. We may reasonably expect that Tunis will be settled by the end of December and Tripolitania by the end of January. We ought not to be dependent on the actual working out of these operations. All prospect of attack in Europe in 1943 depends on early decision.

6. However, everything hangs on whether 'Barkis is willin' '.

*   *   *

He proved unwilling, as the following interchange of telegrams shows.

Prime Minister to Premier Stalin   3 Dec 42

The President tells me he has proposed a meeting for us three in January somewhere in North Africa. This is far better than the Iceland project we talked over in Moscow. You could get to any point desired in three days, I in two, and the President in about the same time as you. I earnestly hope you will agree. We must decide at the earliest moment the best way of attacking Germany in Europe with all possible force in 1943. This can only be settled between the heads of Governments and States with their high expert authorities at their side. It is only by such a meeting that the full burden of the war can be shared according to capacity and opportunity.

Premier Stalin to Premier Churchill   6 Dec 42

I welcome the idea of a meeting between the heads of the Governments of the three countries being arranged in order to fix a common line of military strategy.

To my great regret however I will not be in a position to leave the Soviet Union. I wonder whether it would not be possible to discuss these problems by way of correspondence between us as long as there is no chance of arranging our meeting? I admit that there will be no disagreement between us. These operations will not be relaxed in January, probably to the contrary.

I am waiting your reply to the paragraph of my preceding letter dealing with the establishment of the Second Front in Western Europe in the spring of 1943.

The operations in the Stalingrad area as well as on the central front are developing. In the Stalingrad area we are keeping a large group of the German troops surrounded, and we hope to annihilate them completely.

The President in reply to an identical message expressed his deep disappointment to Stalin, and to me he said:

I think it would be a mistake for our Staff people to discuss in Moscow any major moves planned for this coming summer. From the practical point of view they could not bind your Government or mine, nor could final plans be approved by you or me without careful study with our Staffs at home. What would you think therefore of suggesting that Staff conversations between military officials from U.K., Russia, and America take place in Africa, either in Algiers, Khartoum, or some other suitable place? The results and recommendations of such a meeting would of course have to be taken up in all three capitals before final approval.

My opinion was unchanged. I was glad that the President saw the disadvantages of an expert conference at Moscow, but I did not like one at Khartoum or Algiers much better. I was sure that for the military representatives to meet at some distant place alone and without any prior agreement on our joint affairs between us and the Americans would only waste time, and might well result, after many long telegrams had been sent in cipher, in a deadlock on the spot, and even higher up. Only the heads of States or Governments face to face could settle the fearful questions that were open. Why should the refusal of Stalin to be present at a Three-Power Conference preclude an early Anglo-American meeting? The President however seemed determined to have a triple military meeting, and this I thought it necessary to agree to in principle. On the larger issue he forwarded to me on December 17 his latest news from Stalin.

'I too,' said Stalin,

must express my deep regret that it is impossible for me to leave the Soviet Union either in the near future or even at the beginning of March. Front business absolutely prevents it, demanding my constant presence near our troops. So far I do not know what exactly are the problems which you, Mr. President, and Mr. Churchill intend to discuss at our joint conference. I wonder whether it would not be possible to discuss these problems by way of correspondence between us. As long as there is no chance of arranging our meeting I admit that there will be no disagreement between us.

Allow me also to express my confidence that time is not being lost, and that the promises about the opening of a Second Front in Europe given by you, Mr. President, and by Mr. Churchill in regard to 1942, and in any case in regard to the spring of 1943, will be fulfilled, and that a Second Front in Europe will be actually opened by the joint forces of Great Britain and the United States of America in the spring of next year.

In view of all sorts of rumours about the attitude of the Union of Soviet Socialist Republics towards the use made of Darlan or other men like him, it may not be unnecessary for me to tell you that, in my opinion, as well as in that of my colleagues, Eisenhower's policy with regard to Darlan, Boisson, Giraud, and others is perfectly correct. I think it a great achievement that you succeeded in bringing Darlan and others into the waterway [?main stream] of the Allies fighting Hitler. Some time ago I made this known also to Mr. Churchill.

*   *   *

The President now sent me a very genial letter by courier, asking for an answer, yes or no.

Private

December 14, 1942

Dear Winston,

I have not had an answer to my second invitation to our Uncle Joe, but, on the assumption that he will again decline, I think that in spite of it you and I should get together, as there are things which can be definitely determined only by you and me in conference with our Staff people. I am sure that both of us want to avoid the delays which attended the determination on 'Torch' last July.

1. On the grounds of vile climate and icing on the wings, Iceland must be definitely out for both of us.

2. England must be out for me for political reasons.

3. There will be a commotion in this country if it is discovered that I have flown across any old seas. Therefore Bermuda would be just as much out for me as Africa. However, on condition that I can get away in absolute secrecy and have my trip kept secret until I get back, I have just about made up my mind to go along with the African idea—on the theory that public opinion here will gasp, but be satisfied when they hear about it after it is over.

4. One mitigating circumstance would be the knowledge that I had seen our military leaders in North and West Africa, and that is why I think it would be best if we could meet somewhere in that neighbourhood instead of Khartoum. Incidentally, I could actually see some of our troops.

5. Incidentally also it would do me personally an enormous amount of good to get out of the political atmosphere of Washington for a couple of weeks.

6. My thought is, therefore, that if the time suits your plans we could meet back of Algiers or back of Casablanca about January 15th. That would mean that I would leave about January 11th, and pray for good weather. My route would be either from here to Trinidad and thence to Dakar and thence north, or from here to Natal (Brazil), and across to Liberia or Freetown, and north from there.

7. In view of Stalin's absence, I think you and I need no Foreign Affairs people with us, for our work will be essentially military. Perhaps your three top men and my three top men could meet at the same place four or five days in advance of our arrival and have plans in fairly good tentative shape by the time we get there. I asked General [Bedell] Smith, who left here four or five days ago, to check up confidentially on some possible tourist oasis as far from any city or large population

as possible. One of the dictionaries says 'an oasis is never wholly dry'. Good old dictionary!

8. Here is an alternative plan in case Uncle Joe says he will meet us about March 1st:

I would suggest that your Staff people and mine should meet with the Russian Staff people somewhere in Africa, or even as far as Baghdad, and come to certain recommendations which would at least get the preliminaries of new moves started. The three of us could, when we meet, close up the loose ends, and also take up some of the post-war matters.

With my warm regards,
As ever yours,
FRANKLIN D. ROOSEVELT

To save time Mr. Roosevelt also cabled the substance of his letter.

In spite of Stalin's inability to meet with us, I think we should plan a meeting at once with our respective military staffs. I should like to meet in Africa about January 15. There is, I believe, a satisfactory and safe place just north of Casablanca. It might be wise for some of our military men to precede us by a few days to clear the ground. I should think if we could have four or five days together we could clear up all of our business. Will you let me know what you think of this?

I was naturally pleased with this solution, and was sure it would be better than the purely technical meeting of experts. I hastened to reply:

Former Naval Person to President   21 Dec 42
Yes, certainly. The sooner the better. I am greatly relieved. It is the only thing to do. All arrangements here will be made on basis that it is a Staff meeting only. Suggested code-name 'Symbol'.

*   *   *

The following weeks were spent in drafting Staff appreciations for the forthcoming meeting. There were not only issues of military strategy to be worked out, but also the consideration of the grave political issues arising in North Africa as the result of 'Torch' and the assassination of Darlan. I had obtained the President's agreement to the appointment of Mr. Harold Macmillan to assist the American political representative in North Africa, Mr. Robert Murphy, and he went out to study the position on the spot.

Meanwhile the arrangements for 'Symbol' went smoothly ahead.

Former Naval Person to President Roosevelt   30 Dec 42

I sent Brigadier Jacob to North Africa on Christmas Day to consult with Generals Eisenhower and Bedell Smith about arrangements for 'Symbol'. Jacob has now telegraphed that they have found admirable accommodation, and that General Bedell Smith, who is in full agreement, is telegraphing the results of their reconnaissance to you.

2. I do not think we can do better than accept these proposals, and as time is short I am going ahead on the assumption that you approve.

3. My intention is that H.M.S. *Bulolo*, which is a specially fitted headquarters ship, should leave the United Kingdom on about January 4 with the more junior Staff officers of my delegation, cipher staff, clerical staff, etc. *Bulolo* will be berthed in the harbour and serve as signal ship.

4. You suggested that some of our military men should precede us by a few days to clear the ground. I entirely agree, and will arrange for British Chiefs of Staff to arrive by air at rendezvous on whatever day it may be possible for American Chiefs of Staff to reach there. Can you give me a date?

5. It would also be helpful if you could let me know as soon as possible your own programme, and I will make my own arrangements.

6. Many thanks about Macmillan's appointment. I agree to what you say about Eisenhower's final authority.

The President and I now had a number of agreeable interchanges on questions of security. He proposed to call himself 'Admiral Q'.

Former Naval Person to President   3 Jan 43

However did you think of such an impenetrable disguise? In order to make it even harder for the enemy and to discourage irreverent guesswork, propose Admiral Q and Mr. P.

N.B.—We must mind our P's and Q's.

De Gaulle. I think it far better his visit should be postponed till 'Torch' affairs are 'Symbolised'.

*   *   *

The Chiefs of Staff Committee produced two papers for the War Cabinet summarising their considered views upon future strategy. In reaching their conclusions they emphasised a serious divergence of view between themselves and their American colleagues. It was one of emphasis and priority rather than of principle. It would in fact be the purpose of the coming conference to arrive at a common agreement. The British Chiefs of Staff took the view that the best policy to adopt would be to follow up 'Torch' vigorously, accompanied by as large a 'Bolero' preparation for 'Round-up' as possible, while the American Chiefs of Staff favoured putting our main European effort into 'Round-up' and standing fast in North Africa. In their first paper the British Chiefs of Staff, commenting on the American proposals, set forth their points as follows:

We consider that our policy should be:
1. To exploit 'Torch' as vigorously as possible with a view to
   (a) knocking Italy out of the war,
   (b) bringing Turkey into the war, and
   (c) giving the Axis no respite for recuperation.

2. Increased bombing of Germany.
3. Maintenance of supplies to Russia.
4. The build-up of 'Bolero' on the greatest scale that the above operations admit, in order that we may be ready to re-enter the Continent with about twenty-one divisions in August or September 1943, if the conditions are such that there is a good prospect of success.

We believe that this policy will afford earlier and greater relief, both direct and indirect, to Russia than if we were to concentrate on 'Bolero' to the exclusion of all other operations, observing that at the best we could not put a force of more than twenty-five divisions on to the Continent in late summer of 1943.

I informed Stalin of our plans to meet. He replied:

Premier Stalin to Premier Churchill   5 Jan 43
Many thanks for your communication concerning the impending conversations between you and the President. I will be very grateful for information on the results of these conversations.

The final arrangements were now made.

*   *   *

We did not go empty-handed to the conference on which so much depended. Alexander's and Montgomery's plans for the advance on Tripoli were now complete.

General Alexander to Prime Minister   5 Jan 43
Administrative situation of Eighth Army makes it impos-

sible for its main body to move forward before night January 14–15. Montgomery intends however to move forward in strength on this date. Operations will continue intensively until Tripoli is reached.

2. On January 4 heavy gale caused extensive damage to ships and unloading facilities in Benghazi. This may cause a few days' postponement of forward move or restrict size of force. Am asking him whether his intentions altered.

General Alexander to Prime Minister　　　　6 Jan 43
　　Further to my last. No change in Montgomery's date.

General Alexander to Prime Minister and C.I.G.S.　　9 Jan 43
　　The plan for operations is as follows:

The advance will start night January 14–15 with XXXth Corps. 7th Armoured Division and 2nd N.Z. Division will advance to Sedada. There will probably be opposition from the Gheddahia area. After this has been dealt with direction of advance will be Beni Ulid–Tarhuna, 7th Armoured Division leading. 51st Division will follow the line of the main coastal road; 22nd Armoured Brigade is with Army Command. Xth Corps is not being brought up. Heavy bombing of Tripoli and bottlenecks on coastal road starts January 8.

XXXth Corps will have approximately 500 miles of petrol and ten days' rations and water for the whole force. Ammunition echelons will be full, and generally the administrative situation is reasonably good for a period of ten days. Xth Corps will help by carrying supplies from Tobruk to Benghazi. When we get to Tripoli, until the port is opened we shall be on very short commons. The supplies which can be brought to XXXth Corps by road are about 800 tons a day, which should be sufficient provided we do not have to fight a battle after we have captured Tripoli until the port is opened.

The capture of the port of Tripoli would be a most welcome prize. It would carry the Eighth Army two hundred miles nearer to Tunisia, and thus bring a new favourable factor of decisive importance into the North African scene.

CHAPTER 15

The Casablanca Conference

Flight to Casablanca – The Anfa Suburb – The President Arrives – Generals Eisenhower and Alexander Join Us – Hopes of Taking Tripoli – My First Report to the War Cabinet, January 18 – Differences between the Chiefs of Staff and the Joint Planners – My Talks with General Eaker about the Flying Fortresses – He Converts Me to Their Support – Invitation to General de Gaulle – He Arrives – Stiff Conversations – A Tribute to General de Gaulle – Further Report to the War Cabinet of January 20 –'Unconditional Surrender' – The Full Story – 'Verify Your Quotations' – Final Report on the Conference by the Combined Chiefs of Staff –'Conduct of the War in 1943' – The Press Conference of January 24 – The President and I Motor to Marrakesh – The Villa Taylor – The President Departs at Dawn on the 25th.

On January 12 I left for North Africa. My journey by air was a little anxious. In order to heat the 'Commando' they had established a petrol engine inside which generated fumes and raised various heating points to very high temperatures. I was woken up at two in the morning, when we were over the Atlantic 500 miles from anywhere, by one of these heating points burning my toes, and it looked to me as if it might soon get red-hot and light the blankets. I therefore climbed out of my bunk and woke up Peter Portal, who was sitting in the well beneath, asleep in his chair, and drew his attention to this very hot point. We looked around the cabin and found two others, which seemed equally on the verge of becoming red-hot. We then went down into the bomb alley (it was a converted bomber), and found two men industriously keeping alive this petrol heater. From every point of view I thought this was most dangerous. The hot points might start a conflagration, and the atmosphere of petrol would make an explosion imminent. Portal took the same view. I decided that it was better to freeze than to burn, and I ordered all heating to be turned off, and we went back to rest shivering in the ice-cold winter air about eight thousand feet up, at which we had to fly to be above the clouds. I am bound to say this struck me as rather an unpleasant moment.

When we got to Casablanca we found beautiful arrangements made. There was a large hotel in the suburb of Anfa with ample accommodation for all the British and American Staffs and big conference rooms. Round this hotel were dotted a number of extremely comfortable villas which were reserved for the President, for me, for General Giraud, and also for General de Gaulle, should he come. The whole enclave was wired in and closely guarded by American troops. I and the Staff were there two days before the President arrived. I had some nice walks with Pound and the other Chiefs of Staff on the rocks and the beach. Wonderful waves rolling in, enormous clouds of foam, made one marvel that anybody could have got ashore at the landing. There was not one calm day. Waves fifteen feet high were roaring up terrible rocks. No wonder so many landing-craft and ships' boats were turned over with all their men.

My son Randolph had come across from the Tunisian front. There was plenty to think about, and the two days passed swiftly by. Meanwhile the Staffs consulted together for long hours every day.

*   *   *

The President arrived in the afternoon of the 14th. We had a most warm and friendly meeting, and it gave me intense pleasure to see my great colleague here on conquered or liberated territory which he and I had secured in spite of the advice given him by all his military experts. The next day General Eisenhower arrived, after a very hazardous flight. He was most anxious to know what lines the Combined Chiefs of Staff would take, and to keep in touch with them. Their plane of command was altogether above his. A day or two later Alexander came in, and reported to me and the President about the progress of the Eighth Army. He made a most favourable impression upon the President, who was greatly attracted by him, and also by his news, which was that the Eighth Army would take Tripoli in the near future. He explained how Montgomery, who had two strong Army Corps, had dismounted one and taken all the vehicles to bring the other on alone, and that this would be strong enough to drive Rommel right back through Tripoli to the Mareth frontier line, which was a very serious obstacle. Everyone was much cheered by this news, and the easy, smiling grace of Alexander won all hearts. His unspoken confidence was contagious.

Prime Minister to Deputy Prime Minister and
War Cabinet   18 Jan 43

The Chiefs of Staff have been in session two or three times each day, either alone or with their American colleagues. The whole field of the war is being surveyed theatre by theatre. Admiral King of course considers the Pacific should be a first charge on all resources, and both American Army and Navy authorities are very keen on more vigorous action in Burma to help China, culminating in a large-scale 'Anakim' [Burma] later in the year. General Marshall is also keen on this, but otherwise his emphasis seemed to lie towards building up 'Round-up' [or] 'Sledgehammer' at the expense of the Mediterranean.

On the other hand, I am satisfied the President is strongly in favour of the Mediterranean being given prime place. He also seems increasingly inclined to Operation 'Husky' [Sicily], which he suggested to me last night should be called 'Belly', and I advised 'Bellona'. Although nothing definite has been settled between us pending results of the Staff conversations, I feel sure that we are in solid agreement on the essentials.

Meanwhile at the Combined Staff meetings it has become apparent that the Americans are increasingly turning towards Sicily instead of Sardinia. This is what I should like. Admiral King even went so far as to say that if it was decided to do Sicily he would find the necessary escorts.

The Mediterranean situation is being decisively changed by the victorious advance of the Desert Army. Alexander, who is here, made a great impression on all present at the President's conference on the 15th by his clear, precise, confident accounts of his progress and intentions. He hoped to have Tripoli by the 26th, and to deploy as many as six divisions against the Mareth position by the middle of March. A smaller number of divisions could be deployed at an earlier date. Thus with Anderson's four divisions we may expect ten British divisions in the First and Eighth Armies to be available for the final battle for the Tunisian tip.

As the U.S. will not have more than two divisions in Tunisia by then and the French are so under-equipped, we shall have an overwhelming British preponderance in this theatre. In these circumstances, should all go well in the battle now in progress for Tripoli and should the clearance of Tripoli harbour not be too difficult, the arrival of the Desert Army in the highest fettle in the Tunisian theatre should be decisive. So great a reinforcement of British numbers would evidently justify increased representation for us in the high command. The President received very well last night a suggestion which I made in agreement with C.I.G.S. that at the right time Alexander should fill the vacancy of Deputy C.-in-C. to Eisenhower which has been created by the appointment of Clark to the Fifth U.S. Army. This avoids difficulties with the French which might follow the appointment of a British officer to the command of all forces in Tunisia.

It was fortunate indeed that we all met here and that I brought General Alexander to the scene. General Eisenhower was about to begin an operation most daring and spirited but also most hazardous against Sfax, which he intended to try to hold, supplying himself partly from Malta. This operation ought evidently to be concerted with Alexander's advance, for otherwise the Americans might find themselves heavily attacked in Sfax just at the very period when the Desert Army would be motionless in Tripoli, regathering petrol and supplies and dependent upon the conditions of the port.

I therefore brought together Alexander and Eisenhower, who get on extremely well, both alone and also with C.I.G.S. and Marshall. The result has been a perfect understanding between them and arrangements for visits when necessary. Eisenhower is greatly relieved to realise how soon and with what great forces Alexander can arrive, and instead of an isolated operation to keep things going he is now in a position to make a really good combination. The feeling of all four generally was that we have very good prospects in Tunisia provided we do not make a mistake. Personally I am very well satisfied with the way this has gone.

* * *

Neither I nor the President attended the Staff conferences, but we were informed of the whole position and consulted with our own officers every day. The differences did not run along national lines, but were principally between the Chiefs of Staff and the Joint Planners. I was myself sure that Sicily should be the next step, and the Combined Chiefs of Staff took the same view. The Joint Planners, on the other hand, together with Lord Mountbatten, felt that we should attack Sardinia rather than Sicily, because they thought it could be done three months earlier; and Mountbatten pressed this view on Hopkins and others. I remained obdurate, and, with the Combined Chiefs of Staff solid behind me, insisted on Sicily. The Joint Planners, respectful but persistent, then said that this could not be done until August 30. At this stage I personally went through all the figures with them, and thereafter the President and I gave orders that D-Day was to be during the favourable July moon period, or, if possible, the favourable June moon period. In the event the airborne troops went in on the night of July 9, and the landings started on the morning of July 10.

*   *   *

In these January days I received a request from General Eaker, the Commander of the American Air Forces in England, that he should see me. We discussed the question of the American scheme for the daylight bombing of Germany by the armoured Flying Fortresses. I was personally sceptical of this method. I had regretted that so much effort had been put into the daylight bombing, and still thought that a concentration upon night bombing by the Americans would have resulted in a far larger delivery of bombs on Germany, and that we should have gradually worked up complete accuracy by scientific methods, as we did later. I put these points to Eaker, who knew my view and was much troubled by it. He stated the case for the daylight Fortress bombers with forceful earnestness, and pointed out what immense preparations had already been made in England—the transfer of many squadrons from America, the piling up of men, materials, spare parts, and so forth, and also the preparation of airfields now at length ready.

I said in reply that here we were at the beginning of 1943. The Americans had been in the war for more than a year. They had all the time been building up their air-power in England, but so far they had never thrown a single bomb on Germany by their daylight methods, except perhaps on one occasion when a very short raid was protected by British fighters. We had been led to believe at Washington the year before that in four or five months very heavy deliveries of bombs would be taking place by American aircraft, but nothing had happened, though an immense expenditure of resources had been made. Eaker however pleaded his cause with skill and tenacity. He said it was quite true that they had not yet struck their blow—give them a month or two more and they would come into action on an ever-increasing scale.

Considering how much had been staked on this venture by the United States and all they felt about it, I decided to back

Eaker and his theme, and I turned round completely and withdrew all my opposition to the daylight bombing by the Fortresses. He was much pleased with this, because he had feared that his own Government had already lost a good deal of faith in the daylight bombing method. It was certainly a terrible thing that in the whole of the last six months of 1942 nothing had come of this immense deployment and effort—not a single bomb had been dropped on Germany. There must have been twenty thousand men and five hundred machines all laid out in East Anglia, and nothing so far, as it seemed, to show for it all. However, when I turned round and no longer pressed the formidable point I had been developing there was a great easement and the American plans were no longer subjected to British criticism. They went ahead and soon began to pay dividends. All the same, I still think that if at the beginning they had put their money on night bombing we should have reached our climax much sooner. General Eaker afterwards said on several occasions that I saved the Fortress bombers from abandonment by the United States at the moment when they were about to come into their own. If this is true I saved them by leaving off opposing them.

*   *   *

The question of de Gaulle was then raised. I was now most anxious for him to come, and the President agreed generally with this view. I asked the President also to telegraph inviting him. The General was very haughty and refused several times. I then got Eden to put the utmost pressure upon him, even to the point of saying that if he would not come we should insist on his being replaced by someone else at the head of the French Liberation Committee in London. It is very odd to see the account which the President's son, Elliott Roosevelt, gives of this in the book which he hastened to write about the confidential talks he heard at the meals to which he was brought by his father. He seems to suggest that the President suspected me of trying to stop de Gaulle coming, and objecting to his being brought there, whereas I was putting the utmost possible pressure on him to come. This rubbish has had a wide and long currency. The telegrams dismiss it for ever.

Prime Minister to Foreign Secretary   18 Jan 43
   If you think well you should give the following message to de Gaulle from me. [Begins.]

I am authorised to say that the invitation to you to come here was from the President of the United States of America as well as from me.

I have not yet told General Giraud, who came attended only by two Staff officers, and is waiting here, of your refusal. The consequences of it, if persisted in, will in my opinion be unfavourable for you and your Movement. First we are about to make arrangements for North Africa, on which we should have been glad to consult you, but which must otherwise be made in your absence. The arrangements when concluded will have the support of Great Britain and the United States.

The fact that you have refused to come to the meeting proposed will in my opinion be almost universally censured by public opinion and serve as a complete answer to any complaints. There can of course be no question of your being invited to visit the United States in the near future if you reject the President's invitation now. My attempt to bridge the difficulties which have existed between your Movement and the United States will have definitely failed. I should certainly not be able to renew my exertions in this direction while you remain the leader of the above Movement.

The position of His Majesty's Government towards your Movement while you remain at its head will also require to be reviewed. If with your eyes open you reject this unique opportunity we shall endeavour to get on as well as we can without you. The door is still open. [Ends.]

I leave your latitude to make any alteration in the message which you may think desirable, so long as its seriousness is not impaired. The difficulty is that on account of secrecy we cannot appeal to the French National Committee. Here I have been all these days fighting de Gaulle's battle and making every arrangement for a good reconciliation between the different sections of Frenchmen. If he rejects the chance now offered I shall feel that his removal from the headship of the Free French Movement is essential to the further support of this Movement by H.M.G. I hope you will put as much of this as you think fit to him. For his own sake, you ought to knock him about pretty hard.

*   *   *

At last on January 22 de Gaulle arrived. He was taken to his villa, which was next to Giraud's. He would not call upon Giraud, and it was some hours before he could be prevailed upon to meet him. I had a very stony interview with de Gaulle, making it clear that if he continued to be an obstacle we should not hesitate to break with him finally. He was very formal, and stalked out of the villa and down the little garden with his head high in the air. Eventually he was prevailed upon to have a talk with Giraud, which lasted for two or three hours and must have been extremely pleasant to both of them. In the afternoon he went to see the President, and to my relief they got on unexpectedly well. The President was attracted by 'the spiritual look in his eyes'; but very little could be done to bring them into accord.

*   *   *

In these pages various severe statements, based on events of the moment, are set down about General de Gaulle, and certainly I had continuous difficulties and many sharp antagonisms with him. There was however a dominant element in our relationship. I could not regard him as representing captive and prostrate France, nor indeed the France that had a right to decide freely the future for herself. I knew he was no friend of England. But I always recognised in him the spirit and conception which, across the pages of history, the word 'France' would ever proclaim. I understood and admired, while I resented, his arrogant demeanour. Here he was—a refugee, an exile from his country under sentence of death, in a position entirely dependent upon the goodwill of the British Government, and also now of the United States. The Germans had conquered his country. He had no real foothold anywhere. Never mind; he defied all. Always, even when he was behaving worst, he seemed to express the personality of France—a great nation, with all its pride, authority, and ambition. It was said in mockery that he thought himself the living representative of Joan of Arc, whom one of his ancestors is supposed to have served as a faithful adherent. This did not seem to me as absurd as it looked. Clemenceau, with whom it was said he also compared himself, was a far wiser and more experienced statesman. But they both gave the same impression of being unconquerable Frenchmen.

*   *   *

I made a further report to the War Cabinet.

Prime Minister to the Deputy Prime Minister and War Cabinet   20 Jan 43

Admiral 'Q' [the President] and I called a plenary conference this afternoon, at which the Combined Chiefs of

Staff reported progress. It was a most satisfactory meeting. After five days' discussions and a good deal of apparent disagreement the Combined Chiefs of Staff are now, I think, unanimous in essentials about the conduct of the war in 1943. Their final report is not yet ready, but the following is the gist of the statement which C.I.G.S. made on their behalf. The security of sea communications was agreed to be the first charge upon our combined resources, and the principle reaffirmed that we must concentrate first on the defeat of Germany. Full preparations for taking Sicily are to go ahead at once with a view to carrying out the operation at the earliest possible moment. In addition we hope to mount the Burma plan towards the end of this year. The Americans have undertaken to supply [for this latter] the lion's share of the assault shipping and landing-craft, which will be American-manned, and also to help us out with naval covering forces. At home 'Bolero' is to go ahead as fast as our commitments allow, with a view to a 'Sledgehammer' of some sort this year or a return to the Continent with all available forces if Germany shows definite signs of collapse. In the Pacific operations for the capture of Rabaul and the clearing of New Guinea are to continue in order to retain the initiative and hold Japan. Whether this offensive should subsequently be carried forward to Truk will be a matter for decision later in the year.

Admiral 'Q' and I were in complete agreement with the above outline.

2. Having learned that in the course of the discussions of the Combined Chiefs of Staff the fear had been expressed by the American representatives that we might pull out once Germany was defeated, I thought it right to say in categorical terms that our interest and our honour were alike engaged and that the determination of the British Parliament and people to devote their whole resources to the defeat of Japan after Germany had been brought to her knees was not in doubt. I added that I was sure that the War Cabinet would be fully prepared to enter into a formal treaty or pact with the United States on this point. Admiral 'Q' brushed aside the idea, saying he was confident that the Unites States and the British Empire were entirely of one mind in this matter. He added however that it would be very desirable, if it were at all possible, to get a definite engagement—secret if necessary —from Russia that she would join in the struggle against Japan once Germany was out of the war.

3. Having reached agreement on broad principles, the Chiefs of Staff will have to spend the next ten days examining ways and means. There is a good deal of detailed work to be done,

and I do not think they ought to separate for several days. It will in any event be necessary to have another conference of this kind within the next six months. The necessity for this was particularly stressed by General Marshall.

4. I thought it a good opportunity to broach in plenary session the proposal that at the right time Alexander should become Deputy Commander-in-Chief to Eisenhower. It was warmly welcomed by Marshall and King. The difficult question of air command is under active consideration, and will, I am assured, be settled satisfactorily.

5. The War Cabinet should know that General Marshall asked leave to place on formal record his admiration of the profound contribution which had been rendered to the Allied cause in North Africa by Admiral Cunningham. His naval leadership and skill had been outstanding, and his wisdom and counsel had been of the greatest help to General Eisenhower. Admiral 'Q' also paid a warm tribute to Field-Marshal Sir John Dill. He had come to be regarded by the Americans as an indispensable link between the United States and the British Chiefs of Staff on military policy.

6. We propose to draw up a statement of the work of the conference for communication to the Press at the proper time. I should be glad to know what the War Cabinet would think of our including in this statement a declaration of the firm intention of the United States and the British Empire to continue the war relentlessly until we have brought about the 'unconditional surrender' of Germany and Japan. The omission of Italy would be to encourage a break-up there. The President liked this idea, and it would stimulate our friends in every country.

7. It will also be necessary on the conclusion of the conference to draw up a statement for communication to Premier Stalin. Our idea is that this statement should set out our combined intentions, but should contain no promises.

8. While the above, which has been drawn up under my direction by General Ismay, represents the present position of our discussions and is, as my colleagues know, in the closest harmony with ideas we have shared, it must be admitted that all our military operations taken together are on a very small scale compared with the mighty resources of Britain and the United States, and still more with the gigantic effort of Russia. I am inclined to think that the President shares this view, as Hopkins spoke to me on the subject yesterday, saying in effect, 'It is all right, but it is not enough.' Making all allowances for our tremendous efforts on the sea and in the air, I still feel this most strongly, and during

the remaining days of our conference we must bend ourselves to the task of weighting our blows more heavily.

*   *   *

The reader should note paragraph 6 of the above message, as
the use by the President at the subsequent meeting with the
Press of the words 'unconditional surrender' raised issues which
will recur in this story and certainly be long debated. There is a
school of thought, both in England and America, which argues
that the phrase prolonged the war and played into the dictators'
hands by driving their peoples and armies to desperation. I do
not myself agree with this, for reasons which the course of this
narrative will show. Nevertheless, as my own memory has
proved defective on some points, it will be well to state the facts
as my records reveal them. Elliott Roosevelt asserts in his book
that the words were used by the President at one of our dinners.
He reports that I 'thought, frowned, thought, finally grinned, and
at length announced "Perfect",' and also that the nightcap toast
proposed by me that evening was 'Unconditional surrender'. I
have no recollection of these private and informal interchanges
where conversation was free and unguarded. The matter must
certainly however have cropped up in my official talks with the
President. Hence paragraph 6.

The records of the War Cabinet show that this was brought
before them at their afternoon meeting on January 20. The
discussion seems to have turned, not upon the principle of 'unconditional surrender', but on making an exception in favour
of Italy. Accordingly on January 21 the following message was
sent:

*Deputy Prime Minister and Foreign Secretary to Prime
Minister*

The Cabinet were unanimously of opinion that balance of
advantage lay against excluding Italy, because of misgivings
which would inevitably be caused in Turkey, in the Balkans
and elsewhere. Nor are we convinced that effect on Italians
would be good. Knowledge of all rough stuff coming to them
is surely more likely to have desired effect on Italian morale.

There can therefore be no doubt that the phrase 'unconditional surrender' in the proposed joint statement that was being
drafted was mentioned by me to the War Cabinet, and not dis-
approved in any way by them. On the contrary, their only wish
was that Italy should not be omitted from its scope. I do not
remember nor have I any record of anything that passed be-

tween me and the President on the subject after I received the Cabinet message, and it is quite possible that in the pressure of business, especially the discussions about the relations of Giraud and de Gaulle and interviews with them, the matter was not further referred to between us. Meanwhile the official joint statement was being prepared by our advisers and by the Chiefs of Staff. This was a careful and formally worded document, which both the President and I considered and approved. It seems probable that as I did not like applying unconditional surrender to Italy I did not raise the point again with the President, and we had certainly both agreed to the communiqué we had settled with our advisers. There is no mention in it of 'unconditional surrender'. It was submitted to the War Cabinet, who approved it in this form.

It was with some feeling of surprise that I heard the President say at the Press Conference on January 24 that we would enforce 'unconditional surrender' upon all our enemies. It was natural to suppose that the agreed communiqué had superseded anything said in conversation. General Ismay, who knew exactly how my mind was working from day to day, and was also present at all the discussions of the Chiefs of Staff when the communiqué was prepared, was also surprised. In my speech which followed the President's I of course supported him and concurred in what he had said. Any divergence between us, even by omission, would on such an occasion and at such a time have been damaging or even dangerous to our war effort. I certainly take my share of the responsibility, together with the British War Cabinet.

The President's account to Hopkins seems however conclusive.

We had so much trouble getting those two French generals together that I thought to myself that this was as difficult as arranging the meeting of Grant and Lee—and then suddenly the Press Conference was on, and Winston and I had had no time to prepare for it, and the thought popped into my mind that they had called Grant 'Old Unconditional Surrender', and the next thing I knew I had said it.*

I do not feel that this frank statement is in any way weakened by the fact that the phrase occurs in the notes from which he spoke.

* Sherwood, *Roosevelt and Hopkins*, p. 696.

Memories of the war may be vivid and true, but should never be trusted without verification, especially where the sequence of events is concerned. I certainly made several erroneous statements about the 'unconditional surrender' incident, because I said what I thought and believed at the moment without looking up the records. Mine was not the only memory at fault, for Mr. Bevin in the House of Commons on July 21, 1949, gave a lurid account of the difficulties he had had to encounter in rebuilding Germany after the war through the policy of 'unconditional surrender', on which he said neither he nor the War Cabinet had ever been consulted at the time. I replied on the spur of the moment, with equal inaccuracy and good faith, that the first time I heard the words was from the lips of the President at the Casablanca Press Conference. It was only when I got home and searched my archives that I found the facts as they have been set out here. I am reminded of the professor who in his declining hours was asked by his devoted pupils for his final counsel. He replied, 'Verify your quotations.'

*   *   *

The use of the expression 'unconditional surrender', although widely hailed at the time, has since been described by various authorities as one of the great mistakes of Anglo-American war policy. It requires to be dealt with at this point. It is said that it prolonged the struggle and made recovery afterwards more difficult. I do not believe that this is true. I took occasion at the Guildhall on June 30, 1943, to say:

We the United Nations, demand from the Nazi, Fascist, and Japanese tyrannies unconditional surrender. By this we mean that their will-power to resist must be completely broken, and that they must yield themselves absolutely to our justice and mercy. It also means that we must take all those far-sighted measures which are necessary to prevent the world from being again convulsed, wrecked, and blackened by their calculated plots and ferocious aggressions. It does not mean, and it never can mean, that we are to stain our victorious arms by inhumanity or by mere lust of vengeance, or that we do not plan a world in which all branches of the human family may look forward to what the American Declaration of Independence finely calls 'life, liberty, and the pursuit of happiness'.

President Roosevelt also said on December 24, 1943:

The United Nations have no intention to enslave the German people. We wish them to have a normal chance to develop in peace, as useful and respectable members of the European family. But we most certainly emphasise the word 'respectable', for we intend to rid them once and for all of Nazism and Prussian militarism and the fantastic and disastrous notion that they constitute the 'Master Race'.

My principal reason for opposing, as I always did, an alternative statement on peace terms, which was so often urged, was that a statement of the actual conditions on which the three great Allies would have insisted, and would have been forced by public opinion to insist, would have been far more repulsive to any German peace movement than the general expression 'unconditional surrender'. I remember several attempts being made to draft peace conditions which would satisfy the wrath of the conquerors against Germany. They looked so terrible when set forth on paper, and so far exceeded what was in fact done, that their publication would only have stimulated German resistance. They had in fact only to be written out to be withdrawn.

On this point I submitted a note to my colleagues dated January 14, 1944, just after the Russians had made clear to us their attitude at Teheran.

By 'unconditional surrender' I mean that the Germans have no *rights* to any particular form of treatment. For instance, the Atlantic Charter would not apply to them as *a matter of right*. On the other hand, the victorious nations owe it to themselves to observe the obligations of humanity and civilisation.

The question is whether we should go further at the present time. It is perhaps well to look at what is actually going to happen to Germany before deciding whether more precise statements would induce them to surrender.

First, they are to be completely disarmed and deprived of all power to rearm.

Second, they are to be prohibited from all use of aviation, whether civil or military, and from practising the art of flying.

Third, large numbers of persons alleged to be guilty of atrocities are to be handed over for judgment to the countries where their crimes were committed. Premier Stalin mentioned at Teheran that he would certainly require at least four million Germans to work for many years in building up the ruin they had caused in Russia. I have no doubt the Russians will insist upon the handing over to them of vast quantities of German machinery to make up in a generous fashion for what has been destroyed. It may well be that similar claims will be made by others of the victorious Powers. In view of the great severity practised upon immense numbers of French, Italian, and Russian prisoners of war and internees, such retribution would not appear to be devoid of justice.

Fourth, the British, United States, and Russian Governments are, I understand, agreed that Germany is to be decisively broken up into a number of separate States. East Prussia and Germany east of the river Oder are to be alienated for ever and the population shifted. Prussia itself is to be divided and curtailed. The Ruhr and other great centres of coal and steel must be put outside the power of Prussia.

Fifth, the entire core of the German Army comprised in its General Staff must be entirely broken up, and it may be that the Russians will claim that very large numbers of the General Staff of the German Army shall be either put to death or interned for many years. I have myself wished to publish a list of some fifty to a hundred outlaws of first notoriety with a view to dissociating the mass of the people from those who will suffer capital punishment at the hands of the Allies and of avoiding anything in the nature of mass executions. This would tend to reassure the ordinary people. But these proposals were scouted at Teheran as being far too lenient, though I am not sure how far Marshal Stalin was serious in this part of the conversation.

Enough at any rate is set down above to show that a frank statement of what is going to happen to Germany would not necessarily have a reassuring effect upon the German people, and that they might prefer the vaguer terrors of 'unconditional surrender', mitigated as they are by such statements as the President has made.

Finally I said in the House of Commons on February 22, 1944:

The term 'unconditional surrender' does not mean that the German people will be enslaved or destroyed. It means however that the Allies will not be bound to them at the moment of surrender by any pact or obligation. There will be, for instance, no question of the Atlantic Charter applying to Germany as a matter of right and barring territorial transferences or adjustments in enemy countries. No such arguments will be admitted by us as were used by Germany after the last war, saying that they surrendered in consequences of President Wilson's 'Fourteen Points'. Unconditional surrender means that the victors have a free hand. It does not mean that they are entitled to behave in a barbarous manner, nor that they wish to blot out Germany from among the nations of Europe. If we are bound, we are bound by our own consciences to civilisation. We are not to be bound to the Germans as a result of a bargain struck. That is the meaning of 'unconditional surrender'.

It cannot be contended that in the closing years of the war there was any misconception in Germany.

*   *   *

At length, after ten days' work on the main issues, the Combined Chiefs of Staff reached agreement. Both the President and I kept in daily touch with their work and agreed between ourselves about it. It was settled that we should concentrate all upon taking Tunis, both with the Desert Army and with all forces that could be found by the British, and from Eisenhower's army, and that Alexander should be Eisenhower's Deputy and virtually in charge of all the operations. In addition we had the executive command of the Navy and Air Force, under Admiral Cunningham and Air Marshal Tedder. It was evident that should the Eighth Army succeed in arriving on the scene with its six or seven divisions, these, added to the four or five under General Anderson in the First British Army, would give the British about twelve divisions, compared with the Americans' three and possibly four, which was all that they could spare for the Tunis climax after garrisoning Morocco and Algeria. Two years later General Marshall told me at Malta how astonished he was that we British had not suggested any transfer of the command from Eisenhower to a British commander, although we had such an enormous superiority of divisions engaged in the fighting for Tunis. This idea never crossed my mind. It was contrary to the whole basis on which the President and I had worked. The relations between Eisenhower and Alexander will be referred to later. Both were selfless men and played the game with each other. Eisenhower confided the entire conduct of the battle to Alexander.

*   *   *

We were now to wind up our affairs. Our last formal and plenary meeting with the Chiefs of Staff took place on January

23, when they presented to us their final report on 'The Conduct of the War in 1943'. It may be epitomised as follows:

The defeat of the U-boat must remain a first charge on the resources of the United Nations. The Soviet forces must be sustained by the greatest volume of supplies that can be transported to Russia.

Operations in the European theatre will be conducted with the object of defeating Germany in 1943 with the maximum forces that can be brought to bear upon her by the United Nations.

The main lines of offensive action will be:

In the Mediterranean
    (*a*) The occupation of Sicily, with the object of:

        (i) Making the Mediterranean line of communications more secure.

        (ii) Diverting German pressure from the Russian front.

        (iii) Intensifying the pressure on Italy.

    (*b*) To create a situation in which Turkey can be enlisted as an active ally.

In the United Kingdom
    (*c*) The heaviest possible air offensive against German war effort.

    (*d*) Such limited offensive operations as may be practicable with the amphibious forces available.

    (*e*) The assembly of the strongest possible force in constant readiness to re-enter the Continent as soon as German resistance is weakened to the required extent.

Operations in the Pacific and Far East shall continue with the object of maintaining pressure on Japan, and for the full-scale offensive against Japan as soon as Germany is defeated. These operations must be kept within such limits as will not, in the opinion of the Joint Chiefs of Staff, jeopardise the capacity of the United Nations to take advantage of any favourable opportunity for a decisive defeat of Germany in 1943. Subject to this, plans and preparations shall be made for the recapture of Burma ['Anakim'], beginning in 1943, and for operations against the Marshalls and Carolines, if time and resources allow, without prejudice to 'Anakim'.

In giving our approval to this policy, which we had shaped at each stage with our expert advisers, the President and I added a letter to the respective Chiefs of Staff:

In cordially approving the report of the Combined Chiefs of Staff drawn up after thorough examination of problems, the President and the Prime Minister wish to emphasise the following points, which should be steadily pressed in all preparations:

(i) The desirability of finding means of running the W.J.* Russian convoys even through the 'Husky' period.

(ii) The urgency of sending air reinforcements to General Chenault's forces in China and of finding personnel to make them fully operative.

(iii) The importance of achieving the favourable June moon for Sicily, and the grave detriment to our interest which will be incurred by an apparent suspension of activities during the summer months.

(iv) The need to build up more quickly the U.S. striking force in U.K., so as to be able to profit by favourable August weather for some form of 'Sledgehammer'. For this purpose not only the allowances of initial equipment and monthly maintenance should be searchingly re-examined, but the priorities of material and man-power shipment from U.S. to Great Britain should be adjusted to the tactical situation likely to be presented at the target date.

*   *   *

Finally, on the morning of the 24th we came to the Press Conference, where de Gaulle and Giraud were made to sit in a row of chairs, alternating with the President and me, and we forced them to shake hands in public before all the reporters and photographers. They did so, and the pictures of this event cannot be viewed even in the setting of these tragic times without a laugh. The fact that the President and I were at Casablanca had been a well-kept secret. When the Press reporters saw us both they could scarcely believe their eyes, or, when they were told we had been there for nearly a fortnight, their ears.

After the compulsory, or 'shotgun', marriage (as it is called in the United States) of the bride and bridegroom, about whom such pains had been taken, the President made his speech to the reporters, and I supported him.

*   *   *

The President prepared to depart. But I said to him, 'You cannot come all this way to North Africa without seeing Marrakesh. Let us spend two days there. I must be with you when you

* Winston-Joe.

see the sunset on the snows of the Atlas Mountains.' I worked on Harry Hopkins also in this sense. It happened there was a most delightful villa, of which I knew nothing, at Marrakesh which the American Vice Consul, Mr. Kenneth Pendar, had been lent by an American lady, Mrs. Taylor. This villa would accommodate the President and me, and there was plenty of outside room for our entourages. So it was decided that we should all go to Marrakesh. Roosevelt and I drove together the 150 miles across the desert—already it seemed to me to be beginning to get greener—and reached the famous oasis. My description of Marrakesh was 'the Paris of the Sahara', where all the caravans had come from Central Africa for centuries to be heavily taxed *en route* by the tribes in the mountains and afterwards swindled in the Marrakesh markets, receiving the return, which they greatly valued, of the gay life of the city, including fortune-tellers, snake-charmers, masses of food and drink, and on the whole the largest and most elaborately organised brothels in the African continent. All these institutions were of long and ancient repute.

It was agreed between us that I should provide the luncheon, and Tommy was accordingly charged with the task. The President and I drove together all the way, five hours, and talked a great deal of shop, but touched on lighter matters. Many thousand American troops were posted along the road to protect us from any danger, and aeroplanes circled ceaselessly overhead. In the evening we arrived at the villa, where we were very hospitably and suitably entertained by Mr. Pendar. I took the President up the tower of the villa. He was carried in a chair, and sat enjoying a wonderful sunset on the snows of the Atlas. We had a very jolly dinner, about fifteen or sixteen, and we all sang songs. I sang, and the President joined in the choruses, and at one moment was about to try a solo. However, someone interrupted and I never heard this.

My illustrious colleague was to depart just after dawn on the 25th for his long flight by Lagos and Dakar and so across to Brazil and then up to Washington. We had parted the night before, but he came round in the morning on the way to the aeroplane to say another good-bye. I was in bed, but would not hear of letting him go to the airfield alone, so I jumped up and put on my zip, and nothing else except slippers, and in this informal garb I drove with him to the airfield, and went on the plane and saw him comfortably settled down, greatly admiring his courage under all his physical disabilities and feeling very anxious about the hazards he had to undertake. These aeroplane journeys had to be taken as a matter of course during the war. None the less, I always regarded them as dangerous excursions. However, all was well. I then returned to the Villa Taylor, where I spent another two days in correspondence with the War Cabinet about my future movements, and painting from the tower the only picture I ever attempted during the war.

CHAPTER 16

Adana and Tripoli

Need to Bring Turkey into the War – My Note to the Chiefs of Staff of November 18 – My Telegram to Stalin of November 24 – I Wish to Meet the Turkish President – Objections by the Cabinet – President Roosevelt's Agreement with My Plan – I Repeat My Request to My Colleagues – They At Length Acquiesce – Off Over the Atlas Mountains – The Turkish Government Welcomes the Conference – We Fly to Adana – My Memorandum to the Turks – A Wooing Letter – Full Account to Them of Our Position – Our Discussions in President Inönü's Train – 'Morning Thoughts' – Russian Triumph at Stalingrad – My Telegram to Stalin of February 2 – His Reply February 6 – Lost Opportunities.

The strategic scene in the Mediterranean had been transformed by the Allied occupation of North-West Africa, and with the acquisition of a solid base on its southern shores a forward movement against the enemy became possible. The President and I had long sought to open a new route to Russia and to strike at Germany's southern flank. Turkey was the key to all such plans. To bring Turkey into the war on our side had for many months been our aim. It now acquired new hope and urgency.

As soon as the results of Alamein and 'Torch' were manifest I had sent, on November 18, a note to the British Chiefs of Staff on this sphere. We had considerable forces already stationed in Egypt and the Middle East which must in any case remain in that theatre, but which in the improved situation should be made to play an active part. The following is the substance of my note:

A supreme and prolonged effort must be made to bring Turkey into the war in the spring. We must expect that our naval forces and shipping, landing-craft, etc., will be fully engaged in the Central Mediterranean, and that only minor amphibious facilities will be available in the Levant. Access can however be had to Turkey by the railways through Syria, as well as by coastal shipping, and by a gradual build-up of air protection not only Adalia but the Dardanelles itself might become open to supplies for Turkey. Troops can move by rail and road from Syria.

I wish to record my opinion that Turkey may be won if the proper measures are taken. Turkey is an Ally. She will wish to have a seat among the victors at the Peace Conference. She has a great desire to be well armed. Her Army is in good order, except for the specialised modern weapons in which the Bulgarians have been given so great an advantage by the Germans. The Turkish Army has been mobilised for nearly three years, and is warlike. Hitherto Turkey has been restrained by fear from fulfilling her obligations, and we have taken an indulgent view of her policy on account of our own inability to help. The situation has now changed. By the destruction of Rommel's army large forces may presently become available in Egypt and Cyrenaica. By a strengthened Russian resistance and a possible counter-stroke in the Caucasus, which we should urge upon the Russians with all emphasis, great easement will be secured in Persia, and our Tenth Army may be drawn upon. There is also the Ninth Army in Syria. From all these sources it should be possible, on the assumption of the Russians maintaining themselves in the Caucasus north of the mountain line and holding the Caspian, to build up a powerful British land and air force to assist the Turks. A target date for the concentration should be April or May. Let me have proposals.

The following is the order of procedure, political and military:

(a) Turkey should be offered a Russian–American–British guarantee of territorial integrity and *status quo*. The Russians have already agreed with us upon this. The addition of the United States would probably be a decisive reassurance. This should be followed by the dispatch to Turkey of a strong Anglo-American Military Mission.

(b) All through the winter from now on Turkey must be equipped from Egypt and from the United States with tanks, A.T. and A.A. guns, and active construction of airfields must be undertaken. We have been working upon airfield construction in Turkey for two years. What progress has been made so far? Now that Rommel has been beaten there is evidently a surplus of material in Egypt. We had over 2,500 tanks at the disposal of the Middle East Army. Much enemy material has been captured, both German and Italian. This is also true of anti-tank and A.A. guns. Experts must be provided to assist the Turks in learning to use and maintain this material. A ceaseless flow of weapons and equipment must go into Turkey. We have already promised a consignment, but the moment Turkey agrees secretly with the plan above far greater quantities must be sent. What is the capacity of the railways from Syria to the Bosphorus and the Dardanelles? It would seem a great mistake to attack Rhodes and other islands in enemy hands in the Eastern Mediterranean until we have got Turkey on our side. Any attacks can then be supported by heavy shore-based air-power. We have to creep round this coast by land and sea, building up our air as we go.

(c) In conjunction with the above, we should urge the Russians to develop their strength on their southern flank, to try to clear the Caucasus, to regain Novorossisk, and above all to resume at the earliest date their intention, explained to me by Premier Stalin, of striking south-west from the region north of Stalingrad towards Rostov-on-the-Don. An ultimate result of these operations, if successful, would be the opening of the Dardanelles, under heavy air protection, to the passage of supplies to Russian Black Sea ports, and to any naval assistance the Russians might require in the Black Sea. . . .

This document of mine represented the preliminary stage. On November 24 I informed Stalin of the train of my thought.

I have communicated to President Roosevelt some preliminary ideas about Turkey, and have found that he independently had formed very similar views. It seems to me that we ought all of us to make a new effort to have Turkey enter the war on our side. For this purpose I should like the United States to join in an Anglo-Soviet Guarantee of the territorial integrity and status of Turkey. Secondly, we are already sending Turkey a considerable consignment of munitions, including two hundred tanks, from the Middle East. . . . Thirdly, I hope by the early spring to assemble a considerable army in Syria . . . so as to go to the help of Turkey, either if she were threatened or were willing to join us. It is evident that your operations in the Caucasus or north of it may also exercise a great influence. If Turkey were to join us we could not only proceed with operations designed to open the shipping route to your left flank on the Black Sea, but we could also bomb heavily, from Turkish bases, the Roumanian oilfields, which are of such vital importance to the Axis, in view of your successful defence of the main oil supplies of the Caucasus.

On November 28 Stalin replied that he was in full agreement with the President and myself on the question of Turkey. 'It would be desirable to do everything possible to have Turkey enter the war on our side in the spring. This would be of great importance in order to accelerate the defeat of Hitler and his accomplices.'

*   *   *

There the subject rested until the Casablanca Conference. It had been one of the main points in our discussions. Our general agreement on the need to bring Turkey into the war was set forth in the combined report and covering letter. I now wished to clinch the matter by a personal meeting with President Inönü on Turkish soil. There was also much business to be done in Cairo, and I hoped on the way home to visit the Eighth Army in Tripoli, if it were taken, and also to call at Algiers. There were many things I could settle on the spot, and more which I needed to see with my own eyes. On January 20 therefore I telegraphed from Casablanca to the Deputy Prime Minister and the Foreign Secretary as follows:

> I raised the Turkish question, having explored the ground beforehand, with President Roosevelt. It was agreed that we played the hand in Turkey, whether in munitions or diplomacy, the Americans taking the lead with China, and of course in French North Africa. You will be pleased at this. ... As soon as the President has gone I shall, if the weather is good, fly from Marrakesh to Cairo, where I propose to stay for two or three days and settle several important matters. ... Is this not the opportunity and the moment for me to get into direct touch with the Turks? ... If you both think well of this the Foreign Secretary should make the proposal to the Turks without delay.

On the following day I received a reply to this telegram stating that Mr. Attlee and Mr. Eden had consulted the War Cabinet, and that as a result they urged my return direct to London to give an account to Parliament of my meeting with the President. My colleagues were opposed to my going to Cairo, on the ground of extending my risks unnecessarily. Even more strongly did they resist the Turkish proposal. They were convinced that the moment was not ripe for an approach, and that if I persisted I should court either 'a rebuff or a failure'.

I was by no means content with these arguments.

Prime Minister to Foreign Secretary   21 Jan 43
> I am very sorry about Turkey. I think a golden opportunity may be lost. It had not been my intention to extort any

pledge, but only to explain to them the ways in which we can now help them to place their country in a position of security. They are three: (1) by the guarantees; (2) by substantial munitions aid; (3) by sending them reinforcements in the event of attack—necessary specialist flak units, tanks and aircraft, anti-tank weapons, Radar, and so on. If the Turks were afraid to come I should not feel at all rebuffed.

Mr. Eden sent me a personal message saying that he felt that the arguments put forward by the War Cabinet were sound, and that the results which I thought important could be achieved by other means. I discussed the question with the President in the light of these messages from London. On January 24 therefore I telegraphed again as follows:

Prime Minister to Deputy Prime Minister and
Foreign Secretary   24 Jan 43
I must ask seriously that this matter be reviewed by Cabinet and that I may know as soon as possible their decision. I now wish and ask that the following telegram should be sent, either from me to President Inönü or to the Turkish Prime Minister, as may be thought best.

'I shall shortly be visiting Cairo after my conference in North Africa with President of the U.S. I have been charged with the duty of speaking for both Great Britain and the U.S. on the equipment of the Turkish Army with the latest weapons, which are now at last coming forward in large numbers, and also of touching generally upon the matters affecting general defensive security of Turkey. I should be willing therefore to come to a most secret rendezvous with the Turkish Prime Minister, and I could also arrange, if desired, for C.I.G.S. to meet Marshal Chakmak or other high Turkish military authorities. Cyprus would afford a completely sure and secret meeting-place for a friendly talk about general situation, and I should be quite willing to come there if this were agreeable to you.'

President Roosevelt attaches much importance to action on these lines, and in the event of my colleagues being willing to send the above message he will himself telegraph to President Inönü as follows:

'President Inönü: The Prime Minister, who has been conferring with me, is going shortly to Cairo. He will in all probability wish to confer with you or with your Prime Minister at some convenient secret place. In case Prime Minister Churchill does seek a conference I earnestly hope you or your Prime Minister will find it possible to meet him. Roosevelt.'

Even if the Turks should say 'No' it will do no harm. I have no false pride in these matters. The capture of Tripoli, the increasing Russian victories, and the fact that I speak for the two great Allies creates a most favourable occasion. Do not, I beg you, lightly dismiss it.

The flight from Marrakesh to Cairo has been very carefully reconnoitred and considered, and is not thought to present any difficulties. It does not go over any enemy territory nor near any fighting fronts. The C.A.S. and the pilot think it a perfectly good and simple flight. The Chief of the Imperial General Staff and I need to go there in any case in order to discuss with Wilson the whole question of his new command and the dispositions of the Tenth Army, on which we are now about to draw heavily for Sicily.

I trust that you and my colleagues will give me such latitude in my personal movements as I deem necessary to the public interest.

The War Cabinet reiterated their arguments against my proposed meeting with the Turkish leaders. They were in favour of the Staff talks continuing, and thought that an approach to Turkey on the highest level, without previous preparation, particularly in regard to shipping and communications in the event of supplies being sent as a result of an agreement, would be premature. I got quite upset by the obstruction of the Cabinet as I lay in my luxurious bed in the Villa Taylor looking at the Atlas Mountains, over which I longed to leap in the 'Commando' aeroplane which awaited me so patient and contented on the airfield.

I was moreover convinced of the rightness of my view, and the President was entirely at one with me on this. I therefore replied again on January 25.

Prime Minister to Deputy Prime Minister and
War Cabinet   25 Jan 43

Neither the President nor I are at all convinced by arguments put forward. There never was any idea of persuading Turkey to come into war without regard to circumstances and conditions. These have to be created and prepared beforehand. In the first place, Turkey has to be well kitted up. In the second, the situation developing against Italy and induced by the Russian advances must first of all produce its solid result upon safety of Turkey. However, it seems to me a subject of surprise, if right conditions were created, that any one should have doubt about the advantages of Turkey entering the war on our side. No one would propose to urge the Turks to step outside their bounds, but mere occupation by us and use of Turkish aerodromes would give us the power to paralyse Ploesti oilfields, with consequences judged by Chiefs of Staff to be of far-reaching importance. Besides this, there could surely be no doubt that the arrival of Turkey on the Allied side in four or five months' time, when the great operations on which we are resolved will be afoot, would be an invaluable make-weight to our war effort against our enemies. I have not the slightest doubt that Combined Chiefs of Staff would take this view, but they are unhappily now dispersed. I can only say that C.I.G.S. takes the same view as the President and his advisers.

2. I asked most earnestly that telegram in question should be sent. I am sure, and President agreed with me, that what you call the 'rebuff', if received, which is questionable, would not have any noticeable consequences. If, on other hand, the Turks accept, it would surely not be in their interest to let this important contact with the winning side lapse into a failure. As to their pressing inordinate demands for munitions upon me and the President, I should naturally report these to you before agreeing to them.

3. Therefore I wish to request you should send my telegram. The President, who departs in a few hours (Monday morning), has left me authority to release his as soon as your decision as been made.

This of course brought matters to a head. The same afternoon I received an answer from the War Cabinet acquiescing in my plan, and I telegraphed to London in a more easy mood:

Prime Minister to Deputy Prime Minister and
Foreign Secretary   25 Jan 43
    I am most grateful to you for allowing me to try my plan. We may only get a snub, in which case it will be my fault, but I do not think it will do for me to wait for the Turkish answer. I think there is a shade of odds in favour of their coming. If they come, I think I can get things pushed on a bit. How difficult everything becomes once one cannot talk together!

2. Apart from Turkey, there are tremendous possibilities open in Southern Tunisia. I shall try to make sure that these are exploited to the full. The arrival of the glorious Desert armies, whom I last saw in such despondency and disarray, at this stage in their 1,500 mile march is the greatest factor alive on the North African shore. It is rather odd to think that this morning up to noon I had the option of either answering my questions to-morrow in the House of Commons or of meeting General Wilson in Cairo (D.V.).

I could not resist sending this:

*Prime Minister to Deputy Prime Minister and
Foreign Secretary*   26 Jan 43
We are just over the Atlas Mountains, which are gleaming with their sunlit snows. You can imagine how much I wish I were going to be with you to-morrow on the Bench, but duty calls.

*   *   *

Accordingly on the afternoon of the 26th we sailed off in the 'Commando,' and after having an extremely good dinner, provided by Mr. Pendar at the Taylor Villa, I slept soundly till once again, after an eight months' interval, I went to the co-pilot's seat and sat by Captain Vanderkloot, my young American pilot, and we saw together for the second time dawn gleam upon the waters of the Nile. This time we had not to go so far to the south, because the victory of Alamein had swept our foes fifteen hundred miles farther to the west. We arrived at the airfield, ten miles from the Pyramids, and were welcomed by the Ambassador, Lord Killearn, and received by the Cairo Command. We then repaired to the Embassy. Here I was joined by Sir Alexander Cadogan, Permanent Under-Secretary of State at the Foreign office, sent from England by the Cabinet at my desire. We were all able to contrast the situation with what it had been in August 1942 with feelings of relief and satisfaction.

Messages now reached me to say that the Turkish President, Ismet Inönü, was delighted at the idea of the proposed meeting. Several suggestions were made as to time and place. One plan was that I should go myself to Angora. This was strongly opposed by the Foreign Office, particularly in view of the lack of security, as had been shown by the recent attempt to murder the German Ambassador, von Papen, with a bomb. Another suggestion, made by the Turkish President, was that I should meet his Prime Minister, Mr. Saracoglu, in Cyprus on January 31, whither he would travel after dining at the German Embassy. A much more convenient proposal, made from the Turkish side, was that the President and his staff should meet me in his special train in secrecy anywhere agreeable to me on Turkish territory. Arrangements were therefore made for a meeting to take place at Adana, on the coast near the Turkish-Syrian border, on January 30. I hastened to inform both the President and Stalin of this decision.

Prime Minister to President Roosevelt   27 Jan 43

The Turk is delighted, as you will see from his message to you. I am now in Cairo, and shall start in a day or two for a secret rendezvous in Turkey, name of which I will telegraph later. I will keep you fully informed. Hope all is well with you and that you are not at all fatigued. We seem to have got a good world Press.

And:

Prime Minister to Premier Stalin   27 Jan 43

It was agreed between President Roosevelt and me that I should propose to the Turkish President a meeting between him and me in order to arrange for the better and more speedy equipment of the Turkish Army with a view to future eventualities. The Turkish President has replied cordially welcoming this plan for increasing 'the lateral defensive strength' of Turkey, and he is willing, if I wish, that our meeting should become public in due course after it has taken place. You know my views already in this matter from the telegrams exchanged between us, and you may be sure I shall keep you promptly and fully informed.

Pray accept my renewed expressions of admiration at the continued marvellous feats of the Soviet armies.

*   *   *

I went in the 'Commando' to meet the Turks. It is only a four-hour flight across the Mediterranean, most of it in sight of Palestine and Syria, and we landed at Adana. I had with me in another plane Cadogan and Generals Brooke, Alexander, Wilson, and other officers. We landed not without some difficulty on the small Turkish airfield, and we had hardly completed the salutations and ceremonial before a very long enamelled caterpillar began to crawl out of the mountain defiles, containing the President, the entire Turkish Government, and Marshal Chakmak. They received us with the utmost cordiality and enthusiasm. Several saloon carriages had been put on the train for our accommodation, there being none other in the neighbourhood. We spent two nights in this train, having long daily discussions with the Turks and very agreeable talks at meals with President Inönü. I had meanwhile on the journey prepared a statement addressed to the Turks and written for their consumption. It was meant to be a wooing letter containing an offer of platonic marriage both from me and the President.

The danger to Turkey on her northern flank has been removed for the time being by the shattering victories of the Russians over the Germans, and on her southern flank by the fact that Generals Alexander and Montgomery have chased Rommel 1,600 miles away from Cairo, with the destruction of three-quarters of his army and nine-tenths of his equipment. There remains however the Germans' need of oil and of the *Drang nach Osten*, and they may in the summer try to force their way through the centre. Turkey must be in the best possible condition to resist any such act of aggression by force of arms. We have come here to find out how we can best help our Ally at this serious but at the same time hopeful juncture. To this end we are prepared to speed up and increase the supply of the modern munitions which the Turkish Army unhappily lacks. The President of the United States has asked me to handle this matter for him as well as for my own country. This of course does not mean that I can draw a blank cheque on the United States, and I shall have to refer back on particular points. However, the President was most anxious this meeting should take place, as he is desirous that Turkey should be safe and strong, and that she should be closely associated with the two great Western democracies not only during the concluding stages of the war, but in the general work of world rehabilitation which will follow. I think therefore we may expect most sympathetic consideration for anything we recommend.

2. In what directions can we increase the flow and speed up the efficient use of the weapons we supply? What is the present state of the communications, and what measures should be taken to reduce any congestion on them? What measures should be taken to make sure that the equipment is properly handled by our Ally? We [British] have ourselves no false pride on these points and think only of getting stronger and better equipped. For instance, the Americans have sent out teachers to train us in the use of the various tanks and weapons they have supplied to us in the Middle East. They even sent out a large number of skilled engineers in plain clothes before they came into the war in order to teach us how to keep the machines in running order and how to make repairs. Another instance is the railway through Persia. We thought we were running it very well, but the Americans made a number of criticisms and offered to take it over with larger strength and help us to run it better. They are now taking it over from us section by section. I say this to show that we are not making any derogatory suggestion in asking that a considerable number of experts and technicians in plain clothes should come in to assist in the working up of

the material so that it can get into the hands of the troops and be kept in good condition. Also, we are very ready to send officers with the latest experience in tank warfare, and other branches of technical warfare and to give all possible information that could be desired.

I have been particularly distressed at the spectacle of the Turkish Army, which has the finest infantry and a good field artillery, but has not been able to get during the whole three and a half years of this war the modern equipment which is decisive on the battlefield, and which the Germans, from their looted stores, have been able to give, for instance, to the Bulgarians. This has made me fully comprehend the attitude of Turkey at every stage we have so far travelled. The time has come when these disparities can and must be removed with the greatest speed. . . .

The British and Americans will certainly send together, immediately on Turkey being drawn into the war, at least twenty-five air squadrons. A number of airfields have already been prepared and a good deal of material is already on the sites. However, there is a second series of airfields, the preparation of which was discontinued about a year ago, the construction of which should be actively proceeded with. Material, spare parts, and field workshops must all be put in place. The nests must be made so that the birds can fly there at once. Unless the nests are ready birds cannot live and cannot strike. The work, which is really vital to the defence of Turkey, should be pushed forward with frantic energy, and British and American engineers and Air Force officers volunteer their services to any extent that may be needed. The moment the Staff arrangements have been made not a day should be lost.

5. It is not possible for the Turkish Army fully to equip itself with all the technical weapons should the emergency arise in the early summer of this year. The British could make available certain special units which are already fully trained, which do not involve the movement of great masses of men across the communications, but which are essential to the holding of the airfields and also the repulse of tank attacks. To this end we will hold ready at convenient places, with such American assistance as we may need and can obtain, as many regiments of anti-tank artillery as can be conveniently received, including some of our very latest 17-pounders, which have never yet been in action. We will also have ready a number of regiments of anti-aircraft artillery to reinforce the forces which will already have been moved into position. We will also prepare to move two battle-experienced armoured divisions in at the earliest moment. In

addition to this, there will be the Ninth and Tenth Armies. We are drawing somewhat upon the Tenth Army for future operations in the Central Mediterranean, but the Polish Corps, which is three-quarters equipped and is of very high-class personnel, would be available unless the Russian Caucasian front should break and the Germans be found advancing towards Persia. This is not at all likely. Besides this, the Ninth Army in Syria is being built up to perhaps five divisions. It is felt however that the movement of these masses might congest the communications and that it is far better in the first instance to push the specialised units through with the maximum celerity. . . .

6. I will now tell you about the Casablanca Conference and the great concentration of forces we have decided to make in the Central Mediterranean. Naturally, we cannot give details about the exact plans and dates, but our intention is to destroy Italy ; shatter her entirely ; beat her out of the war, both by terrific bombing from Tunis and from Great Britain and by heavy attacks over the sea, for which great preparations are required and are being made. The breaking down of Italy would lead to contact with the Western Balkans and with the highly hopeful resistance maintained both by General Michailovitch in Serbia and the Partisans in Croatia and Slovenia. According to our expectations and reasonable hopes, we shall drive the enemy from the coasts of Africa into the sea before the summer, and perhaps much earlier. In that event the summer months will see in the Mediterranean the largest operations it is in the power of Great Britain and the United States to conduct. These operations, and above all the Italian attitude, will cause the very greatest agitation throughout the Balkans. The further advance of the Russian armies cannot be excluded. Operations across the black Sea must be considered a possibility, with their superior fleet. It is therefore in the summer that we must consider the crisis temperature will rise very high and the need for Turkey to be secure will be paramount.

7. I know that Premier Stalin is most anxious to see Turkey well armed and ready to defend herself against aggression. I know it is President Roosevelt's wish, as it is certainly that of His Majesty's Government, that Turkey should be a full partner in the Peace Conference, where all questions of changes in the existing *status quo* will have to be settled. It is not possible to say when this world war will end. We British and Americans are quite sure that we shall win. That is why the President has called the Casablanca Conference the 'Unconditional Surrender Conference'. It must be remembered that

we were peaceful nations who had made very little preparation for the war. But we are now becoming warlike nations, with far greater resources of men and munitions than the Germans, Japanese, and Italians can produce. We are absolutely resolved to go on to the end and make a good job of it this time. You probably know as well as we, and perhaps even better, what is the interior state of Germany. We are not counting on an early or sudden collapse, but of course no one can be sure that it will not come suddenly, as it did last time. We must be ready, both for the worst and for the best.

8. I have not been in Turkey since 1909, when I met many of the brave men who laid the foundations of the modern Turkey. There is a long story of the friendly relations between Great Britain and Turkey. Across it is a terrible slash of the last war, when German intrigues and British and Turkish mistakes led to our being on opposite sides. We fought as brave and honourable opponents. But those days are done, and we and our American Allies are prepared to make vigorous exertions in order that we shall all be together and continue together to move forward into a world arrangement in which peaceful peoples will have a right to be left alone and in which all peoples will have a chance to help one another.

This document I handed to the Turkish President at the first meeting in his train on the late afternoon of our arrival.

*   *   *

The general discussion which followed turned largely on to two questions, the structure of the post-war world, and the arrangements for an international organisation, and the future relations of Turkey and Russia. I give only a few examples of the remarks which, according to the record, I made to the Turkish leaders. I said that I had seen Molotov and Stalin, and my impression was that both desired a peaceful and friendly association with the United Kingdom and the United States. In the economic sphere both Western Powers had much to give to Russia, and they could help in the reparation of Russia's losses. I could not see twenty years ahead, but we had nevertheless made a treaty for twenty years. I thought Russia would concentrate on reconstruction for the next ten years. There would probably be changes: Communism had already been modified. I thought we should live in good relations with Russia, and if Great Britain and the United States acted together and maintained a strong air Force they should be able to ensure a period of stability. Russia might even gain by this. She possessed vast undeveloped areas—for instance, in Siberia.

The Turkish Prime Minister observed that I had expressed the view that Russia might become imperialistic. This made it necessary for Turkey to be very prudent. I replied that there would be an international organisation to secure peace and security, which would be stronger than the League of Nations. I added that I was not afraid of Communism. Mr Saracoglu remarked that he was looking for something more real. All Europe was full of Slavs and Communists. All the defeated countries would become Bolshevik and Slav if Germany was beaten. I replied that things did not always turn out as bad as was expected; but if they did so it was better that Turkey should be strong and closely associated with the United Kingdom and the United States. If Russia, without any cause, were to attack Turkey the whole international organisation of which I had spoken would be applied on behalf of Turkey, and the guarantees after the present war would be much more severe, not only where Turkey was concerned, but in the case of all Europe. I would not be a friend of Russia if she imitated Germany. If she did so we should arrange the best possible combination against her, and I would not hesitate to say so to Stalin. Molotov had asked for a treaty by which the Baltic States would be regarded as Russian provinces. We had refused to agree to this, (a) because territorial rearrangements were to be postponed for settlement after the war, and (b) because we felt it necessary to make a reservation for free determination for individuals.

*   *   *

Early the following morning I lay in bed in my saloon on the train composing, in the light of the general discussion which had taken place, a note on my views on post-war security. I called this paper 'Morning Thoughts'. One paragraph is possibly worthy of preservation in the light of subsequent events:

It is the intention of the Chiefs of the United Nations to create a world organisation for the preservation of peace, based upon conceptions of freedom and justice and the revival of prosperity. As a part of this organisation an instrument of European government will be established which will embody the spirit but not be subject to the weaknesses of the former League of Nations. The units forming this body will not only be the great nations of Europe and Asia Minor as long established, but a number of confederations formed among the smaller States, among which a Scandinavian Bloc, a Danubian Bloc, and a Balkan Bloc appear to be obvious. A similar instrument will be formed in the Far East, with different membership, and the whole will be held together by the fact that the victorious Powers intend to continue fully armed, especially in the air, while imposing complete disarmament upon the guilty. No one can predict with certainty that the victors will never quarrel among themselves, or that the United States may not at once again retire from Europe, but after the experiences which all have gone through, and their sufferings, and the certainty that a third struggle will destroy all that is left of the culture, wealth, and civilisation of mankind and reduce us to the level almost of wild beasts, the most intense effort will be made by the leading Powers to prolong their honourable association, and by sacrifice and self-restraint win for themselves a glorious name in human annals. Great Britain will certainly do her utmost to organise a coalition resistance to any act of aggression committed by any Power, and it is believed that the United States will co-operate with her, and even possibly take the lead of the world, on account of her numbers and strength, in the good work of preventing such tendencies to aggression before they break into open war.

*   *   *

During these general political discussions military conversations were conducted by the C.I.G.S. and our other high commanders. The two main points to be considered were the provision of equipment for the Turkish forces, prior and subsequent to any political move by Turkey, and the preparation of plans for the reinforcement of the Turkish forces by British units in the event of their coming into the war. The result of these talks were embodied in a military agreement.

*   *   *

We must now revert to the tremendous drama unfolding around Stalingrad. As has been described, Paulus's Sixth German Army had been caught by the Russian pincers and encircled as the result of the November conflict. Manstein's supreme effort from the south-west in December to break through the Russian cordon and relieve the beleaguered garrison had failed. He pierced the Russian line to a depth of forty miles, but there he was stopped, still fifty miles from Stalingrad. A new Russian offensive from the north threatened his flank and forced him into a retreat which spread to all the German southern front, including the Caucasus, and ended only when it was back behind Rostov-on-the-Don.

There was now no hope of further succour for Paulus. Great efforts were made to supply him from the air, but little got through, and at the expense of heavy losses in aircraft. The cold was intense ; food and ammunition were scarce, and an outbreak of typhus added to the miseries of his men. On January 8 he rejected an ultimatum to surrender, and next day the last phase began with violent Russian attacks from the west. The Germans fought strongly, so that only five miles were gained in as many days. But at last they began to crack, and by January 17 the Russians were within ten miles of Stalingrad itself. Paulus threw into the fight every man who could bear arms, but it was no use. On January 22 the Russians surged forward again, until the Germans were thrown back on the outskirts of the city they had tried in vain to take. Here the remains of a once-great army were pinned in an oblong only four miles deep by eight long. Under intense artillery fire and air bombardment the survivors defended themselves in violent street-fighting, but their plight was hopeless, and as the Russians pressed forward exhausted units began to surrender wholesale. Paulus and his staff were captured on January 31, and on February 2 Marshal Voronov reported that all resistance had ceased and that ninety thousand prisoners had been taken. These were the survivors of twenty-one German and one Roumanian divisions.

This crushing disaster to the German arms ended Hitler's prodigious effort to conquer Russia by force of arms, and destroy Communism by an equally odious form of totalitarian tyranny.

*　　　*　　　*

I kept Stalin informed of the conversations at Adana.

Prime Minister to Premier Stalin　　　　　　2 Feb 42
Thank you for your telegram about Turkey. I met all the chief Turks at Adana on the 30th, and had long and most friendly talks. There is no doubt they have come a long way towards us both, and also that their news from Germany

convinces them of a bad condition there. The first thing is to equip them with modern weapons, of which we have so far been able to spare only a few. I have arranged to press forward everything they can take over the Taurus railway, which is the only road, and also to lend them some ships to carry more supplies from Egypt. I am also giving them some German material which we have captured in the Desert. We are setting up at Angora a Joint Anglo-Turkish Military Commission to improve communications for the transit of munitions. We are making joint plans to aid them if they are attacked by Germany or Bulgaria.

2. I have not asked for any precise political engagement or promise about entering the war on our side, but it is my opinion that they will do so before the year is out, and that possibly earlier, by a strained interpretation of neutrality similar to that of the United States before she came in, they may allow us to use their airfields for refuelling for British and American bombing attacks on the Ploesti oil-wells, which are of vital importance to Germany, especially now that your armies have recovered Maikop. I repeat, I have not asked for or received a definite political engagement, and have told them they are free to say so. Nevertheless, their meeting me, their whole attitude, and the joint communiqué, which I am telegraphing you, ranged them more plainly than before in the anti-Hitler system, and will be so taken all over the world.

3. They are of course apprehensive of their position after the war in view of the great strength of the Soviet Republic. I told them that in my experience the U.S.S.R. had never broken an engagement or treaty, that the time for them to make a good arrangement was now, and that the safest place for Turkey was to have a seat with the victors, as a belligerent, at the peace table. All this I said in our common interest in accordance with our alliance, and I hope you will approve. They would, I am sure, be very responsive to any gesture of friendship on the part of the U.S.S.R. I should be very glad to have your candid opinion on all this. I have established very close personal relations with them, particularly with President Inönü.

4. In your recent telegram which you sent to President Roosevelt you asked about the slowing down of the Allied operations in North Africa. So far as the British Eighth Army is concerned, we have since then taken Tripoli, and hope shortly to enter Tunisia in force and drive the enemy from the Mareth and Gabes positions. The clearing and restoring of the harbour at Tripoli is proceeding with all speed,

---

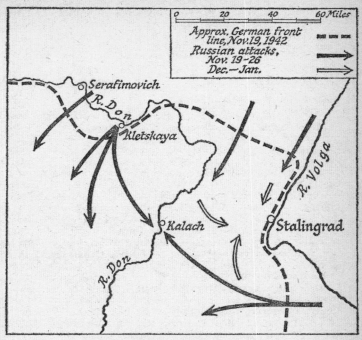

Russian Counter-attacks at Stalingrad

but at present our line of communications runs to Benghazi, and part even to Cairo, 1,500 miles away. Our First Army, reinforced by strong American forces, is bringing its supplies forward, and will attack in conjunction with the Eighth Army as soon as possible. The wet weather is a serious factor, as are also the communications, which, both by road and rail, are slender and 500 miles long. However, it is my hope that the enemy will be completely destroyed or driven from the African shore by the end of April, and perhaps earlier. My own estimate, which is based on good information, is that the Fifth Panzer Army in Tunisia has a ration strength of 80,000 Germans, and with them 25,000 to 30,000 Italians. Rommel has 150,000 Germans and Italians on his ration strength, of which perhaps 40,000 only are fighting troops and weak in weapons. The destruction of these forces is our immediate aim.

5. I will reply later to your most proper inquiries of me and the President about the concrete operations settled at Casablanca.

6. Pray accept my congratulations on the surrender of Field-Marshal Paulus and the end of the German Sixth Army. This is indeed a wonderful achievement.

Victory did not make the Soviet more genial. On February 6 I received a somewhat cool reply.

Premier Stalin to Premier Churchill　　　　　　　　6 Feb 43
Many thanks for information on your talks with the leading Turkish personalities in Adana.

2. In connection with your suggestion that the Turks would reciprocate any friendly gesture from the Soviet Union, I would like to mention that we have already made a number of statements, the friendly character of which is well known to the British Government, some months before the Soviet–German war, as well as after its beginning. However, the Turks did not react to our steps. Apparently they were afraid to incur the wrath of the Germans. I am afraid that a similar reception will be accorded to the gesture suggested by you.

3. The international position of Turkey remains very delicate. On the one hand Turkey has the treaty of neutrality and friendship with the U.S.S.R. and the treaty of mutual assistance against aggression with Great Britain ; on the other hand she has the treaty of friendship with Germany, signed three days before the German attack against the U.S.S.R. It is not clear to me how in the present circumstances Turkey thinks to combine her obligations *vis-à-vis* the U.S.S.R. and Great Britain with her obligations *vis-à-vis* Germany. Still, if Turkey wishes to make her relations with the U.S.S.R. more friendly and intimate let her say so. In this case the Soviet Union would be willing to meet Turkey half-way.

4. Of course I have no objection to your making a statement that I was kept informed on the Anglo-Turkish meeting, although I cannot say that the information was very full.

5. I wish the First and Eighth British Armies, as well as the American troops in North Africa, every success in the coming offensive, and a speedy expulsion of the German–Italian forces from African soil.

6. Let me thank you for your friendly congratulations on the surrender of Field-Marshal Paulus and on the successful annihilation of the encircled enemy troops near Stalingrad.

It was not till March 2 that I received another message from Stalin on Soviet-Turkish relations. Some progress had been made.

On my part I would like to convey to you that on February 13 the Turkish Foreign Minister told the Soviet Ambassador at Angora that the Turkish government would wish to start negotiations with the Soviet Government for the improvement of Soviet-Turkish relations. The Soviet Government replied through their Ambassador at Angora that it welcomes this desire of the Turkish Government, and expressed willingness to commence such negotiations. We expect at present the return of the Turkish Ambassador from Angora. It is contemplated to open negotiations thereafter.

*   *   *

My parleys with Turkey were intended to prepare the way for her entry into the war in the autumn of 1943. That this did not take place after the collapse of Italy and with the further Russian advances against Germany north of the Black Sea was due to unfortunate events in the Ægean later in the year, which will be described in some detail later on.

Of course, when you win everything looks all right, but at this time many long and terrible struggles lay ahead, and I am sure that had I been allowed to carry out my theme, the plain purpose of which was clearly set forth, I could have had Turkey in the war on our side before the end of 1943, without damage to our main plans, and with all kinds of advantages to the Allies, and especially for Turkey. Now in these years after the war, when we see the United States sustaining Turkey with her whole power, all has been put right, except that we did not have the considerable advantages of Turkish aid and all that this implied in the Balkan situation in the early months of 1944.

CHAPTER 17

Home to Trouble

After the failure to conquer Tunis in December the force of our initial blow in North-West Africa was spent, and the German High Command was able temporarily to restore stability in Tunisia. Refusing to recognise that he could not safeguard by sea or air even the short passage between Sicily and Tunis, Hitler ordered the creation of a new army in Tunisia to meet the impending Allied attacks from both east and west. Rommel's battered Afrika Korps was left to continue its retreat under the hard pressure of the Eighth Army.

In the Central Mediterranean Malta had been re-victualled and rearmed and had again sprung into full activity. From our new bases in Algeria and Cyrenaica our naval and air forces ranged widely, protecting Allied shipping and taking heavy toll of enemy supplies and reinforcements. Besides blockading Tunis, where German air forces were still strong, we reached out to the ports on the Italian mainland. Palermo, Naples and Spezia all felt the lash as our strength mounted, and R.A.F. bombers from home took over the attack on Northern Italy. The Italian Fleet made no attempt to interfere. Apart from the presence of the British Fleet, the lack of oil was serious. There were days when there was not one ton of fuel in all Sicily for the escort vessels covering supplies to Tunis.

On land General Eisenhower had seen that his forces in North-West Africa must be given a pause in which to reorganise and build their strength. In the north the ground won by the British 78th and 6th Armoured Divisions had to be consolidated. Farther south the long, tenuous front, held lightly by the French XIXth Corps in the centre and part of the United States IInd Corps on the right, offered the enemy a tempting chance to break through and turn the whole Allied line. Allied units were much intermingled, and the problem was complicated by General Giraud's refusal to allow French troops to be placed under British command. A sharp attack on the French XIXth Corps in mid-January led to the detachment of yet more British and American units to support them, and it became necessary for Eisenhower to issue an order, accepted by Giraud, putting the whole front under the orders of General Anderson, commander of the British First Army.

*   *   *

During January the Eighth Army made good progress in its advance. At the beginning of the month it was halted in front of the enemy position at Buerat. General Montgomery felt it necessary to delay his attack until he was reasonably assured that he could exploit it rapidly. The Army was supplied from Benghazi, Tobruk, and at the earliest moment from Tripoli. On January 15 Montgomery attacked with the 51st Division along the coastal road and the 22nd Armoured Brigade in the centre, while the 7th Armoured and 2nd New Zealand Divisions turned the Desert Flank. Tripoli was taken punctually on January 23. The port was found severely damaged. The entrance had been completely blocked by sunken ships, and the approaches lavishly sown with mines. This had been foreseen, and the first supply ship entered the harbour on February 2. A week later 2,000 tons a day were being handled. Although the Eighth Army had still great distances to travel, its maintenance during the fifteen-hundred-mile advance from Alamein, crowned by the rapid opening up of Tripoli, was an administrative feat for which credit lay with General Lindsell in Cairo and General Robertson with the Eighth Army. At the end of the month the Eighth Army was joined by General Leclerc, who had led a mixed force of Free French about 2,500 strong fifteen hundred miles across the desert from French Equatorial Africa. Leclerc placed himself unreservedly under Montgomery's orders. He and his troops were to play a valuable part in the rest of the Tunisian campaign.

The Eighth Army crossed the frontier into Tunisia on February 4, thus completing the conquest of the Italian Empire by Great Britain. In accordance with the decisions taken at the Casablanca Conference, this Army now came under General Eisenhower, with General Alexander as his deputy in executive command of land operations.

*　　*　　*

I flew back from Adana to Cyprus, where I spent two nights, and inspected for the second time in the war the 4th Hussars, of whom I am Colonel. The last occasion had been a month before Alamein. Everything in Cyprus seemed blooming, and the people as friendly and enthusiastic as I have seen them anywhere. They were all feeling much safer than they had been in 1941, and both the Turkish and Greek elements in the island were very thankful that the Allies were winning and not at all inclined to object to British rule. I made some agreeable contacts with the population, and addressed all the notables in the garden of the Governor's palace. This was my third visit to the island—the first in 1907, as Under-Secretary for the Colonies in Campbell-Bannerman's Government, the second on a cruise in Walter Moyne's yacht in 1936, and now this third visit in 1943. All the time I had followed attentively their affairs and I am glad to have played a part in abolishing the tribute which Treasury rigour had imposed on the island so wrongfully.

We had another two nights in Cairo, and then flew to Tripoli, where Montgomery, a victor at the end of his historic march, awaited me at the airfield. The enemy had been pushed forty or fifty miles west of the city. I spent two days in Tripoli, and witnessed the magnificent entry of the Eighth Army through its stately streets. At their head were the pipers of the 51st Highland Division. Spick and span they looked after all their marching and fighting. In the afternoon I inspected massed parades of two divisions. I stayed in Montgomery's caravan, which I had not slept in since our meeting before Alamein. I addressed about two thousand officers and men of his headquarters. I spoke to them about

> Yet nightly pitch our moving tent
> A day's march nearer home.

But they were still a long way from home; nor was the route to be direct.

I had planned to fly to Malta, and in consequence of the directions I had given at Cairo all had been set in readiness by Montgomery. As the flight was considered dangerous, on account of the presence of the enemy, I was to go in a small two-seater plane with an escort of half a dozen Spitfires. However, when I expressed my pleasure and surprise at these excellent arrangements having been made by Montgomery he realised that he had taken what was only my wish as an order. He then began to make objections about the danger of the flight, and finally I deferred to his advice. I am sorry for this, as I should have liked to have a memory of Malta while it was still in its struggle.

The reader may remember that on leaving Cairo six months earlier I had given General Alexander the following directive:

Prime Minister to General Alexander, Commander-
in-Chief in the Middle East   10 Aug 42
  Your prime and main duty will be to take or destroy at the earliest opportunity the German–Italian army commanded by Field-Marshal Rommel, together with all its supplies and establishments in Egypt and Libya.
  2. You will discharge or cause to be discharged such other duties as pertain to your command, without prejudice to the task described in paragraph 1, which must be considered paramount in His Majesty's interests.*

He now sent me the following reply:

General Alexander to Prime Minister
Sir,
  The orders you gave me on August [10], 1942, have been fulfilled. His Majesty's enemies, together with their impedimenta, have been completely eliminated from Egypt, Cyrenaica, Libya, and Tripolitania. I now await your further instructions.†

After these two long and vivid days I set off with my party from Tripoli to visit Eisenhower and all the others at Algiers.

Prime Minister to General Eisenhower (Africa)   3 Feb 43
  According to my present plans, I should arrive on the 5th. I hope that it will be agreeable to you if I lunch with you in a small circle. I hope to see Giraud and Murphy, and of course

* See facsimile, p. 286–7.
† See facsimile, p. 289

Macmillan. I do not wish General Anderson to be brought back from the front unless you consider it absolutely convenient and desirable. I plan to leave for Gibraltar after early luncheon. I am looking forward very much to seeing you. Please tell only Admiral Cunningham.

At Algiers the tension was acute. The murder of Darlan still imposed many precautions on all prominent figures. The Cabinet continued to show concern about my safety, and evidently wanted me home as soon as possible. This at least was complimentary. On the other hand, I soon saw that I should have to stay longer in Algiers.

Prime Minister to Deputy Prime Minister   5 Feb 43
We are here in the Admiral's villa, which is next door to General Eisenhower's. Both are surrounded by barbed wire and heavily guarded and patrolled. We came here by circuitous route in bullet-proof car. I do not propose leaving precincts. No one considers in these circumstances there is any danger provided precautions are taken.

I am planning flying direct from here to England as soon as thoroughly satisfactory weather conditions are established. I should be glad of a day's rest however, after a very strenuous week. Yesterday I reviewed over 40,000 of our troops in Tripoli. The Italians were second to none in their enthusiasm.

Please do not worry about my personal safety, as I take the utmost care of myself and am very quick to see where danger lies. I hope to take my questions in the House on Tuesday. I must ask a few days' grace on my return before making a statement, which I expect to do on Thursday.

The day was a full one. I had long talks with Eisenhower, and learned from him and from the Admiral much that could not have been put in telegrams. The villas were but a hundred yards apart. At luncheon both de Gaulle and Giraud were present. There was so much to settle that I could not leave till late on Saturday. Eisenhower and I dined together at the Admiral's villa in a small, pleasant circle. On February 6 I met Noguès and Peyrouton. Both these Frenchmen were in positions of authority and of extreme difficulty. In spite of his actions at the American landing Noguès was still Governor-General of Morocco. Peyrouton had just arrived on American invitation from the Argentine, where he had been the Vichy Ambassador, to take up the Governor-Generalship of Algeria. I told them that if they marched with us we would not concern ourselves with past differences. They were dignified, but anxious.

Before midnight I left for the airfield. We all took our places in the plane and waited for it to start; but it would not start. One of my assistant secretaries was of very small stature, and I could not help remarking, 'Your light weight is a great advantage in flying, but if we come down in the desert you will not keep us going very long.' At last I got impatient and decided to drive back to the Admiral's comfortable villa. My physician, Sir Charles Wilson, had already gone to sleep. He did not hear us leave, and was locked up for the night in the plane. He was only liberated at daybreak. It was necessary to spend another day at Algiers. There was no lack of business. To the Foreign Secretary I cabled:

> We were delayed in starting last night for two and a half hours by a magneto failure, and as this would have meant the approach to England in broad daylight probably without escort we all thought it better to wait another twenty-four hours. It was obliging of the magneto to cut out before we started and not later on.

At last, on Sunday night, the 7th, we took off, and this time flew directly and safely home. This was my last flight in 'Commando', which later perished with all hands, though with a different pilot and crew.

*　　*　　*

My first task on getting home was to make a full statement to the House of Commons on the Casablanca Conference, my tour of the Mediterranean, and on the general position. As I wished to announce on this occasion the important military appointments which had been agreed between us, I cabled to the President as follows:

8 Feb 43

> I propose to give the House of Commons some account of our joint affairs on Thursday, 11th, at noon.
> I have received from General Alexander a message saying that the directive I gave him on August 10 has been fully accomplished, as the enemy have been driven out of Egypt, Cyrenaica, and Tripolitania. Moreover, the advance forces of the Desert Army are already advancing into Tunisia. This therefore is the moment when the Eighth Army should come under the command of General Eisenhower. I propose to

announce this, as it should certainly come from this end. I therefore propose to you that Alexander's and Tedder's appointments should be released to synchronise with my statement in Parliament. I hope that no advance information about the Eighth Army will get out before I tell Parliament.

I have just returned from Algiers, where I had very satisfactory talks with Eisenhower, Smith, Giraud, Murphy, and others. I have been travelling almost continuously since I saw you last, and will send you a further report in a few days.

Every good wish to you, Harry, and all friends.

The President replied at once.

President Roosevelt to Prime Minister   9 Feb 43

I agree to your announcing on February 11 the placing of your Eighth Army under the command of General Eisenhower and the appointment of Alexander as Deputy under Eisenhower, and also the appointment of Tedder. It is my opinion that co-operation by French forces will be best if the American Supreme Command in North Africa is stressed, and I consider it inadvisable to release and thereby make available to the enemy any information whatever as to the details of the duties of Alexander or Tedder. I am so glad you are safely back. You have accomplished marvels.

I thought it well that the President should take the rough with the smooth about British public opinion.

Former Naval Person to President Roosevelt   10 Feb 43

I will act in the way you wish, but I cannot guarantee that there will be no criticism. I have received the attached note from Brendan Bracken [Minister of Information], who is in close touch with the British and American Press here.

'I am having quite a lot of trouble in persuading some of the newspapers not to criticise the American handling of the North African campaign. If General Eisenhower's appointment as Supreme Commander is stressed and General Alexander's and Air Chief Marshal Tedder's respective functions are left vaguely undefined, I think we must expect a spate of criticism from the British Press. In this respect I have no doubt that the Press would be reflecting the general feeling in the country, and there would be far too many people who would honestly feel that British commanders and troops have been unfairly ignored for the sake of some move in international politics.

'The British Government is accustomed to criticism and is not likely to be unduly ruffled. But the Americans will very much resent the almost inevitable resulting criticism of

General Eisenhower's appointment or any comparison between his military qualifications and those possessed by General Alexander. I think it is important therefore that the public should be told that General Eisenhower is Generalissimo, that Alexander is commanding the forces of the United Nations fighting in Tunis, and that Tedder is commanding the Air Forces.'

I shall utter the most solemn warning against controversy in these matters, and every effort will be made by Bracken behind the scenes. Please do the like on your side to help your faithful partner. The Russian successes seem to me to be opening altogether a new situation. My hearty congratulations on Guadalcanal.*

*   *   *

It took me more than two hours on February 11 to make my speech. I thought I had a good tale to tell. The high spot was of course my directive to General Alexander of August 1942, and the reply which had reached me at Montgomery's headquarters in Tripoli on February 2, 1943. I proceeded to outline the general situation in French North-West Africa, and made the announcements I had settled with the President about commands and the appointment of General Eisenhower as Supreme Commander.

*   *   *

There were so many complicated questions open that I thought it would be well for the Foreign Secretary to visit Washington for the first time during the war and establish intimate personal relations with the President, and also get into close touch with Mr. Hull and the State Department. The President welcomed the idea, and I prepared myself to take over the Foreign Office in Mr. Eden's absence.

President to Prime Minister   12 Feb 43
    That is an excellent thought about Anthony Eden. Delighted to have him. The sooner the better. Your speech was grand, and will do lots of good everywhere.

*   *   *

I was more tired by my journeying than I had realised at the time, and I must have caught a chill. A few days later a cold and sore throat obliged me to lie up. In the evening of the 16th,

* The conquest of Guadalcanal was completed on February 9. Events there will be described in the next Book.

when I was alone with Mrs. Churchill, my temperature suddenly rose, and Lord Moran, who had been watching me, took a decided view and told me that I had inflammation of the base of a lung. His diagnosis led him to prescribe the drug called M and B. The next day elaborate photographs were taken and confirmed the diagnosis, and Dr. Geoffrey Marshall of Guy's Hospital was called in consultation. All my work had come to me hour by hour at the Annexe, and I had maintained my usual output though feeling far from well. But now I became aware of a marked reduction in the number of papers which reached me. When I protested the doctors, supported by my wife, argued that I ought to quit my work entirely. I would not agree to this. What should I have done all day? They then said I had pneumonia, to which I replied, 'Well, surely you can deal with that. Don't you believe in your new drug?' Doctor Marshall said he called pneumonia 'the old man's friend'. 'Why?' I asked. 'Because it takes them off so quietly.' I made a suitable reply, but we reached an agreement on the following lines. I was only to have the most important and interesting papers sent me, and to read a novel. I chose *Moll Flanders*, about which I had heard excellent accounts, but had not found time to test them. On this basis I passed the next week in fever and discomfort, and I sometimes felt very ill. There is a blank in my flow of minutes from the 19th to the 25th.

The Speaker, Captain Fitzroy, had been taken ill on almost the same day as me. He too developed pneumonia, and at first we interchanged inquiries. I was not reassured by the replies I got. The Speaker was five years older than I, and his case was serious.

* * *

For me the days passed very slowly, but not without some enlivening diversions. A gentleman, Mr. Thompson, kindly presented me with a lion, who sent me a beautiful photograph of himself, with good wishes for my recovery. 'Rota' was the lion's name, and I had to invoke the aid of the Duke of Devonshire, who had been Mr. Thompson's intermediary, to provide him with a home. He was a male lion of fine quality, and in eight years became the father of many children. The assistant secretary who had been with me in the airplane came with some papers. He was a charming man, highly competent, but physically on the small side. Indulging in chaff, I now showed him a magnificent photograph of Rota with his mouth open, saying, 'If there are any shortcomings in your work I shall send you to him. Meat is very short now.' He took a serious view of this remark. He reported to the office that I was in a delirium.

To the Duke I wrote:

> I shall have much pleasure in becoming the possessor of the lion, on condition that I do not have to feed it or take care of it, and that the Zoo makes sure that it does not get loose.
>
> You are quite right in your assumption that I do not want the lion at the moment either at Downing Street or at Chequers, owing to the Ministerial calm which prevails there. But the Zoo is not far away, and situations may arise in which I shall have great need of it.
>
> I hope to come to see the lion some time when the weather is better, also my black swans.
>
> I consider you personally bound to receive the lion at Chatsworth should all else fail.

* * *

Soon the President, General Smuts, and other friends who had heard about my illness sent repeated telegrams urging me to obey the doctor's orders, and I kept faithfully to my agreement. When I finished *Moll Flanders* I gave it to Doctor Marshall to cheer him up. The treatment was successful.

About this time also there arrived from the President a portrait of an American general named Sylvester Churchill, who had died in 1862 and was undoubtedly a direct descendant of the Dorsetshire Churchills. His pedigree was attached to the photograph. The President thought we looked very much alike.

THE WHITE HOUSE
WASHINGTON
March 2, 1943

Dear Winston,

When you and the family have a spare minute give this a glance. It needs no reply. I do think, however, that Mrs. Harrison is right in regard to a certain resemblance. She is the wife of our Minister to Switzerland.

As ever yours,
FRANKLIN D. ROOSEVELT

Enclosure   27 Feb 43

Dear Mr. President,

I am sending you a photograph of a portrait which I have

BRITISH EMBASSY,
CAIRO.

Most Secret

Direction to General Alexander

Commander in Chief in the Middle East

1. Y[our] prime & main duty will be to take or destroy at the earliest opportunity the German & Italian Army commanded by Field Marshal Rommel together with all its supplies & establishments in Egypt & Libya.

2. You will discharge or cause to be discharged such other duties as pertain to yr command as without prejudice to the task described in paragraph 1, do not be considered paramount in this Majesty's interests.

W.S.C.
10. Aug. 42.

10 8 42

Facsimile of Mr. Churchill's Directive to General Alexander.

of our great-great-grandfather, General Sylvester Churchill.*
   So many people who see it in my house, without knowing his name, exclaim, 'Why, there is Winston Churchill!' and I reply, 'He was a Churchill, an *American one*!' They are very interested. Thinking you might be so too, Mr. President, I had the portrait photographed, and here it is.

I replied:

Prime Minister to President   19 Mar 43
   Thank you so much for your letter of March 2. I have shown the photograph and Mrs. Harrison's letter to Mrs. Churchill, and we are both much interested in them. Would you please thank Mrs. Harrison so much for letting us see the photograph?

---

* GENERAL SYLVESTER CHURCHILL
Born Woodstock, Vermont, 1783
Died Washington, D.C., 1862

   General Churchill was a Captain of Infantry in the War of 1812, a Colonel in the Mexican War in 1846, and was credited with having won the Battle of Buena Vista, in which, assuming command, he 'saved the whole army from disaster and won the victory'. For this he was promoted to Brigadier-General by brevet. Until 1856 he was Inspector-General of the Army, and travelled over 10,000 miles a year inspecting frontier posts. He was retired in 1856, and died in Washington in 1862.

CHURCHILLS of
   Dorsetshire
      |
JOHN CHURCHILL,
   London.
   (Merchant,
   supplying
   Geo. Endicott of
   the Mass. Bay
   Colony.)

      |
      |_____

                        JOHN CHURCHILL
                        Born England. Emigrated to
                        Plymouth, Mass., in 1643. Died 1662.

                        JOSEPH CHURCHILL
                        Born Plymouth, Mass., 1647.

                        BARNABAS CHURCHILL
                        Born Plymouth, Mass., 1686.

                        JOSEPH CHURCHILL
                        Born Plymouth, Mass., 1721.

                        JOSEPH CHURCHILL
                        Born Plymouth, Mass, 1748.

                        SYLVESTER CHURCHILL
                        Born Woodstock, Vermont, 1783.
                        Died Washington, D.C., 1862.

MESSAGE INSTRUCTIONS — OUT

GROUPS THIS LINE IS FOR SIGNALS USE ONLY

TO Prime Minister

FROM Gen. Alexander

	Originator's Number	Date	In Reply to Number
			AUG 15th

Sir, the orders you gave me on AUG 15th 1942 have been fulfilled @ His Majesty's enemies together with their impedimenta have been completely eliminated from EGYPT, CYRENAICA, LIBYA and TRIPOLITANIA @ I now await your further instructions

19 55 M/c

Facsimile of General Alexander's Reply

Several good judges think there is a singular resemblance.

* * *

Although the speed of the advance from the east had surpassed expectations, the Allied situation in mid-February was anxious. The severe losses inflicted by sea and air had not prevented the enemy from building up a force of fourteen divisions, including those of Rommel's army. Most of the Germans came in by air. Four divisions, three German and one Italian, were armoured. The Allies had only nine divisions available for operations, of which two of the French XIXth Corps were ill-equipped. The U.S. IInd Corps was still incomplete; of its four divisions only the 1st Infantry and 1st Armoured Division were on the front. The northern sector, from the sea to Bou Arada, was held by the British Vth Corps, of three divisions. On their right was the French XIXth Corps, composed of one French division, the 1st U.S. Infantry Division, and two British brigades. This corps held the passes of the mountainous ridge overlooking the coastal plain. Farther south the line was continued by the U.S. IInd Corps, comprising the U.S. 1st Armoured Division and a French division, with another U.S. infantry division assembling. These also were spread to hold the passes on their front, with the important exception of the Faid Pass, which the Germans had captured on January 30.

Rommel, promoted to command all the Axis troops in Tunisia, concentrated a striking force of two German armoured divisions east of Faid in order to throw back the U.S. IInd Corps and prevent them from coming down on his flank and rear while he was engaged against the Eighth Army. The attack began on February 14. It had been mistakenly expected that the main blow would come through Fondouk and not Faid. Consequently the 1st U.S. Armoured Division, under General Anderson's orders, was much dispersed; only half of it was south of Fondouk to take the shock. It was overborne and there was much confusion. On the 17th Kasserine, Feriana, and Sbeitla were in German hands.

Rommel now had a choice: he could advance through the Kasserine pass on Tebessa, a main centre of communications, with the important airfield of Youks-les-Bains behind it, or strike northwards. He struck northwards. He was met and held by the 1st Guards Brigade and a detachment of the U.S. 9th Division which Anderson had hastened there. On the Thala road the 21st Panzer Division, which led the attack, encountered our 26th Armoured Brigade and two British battalions, together with American infantry and artillery. A fierce fight ensued, but by noon on the 22nd Rommel began a general withdrawal in good order. Kasserine and Feriana were reoccupied by our forces on February 27, and Sbeitla on the 28th. Later our original line was re-established.

But Rommel had not yet finished his aggressive attempts to retain at least a foothold in Tunisia. On February 26 he began a series of strong attacks on the front of the British Vth Corps. South of Medjez the enemy were repulsed without significant gains; to the north they won several miles, leaving the town itself in an awkward salient. Near the coast our troops were forced back twenty miles to Djebel Abiod, but at this point they held firm.

* * *

I now received a letter from the King, who followed the course of the war with the closest attention, and was not without anxiety on some aspects of it.

BUCKINGHAM PALACE
February 22, 1943

My dear Winston,

I am very sorry to hear that you are ill, and I hope that you will soon be well again. But do please take this opportunity for a rest, and I trust you will not forget that you have earned one after your last tour, and you must get back your strength for the strenuous coming months. I missed being able to have a talk to you last Tuesday, and I understand we may not meet next Tuesday either, so I am writing to you instead.

I do not feel at all happy about the present political situation in North Africa. I know we had to leave the political side of 'Torch' to the Americans, while we were able to keep Spain and Portugal friendly during the time the operation was going on. I know we had to tread warily at the start, but is there nothing we can do now to strengthen Macmillan's and Alexander's hands in both the political and military sphere, to make the two French sides come together?

Now I hear that from the American point of view the date of 'Husky' will have to be postponed to the later one, whereas we can plan for the earlier one, which will be an aggravation of our difficulties in preparing the operation.

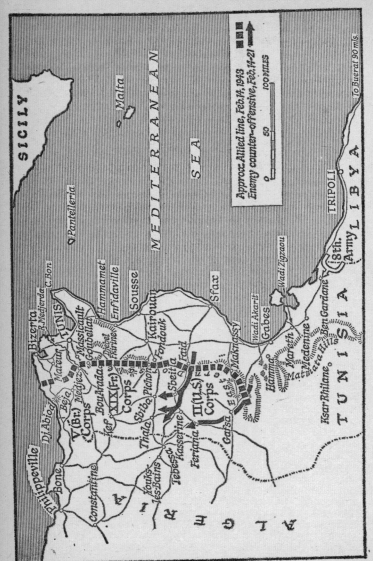

Tunisia.

This fact will throw out all our careful calculations for convoys and escorts, and will upset our import programme again. I should not think of bothering you with these questions at this moment, but I do feel worried about them, and I would like an assurance from you that they are being carefully watched.

I cannot discuss these vital matters with anyone but yourself.

Believe me,

Yours very sincerely,

GEORGE R.I.

I replied forthwith, and once I began dictating it seemed easy to cover the ground.

February 22, 1943

Sir,

It is very good of Your Majesty to write with your own hand to me.

I do not feel seriously disturbed by the course of events in North Africa, either political or even military, although naturally there is much about both aspects which I would rather have different.

I have been reading all the key telegrams with attention up till two days ago, when I must admit I have fallen a little behind. I am sure that Murphy's aim is to uphold Giraud and to procure a quiet, tranquil government for the sixteen million people living in French North Africa. In this way alone would he gain any credit. It is quite true that we have for this purpose and to safeguard our vital communications to work with a mass of French officials who were appointed by Vichy; but without them I really do not know how the country could be governed. Even in Syria we have done this to some extent. I do not myself see any danger of these officials changing their sides or obstructing our operations. Their own bread-and-butter depends upon their good behaviour, and possibly their lives as well.

The irruption of de Gaulle or his agents into this field, especially if forcibly introduced by us, would cause nothing but trouble. It is entirely his fault that a good arrangement was not made between the two French factions. The roughness with which he refused the President's invitation (and mine) to come and make a friendly settlement at Casablanca has put him and his French National Committee practically out of court with the Americans.

As I told Your Majesty the last time we met, I tried all I could to bring the operation 'Husky' forward to June. In this

I was splendidly seconded by the Chiefs of Staff and all concerned. General Eisenhower however expressed a decided opinion that a June operation would be 'unlikely to succeed', and was for July at the earliest. Our Chiefs of Staff therefore sent their paper to the Combined Chiefs of Staff in Washington, and I also telegraphed to Hopkins asking him to put this through, with the result that, according to my latest information, the Combined Chiefs of Staff—who are the supreme and official body through which command is exercised—have ordered General Eisenhower to prepare for the June operation with the utmost zeal, and to report to them by April 10 what progress has been made. Thus you see the American Chiefs of Staff took the same view as ours did, and, if I may say so, as I did. That is how the matter stands now.

As to the battle, I suspend judgment till we hear from Alexander. The IInd American Army Corps sustained a heavy defeat, and apparently was deprived of about half of its important weapons without inflicting any serious loss upon the enemy. However, we have about six of our finest infantry brigade groups and the 6th Armoured Division as well as a brigade of heavy Churchill tanks there. More are on the way. The supplies have come in better. Already the 1st Guards Brigade have come into action at Sbeitla, and have made the enemy feel that they have come up against bone.

In order to make this new offensive, not foreseen in their original plan, the enemy have stripped the Mareth Line pretty thin. Montgomery, who has the whole picture before him, and who has been receiving splendid daily deliveries in Tripoli harbour as well as from Benghazi, sometimes reaching a total of 6,000 tons from the two ports together, will soon be able to bring up the Xth Corps, whose transport he has had to use to maintain himself so far, and to build up reserves. I look forward to both the Xth and XXXth Corps being in action in Tunisia by the middle of March, or it may be earlier. Nevertheless, matters may not wait so long, because if Montgomery feels the enemy is wilting on his front he will certainly use his strength against them.

I suppose Your Majesty realises that these two corps of the Eighth Army, comprising together about 160,000 men, are perhaps the best troops in the world. Therefore I look confidently forward to their entry into action. Moreover, we have General Alexander under Eisenhower to concert and combine the entire movements. It may well be that the enemy is wasting strength on a false assumption and will give Montgomery an earlier chance.

I need scarcely say that no word of mine is intended in disparagement of the Americans. They are brave but not seasoned troops, who will not hesitate to learn from defeat, and who will improve themselves by suffering until all their strongest martial qualities have come to the front. What a providential thing it was that I perpetually pressed for General Eisenhower to take the command, as the defeat of the American corps, if it had been under a British general, would have given our enemies in the United States a good chance to blaspheme.

Generally I feel we may await with reasonable confidence the development of the situation in North Africa, and I look forward to an improvement before long.

Although I have been hampered by fever from reading all the telegrams, I think I have the picture truly in my mind, and I wish indeed that I could have given this account to Your Majesty verbally at luncheon. I send this instead.

With my humble duty,
WINSTON S. CHURCHILL

*   *   *

The Tripoli tonnage rate mounted magnificently. I telegraphed to the Port Commandant on the 24th: 'Tell them from me they are unloading history.'

From what I read in the boxes, which kept a steady though diminished flow, I formed an unfavourable picture of the manner in which the British First Army had been handled in the severe battle which had developed in Tunisia.

Prime Minister to General Alexander   24 Feb 43

About Christmas-time all ideas of offensive were given up in the First Army, and for the last two months every effort has been made to push supplies forward and bring up reinforcements. It is quite true the French falling out of the line was a complication, but the Americans came in in large force. However, these same Americans came under Anderson's command, and were spread about by him or someone over a large, loosely held line in bits and pieces as you yourself describe. It might have been wise to withdraw the line in the south to the hills, but neither a vigorous front was made nor a prudent withdrawal. Before the attack took place our Intelligence gave ample warning. Even then a withdrawal would have been very sensible. Nobody cared about these places, whose names had never been heard of till they were lost. A kind of false-front manœuvre might have been very clever, but there was none of this, with the result that the

American IInd Army Corps was left to be mauled, and took it very badly under the attack of the 150 enemy tanks set against them.

2. The situation has now been restored, but the past must be searchingly reviewed. I am relying upon you and your judgment, feeling sure that you will not shield incompetence or inadequacy.

3. I am so glad to read that the much-abused Churchills acquitted themselves well. Of course my main idea in them was armour, and I believe they can take a lot of punishment. Any information you can send or have sent by one of your officers would interest me.

4. I have been free of the fever for a few hours to-day, and I hope this is the beginning of recovery from a very disagreeable experience. Every good wish to you. I am sure you have in your hands now all the threads necessary to bring about a very fine event before the middle of April. How glad I am you are there! The unloadings at Tripoli are splendid. Please keep me informed.

To Mr. Harry Hopkins   24 Feb 43
Have had a bad time, and might easily have been worse. Am feeling definitely better now. I think the Tunis battle is good, and going to be better ; and our men, British and American, are fighting like brothers, mingled together and side by side. A reward lies ahead of them all. Tripoli unloaded 6,300 tons yesterday. Montgomery is sharpening his claws.

Thank you so much for helping to get the target date [for Sicily] settled for June. None of this recent fighting should affect it, though some will try to say so.

My warmest regards to the President.

To General Eisenhower (Algiers)   25 Feb 43
Thank you so much for your kind message. I was sure the Kasserine battle would turn out all right in the end.

It was now the President's turn to be laid up.

Former Naval Person to President   27 Feb 43
I do hope you are all right and that the fever will soon go. I have got rid of mine, which was heavy and long, I hope for good. Every good wish.

*   *   *

While I was myself hard-pressed I had to think deeply about the health of another invalid whose bulletins filled the papers. Several hundred Indian Congress members had been arrested and interned by the Viceroy, with the full authority of the War Cabinet, given during my absence in Cairo. Early in February Mr. Gandhi announced he would fast for three weeks. He was in detention under the most favourable conditions in a small palace at Poona, watched with ceaseless vigilance both by British and his own Indian doctors. He continued obdurately to fast, and most active world-wide propaganda was set on foot that his death was approaching. Nearly all the Indian members of the Viceroy's Executive Council demanded his release, and resigned in protest at our refusal. In the end, being quite convinced of our obduracy, he abandoned his fast, and his health, though he was very weak, was not seriously affected.

I kept the President fully informed throughout and no pressure was put upon us from the United States. The incident was one which at the time caused me much anxiety, because Mr. Gandhi's death would have produced a profound impression throughout India, where his saintly qualities commanded intense admiration. We however had judged the situation rightly.

*　　*　　*

Stalin at this time sent me a film of the Stalingrad victory, with all its desperate fighting wonderfully portrayed, and with the final surrender of Field-Marshal Paulus and his appearance before the Soviet court-martial. The Russian Government treated this important German war chief with the greatest consideration, and he has been in their service ever since. A less agreeable fate awaited the endless lines of German prisoners, whom the film shows marching wearily forward over the limitless wastes of snow.

I had a cinema installed near my bedroom, and was able to go from my bed to see it about February 24. It was a production of the highest merit, and well commemorates this glorious episode in the struggle on the Eastern Front. I was able in return to send to Stalin, to the President, and to the Dominion Governments our own film, just completed, of the Battle of Alamein, called *Desert Victory*. These photographs, like the Russian, were all taken by the operators under heavy fire and with some loss of life. The sacrifice was not made in vain, for the fruits of their work excited the greatest admiration and enthusiasm throughout the Allied world and brought us all closer together in our common task.

To the President, who was still ailing, I wrote:

I hope you will accept the accompanying copy of the new film *Desert Victory*, which I saw last night and thought very good. It gives a vivid and realistic picture of the battles, and I know that you will be interested in the photographs of the Sherman tanks in action. I am having the film sent to you by air so that you may see it as soon as possible.

I was so sorry to see that you have been ill, and I hope that you have fully recovered. I am feeling very much better, and hope soon to return to full work.

With kindest regards, and all best wishes to Mrs. Roosevelt, Harry, and yourself. . . .

The President replied:

Dear Winston,   17 *March*, 1943

That new film *Desert Victory* is about the best thing that has been done about the war on either side. Everyone here is enthusiastic. I gave a special showing for the White House staff, and to-night the Interior Department employees are having a special showing, because everybody in town is talking about it ; and I understand that within ten days it will be in the picture houses. Great good will be done.

I think I picked up sleeping sickness or Gambia fever or some kindred bug in that hell-hole of yours called Bathurst. It laid me low—four days in bed—then a lot of sulpha-thiazole, which cured the fever and left me feeling like a wet rag. I was no good after 2 p.m., and after standing it for a week or so I went to Hyde Park for five days ; got full of health in glorious zero weather—came back here last week, and have been feeling like a fighting cock ever since.

Anthony has spent three evenings with me. He is a grand fellow, and we are talking everything, from Ruthenia to the production of peanuts!

It is an interesting fact that we seem to agree on about 95 per cent. of all the subjects—not a bad average.

He seems to think that you will manage rather well with the Leadership in the House of Commons—but both of us are concerned over what you will do with the Foreign Office! We fear that he will not recognise it when he gets back.

Please, please, for the sake of the world, don't overdo these days. You must remember that it takes a month of occasional let-ups to get back your full strength.

Harry is in grand form and all goes well here.

Tell Mrs. Churchill that when I was laid up I was a thoroughly model patient, and that I hope you will live down the reputation in our Press of having been the 'world's worst patient'.

God bless you.

CHAPTER 18

Russia and the Western Allies

The Russian Victories – Anglo-American Efforts – Stalin's Complaints, Feburary 16 – The President's Reply to Stalin, March 5 – My Telegram to Stalin, March 11 – Full Account of Our Resources and Dispositions – Further Correspondence with Stalin – The Position of Finland – Stalin's Telegram of March 15 – My Reply of March 20 – Mr. Eden's Conversations with the President in Washington – Our Efforts to Maintain the Arctic Convoys – A More Agreeable Note in My Correspondence with Stalin – He Begins to Appreciate Importance of Our Tunis Operations – Katyn: the Fate of the Polish Officers – The Camps near Smolensk – A Sinister Silence – M. Maisky Visits Me – Breach of Polish and Soviet Relations – The Nuremberg Omission.

The spring of 1943 marked the turning-point of the war on the Eastern Front. Even before the German Army at Stalingrad had been overwhelmed the mounting Russian tide had swept the enemy back all along the line. The German army of the Caucasus was skilfully withdrawn, half of it to Rostov ; the rest formed strong bridgeheads at Novorossisk and in the Kuban peninsula. The Russians pressed the enemy from the Don and back beyond the Donetz river, the starting line of Hitler's offensive of the previous summer. Farther north again the Germans lost ground, until they were more than two hundred and fifty miles from Moscow. The investment of Leningrad was broken. The Germans and their satellites suffered immense losses in men and material. The ground gained in the past year was taken from them. They were no longer superior to the Russians on land. In the air they had now to reckon with the growing power of the British and American Air Forces, operating both from Britain and in Africa.

If Stalin could have come to Casablanca the three Allies might have worked out a common plan face to face. But this could not be, and discussions were pursued by telegram. On January 26 we had told him of the military decision taken at our conference.

President Roosevelt and Prime Minister to Premier Stalin   26 Jan 43

We have been in conference with our military advisers, and have decided on the operations which are to be undertaken by American and British forces in the first nine months of 1943. We wish to inform you of our intentions at once. We believe that these operations, together with your powerful offensive, may well bring Germany to her knees in 1943. Every effort must be made to accomplish this purpose.

2. We are in no doubt that our correct strategy is to concentrate on the defeat of Germany, with a view to achieving an early and decisive victory in the European theatre. At the same time we must maintain sufficient pressure on Japan to retain the initiative in the Pacific and Far East, sustain China, and prevent the Japanese from extending their aggression to other theatres, such as your maritime provinces.

3. Our main desire has been to divert strong German land and air forces from the Russian front and to send to Russia the maximum flow of supplies. We shall spare no exertion to send you material assistance by every available route.

4. Our immediate intention is to clear the Axis out of North Africa and set up naval and air installations

    (i) to open an effective passage through the Mediterranean for military traffic, and

    (ii) to maintain an intensive bombardment of important Axis targets in Southern Europe.

5. We have made the decision to launch large-scale amphibious operations in the Mediterranean at the earliest possible moment. Preparation for these is now under way, and will involve a considerable concentration of forces, including landing-craft and shipping in Egyptian and North Africa ports.

In addition, we shall concentrate in the United Kingdom a strong American land and air force. These, combined with the British forces in the United Kingdom, will prepare themselves to re-enter the continent of Europe as soon as practicable. All this will certainly be known to our enemies, but they will not know where or when, or on what scale, we propose striking. They will therefore be compelled to divert both land and air forces to all the shores of France, the Low Countries, Corsica, Sardinia, Sicily, the heel of Italy, Yugoslavia, Greece, Crete, and the Dodecanese.

6. In Europe we shall increase the Allied bomber offensive from the United Kingdom against Germany at a rapid rate, and by midsummer it should be more than double its present strength. Our experiences to date have shown that the day bombing attacks result in destruction and damage to

The Front in Russia, April 1942–March 1943

large numbers of German fighter aircraft. We believe an increased tempo and weight of daylight and night attacks will lead to greatly increased material and moral damage in Germany and rapidly deplete German fighter strength. As you are aware, we are already containing more than half the German Air Force in Western Europe and the Mediterranean. We have no doubt our intensified and diversified bombing offensive, together with the other operations which we are undertaking, will compel further withdrawals of German air and other forces from the Russian front.

7. In the Pacific it is our intention to eject the Japanese

from Rabaul within the next few months, and thereafter to exploit the success in the general direction of Japan. We also intend to increase the scale of our operations in Burma in order to reopen our channel of supply to China. We intend to increase our Air Force in China at once. We shall not however allow our offensives against Japan to jeopardise our capacity to take advantage of every opportunity that may present itself for the decisive defeat of Germany in 1943.

8. Our ruling purpose is to bring to bear upon Germany and Italy the maximum forces by land, sea, and air which can be physically applied.

And further on my return home, with the President's authority, I sent the following additional explanation:

9 Feb 43

(*a*) There are a quarter of a million Germans and Italians in Eastern Tunisia. We hope to destroy or expel these during April, if not earlier.

(*b*) When this is accomplished we intend in July, or earlier if possible, to seize Sicily, with the object of clearing the Mediterranean, promoting an Italian collapse, with the consequent effect on Greece and Yugoslavia, and wearing down the German Air Force. This is to be closely followed by an operation in the Eastern Mediterranean, probably against the Dodecanese.

(*c*) These operations will involve all the shipping and landing-craft we can get together in the Mediterranean, and all the troops we can have trained in assault-landing, and will be of the order of 300,000 or 400,000 men. We shall press any advantage to the utmost once ports of entry and landing bases have been established.

(*d*) We are also pushing preparations to the limit of our resources for a cross-Channel operation in August, in which both British and United States would participate. Here again shipping and assault landing-craft will be limiting factors. If the operation is delayed by weather or other reasons it will be prepared with stronger forces for September. The timing of this attack must of course be dependent upon the condition of German defensive possibilities across the Channel at that time.

(*e*) Both the operations will be supported by very large United States and British air forces, and that across the Channel by the whole Metropolitan Air Force of Great Britain. Together these operations will strain to the very utmost the shipping resources of Great Britain and the United States.

(*f*) The President and I have enjoined upon our Combined Chiefs of Staff the need for the utmost speed and for reinforcing the attacks to the extreme limit that is humanly and physically possible.

And a few days later:

Prime Minister to Premier Stalin   14 Feb 43
   The series of prodigious victories which to-night brings us the news of the liberation of Rostov-on-the-Don, leaves me without power to express to you the admiration and the gratitude which we feel to the Russian arms. My most earnest wish is to do more to aid you.

He replied promptly.

Premier Stalin to Premier Churchill   16 Feb 43
   I received your message concerning the contemplated Anglo-American military operations on February 12. Many thanks for your additional information on the Casablanca decisions. I cannot refrain however from making certain observations on your message, which, as you state, represents also the view-point of the President.
   2. It is evident from your message that, contrary to your previous calculations, the end of operations in Tunis is expected in April instead of February. I hardly need to tell you how disappointing is such a delay. Strong activity of the Anglo-American troops in North Africa is more than ever necessary at this moment, when the Soviet armies are still in a position to maintain their powerful general offensive. With simultaneous pressure on Hitler from our front and from your side we could achieve great results. Such a situation would create serious difficulties for Hitler and Mussolini. In this way the intended operations in Sicily and the Eastern Mediterranean could be expedited.
   3. It is evident from your message also that the establishment of the Second Front, in particular in France, is envisaged only in August-September. It seems to me that the present situation demands the greatest possible speeding up of the action contemplated—*i.e.*, of the opening of the Second Front in the West at a considerably earlier date than indicated. In order not to give the enemy any respite it is extremely important to deliver the blow from the West in the spring or in the early summer and not to postpone it until the second half of the year.
   4. We have reliable information to the effect that since the end of December, when the Anglo-American operations in Tunis for some reason were slowed down, the Germans

transferred twenty-seven divisions, including five Panzer divisions, from France, Belgium, Holland, and Germany herself to the Soviet-German front. Thus instead of helping the Soviet Union by diversion of the German forces from the Soviet-German front the position of Hitler was alleviated. It is just because the military operations in Tunis slackened that Hitler was able to throw in some additional troops against the Russians.

5. All this brings us to the conclusion that the sooner we jointly take advantage of Hitler's difficulties at the front the more reasons we shall have to expect his early defeat. Unless we take all this into consideration, unless we use the present moment to our common interest, it may happen that the Germans, after having a respite, which will enable them to re-muster their forces, may once more recover their strength. It is clear to every one of us how undesirable it would be to allow this to occur.

I deemed it necessary to send this reply also to Mr. Roosevelt.

Many thanks for your very warm congratulations on the liberation of Rostov. Our troops to-day captured Kharkov.

This message reached me during my illness:

Prime Minister to Premier Stalin   24 Feb 1943
I much regret I have not been able to answer your last telegram to me. I had the answer all in draft, but my fever got so high that I thought it better to leave it for a while. In a few days I hope to send you more information on the whole scene. Meanwhile what you are doing is simply indescribable. The battle in Tunisia is all right. The enemy have shot their bolt and will now be brought into the grip of the vice. Every good wish.

The President sent me on March 5 a copy of his own reply to Stalin.

I have received your message of February 16, in which you present certain considerations that you have communicated to Mr. Churchill in reply to his message to you of February 9.

I regret equally with you that the Allied effort in North Africa did not proceed in accordance with the schedule, which was interrupted by unexpected heavy rains that made the roads extremely difficult for both troops and supplies *en route* from our landing ports to the front lines, and made the fields and mountains impassable.

I realise fully the adverse effect of this delay on the common Allied effort, and I am taking every possible step to begin

at the earliest possible moment successful aggressive action
against the Axis forces in Africa with the purpose of accomplishing their destruction.

You are fully informed in regard to the wide dispersion
of American transportation facilities at the present time,
and I can assure you that we are making a maximum effort
to increase the output of ships to improve our transportation.

I understand the importance of a military effort on the
continent of Europe at the earliest practicable date in order
to reduce Axis resistance to your heroic army, and you
may be sure that the American war effort will be projected
on to the continent of Europe at as early a date, subsequent to success in North Africa, as transportation facilities
can be provided by our maximum effort.

We hope that the success of your heroic army, which is an
inspiration to all of us, will continue.

I thought it right to present our whole case in my own words.

Prime Minister to Premier Stalin   11 Mar 43
Mr. Roosevelt has sent me a copy of his reply to your full
message of February 16. I am now well enough to reply myself.

2. Our first task is to clear the Axis out of North Africa by
an operation the code-name of which is 'Vulcan'. We hope
this will be accomplished towards the end of April, by which
time about a quarter of a million Axis troops will be engaged
by us. . . .

5. The Anglo-American attempt to get Tunis and Bizerta
at a run was abandoned in December because of the strength
of the enemy, the impending rainy season, the already sodden
character of the ground, and the fact that the communications stretched 500 miles from Algiers and 160 miles from
Bone through bad roads and a week of travelling over single-
track French railways. It was only possible to get supplies
up to the Army by sea on a small scale owing to the strength
of the enemy air and submarine attack. Thus it was not possible to accumulate the petrol or other supplies in the forward
areas. Indeed, it was only just possible to nourish the troops
already there. The same was true of the air, and improvised
airfields became quagmires. When we stopped attacking there
were about 40,000 Germans in Tunisia, apart from Italians
and from Rommel, who was still in Tripoli. The German
force in North Tunisia is now more than double that figure,
and they are rushing over every man they can in transport
aircraft and destroyers. Some sharp local reverses were

suffered towards the end of last month, but the position
has now been restored. We hope that the delays caused by
this setback will be repaired by the earlier advance of Montgomery's army, which should have six divisions (say 200,000
men) operating from Tripoli, with sufficient supplies, against
the Mareth position before the end of March. Already on
March 6 Montgomery's army repulsed Rommel's forestalling attack with heavy losses. The British and American
army in the northern sector of Tunisia will act in combination
with Montgomery's battle.

6. I thought that you would like to know these details of
the story, although it is on a small scale compared with the
tremendous operations over which you are presiding.

7. The British Staffs estimate that about half the number
of divisions which were sent to the Soviet-German front from
France and the Low Countries since last November have already been replaced mainly by divisions from Russia and
Germany and partly by new divisions formed in France.
They estimate that at the present time there are thirty German divisions in France and the Low Countries.

8. I am anxious that you should know, for your own most
secret information, exactly what our military resources are
for an attack upon Europe across the Mediterranean or the
Channel. By far the larger part of the British Army is in
North Africa, in the Middle East, and in India, and there is
no physical possibility of moving it back by sea to the
British islands. By the end of April we shall have about
200,000 men in Northern Tunisia, in addition to General
Montgomery's army of some six divisions, and we are bringing two specially trained British divisions from Persia and
sending one from this country to reinforce them for the attack
on Sicily, a total of fourteen. We have four mobile British
divisions, the two Polish divisions, one Free French division,
and one Greek division in the Middle East. There is the equivalent of four static divisions in Gibraltar, Malta, and Cyprus.
Apart from garrison and frontier troops, there are ten or
twelve divisions formed and forming in India for reconquering Burma after the monsoon and reopening contact with
China (Operation 'Anakim'). Thus we have under the British
command, spread across a distance of some 6,300 miles from
Gibraltar to Calcutta, thirty-eight divisions, including strong
armour and powerful proportionate air forces. For all these
forces active and definite tasks are assigned for 1943.

9. The gross strength of a British division, including corps,
army, and line of communication troops, may be estimated
at about 40,000 men. There remain in the United Kingdom
about nineteen formed divisions, four Home Defence divi-

sions, and four drafting divisions, of which sixteen are being prepared for a cross-Channel operation in August. You must remember that our total population is forty-six millions, and that the first charge upon it is the Royal Navy and Mercantile Marine, without which we could not live. Thereafter come our very large Air Force, about twelve hundred thousand strong, and the needs of munitions, agriculture, and air-raid defence. Thus the entire manhood and womanhood of the country is and has been for some time fully absorbed.

10. The United States had the idea in July last to send twenty-seven divisions, of a gross strength each of between forty and fifty thousand men, to the United Kingdom for the invasion of France. Since then they have sent seven divisions to the operation 'Torch', and three more are to go. In this country there is now only one, in addition to a strong Air Force. This is no disparagement of the American effort. The reason why these performances have fallen so far short of the expectations of last year is not that the troops do not exist but that the shipping at our disposal and the means of escorting it do not exist. There is in fact no prospect whatever of bringing anything more than I have mentioned into the United Kingdom in the period concerned. . . .

After a paragraph describing the bombing offensive against Germany I ended:

12. With regard to the attack across the Channel, it is the earnest wish of the President and myself that our troops should be in the general battle in Europe which you are fighting with such astounding prowess. But in order to sustain the operations in North Africa, the Pacific, and India, and to carry supplies to Russia, the import programme into the United Kingdom has been cut to the bone and we have eaten, and are eating, into reserves. However, in case the enemy should weaken sufficiently we are preparing to strike earlier than August, and plans are kept alive from week to week. If he does not weaken a premature attack with inferior and insufficient forces would merely lead to a bloody repulse, Nazi vengeance on the local population if they rose, and a great triumph for the enemy. The Channel situation can only be judged nearer the time, and in making this declaration of our intentions there for your own personal information I must not be understood to limit our freedom of decision.

* * *

It was clear that the most effective aid which we could offer the Russians was the speedy clearing of the Axis forces from

North Africa and the stepping up of the air war against Germany. Stalin of course repeated his demands for a Second Front.

Premier Stalin to Premier Churchill   15 Mar 43

It is evident that the Anglo-American operations in North Africa have not only not been expedited, but on the contrary they have been postponed till the end of April. Even this date is not quite definite. Thus at the height of our fighting against the Hitler forces—*i.e.*, in February–March—the weight of the Anglo-American offensive in North Africa has not only not increased, but there has been no development of the offensive at all, and the time-limit for the operations set by yourself was extended. Meanwhile Germany succeeded in transferring thirty-six divisions (including six armoured divisions) from the West against the Soviet troops. It is easy to see what difficulties this created for the Soviet armies and how the position of the Germans on the Soviet-German front was alleviated.

Fully realising the importance of Sicily, I must however point out that it cannot replace the Second Front in France. Still, I welcome by all means the contemplated acceleration of this operation.

Now as before I see the main task in hastening of the Second Front in France. As you remember, you admitted the possibility of such a front already in 1942, and in any case not later than the spring of 1943. There were serious reasons for such an admission. Naturally enough I underlined in my previous message the necessity of the blow from the West not later than the spring or the early summer of this year.

The Soviet troops spent the whole winter in the tense fighting, which continues even now. Hitler is carrying out important measures with a view to replenish and increase his army for the spring and summer operations against the U.S.S.R. In these circumstances it is for us extremely important that the blow from the West should not be put off, that it should be struck in the spring or in the early summer.

I studied your observations, contained in the paragraphs 8, 9, and 10, on the difficulties of the Anglo-American operations in Europe. I recognise these difficulties. Notwithstanding all that, I deem it my duty to warn you in the strongest possible manner how dangerous would be from the view-point of our common cause further delay in the opening of the Second Front in France. This is the reason why the uncertainty of your statements concerning the contemplated Anglo-

American offensive across the Channel arouses grave anxiety in me, about which I feel I cannot be silent.

*   *   *

At this time the Russian Government, doubtless as a result of their successful spring offensive against the Germans, had been sounding both the British and American Foreign Offices upon the post-war arrangements on Russia's western frontier. American opinion was sensitive to any suggestion of recognising the Russian position in the Baltic States, and the cause of Finland had considerable support in Washington. The Russians had refused an American offer of mediation between Finland and the Soviet Union with the object of drawing the Finns out of the war.

Premier Stalin to Premier Churchill   15 Mar 43

On March 12 the American Ambassador, Admiral Standley, on behalf of the U.S.A. Government, conveyed to Mr. Molotov the following message:

'The Government of the U.S.A. offers its good offices as intermediary between the U.S.S.R. and Finland in order to explore the possibility of a separate peace.'

On Mr. Molotov's question whether the American Government has information that Finland desires peace and what is her real position, Admiral Standley replied that he cannot say anything on the matter. As is well known, the Anglo-Soviet Treaty of May 26, 1942, stipulates that our countries cannot negotiate on the conclusion of a separate peace with Germany or her Allies otherwise than by mutual agreement. I consider this as a fundamental and unalterable principle. In view of this I felt it is my duty first to inform you about the American proposal and second to ask your opinion on the matter.

I have no reasons to believe that Finland really desires peace, that she has decided already to part with Germany and to offer acceptable conditions. It seems to me that Finland has not yet escaped from Hitler's claws, if she has this intention at all. The present Finnish Government, which concluded a peace treaty with the Soviet Union and then violated it and attacked the Soviet Union in alliance with Germany, is hardly able to break with Hitler.

Notwithstanding all that, in view of the proposal made by the Government of the U.S.A., I deemed it my duty to inform you of the above.

To this I sent the following answer:

Prime Minister to Premier Stalin   20 Mar 43
  You can best judge of how much military value it would
be in the struggle against the Germans on your front to get
Finland out of the war. I should suppose that it would have
the effect of releasing more Soviet divisions than German
divisions for use elsewhere. Further, the defection of Finland
from the Axis might have considerable effect on Hitler's other
satellites. . . .
  Generally speaking, I should have thought that the Finns
would be anxious to withdraw from the war as soon as they
are convinced that Germany must be defeated. If so, it seems
to me that it might not be altogether premature for you to ask
the United States Government whether they know or could
find out, without disclosing your interest, what terms the
Finns would be prepared to accept. But you will be the best
judge of the right tactics.

                    *   *   *

Our plans for Sicily strained our shipping resources to the
point where it might be necessary to postpone the convoys to
Russia. We consulted the Americans on this through Mr. Eden
who was still in Washington.

Mr. Eden to Prime Minister   19 Mar 43
  I saw the President this morning and gave him your message about Russian convoys. He agrees that in the light of
enemy dispositions it is right to postpone the March convoy. He was doubtful however whether it would be wise now
to decide on no further convoy until after Sicily. He felt that
this would be a severe additional blow to Stalin, and that if
the enemy concentrations were to disperse, for whatever
reason, within the next few weeks, we might still be in a position to run a convoy. He will however think the whole matter
over further and send you a personal message very shortly.
  The President has had a message from Stalin similar to
your rough one. This he had apparently anticipated.

This came the next day:

President Roosevelt to Former Naval Person   20 Mar 43
  In the face of known German naval and Air Force concentration on route of March convoy there appears to be no
military justification for its departure at scheduled time. . . .
In another three or four weeks it may of course be necessary
to break the news to Stalin that convoys to Russia must be
interrupted until August or September in order to provide for
the Sicily effort, but it seems to me now that a delay in giving

him the bad news would be the wiser course. Incidentally, none of us can be positive about the situation four or five months hence.

*   *   *

A more agreeable note now crept into my correspondence with Stalin.

Premier Stalin to Premier Churchill   27 Mar 43
I received your message on the main battle in Tunis. I wish British and American troops full and speedy success. I hope that you will be able now to break and defeat the enemy and completely drive him out of Tunis.
I hope also that the air offensive against Germany will go on inexorably increasing. I will be very grateful if you will send me your photographs of the destructions in Essen.

Premier Stalin to Premier Churchill   29 Mar 43
I congratulate the British Air Force on the new big and successful bombing of Berlin.
I hope that the British armoured units will be able to use to the full the improvement in the Tunis situation and not give any respite to the enemy.
Yesterday, together with my colleagues, I have seen the film *Desert Victory*, which you have sent me. It makes a very strong impression. The film depicts magnificently how Britain is fighting, and stigmatises those scoundrels (there are such people also in our country) who are asserting that Britain is not fighting at all, but is merely an onlooker. Impatiently I will wait a similar film on your victory in Tunis.
The film *Desert Victory* will be widely shown in all our armies at the front and among the widest masses of our population.

I thought this was the moment to tell him the bad news about the convoys.

Prime Minister to Premier Stalin   30 Mar 43
The Germans have concentrated at Narvik a powerful battle fleet consisting of *Tirpitz, Scharnhorst, Lützow,* one 6-inch cruiser, and eight destroyers. Thus danger to Russian convoys which I described in my message to you of July 17 last year has been revived in even more menacing form. I told you then that we did not think it right to risk our Home Fleet in the Barents Sea, where it could be brought under attack of German shore-based aircraft and U-boats without adequate protection against either, and I explained that

if one or two or our most modern battleships were to be lost or even seriously damaged while *Tirpitz* and other large units of the German battle fleet remained in action the whole command of the Atlantic would be jeopardised, with dire consequences to our common cause.

2. President Roosevelt and I have therefore decided with the greatest reluctance that it is impossible to provide adequate protection for the next Russian convoy, and that without such protection there is not the slightest chance of any of the ships reaching you in the face of the known German preparations for their destruction. Orders have therefore been issued that the sailing of the March convoy is to be postponed.

3. It is a great disappointment to President Roosevelt and myself that it should be necessary to postpone this convoy. Had it not been for German concentration it had been our firm intention to send you a convoy of thirty ships in March and again early in May. At the same time we feel it only right to let you know at once that it will not be possible to continue convoys by the Northern route after early May, since from that time onward every single escort vessel will be required to support our offensive operations in the Mediterranean, leaving only a minimum to safeguard our life-line in the Atlantic. In the latter we have had grievous and almost unprecedented losses during the last three weeks. Assuming Sicily goes well, we should hope to resume the convoys in early September, provided that the disposition of German main units permits and that the situation in the North Atlantic is such as to enable us to provide the necessary escorts and covering force.

4. We are doing our utmost to increase the flow of supplies by the Southern route. The monthly figure has been more than doubled in the last six months. We have reason to hope that the increase will progress and that figures for August will reach 240,000 tons. If this is achieved the monthly delivery will have increased eightfold in twelve months. Furthermore, the United States will materially increase shipments via Vladivostok. This will in some way offset both your disappointment and ours at the interruption to the Northern convoys.

Premier Stalin to Prime Minister   2 Apr 43
I received your message of March 30 conveying to me that necessity compels you and Mr. Roosevelt to stop convoys to the U.S.S.R. till September.

I understand this unexpected action as a catastrophic diminution of supplies of arms and military raw materials to the U.S.S.R. on the part of Great Britain and the United States of America, as transport via Pacific is limited by the tonnage and not reliable and the Southern route has a small transit capacity. In view of this both just mentioned routes cannot compensate for the discontinuation of transport via the Northern route.

You realise of course that the circumstances cannot fail to affect the position of the Soviet troops.

Prime Minister to Premier Stalin   6 Apr 43
I acknowledge the force of all you say in your telegram about the convoys. I assure you that I shall do my utmost to make any improvement which is possible. I am deeply conscious of the giant burden borne by the Russian armies and their unequalled contribution to the common cause.

2. We sent 348 heavy bombers to Essen on Saturday, casting 900 tons of bombs in order to increase the damage to Krupp's, which was again effectively hit, and to carry ruin into the south-western part of the city, which had previously suffered little. Last night 507 aircraft, all but 166 being heavies, carried 1,400 tons to Kiel. This is one of the heaviest discharges we have ever made. The cloud layers were thicker than we expected, but we hope the attack got home. The American daylight bombing with the Flying Fortresses is becoming more effective. Yesterday they struck at the Renault works near Paris, which had begun to spring to life again. Besides the bombing, which they do from great altitudes with remarkable precision by daylight, they provoke the enemy fighters to attacks in which many are destroyed by the heavy armament of the Flying Fortresses. Four American and about thirty-three British bombers were lost in these three enterprises. I must again emphasise that our bombing of Germany will increase in scale month by month, and that we are able to find the targets with much more certainty.

3. This present week the general battle in Tunisia will begin, and the British Eighth and First Armies and the American and French forces will all engage according to plan. The enemy is preparing to retire into his final bridgehead. He has already begun demolitions and the removal of coastal batteries from Sfax. Under the pressure about to be renewed upon him he seems likely to retire, perhaps rapidly, to a line he is fortifying from Enfidaville, in the Gulf of Hammamet. This new position will run into the main front he now holds in Northern Tunisia, facing west, and which rests its northern flank on the Mediterranean about thirty miles from Bizerta. At this northern flank also we are striking. I shall keep you informed of how we get on, and whether we are able to cut

off any large body of the so-called 'Rommel's Army' before they reach the final bridgehead.

4. Hitler, with his usual obstinacy, is sending the Hermann Goering and the 9th German Divisions into Tunisia, chiefly by air transport, in which at least a hundred large machines are employed. The leading elements of both of these divisions have already arrived. Therefore we must expect a stubborn defence of the Tunisian tip by about a quarter of a million men, less any they lose on the way. Our forces have a good superiority both in numbers and equipment. We are bringing a very heavy constant air attack to bear upon the ports, and we are making every preparation to prevent a Dunkirk escape. This is particularly important in the interests of the Sicilian operation. In about a month after we are masters at Bizerta and Tunis we hope to be able to pass storeships through the Mediterranean, thus shortening the voyage to Egypt and the Persian Gulf.

My full explanations and accounts were not wholly unrewarded. The answer was more friendly than usual.

Premier Stalin to Premier Churchill   12 Apr 43
The speedy development of the Anglo-American advance in Tunis constitutes an important success in the war against Hitler and Mussolini. I wish to kill the enemy and capture as many prisoners and trophies as possible.

We are delighted that you are not giving respite to Hitler. To your strong and successful bombing of the big German cities we add now our air raids on the German industrial centres of East Prussia. Many thanks for the film depicting the results of the bombing of Essen. This film, as well as all the other films which you promise to send, will be widely shown to our Army and population.

The contemplated deliveries of fighters from the cancelled convoys are of great value to us. I am also very grateful for your offer to send us sixty Hurricanes armed with 40-mm cannon. Such planes are very needed, especially against heavy tanks. I hope that your and Mr. Harriman's efforts to secure the dispatch of planes to the U.S.S.R. will be crowned with a speedy success.

Our people highly appreciate the warm feelings and sympathy of the British people which have found expression in the creation of the Aid to Russia Fund mentioned by you.* Please convey to your wife, who is at the head of the fund, my thanks for her untiring activities in this sphere.

*   *   *
* See Book 6, end of Chapter 5.

A breach now occurred between the Soviet Government and the Polish Government in exile in London. After the overrunning of Poland by the German and Russian Armies, following the Ribbentrop-Molotov agreement of September 1939, many thousands of Poles had given themselves up to the Russians, with whom Poland was not at war, and were interned. By further Nazi-Soviet agreements many of these were handed over to the Germans for forced labour purposes. Under the Geneva Convention prisoners of officer status cannot be so treated, and of the 14,500 Poles held by the Soviets in three camps in the Smolensk region 8,000 were officers. A considerable number of these officers were members of the *intelligensia,* including university professors, engineers, and leading citizens who had been mobilised as reservists. Until the spring of 1940 there had been intermittent news of the existence of these prisoners. From April 1940 silence descended upon the three camps. Not a single sign or trace of their occupants ever appeared for thirteen or fourteen months. They were certainly in Soviet power, but no letter, message, escapee, or scrap of information ever came from them.

When Hitler surprised the Russians by his invasion on June 20, 1941, the relations between Russia and Poland changed overnight. They became allies. General Anders and other Polish generals, who had hitherto been confined under rigorous conditions, including beatings, in Russian prisons, were now washed, clothed, released, welcomed, and given high commands in the Polish forces which the Soviets were now raising to fight the German invaders. The Poles, who had long been anxious about the fate of the large group of officers in the three internment camps, asked for their release in order that they might join the new Polish Army, to which they would have been invaluable. About four hundred officers were collected from other parts of Russia, but not one from the three camps now in German throes could ever be found. No explanation could be offered to repeated Polish inquiries by their new comrades-in-arms. Polish leaders, who now had access to many Soviet authorities, with whom they were working and who were helping them form their Army, were conscious on numerous occasions of embarrassment on the part of the Russian officials, but no news of the whereabouts of the 14,500 occupants of the three camps was ever forthcoming, and no survivor ever appeared. This naturally led to suspicion and friction between the Polish and the Soviet Governments.

The war rolled on. The Germans held the territory in which the camp had stood. Nearly another year passed.

Early in April 1943 Sikorski came to luncheon at No. 10. He told me that he had proofs that the Soviet Government had murdered the 15,000 Polish officers and other prisoners in their hands, and that they had been buried in vast graves in the forests, mainly around Katyn. He had a wealth of evidence. I said, 'If they are dead nothing you can do will bring them back.' He said he could not hold his people, and that they had already released all their news to the Press. Without informing the British Government of its intention, the Polish Cabinet in London issued a communiqué on April 17 stating that an approach had been made to the International Red Cross in Switzerland to send a delegation to Katyn to conduct an inquiry on the spot. On April 20 the Polish Ambassador in Russia was instructed by his Government to ask for the comments of the Russians on the German story.

On April 13 the German wireless publicly charged the Soviet Government with the murder of the 14,500 Poles in the three camps, and proposed to hold an international inquiry on the spot into their fate. We cannot wonder that the Polish Government was attracted by this plan, but the International Red Cross announced from Geneva that they could not undertake any inquiry into the German allegations unless a corresponding invitation to do so was received from the Soviet Government. The Germans therefore conducted their own investigations, and a committee of experts, drawn from the countries under German influence, produced a detailed report claiming that upwards of 10,000 bodies had been found in mass graves, and that the evidence of documents found on them and the age of the trees planted over the graves showed that the executions dated back to the spring of 1940, when the area was under Soviet control.

Eventually in September 1943 the region of Katyn was occupied by the Russians. After the recapture of Smolensk a committee composed exclusively of Russians was appointed to inquire into the fate of the Poles at Katyn. Their report, issued in January 1944, claims that the three camps were not evacuated in time, owing to the rapidity of the German advance, and that the Polish prisoners fell into German hands and were later slaughtered by them. This version, to be believed, involves acceptance of the fact that nearly 15,000 Polish officers and men of whom there was no record since the spring of 1940 passed into German hands in July 1941 and were later destroyed by the Germans without one single person escaping and reporting, either to the Russian authorities or to a Polish Consul in Russia or to the Underground Movement in Poland. When we remember the confusion caused by the German advance, that the guards of the camps must have fled as the invasion came nearer, and all the contacts afterwards during the period of Russo-Polish co-operation, belief seems an act of faith.

* * *

I made one of my rare visits to Chartwell to spend the night at my cottage. The telephone announced that the Soviet Ambassador must see me at once and was on his way. Maisky arrived in unusual perturbation. He brought me a message from Stalin that after the hideous charges which the Polish Government in London had published and sponsored against Russia of the wholesale murder of the Polish officer prisoners the agreement of 1941 would be immediately denounced. I said I thought the Poles had been unwise to make or lend themselves to such accounts, but that I earnestly hoped a blunder of this kind would not entail a breach in their relations with the Soviets. I drafted a telegram to Stalin in this sense. M. Maisky proceeded to argue the falsity of the accusation, and gave various reasons to prove the physical impossibility of the crime having been committed by Russia. I had heard a lot about it from various sources, but I did not attempt to discuss the facts. 'We have got to beat Hitler,' I said, 'and this is no time for quarrels and charges.' But nothing I could say or do prevented the rupture between the Russian and Polish Governments. Many inconveniences resulted from this. Anyhow, we had got a lot of the Polish fighting men and many of their women and children out of Russia. This beneficial process still went on fitfully, and I continued the formation and equipment in Persia of three Polish divisions under General Anders.

In the trials of Germans at Nuremberg for war crimes the murder of the Poles at Katyn was mentioned in the indictment of Goering and others, who laid the White Book of the German investigation before the court. It was decided by the victorious Governments concerned that the issue should be avoided, and the crime of Katyn was never probed in detail. The Soviet Government did not take the opportunity of clearing themselves of the horrible and widely believed accusation against them and of fastening the guilt conclusively upon the German Government, some of whose principal figures were in the dock on trial for their lives. In the final judgment of the International Tribunal at Nuremberg Katyn is not mentioned in the section dealing with the treatment of prisoners of war by Nazi Germany. Everyone is therefore entitled to form his own opinion, and there is certainly no lack of material in the many books that have been published by the Polish leaders still in exile from their country, and in particular those written by Mr. Mikolajczyk, the former Polish Prime Minister, who joined the first Polish Government after the war, and by General Anders.

Victory in Tunis

General Alexander took command of the whole front in the last week of February. At the same time, in accordance with the Casablanca agreement, Air Marshal Tedder assumed control of the Allied Air Forces. The battle in Tunisia was then at its height. General Eisenhower, with supreme responsibility, could not conduct operations of this complex and convulsive character, by British, American, and French troops, from his headquarters at Algiers, nearly four hundred miles away. There must be a man on the spot. He had now arrived with plenary powers.

General Alexander to Prime Minister   27 Feb 43

Have just returned from three days on the American and French front lines. Regrouping, sort out, and reorganisation is now under way, but is being somewhat delayed by enemy action in north. Broadly speaking, Americans require experience and French require arms. For Americans I am sending best officers available to give instruction in battle technique and to help them train for war. For French I have wired to home and mid-East for essential arms and light equipment to be flown here, and am helping as far as possible from my own resources. The repulse of the enemy in the south and re-establishment of former positions have put heart into Americans. I have ordered vigorous but in meantime minor offensive action in south to regain initiative. I am frankly shocked at whole situation as I found it. Although Anderson should have been quicker to realise true state of affairs and to have started what I am now doing, he was only put in command of whole front on January 24.

I am regrouping whole force into three parts, as follows: British and French under Anderson, all Americans under Friedendall, Eighth Army under Montgomery.

Hate to disappoint you, but final victory in North Africa is not just around the corner. A very great deal is required to be done both on land and in the air. General Eisenhower could not be more helpful.

Am glad to hear you are better. Best wishes.

* * *

Until the port of Tripoli was working fully Montgomery was able to advance into Tunisia only with a part of his forces. Realising that as soon as the Kasserine battle was over Rommel would certainly turn upon him, he established his three forward divisions, the 7th Armoured, 51st British, and 2nd New Zealand, in position about Medenine. There had been no time to put out minefields or wire, but no fewer than five hundred anti-tank guns were deployed in readiness.

General Montgomery to Prime Minister   28 Feb 43
Xth Corps has got back all its transport, and is now on the move forward from Benghazi. Leading [units] will be complete in Tripoli area by March 10, and others in succession. Whole Xth Corps will be concentrated up with me in forward area by March 19. I am taking the necessary steps to fight Rommel in my present positions, and see him off should he attempt any dirty work before I am ready to resume my own offensive against him. I intend to hold my present positions firm, as they are exactly what I require for the development of my own offensive against Mareth position in due course.

On March 6 Rommel made four major attacks, using all three of the German Panzer divisions. Every attack was beaten off with heavy loss. The enemy withdrew, leaving on the field fifty-two tanks destroyed by gunfire. We lost no tanks, and only

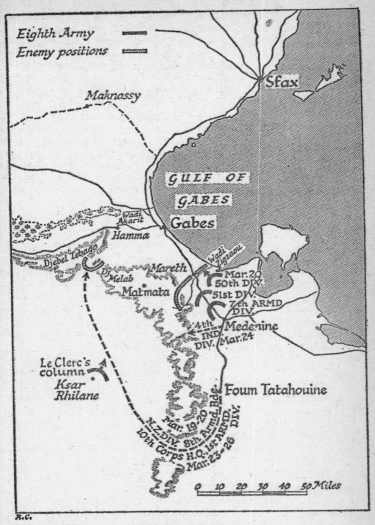

Forcing the Mareth Line.

130 killed and wounded. Nothing like this example of the power of massed anti-tank artillery had yet been seen against armour. This was probably Rommel's sharpest rebuff in all his African exploits. Morover, it was his last action there. Shortly afterwards he was invalided to Germany, and von Arnim succeeded him.

The Eighth Army now moved forward to close with the enemy's main position, the Mareth Line. This was a highly organised twenty-mile-long defence system constructed by the French before the war to prevent Italian incursion into Tunisia. Now Italians were manning it against the British! At its seaward end the steep-sided Wadi Zigzaou was a formidable anti-tank obstacle immediately in front of the main defences; farther south concrete pill-boxes, anti-tank ditches, and wire continued the front to the Matmata hills. There was no chance of an outflanking movement except by a long *détour* leading to the narrow defile between the Djebels Tebaga and Melab. The route had formerly been pronounced by the French as impossible for vehicles, but it had been reconnoitred in January by the Long Range Desert Group and declared feasible, if very difficult. Here was not the least valuable of the many services rendered throughout the African campaign by this hardy and highly mobile reconnaissance unit. Clearly the enemy were not under any illusions, for they had fortified the pass and occupied it with a German Panzer division and Italian infantry. But in view of the frontal strength of the Mareth position, held as it was by six divisions, two of them German, with the 15th Panzer Division in reserve, Montgomery decided to include in his plan a flanking column to break through the pass and establish itself behind the main enemy front.

A fortnight was needed for preparing a deliberate assault against such strongly held defences. During that time the U.S. IInd Corps recaptured Gafsa and thrust eastwards. Although they were unable to break into the coastal plain, they pinned the 10th Panzer Division to this front throughout the Mareth battle. On March 10 also General Leclerc's troops were severely attacked by a mixed force of armoured cars and artillery, supported by air action. The French stood firm, and, helped by the R.A.F., drove off the enemy with considerable loss.

The stage was thus set for the battle of the Mareth Line. The operation was called 'Pugilist'. An intensive day bombing programme had been ordered to pave the way, but bad weather

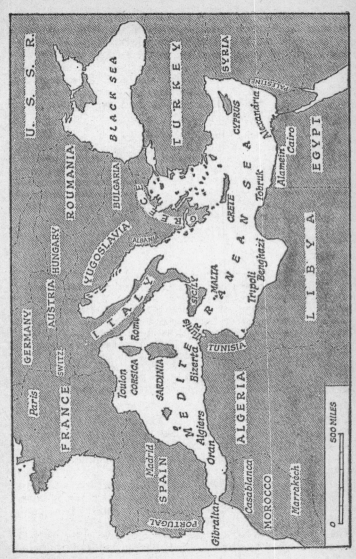

Map to Illustrate the Mediterranean Campaigns, 1942.

prevented the bomber forces working till the 20th. A preliminary attack by the 201st Guards Brigade on March 16 proved unsuccessful and costly. Montgomery pressed on with the rest of his plan. On the night of the 19th he dispatched on its long flank march a force under General Freyberg, which included the 2nd New Zealand Division, the 8th Armoured Brigade, and a medium artillery regiment. By next evening, the 20th, they were approaching the defile.

General Alexander to Prime Minister   21 Mar 43
 'Zip' is timed by Eighth Army for to-night. The stage is set, and you will receive confirmation when the curtain goes up. American IInd Corps has taken Gafsa, and their 1st Armoured Division is moving on Maknassy. So far Germans have not reacted to this threat, which was designed to draw them off from Eighth Army, but to-morrow may tell us more. Montgomery will communicate with you direct to-morrow.

General Alexander to Prime Minister   21 Mar 43
 'Zip'.

General Montgomery to Prime Minister   21 Mar 43
 'Pugilist' launched successfully yesterday. New Zealand Corps moved round enemy west flank, and to-day is fifteen miles south-west of El Hamma and is directed on Gabes. XXXth Corps attacked enemy east flank last night and established a bridgehead through the main obstacles and minefields of Mareth position, and this bridgehead is being widened and its success exploited. Enemy clearly intends to stand and fight, and I am preparing for a dog-fight battle in Mareth area, which may last several days. Action of New Zealand Corps in Gabes area may have a decisive effect on the battle.

Just before midnight the XXXth Corps delivered the main attack on the coastal sector of the Mareth defences. The 50th Division crossed the Wadi Zigzaou, and gained a footing beyond. The Wadi proved an even more severe obstacle than had been expected ; neither tanks nor anti-tank guns could cross, despite the unsparing efforts of the engineers. All next day the division held its ground, but on the 22nd a violent counter-attack by the 15th Panzer Division and German infantry forced them back. During the night of the 23rd they were withdrawn across the Wadi.

The frontal attack having failed, Montgomery swiftly changed his plan. He gave the divisions confronting the Mareth Line a containing rôle and transferred the main weight to his left wing. The headquarters of the Xth Corps and the 1st Armoured Division were dispatched to join Freyberg at the defile by the same long and arduous route, while the 4th Indian Division opened up a way across the Matmata hills west of Medenine.

The problem of breaking through the defile to El Hamma was formidable, even with the strong reinforcements that Freyberg received. The enemy became aware of the danger, and reinforced this flank with the German 164th Infantry Brigade and part of the 15th Panzer Division. Only heavy pounding could force a passage, and in this the Western Desert Air Force, which had given unfailing support to the Eighth Army in all its battles, rose to a supreme endeavour. Thirty of its squadrons, eight of them American, inflicted a series of intense air bombardments on the defences of the pass. This culminated on the afternoon of March 26 in a two-and-a-half-hour continuous attack by relays of bombers and low-flying fighters. Sustained by this and a strong artillery barrage, the New Zealanders and the 8th Armoured Brigade broke into the enemy defences. They were followed by the 1st Armoured Division, which, when the moon rose, passed through them, and by dawn had nearly reached El Hamma. Caught between the New Zealanders in front and the Armoured Division behind them, the enemy fought desperately, but in vain. Their losses were crippling ; 7,000 prisoners were taken. Thus was gained a fine victory, in which not only the quality of the troops, but also the skill of their commander was prominent.

General Montgomery to Prime Minister　　　　28 Mar 43
　　After seven days of continuous and heavy fighting Eighth Army has inflicted a severe defeat on enemy. Enemy resistance south of line El Hamma-Gabes is disintegrating. My troops are in possession of whole Mareth defences.

Faced with the danger of having his retreat cut off, the Italian General Messe, in command on this front, hastily withdrew his forces and formed front again ten miles north of Gabes, on the Wadi Akarit, which lies athwart a gap between the sea and marshes to the west. The Eighth Army closed on the enemy, but before it was ready to attack there were significant events farther north. At the end of March the British 46th Division in the coastal sector began an advance, and after several days of fighting regained all the ground previously lost. East of Beja the British 4th and 78th Divisions also attacked successfully. In a fortnight the whole position north of Medjez had been substantially restored to the line held before the German offensive had forced it back. On March 31 the U.S. IInd Corps renewed their thrust down the Gafsa-Gabes road, threatening the rear of the enemy on the Wadi Akarit. They did not succeed in breaking through, but the operation had the important result of drawing in the 21st Panzer Division to reinforce the 10th. Both of these divisions were thus fully occupied against the Americans while the assault upon the Wadi Akarit was taking place. At the same time the Tactical Air Force began a series of attacks against enemy landing-grounds. These were most successful, and indeed eventually drove the enemy Air Force out of Tunisia.

*   *   *

On April 5 General Alexander submitted his plan in full detail to General Eisenhower. By April 6 the Eighth Army was set for its new attack. The Wadi Akarit, itself a considerable obstacle, was overlooked by hills to the north, and the whole formed a naturally strong defensive position. Montgomery made his characteristic use of the artillery. Before dawn the 51st and 50th British and 4th Indian Divisions, supported by massed artillery, were launched against fierce opposition. The enemy made determined counter-attacks, and it was not till nightfall that the battle was won.

General Montgomery to Prime Minister   6 Apr 43
I delivered a heavy attack against enemy in Akarit position early this morning. I did two things not done by me before, in that I attacked centre of enemy position, and in the dark with no moon. Attack delivered by about three infantry divisions, supported by 450 guns, and enemy was surprised and overwhelmed and all objectives were captured. Through the hole thus made I am passing Xth Corps, consisting of New Zealand Division and one armoured division, and this movement has now just begun at the time of sending you this. The prisoners are estimated at 2,000 after only six hours' fighting, and many more are flowing in.

I shall endeavour to fight the enemy to a standstill in this area and inflict damage on him here, so that he will have all the less troops and material to fight on rearward positions. Heavy fighting is going on, and when enemy recovers from his surprise he will probably fight desperately. But he cannot fight any longer on the Akarit position, as I have driven a deep wedge into the centre of it, and the dominating key points are all in my possession.

My troops are in TREMENDOUS form and have fought splendidly.

Will press on northwards when I have finished here.

The enemy were followed up next day on both the roads running northwards, and all available British and American aircraft punished their retreating columns. On April 7 a patrol of the 4th Indian Division met one from the U.S. IInd Corps. The American greeting 'Hello, Limey',* although not understood, was accepted with the utmost cordiality. The two armies which had started nearly two thousand miles apart were now at last joined together. The same day, in order to cut off the enemy's northward retreat, the IXth British Corps, with the British 6th Armoured Division, a brigade of the 46th Division, and the U.S. 34th Infantry Division, tried to break through the Fondouk Pass. Pichon was taken, but it was not till the 9th that the Armoured Division penetrated the defences, entering Kairouan on the 11th after a successful action against the 10th and 21st Panzer Divisions.

The enemy's withdrawal before the Eighth Army was skilfully conducted, though the bold action of our 6th Armoured Division doubtless accelerated its time-table. Sfax, important for its port facilities now that Tripoli was three hundred miles behind, was taken on April 10, and Sousse two days later. On April 13 contact was made with the enemy's final position on the mountains north of Enfidaville. The first probing attacks found them strongly held.

We had possession of the forward airfields and General Eisenhower could intensify the sea and air blockade of Tunisia. The enemy had increased their use of air transport as our sea blockade tightened ; large convoys of transport aircraft, escorted by fighters, were arriving every day. Our own fighters, British and American, were given these tempting targets as a primary task. On April 10 and 11 seventy-one transport aircraft were claimed as destroyed. On the 18th a great convoy a hundred strong was set upon by our Spitfires and four squadrons of American Warhawks off Cape Bon. The convoy was scattered in confusion ; over fifty were brought down. Next day South African Kitty-

---

* A name for British sailors in vogue in the United States Navy, arising from the use of lime-juice on British ships in bygone days to prevent scurvy.

hawks destroyed fifteen out of eighteen; and finally on April 22 a further thirty, including many laden with petrol, went flaming into the sea. This virtually ended Hitler's obstinate attempt, which Germany could ill afford. No more transport aircraft dared to fly by day. Their achievement had been great. In the four months December to March they had ferried more than 40,000 men and 14,000 tons of supplies to Africa.

Realising the strength of the Enfidaville position, Alexander decided that the main attack on Tunis must come from the west. The U.S. IInd Corps, freed from the southern front, was brought up during the first weeks of April and relieved the British Vth Corps in the sector from Beja to the sea. The 1st British Armoured Division was transferred from the Eighth to the First Army. The Eighth Army however still had the task of containing the enemy holding the Enfidaville front, and while the main blow was being prepared it attacked on the night of April 19 with three divisions, strongly supported by artillery and the Air Force. In two days of heavy fighting appreciable gains were made, but it was becoming clear that further progress from this direction could be made only at the cost of heavy casualties.

*   *   *

The main attack of the First Army began on April 22. On the right, south of Goubellat, the IXth Corps advanced with the 46th Infantry and the 1st and 6th Armoured Divisions; north of them was the Vth Corps, the 1st, 4th, and 78th Divisions, moving astride the Medjerda river towards Massicault. Five days of hard fighting failed to break the enemy's resistance, but his losses were heavy, and important ground was gained which was to prove of value a week later. South of the British sector the French XIXth Corps occupied the Djebel Fkirine, while in the north the U.S. IInd Corps, attacking on the 23rd, made steady progress towards Mateur. Despite the physical difficulties of the ground the Americans kept up unremitting pressure, and gradually forced the Germans back.

General Alexander to Prime Minister   30 Apr 43
I had a long conference with Montgomery to-day, and have decided that owing to the extreme difficulties of the ground and the fact that the enemy has concentrated a strong force of guns against Eighth Army in the coastal sector his

operations towards Bou Ficha would have been very costly in casualties and were not certain of success. I have therefore cancelled his large-scale operations, and Eighth Army will undertake active local action, with the chief object of preventing the enemy transferring troops from their front to First Army front. 4th Indian Division, 7th Armoured Division, and 201st Guards Brigade are moving over to First Army, starting to-night. A very strong attack with all available air and artillery support will be launched by Vth Corps probably on May 4, on the axis Medjez-Tunis. IXth Corps, with two or three armoured divisions, to pass through Vth Corps, directed on Tunis. I have every hope that this attack will lead to decisive results.

The last two days have been days of continuous enemy counter-attacks on the front of the 4th and 1st Divisions, and also on IInd U.S. Corps front. On Vth Corps front fighting has been particularly fierce and bitter. Localities have changed hands several times. Both 1st and 4th Divisions have fought very well, and our positions are in the main intact. The enemy's losses have been very heavy. He has used tanks in several of these counter-attacks, and about seven [of his] Mark VI's have been knocked out.

As an instance of the desperate nature of the enemy's resistance, fifty men of the Hermann Goering Division had just surrendered, when one of them persuaded them to take up arms again, and the whole party started fighting and had to be shot to a man.

General Crocker has been wounded, and Horrocks is taking over the command of IXth Corps and Freyberg the Xth Corps.

Prime Minister to Marshal Stalin   3 May 43

The battle in the Tunisian tip continues at a high pitch, and with considerable casualties on both sides. Since we entered Tunisia we have taken about 40,000 prisoners ; in addition, the enemy have suffered 35,000 dead and wounded. The casualties in the First Army have been about 23,000, and in the Eighth Army about 10,000. The total Allied casualties are about 50,000, of which two-thirds are British. The battle will be maintained along the whole front with the utmost intensity, and General Alexander is re-grouping for a strong thrust very soon. The enemy have just under 200,000 encircled. They are still steadily reinforcing, but in the last few days our Air, which is growing ever stronger and coming closer, has cut into them well. So many destroyers and transports have been sunk, including several carrying German reinforcements, that all traffic was temporarily suspended. Unless it can be immediately reopened the supply situation of the enemy will be very serious for him. Also, his chances of getting away by sea in any numbers are not good. The peculiar mountainous character of the country, with flat plains commanded by rugged, upstanding peaks, each of which is a fortress aids the enemy's defence and slows up our advance. I hope however to have good news for you before the end of this month. Meanwhile the whole campaign is most costly to the enemy on account of his additional losses in transit.

*　　*　　*

It was clear that yet one more heavy punch would be needed before the enemy would break. A final attack by the Eighth Army on April 24 had proved that the Enfidaville position was too strong to be overcome without heavy loss. As we have seen, General Alexander transferred to the First Army three of their veteran divisions who had fought in the Desert since the earliest days. On May 6 the culminating attack was launched. The IXth Corps made the principal assault, on a narrow front on either side of the Medjez-Tunis road. The leading infantry, the 4th British and 4th Indian Divisions, were closely followed by the 6th and 7th Armoured Divisions. On their left the Vth Corps protected the flank of the advance. The Allied Air Forces again put forth a supreme effort, with 2,500 sorties in the day. The Axis Air Force had been gradually worn down over many weeks, and at this crisis was able to make only sixty sorties in reply. The climax was at hand. The relentless blockade by sea and air was fully established. Enemy movement over the sea was at a standstill, their air effort ended. To quote from a subsequent German report:

The Anglo-American Air Forces played a decisive part in the enemy operational success which led to the destruction of the German-Italian bridgehead in Tunisia. They took part in the ground fighting to an extent never before attempted.

The IXth Corps made a clean break in the enemy front. The two armoured divisions passed through the infantry and reached Massicault, half-way to Tunis. Next day, May 7, they pressed on, and the 7th Armoured Division entered Tunis, and then swerved north to join hands with the United States forces. Resistance on the main American front had cracked at the same time, and their 9th Infantry Division reached Bizerta. Three German divisions were thus trapped between the Allied troops. and surrendered on May 9.

General Alexander to Prime Minister   8 May 43

Things have gone even better than I could have hoped. So as to give the Americans Bizerta for themselves, I had regrouped, and, as you know, they entered it at the same hour as the First Army took Tunis. I have sent a French regiment into Tunis to take over the guards and to run up the Tricolour. We had a deception plan to mislead the enemy into thinking the blow was in the south, and it worked well, as they sent the majority of their tanks and a number of their 88-mm. guns down opposite 1st British Armoured Division, weakening the front facing IXth Corps. IXth Corps attacked with a huge weight of arms and armour, supported by practically the entire Air Force: it was a real thunderbolt. As a result IXth Corps reached Tunis, a distance of thirty miles, in thirty-six hours.

The Axis front has completely collapsed and disintegrated. We shall have to mop up pockets of Germans, but up to date probably 20,000 prisoners have been taken, besides many guns, lorries, and dumps. Our casualties both in men and tanks are light. First Army casualties are estimated at some 1,200.

Coningham and I have just returned from Tunis, where we were greeted enthusiastically by the population. We then went to IXth Corps front, where 26th Armoured Brigade were attacking Hamman Lif. 1st Guards Brigade is clearing some high ground south of that place. 1st British Armoured Division reached the road. The French tanks are operating just west of Zaghouan.

Our main object now is to cut off as many enemy as possible from gaining the Cape Bon peninsula. R.A.F. work has been quite magnificent, and all troops are in terrific heart.

The 6th Armoured Division, followed by the 4th British Division and with the 1st Armoured on their right, drove east, through and beyond Tunis. They were held up by a hastily organised resistance at a defile by the sea a few miles east of the city, but their tanks splashed through along the beach, and at nightfall on May 10 reached Hammamet, on the east coast. Behind them the 4th Division swept round the Cape Bon peninsula, meeting no opposition. All the remaining enemy were caught in the net to the south.

General Alexander to Prime Minister   10 May 43

Coningham and I have just returned from motoring and flying over area between Bizerta and Tunis, where ground is littered with enemy vehicles, guns, and equipment of all

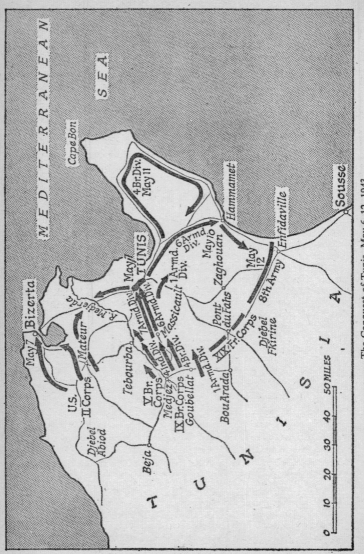

The Conquest of Tunis, May 6–12, 1943

sorts, some abandoned and much destroyed. 50,000 prisoners already counted through cages, and still coming in. Nine German generals so far. Advanced elements of First Army reached Grombalia by 6 p.m. to-day. With luck all Axis forces opposite Eighth Army will be completely surrounded.

Prime Minister to General Alexander 10 May 43

It has fallen to you to conduct series of battles which have ended in destruction of the German and Italian power in Africa. All the way from Alamein to Tunis in ceaseless fighting and marching of last six months you and your brilliant lieutenant Montgomery have added a glorious chapter to annals of British Commonwealth and Empire. Your combinations in the final great battle will be judged by history as a model of the military art. But more than this, you have known how to inspire your soldiers with confidence and ardour which overcame all obstacles and outlasted all fatigue and hardship. They and their trusty United States and French Allied soldiers and airmen together can now be told of the admiration and gratitude with which entire British nation and Empire regard them and their famous deeds. The generous rivalry in arms of the First and Eighth British Armies has achieved victory, full honour for each and all.

General Alexander to Prime Minister 11 May 43

... I expect all organised resistance to collapse within the next forty-eight hours, and final liquidation of whole Axis forces in the next two or three days. I calculate that prisoners up to date exceed 100,000, but this is not yet confirmed, and they are still coming in. Yesterday I saw a horse-drawn gig laden with Germans driving themselves to the prisoners' cage. As they passed we could not help laughing, and they laughed too. The whole affair was more like Derby Day. The equipment of all sorts will take some time to count up; some is destroyed, but a lot intact.

No one has got away except a mere handful by air.

We have recovered 2,000 of our own prisoners, including wounded. It is all very satisfying and augurs well for the future.

Prime Minister to General Eisenhower (Algiers) 11 May 43

Let me add my heartfelt congratulations to those which have been sent to you by His Majesty and the War Cabinet on the brilliant result of the North African campaign by the army under your supreme direction.

The comradeship and conduct with which you have sustained the troops engaged in the fierce and prolonged battle in Tunisia and the perfect understanding and harmony preserved amidst the shock of war between British and United States forces and with our French Allies have proved solid foundation of victory.

The simultaneous advance of British and United States Armies side by side into Tunis and Bizerta is an augury full of hope for the future of the world. Long may they march together, striking down the tyrants and oppressors of mankind.

General Eisenhower to Prime Minister   11 May 43
Yesterday I wrote you a letter attempting to express in some small degree the depth of my appreciation for the unwavering support and the confidence that you have shown in me and in this Allied force. To-day your heart-warming telegram arrived, and I regret that I have *no* words to tell you how pleased I am. I can only say 'Thank you', and assure you that this Army will never stop pounding until Hitlerism is abolished from the earth.

Prime Minister to General Giraud (Algiers)   12 May 43
It cheers all our hearts to see a line of French divisions advancing triumphantly against the common foe and leading German prisoners by the thousand to the rear. Accept my most hearty congratulations on the fighting spirit of the French Army under your command, and the tenacity in defence and aggression in assault which it has displayed in spite of being at a disadvantage in equipment. Every good wish.

*   *   *

Admiral Cunningham had made full preparation for the final collapse, and on May 7 he ordered all available naval forces to patrol the straits to prevent any Axis attempt to stage a 'Dunkirk' evacuation. The appropriate code-name of this operation was 'Retribution'. On the 8th he signalled, 'Sink, burn, and destroy. Let nothing pass.' But only a few barges tried to escape, and nearly all were captured or sunk. Day and night destroyers and coastal craft, together with the R.A.F., continued the ruthless work. In all 879 men surrendered to the Navy, and only 653 are known to have escaped, mostly by air and at night. Our casualties were negligible.

It was not till I visited Algiers a month later that I was able to do justice to the share of all branches of the Navy in our success.

Prime Minister to Admiral Cunningham   11 June 43
The daring and devotion of our submarines succeeded in

sinking forty-seven ships and our surface forces forty-two
ships of an aggregate tonnage of 268,600. When to this is
added sinkings by air, a grand total of one hundred and
thirty-seven ships and 433,400 tons is reached. This was 32
per cent. of the estimated shipping initially available to the
Axis at the beginning of the Tunisian campaign.

During the long struggle on the mainland the Navy and
Air Force, working in closest co-operation, sank twenty-one
destroyers or torpedo-boats and many small craft, and prevented 35 per cent. of enemy supply ships and transports
from reaching Tunisia.

To the minesweepers fell the honour of reopening the
Mediterranean by clearing the channels, 600 miles long, between May 9 and 21.

The protection of our own convoys was carried to very
highest point. Over the whole vast mass of shipping which
entered the Mediterranean between November 8, 1942, and
May 8, 1943, losses were less than $2\frac{1}{4}$ per cent. . . .

The first through convoy to complete the Mediterranean passage since 1941 left Gibraltar on May 17, 1943, and reached
Alexandria without loss on May 26. The reopening of this
route to the Middle East reduced the length of the journey
by nearly 9,000 miles, representing a saving of about forty-five
days in the time spent by an average store ship on passage.

* * *

On May 12 I received the following telegram:

General Alexander to Prime Minister   12 May 43
The end is very near. Von Arnim has been captured, and
prisoners will most likely be over 150,000. All organised resistance has collapsed, and only pockets of enemy are still
holding out. It appears that we have taken over 1,000 guns,
of which 180 are 88-mm., 250 tanks, and many thousands of
motor vehicles, many of which are serviceable. German prisoners driving their own vehicles formed a dense column on
the road from Grombalia to Medjez el Bab all day to-day.

My next telegram, denoting the formal end of the campaign, will follow, I hope, in a few hours.

That day the 6th Armoured Division joined hands with the
Eighth Army. The encircling ring was closed. The enemy laid
down their arms. In the words of Alexander's dispatch:

It was an astonishing sight to see long lines of Germans

driving themselves in their own transport or in commandeered horse-carts westwards in search of prisoner-of-war cages.

At 2.15 p.m. on May 13 he signalled to me:

Sir:
It is my duty to report that the Tunisian campaign is over. All enemy resistance has ceased. We are masters of the North African shores.

*   *   *

No one could doubt the magnitude of the victory of Tunis. It held its own with Stalingrad. Nearly a quarter of a million prisoners were taken. Very heavy loss of life had been inflicted on the enemy. One-third of their supply ships had been sunk. Africa was clear of our foes. One continent had been redeemed. In London there was, for the first time in the war, a real lifting of spirits Parliament received the Ministers with regard and enthusiasm, and recorded its thanks in the warmest terms to the commanders. I had asked that the bells of all the churches should be rung. I was sorry not to hear their chimes, but I had more important work to do on the other side of the Atlantic.

I was already at the White House when I received the following gracious message from the King:

13 *May*, 1943
Now that the campaign in Africa has reached a glorious conclusion, I wish to tell you how profoundly I appreciate the fact that its initial conception and successful prosecution are largely due to your vision and to your unflinching determination in the face of early difficulties. The African campaign has immeasurably increased the debt that this country, and indeed all the United Nations, owe to you.

GEORGE R.I.

My Third Visit to Washington

The reasons which led me to hasten to Washington, once the decision in Africa was certain, were serious. What should we do with our victory? Were its fruits to be gathered only in the Tunisian tip, or should we drive Italy out of the war and bring Turkey in on our side? These were fateful questions, which could only be answered by a personal conference with the President. Second only to these were the plans for action in the Indian theatre. I was conscious of serious divergences beneath the surface which, if not adjusted, would lead to grave difficulties and feeble action during the rest of the year. I was resolved to have a conference on the highest possible level.

On April 29 I telegraphed to President Roosevelt:

It seems to me most necessary that we should all settle together now, first, Sicily and then exploitation thereof, and, secondly, the future of the Burma campaign in the light of our experiences and the shipping stringency. There are also a number of other burning questions which you and I could with advantage bring up to date. I think I could manage to be with you by Tuesday, May 11. Please say whether you would like this, or whether you would prefer to send your people over here, which of course would be easier for us.

* * *

The doctors did not want me to fly at the great height required in a bomber, and the Northern route clipper seaplanes could not take off on account of late ice till after May 20. It was therefore decided to go by sea. We left London on the night of May 4, and went aboard the *Queen Mary* in the Clyde on the following day. The ship had been admirably fitted up to meet all our needs. The whole delegation was accommodated on the main deck, which was sealed off from the rest of the ship. Offices, conference rooms, and of course the Map Room, stood ready for immediate use. From the moment we got on board our work went forward ceaselessly.

All kinds of clever precautions had been taken to conceal the identity of the passengers in the *Queen Mary*. A number of notices had been put up in Dutch to suggest that Queen Wilhelmina and her suite were travelling to America in the ship. Ramps were ostentatiously built in the passages so that a wheel chair could traverse them smoothly. This was in order to start a rumour that the President of the United States and a considerable staff were to be brought to England on the return voyage. The more tales, the more safety. So effective were the cover plans that even some members of the Cabinet Office staff, who had embarked in the *Queen Mary* for the Hot Springs Food Conference, were dumbfounded to see us board the ship. About five thousand German prisoners were already on board. It had been suggested that they should be transferred to another ship, but I could not see what harm they could do to us, under due control and without weapons, and, since the point was referred to me, had given instructions that they should come along.

* * *

The conference, which I had christened 'Trident', was to last at least a fortnight, and was intended to cover every aspect of the war. Our party had therefore to be a large one. The 'regulars' were in full force: the Chiefs of Staff, with a goodly number of Staff Officers; Lord Leathers, with senior officials of the Ministry of War Transport; and Ismay, with members of my Defence Office. The Commanders-in-Chief in India, Field-Marshal Wavell, Admiral Somerville, and Air Chief Marshal Peirse, were also with us. I had summoned them because I was sure that our American friends would be very anxious that we should do everything possible—and even impossible—in the way of immediate operations from India. The conference must hear at first hand the views of the men who would have to do whatever task was chosen.

There was much to be settled among ourselves before we reached Washington, and now we were all under one deck. The Joint Planning and Intelligence Staffs were in almost continuous session. The Chiefs of Staff met daily, and sometimes twice a day. I adhered to my usual practice of giving them my thoughts each morning in the shape of minutes and directives, and I generally had a discussion with them each afternoon or evening. These processes of probing, sifting, and arguing continued throughout the voyage, and grave decisions were reached in measured steps.

We had to think about all the theatres at once. Upon the operations in Europe, following the victory in Africa, we were in complete agreement. It had been decided at Casablanca to attack Sicily, and, as had been seen, all preparations were far advanced. The Chiefs of Staff were convinced that an attack upon the mainland of Italy should follow, or even overlap, the capture of Sicily. They proposed the seizure of a bridgehead on the toe of Italy, to be followed by a further assault on the heel as prelude to an advance on Bari and Naples. A paper setting out these views and the arguments which led up to them was prepared on board ship and handed to the American Chiefs of Staff as a basis for discussion on our arrival in Washington.

*   *   *

We anticipated more difficulties in reaching agreement with our American friends over the second great sphere of British military action, namely, the operations from India. At Casablanca it had been agreed to aim at the capture of Akyab before May 1943,* in order by a limited advance from Assam to gain new starting-points for improving the air route and air-lift to

* Called Operation 'Cannibal'.

China. A provisional date of November 15, 1943, for an assault on Burma had also been fixed, subject to a review of forces available in July. All this had been set forth on paper, but we had little to show in fact. The advance on Akyab had failed, and its capture before the monsoons had now to be ruled out. The advance from Assam had not been undertaken because of administrative difficulties and the inability of the Chinese to advance to Yunnan during the spring. Some increase had been made in the air transport available for the China route, but the full development of the air route and the requirements for a land advance towards Central Burma had proved utterly beyond our resources. It therefore seemed clear beyond argument that the full 'Anakim' operation could not be attempted in the winter of 1943–44.

I was sure that these conclusions would be very disappointing to the Americans. The President and his circle still cherished exaggerated ideas of the military power which China could exert if given sufficient arms and equipment. They also feared unduly the imminence of a Chinese collapse if support were not forthcoming. I disliked thoroughly the idea of reconquering Burma by an advance along the miserable communications in Assam. I hated jungles—which go to the winner anyway—and thought in terms of air-power, sea-power, amphibious operations, and key points. It was however an essential to all our great business that our friends should not feel we had been slack in trying to fulfil the Casablanca plans and be convinced that we were ready to make the utmost exertions to meet their wishes. I therefore prepared in the early days of the voyage a very lengthy paper on the whole position in the Indian and Far Eastern spheres, and especially of those regions for which we bore the main responsibility.

... 'Anakim' as planned is recognised by all of us to be physically impossible for 1943, and the Chiefs of Staff are rightly searching for variants or alternatives. On these a few general observations may be made.

5. Going into swampy jungles to fight the Japanese is like going into the water to fight a shark. It is better to entice him into a trap or catch him on a hook and then demolish him with axes after hauling him out on to dry land. How then to deceive and entrap the shark?

6. The strategic virtues of 'Torch' compelled or induced the enemy to fight in a theatre most costly to himself. It

gained us important territories, bases, and a new French Army, ultimately perhaps of eight or ten divisions. Its success opens the Mediterranean, thus freeing a vital part of our sea communications. Can we not seize in the A.B.D.A. area some strategic point or points which will force the Japanese to counter-attack under conditions detrimental to them and favourable to us? For this purpose the naval command of the Bay of Bengal must be secured. It will next be necessary to establish effective shore-based air command radiating from the key point captured. Thus protected, comparatively small numbers of troops can maintain themselves, unless the enemy brings a disproportionate army to bear, in which case our people can either be reinforced or withdrawn, according to our general plans.

7. The surest way to make a successful landing is to go where you are not expected. It should be possible to carry up to thirty thousand or forty thousand men across the Bay of Bengal, as required, to one or more points of the crescent from Moulmein to Timor. This crescent would include: (i) the Andaman Islands; (ii) Mergui, with Bangkok as objective; (iii) the Kra Isthmus; (iv) assault of Northern Sumatra; (v) the southern tip of Sumatra; (vi) Java.

8. The method of landing should first of all have regard to the importance of getting ashore and establishing rapidly by a carefully prepared evolution a powerful air base. It is not always necessary to conquer in the first stage the real objective. This may be more surely achieved as a second step under the effective shore-based air cover. But in any case the landing, if likely to be opposed, can only be achieved by the provision of a large seaborne air force in carriers of all classes. This seaborne air cover can be withdrawn for use elsewhere once the shore-based air is established under improvised or permanent conditions. The seizure of even one key point intolerable to the enemy would impose upon him not only operations to recapture it, but a dispersion of his forces over the immense coastline exposed to the menace of sea-power. Nothing less than a definite attack on some point will enforce this dispersion. Otherwise the enemy rests at his ease, disposed to advantage in selected best defensive positions. He is content with the valuable property which he has seized, while we have to find a means to recapture it by the offensive. All the alternatives should be examined in a hopeful spirit, resolute to overcome the real difficulties and brush away the still more numerous imaginary difficulties which always weigh on action.

9. Once the Italian Fleet has been destroyed or neutralised

and air control of our routes through and across the Mediterranean is established powerful British naval forces will be available to reconstitute the Eastern Fleet in battleships, aircraft-carriers, and ancillary vessels. We must not exaggerate the Japanese strength. They cannot possibly be strong enough at all points to resist the concentrated impact of a seaborne air-sustained descent. Their own Air Force is dwindling steadily, and will be under great strain through the American and Australian campaign in the Pacific. It should be easy after one point has been attacked to compel still greater dispersion of enemy forces.

10. Our reports show only about 20,000 Japanese in Sumatra, which is 600 miles long, and 40,000 in Java. The Japanese themselves conquered Sumatra and Java with comparatively small forces against much larger garrisons than they have themselves installed. Why should we assume that we are not capable of planning and executing operations of the same vigour, and with the same close combination of naval, army, and air forces? We have larger forces available ; sea-power gives us almost unlimited choice of the point of attack, and we also ought to have learnt a lot from what has happened in the last fifteen months. Let us not rest content with the bleak and skinny programme set out. It could only be said of this that it is better than nothing and will serve to fill in time.

11. Notwithstanding the foregoing, we should be chary of committing ourselves in the forthcoming meeting to any particular plan. It is certain that prejudice will discredit every plan. Moreover, if we show ourselves unduly keen on any one plan others will be pressed as superior alternatives owing to the natural contrariness of allies. We should first confront our friends with the reasons which require modification of 'Anakim'. We should assert our earnest desire to maintain the operations in this theatre on the level of the priorities and status which they occupied at the Casablanca Conference. We should invite their views upon alternatives, and only become involved in detailed argument if and when the discussion reaches this stage. My own impression is that the Americans will require to be satisfied that the maximum action is taken in this theatre and that it is not being displaced in its importance in our minds, and that once reassured on these points they will be ready to consider variants and alternatives. It is for this moment that our studies must be ready.

12. I agree that the time and occasion have come to make a long-term plan for the defeat of Japan, and to interweave that plan as far as is humanly possible with the phases of the prime struggle against Hitler. . . .

15. The unsatisfactory course of the recent Burma cam-

paign cannot be repeated on a far larger scale in 1943–44. Unless there is complete confidence in our ability to carry out the campaign as planned and in reasonable time, we must seek the only two other alternatives for action, namely, (*a*) a vast increase in the air route to China, and (*b*) an overseas expedition to one or more of the key points mentioned in paragraph 7.

There were no serious differences of view among ourselves, and a Chiefs of Staff statement was prepared for presentation in Washington.

* * *

Another burning question for us was how to obtain the use of the Portuguese Atlantic islands. We wanted facilities in the Azores for operating our Long and Very Long Range aircraft from Terceira and San Miguel Islands. We wanted to be allowed to refuel our naval escorts at either San Miguel or Fayal, and to have freedom to use the Cape Verde Islands for reconnaissance aircraft. All these facilities would give far better and wider air cover to our convoys, and consequently more scope for evasive routeing. They would increase our carrying power by enabling us to come more directly through the middle of the Atlantic. They would give us the power to attack U-boats not only going to and from the Biscay bases, but also while they were resting, refuelling, and recharging their batteries in mid-ocean. We were to find the Americans even more ardent than ourselves on all these points.

* * *

On May 8 I cabled to Stalin:

I am in mid-Atlantic on my way to Washington to settle further exploitation in Europe after Sicily, and also to discourage undue bias towards the Pacific, and further to deal with the problem of the Indian Ocean and the offensive against Japan there.

I also telegraphed to the President, who had brushed aside my suggestion that I should stay at the Embassy:

10 May 43

Since yesterday we have been surrounded by the United States Navy, and we all greatly appreciate the high value you evidently set on our continued survival. I look forward to being at the White House to-morrow afternoon, and also going to Hyde Park with you at the week-end. The voyage has so far been most agreeable, and the staff have done a vast amount of work.

On May 11 we arrived off Staten Island. Harry Hopkins was there to meet us, and we immediately entrained for Washington. The President was on the platform to greet me, and whisked me off to my old rooms at the White House. The next afternoon, May 12, at 2.30 p.m., we all met in his oval study to survey and lay out our work at the conference.

Here is a summary of the agreed Anglo-American record of the meeting:

There were present:

British	United States
The PRIME MINISTER.	The PRESIDENT.
Field-Marshal Sir JOHN DILL.	Admiral WM. D. LEAHY.
General Sir ALAN F. BROOKE.	General G. C. MARSHALL.
Admiral of the Fleet Sir DUDLEY POUND.	Admiral E. J. KING.
Air Chief Marshal Sir CHARLES F. A. PORTAL.	Lieut-General J. T. MCNARNEY.
Lieut.-General Sir HASTINGS ISMAY.	Mr. HARRY L. HOPKINS.

Secretaries
Brigadier-General J. R. DEANE.
Brigadier E. I. C. JACOB.

The President welcomed us. It was less than a year ago, he said, that we had all met in the White House, and had set on foot the moves leading up to 'Torch'. It was very appropriate that we should meet again just as that operation was coming to a triumphant conclusion. The meeting at Casablanca had set on foot Operation 'Husky', and he hoped that this would meet with similar good fortune. He thought that the keynote of our plans at the present time should be an intention to employ every resource of men and munitions against the enemy. Nothing that could be brought to bear should be allowed to stand idle.

He then asked me to open the discussion. According to the records, I spoke as follows:

The Prime Minister recalled the striking change which had taken place in the situation since he had last sat by the President's desk and had heard the news of the fall of Tobruk. He could never forget the manner in which the President had sustained him at that time, and the Shermans which had been handed over so generously had made their reputation in Africa. The British came to the present meeting adhering to the Casablanca decisions. There might have to be adjustments made necessary by our success, which also enabled us to take a longer forward view. 'Torch' was over, Sicily was near ; what should come next? We had been able by taking thought together to produce a succession of brilliant events which had altered the whole course of the war. We had the authority and prestige of victory. It was our duty to redouble our efforts and to grasp the fruits of our success. The only questions outstanding between the two Staffs were questions of emphasis and priority. He felt sure that these could be solved.

He did not propose to deal with the U-boat war and the aerial bombardment of Germany. There were no differences of opinion on these subjects. He would like to put forward for consideration a number of objectives, and questions which might focus subsequent study. The first objective was in the Mediterranean. The great prize there was to get Italy out of the war by whatever means might be the best. He recalled how in 1918, when Germany might have retreated to the Meuse or the Rhine and continued the fight, the defection of Bulgaria brought the whole of the enemy structure crashing to the ground. The collapse of Italy would cause a chill of loneliness over the German people, and might be the beginning of their doom. But even if not immediately fatal to Germany, the effects of Italy coming out of the war would be very great, first of all on Turkey, who had always measured herself with Italy in the Mediterranean. The moment would come when a joint American–Russian–British request might be made to Turkey for permission to use bases in her territory from which to bomb Ploesti and clear the Ægean. Such a request could hardly fail to be successful if Italy were out of the war, and the moment were chosen when Germany could take no powerful action against Turkey. Another great effect of the elimination of Italy would be felt in the Balkans, where patriots of various nationalities were with difficulty held in check by large Axis forces, which included twenty-five or more Italian divisions. If these withdrew the effect would be either that Germany would have to give up the Balkans, or else that she would have to withdraw large forces from the Russian front to fill the gap. In no other way could relief be given to the Russian front on so large a scale this year. The third effect would be the elimination of the Italian Fleet. This would immediately release a considerable British squadron of battleships and aircraft-carriers to proceed either to the Bay of Bengal or the Pacific to fight Japan.

Certain questions presented themselves in relation to the Mediterranean. Need we invade the soil of Italy, or could we crush her by air attack? Would Germany defend Italy? Would Italy be an economic burden to us? He did not think so. Would arguments against a general conquest of Italy apply equally against a 'toe and heel' operation to establish contact with Yugoslavia? Finally, there was a large political question for the British and United States Governments. What sort of life after the war should we be willing to accord to Italy if she placed herself unreservedly in our hands? Mr. Churchill said that if Italy made a separate peace we should have the use of Sardinia and the Dodecanese without having to fight for them.

The second objective was the taking of weight off Russia. He was much impressed by Stalin's attitude, in spite of the stopping of the Arctic convoys. For the first time, in his recent speech, Stalin had acknowledged the efforts and victories of his Allies. But we should never forget that there were 185 German divisions on the Russian front. We had destroyed the German army in Africa, but soon we should not be in contact with them anywhere. The Russian effort was prodigious, and placed us in their debt. The best way of taking the weight off the Russian front in 1943 would be to get, or knock, Italy out of the war, thus forcing the Germans to send a large number of troops to hold down the Balkans.

The third objective had already been mentioned by the President in his opening remarks. It was to apply our vast armies, air forces, and munitions to the enemy. All plans should be judged by this test. We had a large army and the Metropolitan Fighter Air Force in Great Britain. We had our finest and most experienced troops in the Mediterranean. The British alone had thirteen divisions in North-West Africa. Supposing that Sicily was completed by the end of August, what should these troops do between that time and the date [in 1944], seven or eight months later, when the cross-Channel operation might first be mounted? They could not possibly stand idle, and so long a period of apparent inaction would have a serious effect on Russia, who was bearing such a disproportionate weight.

Mr. Churchill said that he could not pretend that the problem of landing on the Channel coast had been solved. The difficult beaches, with the great rise and fall of tide, the strength of the enemy's defences, the number of his reserves and the ease of his communications, all made the task one which must not be underrated. Much however would be learnt from Sicily. He wished to make it absolutely clear that His Majesty's Government earnestly desired to undertake a full-scale invasion of the Continent from the United Kingdom as soon as a plan offering reasonable prospects of success could be made.

The next objective was aid to China. The difficulties of fighting in Burma were apparent. The jungle prevented the use of our modern weapons. The monsoon strictly limited the length of the campaigning season, and there was no means of bringing sea-power to bear. ... If further study showed that it would be better to by-pass Burma, he was anxious that another means should be found of utilising the large forces standing in India. He thought that this alternative might well be found in an operation against the tip of Sumatra and the waist of Malaya at Penang. He was most anxious that we should find in that theatre some means of making use of those advantages which had been so valuable in 'Torch'. In that operation sea-power had played its full part ; complete surprise had been possible ; we had been able to seize a territory of importance which not only brought in a new army on our side, but forced the enemy to fight in a place most disadvantageous to him. These conditions might apply [elsewhere].

He felt that the time had now come to study the long-term plan for the defeat of Japan. He would like once more to state the British determination to carry the struggle home to Japan. The only question was how best to do it. He thought that the United States Chiefs of Staff should lead in a joint study, on the assumption that Germany would be out of the war in 1944, and that we could concentrate on the great campaign against Japan in 1945. . . .

The President, in his reply, pointed out that the United Nations were already producing more than both the Germans and Japanese. It was therefore most important to keep the large army and naval forces actively engaged. He was optimistic about Turkey. The entry of that country into the war would provide an important base for air operations against the German lines of communication to the Russian front. It was particularly urgent to consider 'Where do we go from Sicily?' It was clearly necessary to keep employed the Anglo-American forces of over twenty divisions in the Mediterranean area. The drain on Allied resources which might follow the occupation of Italy must be carefully considered in the light of any future operations in the Mediterranean. In any case, after the completion of 'Husky' there would be a surplus of man-power. This should be used to build up 'Bolero', and should start at once. He felt that everyone was agreed that there was no possibility of a cross-Channel enterprise this year, but the operation must be carried out on the largest scale in the spring of 1944.

In the Pacific area the President said that the Japanese were being steadily worn down. The Americans had landed in the Aleutians, and operations in the Solomons and in New Guinea were being carried out. It was particularly important to concentrate on the lengthy Japanese supply lines. Since the war started Japan had lost a million tons of shipping, and if this continued their field of operations would be restricted. They had suffered similar losses in the air. In order to keep up the offensive at sea it was important to establish air bases in China. The President said that the conference was not justified in ignoring the possibility of a Chinese collapse. Priority for aid to China in 1943 and 1944 must be considered. Regaining Burma would not be enough. China could only be helped immediately by air. To do this airfields in Assam must be secured, regardless of the cost. The strengthening of the United States Air Force operating from Chinese bases would mean increased pressure against Japanese shipping. The President ended by saying that in order to relieve Russia we must engage the Germans. For this reason he questioned the occupation of Italy, which would release German troops to fight elsewhere. He thought that the best way of forcing Germany to fight would be to launch an operation across the Channel.

I now replied that as we were agreed that the cross-Channel operation could not take place till 1944, it seemed imperative to use our great armies to attack Italy. I did not think that an occupation of all Italy would be necessary. If Italy collapsed the United Nations would occupy the ports and airfields needed for further operations into the Balkans and Southern Europe. An Italian Government could control the country, subject to Allied supervision.

All these grave issues were now to be thrashed out by our combined Staffs and their experts.

*　　　*　　　*

For the week-end of May 15 the President proposed to take me, not to Hyde Park, but to Shangri-La, which was the name he gave the mountain refuge, about 2,000 ft. high, in the Catoctin Hills, in Maryland, where he sheltered whenever the chance offered itself, from the stifling heat and buzz of Washington. We had a dispute about where we should sit in the car for this three-hour journey. Alike by his rank and from his infirmity there was only one place for the President. Mrs. Roosevelt wished to sit in one of the small front seats, and put me next to the President. I would not have this, and the British Empire went into action. After about three minutes' conflict of wills I won, and Mrs. Roosevelt took her proper place by her husband's side. Harry Hopkins filled the fourth seat, and we whirled off amid our cyclist escort. In about two hours we approached the town of Frederick. I had of course visited the famous battlefield of Gettysburg some years before, but I now made inquiries about Barbara Frietchie and her house. This moved Harry Hopkins to quote the famous lines

> ' "Shoot if you must this old grey head,
> But spare your country's flag," *she said*.'

When it was clear that no one else in the car could add to this quotation I started out:

> 'Up from the meadows rich with corn,
> Clear in the cool September morn,
> The clustered spires of Frederick stand . . .'

and sailed steadily on:

> 'Up rose old Barbara Frietchie then,
> Bowed with her threescore years and ten ;
> Bravest of all in Frederick town,
> She took up the flag that the men hauled down.
>
> . . . .
>
> Halt! The dust-brown ranks stood fast.
> Fire! Out blazed the rifle-blast.
> It shivered the window with frame and sash.
> It rent the banner with many a gash.
> Quick as it fell from the broken staff,
> Dame Barbara seized the silken scarf.
> She leant full out of the window-sill,
> And she shook it forth with a right good will.
> "Shoot if you will this old grey head,
> But spare your country's flag" . . .'

At this point they all joined in the chorus:

> '*she said*.'

I went on:

> 'A shade of sadness, a touch of shame
> Over the face of the leader came,
> And a nobler nature within him stirred
> At the sight of this woman's deed and word.
> "Who touches a hair on yon grey head

[he is said to have exclaimed, somewhat inconsistently with his previous instructions]

> Dies like a dog. March on," he said.

> So all day long through Frederick's street
> Sounded the tramp of marching feet,
> And all day long that free flag tossed
> Over the heads of the rebel host.'

I got full marks for this from my highly select American audience, none of whom corrected my many misquotations, and was encouraged to discuss at some length the characters of Stonewall Jackson and Robert E. Lee, two of the noblest men ever born on the American continent.

After a while silence and slumber descended upon the company, as we climbed with many a twist and turn up the spurs of the Alleghenies. Soon we arrived at Shangri-La, which was in principle a log cabin, with all modern improvements. In front was a fountain and a pool of clear water, in which swam a number of large trout, newly caught in the neighbouring stream and awaiting the consummation of their existence.

The President had been looking forward to a few hours with his stamp collection. General 'Pa' Watson, his personal aide, brought him several large albums and a number of envelopes full of specimens he had long desired. I watched him with much interest and in silence for perhaps half an hour as he stuck them in, each in its proper place, and so forgot the cares of State. But soon another car drove up to the door, and out stepped General Bedell Smith, quick-winged from Eisenhower's headquarters, with a budget of serious questions on which decisions were urgently required. Sadly F.D.R. left his stamp collection and addressed himself to his task. By the evening we were all tired out, and went to bed at ten.

* * *

On this week-end was discussed the question of my meeting Madame Chiang Kai-shek, who was making an extensive tour of the United States. She was at this time in New York, and intimated that she would be glad to receive me there. Amid the pressures under which we were working and in the few days that remained before I must leave I did not feel able to make so long a journey. The President therefore invited the lady to lunch with him to meet me at the White House. The invitation was refused with some hauteur. Madame was of the opinion that I should make the pilgrimage to New York. The President was somewhat vexed that she had not adopted his plan. It was my strong desire to preserve unity in the Grand Alliance, and I offered to go half-way if she would do the same. This offer was however considered facetious, so I never had the pleasure and advantage of meeting this lady until the Cairo Conference.

* * *

On Sunday the President wanted to fish in a stream which flowed through lovely woods. He was placed with great care by the side of a pool, and sought to entice the nimble and wily fish. I tried for some time myself at other spots. No fish were caught, but he seemed to enjoy it very much, and was in great spirits for the rest of the day. Evidently he had the first quality of an angler, which is not to measure the pleasure by the catch. On the Monday we had to leave this agreeable cool abode, and descended the Alleghenies for the really great heat of Washington. On the journey back through Frederick I asked to be shown Barbara Frietchie's house. I was surprised to see it was only one and a half storeys high. I had always pictured it as at least three, if not four, and I had considered exactly how far the heroic dame would have to stand back from the sill to be safe from an upward volley from the street. It now appeared that the famous window, which I saw for the first time, was only about twelve feet from the ground, and it was clear the Confederates must have taken great care to avoid doing her any harm. Thus the story ended well for both sides, and Harry Hopkins solemnly repeated:

> ' "Shoot if you must this old grey head,
> But spare your country's flag," *she said*.'

In the regretted absence of Madame Chiang Kai-shek, the President and I lunched alone in his own room, and made the best of things.

* * *

I had undertaken, at the invitation of the Speaker of the House of Representatives, to address Congress on Wednesday, the 19th, at noon. It was seventeen months since I had last spoken to this august assembly. The speech, in which I tried to cover the whole field, is on record. It was also broadcast to the world. I shall quote only a brief extract.

In North Africa we builded better than we knew. The unexpected came to the aid of the design and multiplied the results. For this we have to thank the military intuition of Corporal Hitler. We may notice, as I predicted in the House of Commons three months ago, the touch of the master-hand. The same insensate obstinacy which condemned Field-Marshal von Paulus and his army to destruction at Stalingrad has brought this new catastrophe upon our enemies in Tunisia. . . .

The African excursions of the two Dictators have cost their countries in killed and captured 950,000 soldiers. In addition nearly 2,400,000 gross tons of shipping have been sunk and nearly 8,000 aircraft destroyed, both of these figures being exclusive of large numbers of ships and aircraft damaged. There have also been lost to the enemy 6,200 guns, 2,550 tanks, and 70,000 trucks. . . . Arrived at this milestone in the war, we can say, 'One continent redeemed.' . . .

I was driving the other day not far from the field of Gettysburg, which I know well, like most of your battlefields. It was the decisive battle of the American Civil War. No one after Gettysburg doubted which way the dread balance of war would incline, yet far more blood was shed after the Union victory at Gettysburg than in all the fighting which went before. It behoves us therefore to search our hearts and brace our sinews and take the most earnest counsel one with another, in order that the favourable position which has already been reached both against Japan and against Hitler and Mussolini in Europe shall not be let slip. . . .

This statement was well received by Congress, and the President, who had listened on the radio, seemed very pleased with me when I returned to the White House.

Problems of War and Peace

The Staffs engaged in perpetual discussion. Sometimes there were four meetings a day. At first the differences seemed insuperable and it looked like a hopeless breach. During this period leakages from high American officers were made to Democratic and Republican senators, leading to a debate in the Senate. By patience and perseverance our difficulties were gradually overcome. In a speech to Congress on May 20 I tried to put the whole picture in true perspective and proportion so far as was possible in public. The fact that the President and I had been living side by side seeing each other at all hours, that we were known to be in close agreement, and that the President intended to decide himself on the ultimate issues—all this, together with the priceless work of Hopkins, exercised throughout a mollifying and also a dominating influence on the course of Staff discussions. After a serious crisis of opinions, side by side with the most agreeable personal relations between the professional men, an almost complete agreement was reached about invading Sicily.

There was profound dissatisfaction in Washington, which we all shared, at the lack of vim in the recent operations in Burma. I considered re-modelling the commands by making Wavell C.-in-C. in India, with Auchinleck as his deputy and one of the best younger Corps Commanders as C.-in-C. of the East Asian front. I was sure changes of this character were

indispensable if we were to treat the problems of this theatre
with the gravity they deserved.

*   *   *

A very stern mood developed in Washington about de Gaulle.
Not a day passed that the President did not mention the subject to me. Although this was done in a most friendly and often
jocular manner, I saw he felt very strongly indeed upon it. Almost every day he handed me one or more accusing documents
against de Gaulle from the State Department or the American
Secret Service. De Gaulle was alleged to have used British money
to offer inducements to the sailors of the *Richelieu* to come
over to him personally. Only politeness prevented our hosts
from suggesting that our financial relations with the United
States make it in a certain sense almost American money.
I was at this time most indignant with de Gaulle. I felt that
our continued support of him might lead to an estrangement
between the British and United States Governments, and that
no one would like this better than de Gaulle. I brought all this
forcibly to the notice of my colleagues at home. It hung in the
balance whether we should not break finally at this juncture
with this most difficult man. However, time and patience
afforded tolerable solutions.

Another very difficult question arose about the Atlantic
Islands. The War Cabinet wished to invoke the ancient alliance
and request the Portuguese Government to give us the facilities
to which both the President and I, strongly pressed by the Combined Chiefs of Staff, attached the greatest importance. It was
estimated by the experts that a million tons of shipping and
many thousands of lives might be saved. I had a particular regard for the rights of Portugal, but felt we were fighting for her
life and independence as well as our own. It was not until six
months had passed and substantial loss had been suffered that
we obtained the sorely needed relief. However, the result was
achieved by long and friendly negotiation, aided by the general
progress of our arms.

*   *   *

On May 22 I had an important conversation on the structure of a post-war settlement at luncheon at the British Embassy. I had asked the Ambassador to gather those whom he
thought most necessary to a discussion of this immense theme.

The Vice-President, Mr. Wallace, the Secretary of War, Mr. Stimson, the Secretary of the Interior, Mr. Ickes, the Chairman of the Foreign Relations Committee of the Senate, Senator Connally, and the Under-Secretary of State, Mr. Sumner Welles, were invited, and apprised of the topic beforehand. The Embassy staff kept a full record of what passed and of the statement which I made at the formally expressed desire of our guests.

In the course of a general talk I said that the first preoccupation must be to prevent further aggression in the future by Germany or Japan. To this end I contemplated an association of the United States, Great Britain, and Russia. If the United States wished to include China in an association with the other three, I was perfectly willing that this should be done ; but, however great the importance of China, she was not comparable to the others. On these Powers would rest the real responsibility for peace. They together, with certain other Powers, should form a Supreme World Council.

Subordinate to this World Council there should be three Regional Councils, one for Europe, one for the American Hemisphere, and one for the Pacific.

As for Europe, I thought that after the war it might consist of some twelve States or Confederations, who would form the Regional European Council. It was important to re-create a strong France ; for the prospect of having no strong country on the map between England and Russia was not attractive. Moreover, I said that I could not easily foresee the United States being able to keep large numbers of men indefinitely on guard in Europe. Great Britain could not do so either. No doubt it would be necessary for the United States to be associated in some way in the policing of Europe, in which Great Britain would obviously also have to take part.

I also hoped that in South-Eastern Europe there might be several Confederations—a Danubian Federation based on Vienna and doing something to fill the gap caused by the disappearance of the Austro–Hungarian Empire. Bavaria might join this group. Then there should be a Balkan Federation.

I said that I should like to see Prussia divided from the rest of Germany, forty million Prussians being a manageable European unit. Many people wished to carry the process of division further and divide Prussia itself into component parts, but on this I reserved judgment. Poland and Czechoslovakia should stand together in friendly relations with Russia. This left the Scandinavian countries and Turkey, which last might or might not be willing, with Greece, to play some part in the Balkan system.

Mr. Wallace asked about Belgium and Holland, suggesting that they might join France. I said that they might form a group of the Low Countries with Denmark. Mr. Wallace also asked whether I contemplated the possibility of Switzerland joining with France, but I said that Switzerland was a special case. Each of the dozen or so of the European countries should appoint a representative to the European Regional Council. thus creating a form of United States of Europe. I thought Count Coudenhov Kalergi's ideas on this subject had much to recommend them.

Similarly, there might be a Regional Council for the Americas, of which Canada would naturally be a member and would represent the British Commonwealth. There should also be a Regional Council for the Pacific, in which I supposed that Russia would participate. When the pressure on her western frontiers had been relieved Russia would turn her attention to the Far East. These Regional Councils should be subordinate to the World Council. The members of the World Council should sit on the Regional Councils in which they were directly interested, and I hoped that in addition to being represented on the American Regional Council and the Pacific Regional Council the United States would also be represented on the European Regional Council. However this might be, the last word would remain with the Supreme World Council, since any issues that the Regional Councils were unable to settle would automatically be of interest to the World Council.

Mr. Wallace thought that the other countries would not agree that the World Council should consist of the four major Powers alone. I agreed, and said that to the four Powers should be added others by election in rotation from the Regional Councils. The central idea of the structure was that of a three-legged stool—the World Council resting on three Regional Councils. But I attached great importance to the regional principle. It was only the countries whose interests were directly affected by a dispute who could be expected to apply themselves with sufficient vigour to secure a settlement. If countries remote from a dispute were among those called upon in the first instance to achieve a settlement the result was likely to be merely vapid and academic discussion.

Mr. Wallace asked what in practice would be the procedure if, for example, there was a dispute between Peru and Ecuador. I answered that it would be dealt with in the first place by the American Regional Council, but always under the general overriding authority of the World Council. In such an instance the interests of countries outside the American Hemisphere would hardly be affected; but plainly a dispute which threatened the peace of the world might very well not be susceptible to being treated only on a regional basis and the Supreme World Council would quickly be brought in.

I was asked whether the association of nations which I contemplated would be confined to the United Nations, or include the neutrals. I replied that there was advantage in trying to induce those nations at present neutral to join the United Nations before the end of the war, and that we ought to use all possible persuasion and pressure to secure this when it could be done with safety to the nation concerned. An example was Turkey. My policy was to help Turkey to build up her own forces to the point where, at the right moment, she could and would effectively intervene. When the United Nations brought the guilty nations to the bar of justice, I could see little but an ineffective and inglorious rôle for Mr. de Valera and others who might remain neutral to the end.

We had much to learn, I said, from the experience of the League of Nations. It was wrong to say that the League had failed. It was rather the member States who had failed the League. Senator Connally agreed, and pointed to the achievements of the League in the years immediately after 1919. So did Mr. Stimson, who thought that if the original guarantee to France had not fallen through subsequent French policy, and also the history of the League, would have been very different.

Force would clearly be required to see that peace was preserved. I suggested an agreement between the United Nations about the minimum and maximum armed forces which each would maintain. The forces of each country might be divided into two contingents, the one to form the national forces of that country, and the other to form its contingent to an international police force at the disposal of the Regional Councils under the direction of the Supreme World Council. Thus, if one country out of twelve in Europe threatened the peace, eleven contingents would be ready to deal with that country if necessary. The personnel of the international contingent provided by each country would be bound, if it were so decided by the World Council, to undertake operations against any country other than their own.

Mr. Wallace said that bases would be required for these contingents. I said that there was something else in my mind which was complementary to the idea I had just expressed. The proposals for a world security organisation did not exclude special friendships devoid of sinister purpose against others. Finally I said I could see small hope for the world unless the United States and the British Commonwealth worked together in fraternal association. I believed that this could take a form which would confer on each advantages without sacrifice. I should like the citizens of each, without losing their present nationality, to be able to come and settle and trade with freedom and equal rights in the territories of the other. There might be a common passport, or a special form of passport or visa. There might even be some common form of citizenship, under which citizens of the United States and of the British Commonwealth might enjoy voting privileges after residential qualification and be eligible for public office in the territories of the other, subject, of course, to the laws and institutions there prevailing.

Then there were bases. I had welcomed the destroyer bases deal, not for the sake of the destroyers, useful as these were, but because it was to the advantage of both countries that the United States should have the use of such bases in British territory as she might find necessary to her own defence ; for a strong United States was a vital interest of the British Commonwealth, and *vice versa*. I looked forward therefore to an extension of the common use of bases for the common defence of common interests. In the Pacific there were countless islands possessed by enemy Powers. There were also British islands and harbours. If I had anything to do with the direction of public affairs after the war, I should certainly advocate that the United States had the use of those that they might require for bases.

* * *

All the American guests present said that they had been thinking on more or less the lines which I had propounded, and thought that it was not impossible that American opinion would accept them or something like them. Lord Halifax asked Mr.

Welles whether he thought that the establishment of a Regional Council for Europe would have the effect of leading United States opinion to disinterest itself in European affairs. Mr. Welles was not afraid of this, having regard to the overriding responsibility of the Supreme World Council and the relation between it and the Regional Councils. Mr. Stimson said most emphatically that in his opinion there would be a tendency to relax after hostilities ceased, and a reluctance to embark upon new international experiments. He believed that it would be much easier to secure American agreement during the war; indeed, that it was a case of during the war or never. The others were disposed to agree, and we all felt that the best approach was to present such plans for the future as a continuation of our present co-operation, and to do so while the war was still proceeding.

I made two other suggestions, both of which carried warm assent. First, that after the war we should continue the practice of Combined Staff conversations, and, second, that we should by constant contact take whatever steps were necessary to ensure that the main lines of our foreign policy ran closely together.

Mr. Wallace said to the Ambassador as he left that it was the most encouraging conversation in which he had taken part for the last two years. I was of course careful to explain that I was expressing only personal views.

* * *

The Vice-President at luncheon with the President and me next day seemed a little anxious lest other countries should think that Britain and the United States were trying to boss the world. I made it perfectly clear that they ought not to be put off necessary and rightful action by such suggestions. It was the essence of my idea that citizenship should be retained in the Anglo-American sphere even if this were wholly exceptional. The President liked the ventilation of these ideas, especially the military aspect. We both thought it essential that the institution of the Anglo-American Combined Staff should be continued for a good long time after the war—at any rate, until we could all be sure that the world was safe.

* * *

On the main issues of war strategy we had six plenary meetings during 'Trident', at which the President and I were present. The Combined Chiefs of Staff presented us each day with the questions on which they desired decisions as a result of their ceaseless labours. Thus all moved forward smoothly, and at the last meeting, on the morning of May 25, we were presented with their report. I had suggested a number of amendments, with which the Combined Chiefs of Staff declared themselves in agreement. The President and I then gave formal approval to the report, as amended, which follows.

OVERALL STRATEGIC CONCEPT FOR THE PROSECUTION OF THE WAR

1. In co-operation with Russia and other Allies, to bring about at the earliest possible date the unconditional surrender of the Axis in Europe.

2. Simultaneously, in co-operation with other Pacific Powers concerned, to maintain and extend unremitting pressure against Japan, with the purpose of continually reducing her military power and attaining positions from which her ultimate surrender can be forced. The effect of any such extension on the overall objective to be given consideration by the Combined Chiefs of Staff before action is taken.

3. Upon the defeat of the Axis in Europe, in co-operation with other Pacific Powers, and, if possible, with Russia, to direct the full resources of the United States and Great Britain to bring about at the earliest possible date the unconditional surrender of Japan.

Basic Undertakings in Support of Overall Strategic Concept

Whatever operations are decided on in support of the overall strategic concept, the following established undertakings will be a first charge against our resources, subject to review by the Combined Chiefs of Staff in keeping with the changing situation:

1. Maintain the security and war-making capacity of the Western Hemisphere and the British Isles.

2. Support the war-making capacity of our forces in all areas.

3. Maintain vital overseas lines of communication, with particular emphasis on the defeat of the U-boat menace.

4. Intensify the air offensive against the Axis Powers in Europe.

5. Concentrate maximum resources in a selected area as early as practicable for the purpose of conducting a decisive invasion of the Axis citadel.

6. Undertake such measures as may be necessary and practicable to aid the war effort of Russia.

7. Undertake such measures as may be necessary and practicable in order to aid the war effort of China as an effective Ally and as a base for operations against Japan.

8. Prepare the ground for the active or passive participation of Turkey in the war on the side of the Allies.

9. Prepare the French forces in Africa to fulfil an active rôle in the war against the Axis Powers.

* * *

I was able to cable home that an agreement most satisfactory to our Chiefs of Staff was being reached over the whole strategic field. 'This is a tribute to the authority of the President and to my close contact with him, the Staff differences of view at one time having been most serious. Moreover, we now hope to obtain a promise for the war-time transfer of twenty new American ships a month to our flag for ten months, thus affording full employment for our surplus seafaring crews. This could certainly not be arranged without the President overruling much opposition.'

I was also able to send the following message to Sir John Anderson about the atomic bomb and the Anglo-American research:

Prime Minister to Lord President   26 May 43
The President agreed that the exchange of information on Tube Alloys should be resumed, and that the enterprise should be considered a joint one, to which both countries would contribute their best endeavours. I understood that his ruling would be based upon the fact that this weapon may well be developed in time for the present war, and that it thus falls within the general agreement covering the interchange of research and invention secrets.

Lord Cherwell to be informed.

* * *

Although so much had gone well, I was extremely concerned that no definite recommendations had been made by the Combined Staffs to follow up the conquest of Sicily by the invasion of Italy. The best I had been able to get was the following resolution by the Combined Chiefs of Staff:

That the Allied Commander-in-Chief North Africa will be instructed, as a matter of urgency, to plan such operations in exploitation of 'Husky' as are best calculated to eliminate Italy from the war and to contain the maximum number of German forces. Which of the various specific operations should be adopted, and thereafter mounted, is a decision which will be reserved to the Combined Chiefs of Staff.

I knew that the American Staff's mind had been turned to Sardinia. They thought that this should be the sole remaining objective for the mighty forces which were gathered in the Mediterranean during the whole of the rest of 1943. On every ground, military and political, I deplored this prospect. The Russians were fighting every day on their enormous front, and their blood flowed in a torrent. Were we then to keep over a million and a half fine troops, and all their terrific air and naval power, idle for nearly a year?

The President had not seemed ready to press his advisers to become more precise on the invasion of Italy, but as this was the main purpose for which I had crossed the Atlantic I could not let the matter rest. Hopkins said to me privately, 'If you wish to carry your point you will have to stay here another week, and even then there is no certainty.' I was deeply distressed at this, and on May 25 appealed personally to the President to let General Marshall come to Algiers with me. At the final conference therefore Mr. Roosevelt said the Prime Minister would shortly have an opportunity of talking to the Commanders-in-Chief in North Africa on 'Post-Husky' policy, and had suggested that it would be of great value if General Marshall could go there too. He had accordingly spoken to General Marshall, and asked whether he could defer his visit to the South-West Pacific in order to fall in with the Prime Minister's request. General Marshall had said that he was perfectly willing to do this.

I then explained to the conference that I should feel awkward in discussing these matters with General Eisenhower without the presence of a United States representative on the highest level. If decisions were taken it might subsequently be thought that I had exerted an undue influence. It was accordingly a source of great gratification to me to hear that General Marshall would accompany me, and I was sure that it would now be possible to arrange everything satisfactorily in Algiers, and for a report to be sent back to the Combined Chiefs of Staff for their consideration.

*   *   *

It had been agreed that the President and I should draft the statements to be made to Russia about the conference. We made several drafts, which were typed at once and brought back. These were corrected again and again, until they were almost illegible with our scribbles. We were puzzling what to put in and what to leave out. Finally, at two o'clock in the morning, I said, much to the President's relief, 'Let me take it away with me to-morrow. I will tidy it up and send it back to you from Botwood.' He was content with this. I added, 'It would be a good thing if Marshall came with me. There is plenty of room in the plane.' We rose to go to bed, worn out by the ceaseless mental toil. At this moment General Marshall appeared. Although it had been decided that he should come to North Africa, he had not apparently expected to fly in the same plane with me or at exactly the same time. He had therefore come to say good-bye. But now the President said to him, 'Why don't you go with Winston? You can talk over the Russian communiqué to-gether.' The General was surprised, but waved his hand agreeably and said, 'I will be there.'

CHAPTER 22

Italy the Goal

We Start for North Africa, May 26 – General Marshall and the Russian Communiqué – A Long Hop to Gibraltar – The Flying-Boat Struck by Lightning – Arrived at the 'Convent' – Marshall Inspects the Gibraltar Defences – Evening Landing at Algiers – Our Determination to Invade Sicily and Italy – British Strength in the Mediterranean – Conference with General Eisenhower, May 29 – 'Hobgoblin' – A Crucial Issue: The Cross-Channel Assault – General Brooke and the Invasion of Italy – Twenty-seven Allied Divisions in the Mediterranean Area – My 'Background Notes' – Turkey and a Balkan Front – An Impressive Statement by General Alexander – My Trip to Carthage – Our Final Meeting, June 3 – Montgomery's Confidence About the Attack on Sicily – We Part in Accord – A Distressing Tragedy – The Hinge Turns.

Early the next day, May 26, General Marshall, the C.I.G.S., Ismay, and the rest of my party took off from the Potomac River in the flying-boat. The President came to see us off.

As soon as we were in the air I addressed myself to the Russian communiqué. As I found it very hard to make head or tail of the bundle of drafts, with all our emendations in the President's scrawls and mine, I sent it along to General Marshall, who two hours later presented me with a typed fair copy. I was immensely impressed with this document, which exactly expressed what the President and I wanted, and did so with a clarity and comprehension not only of the military but of the political issues involved. It excited my admiration. Hitherto I had throught of Marshall as a rugged soldier and a magnificent organiser and builder of armies—the American Carnot. But now I saw that he was a statesman with a penetrating and commanding view of the whole scene. I was delighted with his draft, and also that the task was done. I wrote to the President that it could not be better, and asked him to send it off with any alterations he might wish, without further reference to me. We landed to refuel at Botwood, in Newfoundland, and from there Marshall's draft and my letter were flown back to Washington. The President did not alter a word.

After an early dinner we took off again on our flight of 3,000 miles across the ocean to Gibraltar. It looked a very long hop, but Commander Thompson ('Tommy'), who kept me informed about the arrangements for my journey, explained that we should be nearly following the Great Circle, so apparently it was not so long as it looked. It was dark by the time we took off, and we were all ready for sleep. The large double bed in the bridal suite of the Boeing was most comfortable, and I slept sound for a good many hours. All at once there was a sudden shock and bump. I awoke. Something had happened. There were no consequences, which after all are what is important in air journeys. Nevertheless, being thoroughly awake, I put on my zip suit and went forward down the long central gallery of our spacious machine, and climbed the staircase to the navigating controls. I sat in the co-pilot's seat. It was by now a lovely moonlight night. After a while I asked the pilot what caused the bump. 'We were struck by lightning,' he said, 'but there's nothing wrong.' This was good news. We had not caught fire or broken up in the air ; there was no need to make a forced landing a thousand miles from anywhere. I had always wondered why aircraft did not mind being struck by lightning. To a groundsman it would seem quite a dangerous thing. Afterwards I learned that there had been a good deal of anxiety.

I looked down upon the calm ocean, 7,000 feet below ; but an ocean always looks calm at that height. Almost underneath us was what looked like a little tramp steamer. I was conscious of a distinct sense of comfort from her presence. Under this reassuring illusion I returned to my bed, and did not wake until just before dawn.

I went forward again, as I love to see the daylight come. When you are flying east at 160 miles an hour you meet the sun very early and he rises quickly. I adhered to my rule in these long flights that meals should be regulated by stomach-time. When one wakes up after daylight one should breakfast ; five hours after that, luncheon. Six hours after luncheon, dinner. Thus one becomes independent of the sun, which otherwise meddles too much in one's affairs and upsets the routine of work. General Marshall and I had some very agreeable talks. He questioned me closely on the difference between Impeachment, which is allowed by the United States Constitution, and Attainder, which the British Parliament still preserves. I had no difficulty in convincing him of the necessity of retaining this sovereign procedure. We both took advantage of our leisure to clear away some accumulation of papers. As we approached Gibraltar we looked around for our escort. There was no escort. Everyone's attention was attracted by an unknown aircraft, which we thought at first was taking an interest in us. As it came no closer we concluded it was a Spaniard; but they all seemed quite concerned about it till it disappeared. On alighting, at about 5 p.m., we were met by the Governor. It was too late to continue our journey to Algiers that night, and he conveyed us to the Convent, where he resides, the nuns having been removed two centuries ago.

There is a story attached to the name. Up till 1908 the Governor's residence was always called the Convent. In that year however King Edward VII's Private Secretary, Sir Henry Ponsonby, wrote to the Governor and told him that the King thought it advisable to change the name to 'Government House'. The reason given was that during the King's visit to Gibraltar in Sir George White's Governorship a paragraph had appeared in the English newspapers to the effect that the King had had luncheon at the Convent. Ten days afterwards His Majesty received a resolution passed by a Protestant association deploring the fact that the King should have thought it necessary not only to visit but even to have luncheon at a Roman Catholic institution. However, when King George VI visited North Africa in June 1943 he expressed the wish that the Governor's residence should be renamed the Convent, so the Convent it still is.

We did not leave Gibraltar for Algiers until the following afternoon. There was therefore an opportunity to show General Marshall the Rock, and we all made a few hours' pilgrimage, and inspected the new distillery which assures the fortress a permanent supply of fresh water, and various important guns, some hospitals, and a large number of troops. I finally went below to see the Governor's special pet, the new Rock gallery, cut deep in the rock, with its battery of eight quick-firing guns commanding the isthmus and the neutral ground between Britain and Spain. An immense amount of work had been put into this, and it certainly seemed, as we walked along it, that whatever perils Gibraltar might have to fear attack from the mainland was no longer one of them. The Governor's pride in his achievement was shared by his British visitors. It was not until we said good-bye upon the flying-boat that General Marshall somewhat hesitatingly observed, 'I admired your gallery, but we had one like it at Corregidor. The Japanese fired their artillery at the rock several hundred feet above it, and in two or three days blocked it off with an immense bank of rubble.' I was grateful to him for his warning, but the Governor seemed thunderstruck. All the smiles vanished from his face.

We flew off in the early afternoon with a dozen Beaufighters circling far above us, and in the evening light reached the Algiers airfield, where Generals Eisenhower and Bedell Smith, Admiral Andrew Cunningham, General Alexander, and other friends were waiting for us. I motored straight to Admiral Cunningham's villa, next door to General Eisenhower, which he placed at my disposal.

* * *

I have no more pleasant memories of the war than the eight days in Algiers and Tunis. I telegraphed to Eden to come out and join me so as to make sure we saw eye to eye on the meeting we had arranged between Giraud and de Gaulle, and all our other business. I explained to the Cabinet why his presence was particularly required.

Prime Minister to Deputy Prime Minister   29 May 43
and Dominions Secretary
... It seems to me important that Eden should come here for a few days. He is much better fitted than I am to be best man at the Giraud–de Gaulle wedding. He ought to be conscious of the atmosphere and in touch with the actors in what may easily be a serious drama. General Georges has just visited me. He is in great form and working closely with Giraud.

I propose to stay here or hereabouts till about the 6th, as I need some rest in this sunshine after the hustle of Washington. Opinion here must be allowed to form itself naturally upon the important military issues now open. With a little patience, we British, being all agreed, will probably obtain the desired solutions, as we did at Washington.

I was determined to obtain before leaving Africa the decision to invade Italy should Sicily be taken. General Brooke and I imparted our views to General Alexander, Admiral Andrew Cunningham, and Air Marshal Tedder, and later to General Montgomery. All these leading figures in the recent battles were inclined to action on the greatest scale, and saw in the conquest of Italy the natural fruition of our whole series of victories from Alamein onwards. We had however to procure the agreement of our great Ally. General Eisenhower was very reserved. He listened to all our arguments, and I am sure agreed with their purpose. But Marshall remained up till almost the last moment silent or cryptic.

The circumstances of our meeting were favourable to the British. We had three times as many troops, four times as many warships, and almost as many aeroplanes available for actual operations as the Americans. We had since Alamein, not to speak of the earlier years, lost in the Mediterranean eight times as many men and three times as many ships as our Allies. But what ensured for these potent facts the fairest and most attentive consideration with the American leaders was that notwithstanding our immense preponderance of strength we had continued to accept General Eisenhower's Supreme Command and to preserve for the whole campaign the character of a United States operation. The American chiefs do not like to be outdone in generosity. No people respond more spontaneously to fair play. If you treat Americans well they always want to treat you better. Nevertheless I consider that the argument which convinced the Americans was on its merits overwhelming.

* * *

We held our first meeting at General Eisenhower's villa in Algiers at five o'clock on May 29. General Eisenhower, as our host, presided, and had with him Marshall and Bedell Smith, as his two principals. I sat opposite to him, with Brooke, Alexander, Cunningham, Tedder, Ismay, and some others.

The first topic was 'Hobgoblin'. General Eisenhower explained that this was the code-name for the island of Pantelleria. Its capture was proposed for June 11. The military advantages were obvious from a glance at the map. The possession of the airfield was judged almost essential for the southern assault on Sicily. There was no reason to suppose that this attack would prejudice surprise in Sicily, since the operation was also a necessary step in clearing the Sicilian Narrows. Admiral Andrew Cunningham stated that his present plan was to support the aerial bombardment with 6-inch-gun cruisers, but he was ready to bring in a 14-inch battleship if this appeared desirable. I said that 'the operation would provide a very useful experiment as to the extent to which coast defences could be neutral-

ised by air attack. There was a school of thought in the United
Kingdom which thought that air forces could knock out coast
defences sufficiently to admit practically unopposed landings.'
Brooke observed that the difficulty lay in the fact that there was
a time-lag between the end of the aerial bombardment and the
arrival of the assaulting troops, which gave the enemy time to
recover. The Admiral said that eight destroyers would go right
in with the landing-craft and cover the landings at point-blank
range. I was also assured that nineteen Sherman tanks were included in the assaulting forces. The Italian strength was thought
to be about 10,000 men, including coast defence troops, together
with about a hundred tanks.

General Eisenhower, at my request, gave a brief description
of the plan for invading Sicily, for which all the resources
seemed to be coming forward punctually and in adequate numbers. We then came to the crucial issue. General Eisenhower told
us he had had a long talk with Sir Alan Brooke, who had emphasised that the Russian Army was the only land force that
could produce decisive results (in 1943). The efforts of our
armies should therefore be directed towards diverting the Germans from the Russian front in order to enable the Russian
armies to inflict decisive defeat upon them. General Eisenhower,
speaking of 1944, said that he himself thought that if we had
the command of the air an Anglo-American force of, say, fifty
divisions would probably be able to hold a force of seventy-five
divisions on the Continent. If we were going to knock out Italy
we ought to do so immediately after Sicily and with all the
means at our disposal. This would give a good indication of the
type of resistance likely to be encountered on the mainland of
Italy itself. If capturing Sicily proved to be easy we ought to go
directly into Italy. This would yield far greater prizes than any
attack on islands.

I then said on the major question that it was true that there
was no chance of our putting into Europe an Anglo-American army in any way comparable in size to that of the Russians, who were now holding 218 German divisions on their
front. By May 1, 1944, however we should have an expeditionary
force of twenty-nine divisions in the United Kingdom, seven of
which would have come from North Africa. The United Kingdom must be the assembly-point of the largest force which we
could accumulate. It was also necessary to have plans ready
to cross the Channel in force at any time in case the Germans

were to crack. As General Marshall had frequently pointed out, Northern France was the only theatre in which the vast British Metropolitan and United States Air Forces in the United Kingdom could be brought into full play. I emphasised that both the British people and the British Army were anxious to fight across the Channel.

General Marshall said that a definite date for the cross-Channel operation had been settled by the Combined Chiefs of Staff and that five divisions would be used in the assault phase. General Eisenhower had asked for information as to when he should submit his (Mediterranean) plan for knocking Italy out of the war. The United States Chiefs of Staff felt that no decision could be made until the result of the attack on Sicily and the situation in Russia were known. The logical approach would be to set up two forces, each with its own staff, in separate places. One force would train for an operation against Sardinia and Corsica, and the other for an operation on the mainland of Italy. When the situation was sufficiently clear to enable a choice to be made, the necessary air forces, landing-craft, etc., would be made over to the force charged with implementing the selected plan. Eisenhower said at once that if Sicily was polished off easily he would be willing to go straight to Italy. General Alexander agreed.

The C.I.G.S. then made his general statement. A hard struggle between the Russians and the Germans was imminent, and we should do all in our power to help the former and disperse the latter. The Germans were threatened at many points. We had already made them disperse their forces by our presence in North Africa and the skilful use of cover plans. Taking Sicily would be another step in the right direction. The Germans were faced with operations in Russia, with possible trouble in the Balkans, and with dangers in Italy, France, and Norway. Their forces were already widely stretched, and they could not further reduce them either in Russia or in France. The place where they could most conveniently do this was Italy. If the foot of Italy were found to be packed with troops we should try elsewhere. If Italy were knocked out of the war Germany would have to replace the twenty-six Italian divisions in the Balkans. They would also have to reinforce the Brenner Pass, along the Riviera, and on the Spanish and Italian frontiers. This dispersal was just what we needed for a cross-Channel operation, and we should do everything in our power to increase it. The defences on the coast of France would present no difficulty unless they were held by determined men and the Germans had mobile reserves with which to counter-attack.

Eisenhower then declared that the discussion had seemed to simplify his problem. If Sicily were to succeed, say within a week, he would at once cross the straits and establish a bridge-head. The coast defences of Southern Italy would probably be easier to crack than those of Sicily.

I expressed a personal view that Sicily would be finished by August 15. General Marshall thought we ought to have a good idea of this by the end of July. I said that if we were masters of Sicily by August, and the strain had not been too heavy, we should at once go for the toe of Italy, provided that not too many German divisions had been moved there. The Balkans represented a greater danger to Germany than the loss of Italy, as Turkey might react to our advantage.

Brooke raised the possibility of a crack-up in Italy during the Sicily fighting. In that case we ought to have a scheme of action, and he felt that General Eisenhower should give some thought to the consideration of armistice terms and how far up into Italy we should go. This was getting on very fast. Surveying the forces at our disposal, I said that, apart from the British Army, there were nine United States divisions in North Africa, including an airborne division. Seven divisions, including some British and United States, would begin to leave around November 1. There were two and a half well-armed Polish divisions in Persia, and they wished to take part in any move directed against Italy. The New Zealand Parliament had agreed that their division should be available by September, and that an armoured brigade would be ready by October. The Poles and the New Zealanders would thus provide four divisions.

The Chief of the Imperial General Staff thereupon set out our whole Mediterranean strength, which would amount to twenty-seven British and British-controlled divisions, nine United States and four French divisions. Allowing for casualties, the total would be equivalent to thirty-six divisions. Deducting the seven divisions to be sent home for the cross-Channel operation and two to cover British commitments to Turkey, there would thus be twenty-seven Allied divisions available in the Mediterranean area. I added at this point that the strength of one of our divisions was almost double that of a German division, which was little more than a glorified brigade group. With such forces in our hands it would be bad indeed if nothing happened between August or September and the following May.

*　　　*　　　*

Although much lay in the balance, I was well satisfied with this opening discussion. The desire of all the leaders to go forward on the boldest lines was clear, and I felt myself that the reservations made on account of the unknowable would be settled by events in accordance with my hopes. I now prepared what I called 'Background Notes', setting forth the whole case for the attack on Italy, together with tables of the forces available. I circulated this document to the principals before we met again on Monday, May 31.

I set forth in detail the divisions or their equivalent in the Mediterranean theatre, showing a total of 9 Americans, $3\frac{1}{4}$ French, and $27\frac{3}{4}$ British or British-controlled. From this 7 were to be sent home for 'Bolero', of which 3 were British. Of the remaining $24\frac{3}{4}$ British only $11\frac{1}{2}$ had so far been placed under General Eisenhower or earmarked for Sicily. With Brooke's assent I now offered to transfer to General Eisenhower $8\frac{3}{4}$ additional British and British-controlled divisions, making a total British contribution of 20 divisions, compared with $12\frac{1}{4}$ from all other sources. On this basis I proceeded:

> ... His Majesty's Government feel most strongly that this great force, which comprises their finest and most experienced divisions and the main part of their army, should not in any circumstances remain idle. Such an attitude could not be justified to the British nation or to our Russian allies. We hold it our duty to engage the enemy as continuously and intensely as possible, and to draw off as many hostile divisions as possible from the front of our Russian allies. In this way, among others, the most favourable conditions will be established for the launching of our cross-Channel expedition in 1944.
>
> 3. Compelling or inducing Italy to quit the war is the only objective in the Mediterranean worthy of the famous campaign already begun and adequate to the Allied forces available and already in the Mediterranean basin. For this purpose the taking of Sicily is an indispensable preliminary, and the invasion of the mainland of Italy and the capture of Rome are the evident steps. In this way the greatest service can be rendered to the Allied cause and the general progress of the war, both here and in the Channel theatre.

4. We cannot tell at present what degree of resistance the enemy will oppose to our action. Germany may make the strongest effort to defend Sicily and Italy. We are told one division a week could be transported to Sicily or the southern part of Italy. It is desirable that this possibility should be reviewed in the light of the latest information, and stated in precise terms—*i.e.*, the strength, gross and net, of the German divisions, the number of guns, tanks, and vehicles accompanying them, the areas from which they would most likely be drawn during the next twelve weeks, and whether they will come by rail, march, or sea. There are no signs at present of any movement of this character or on this scale. In order to have six divisions in Sicily before the operation, the enemy decisions and preparations must already have been made and their movement should already now be apparent. Moreover, if these six divisions are to move to Sicily the southern parts of Italy must remain denuded. It is asked that the most searching re-examination of the German movements and capacity to move in the direction mentioned should be made by the Staffs.

5. If the Germans decide to move forces of the order of between six and twelve divisions into Sicily and Italy we shall certainly have achieved part of our task in drawing, directly or indirectly, forces off our Russian allies. If they do not do so, but only send one or two divisions to stimulate Italian effort, the tasks mentioned in paragraph 3 should not be beyond our strength in the next three or four months. If, on the other hand, the Germans elect to fight a major battle for Sicily or for the Italian toe, or both, our armies will be fully engaged and we shall bring about that intensity of air fighting which from our growing relative strength is so greatly to our advantage. If after we have established ourselves in the southern parts of Italy she still continues to fight and the Germans send belated reinforcements on a large scale we might have to withdraw towards the tip, forcing them to attack successive prepared positions at heavy cost, with all the advantages of a procured diversion and of the air battle aforesaid. There would be no reason to regard this as a disaster. As long as we are fighting heavily with the Germans or even with the Italians we shall be playing our part.

I then set out the believed distribution of the Italian Army, amounting to fifty-eight field and fourteen coastal divisions.

6. It will be seen that there are only eleven Italian divisions in the mainland of Italy, about four in Sicily, and five along the Riviera, and that no fewer than twenty-eight are

tied up in Yugoslavia, Albania, and Greece. To these twenty-eight must be added eight Roumanian and eleven German divisions, making a total of forty-seven held in the Balkan peninsula by the guerrilla activities of the Serbian Michailovitch, the Croatian partisans, the general disorders in Greece, and the unrest in these enslaved countries.

7. Should Italy be made to quit the war the following practical advantages would be gained by us. The Germans would be forced to provide troops to occupy the Riviera, to maintain a new front along the Po or on the Brenner, and above all to fill the void in the Balkans caused by the demobilisation and withdrawal of Italian divisions. Up to the present the guerrillas, etc., have only been nourished by parachute packets dropped from less than a dozen aeroplanes. Nevertheless they are accomplishing the prodigious feat of immobilising forty-seven enemy divisions. The occupation of the southern parts of Italy, or even merely of the whole of the toe or heel, would give us access to the Adriatic and the power to send shiploads of munitions to Adriatic ports, and also agents and possibly small Commando bands. We should not have the troops to engage in any serious operations there, and His Majesty's Government do not contemplate or desire the provision of any organised armed force for the Balkan theatre, either this year or in any period with which we are now concerned. Nevertheless, the aiding, within the limits proposed, of the patriot bands in Yugoslavia and the fomenting of revolt in Greece and Albania are measures of high importance, all of which, together with our main operations, will influence the action of Turkey. In this way the utmost aid in our power will be given to Russia and also to 'Bolero'. It is only if and when these prospects are decisively closed to us that we should consider secondary or minor alternatives for Mediterranean action.

8. All attempts to forecast the German action in the Mediterranean are of course highly speculative. Importance should however be attached to the painful impression certainly sustained by the German High Command of the complete destruction of an army of over a quarter of a million men. In the light of this event it may be doubtful whether they would court the repetition in Sicily of a similar disaster though on a smaller scale. Our situation has vastly improved: first, by the inspiring of the Allied armies through their recent victories; secondly, by the fact that only a few hundred of the enemy escaped from Tunisia to Sicily; thirdly, by the psychological effects produced on Spain and Portugal, on Metropolitan France, in Italy and in Turkey, and indeed throughout the whole area of the war. The German position

has proportionately deteriorated. The series of immense
battles impending on the Russian front must absorb their
main strength. If the Germans do not attack, the Russians
certainly will, and may indeed even forestall their enemy. We
cannot foretell the results of these battles, but there is no
reason to suppose that the conditions are not more favourable to the Russians than they were at this time last year. It
must therefore be considered unlikely (a) that the Germans
will attempt to fight a major battle in Sicily, or (b) that they
will send strong forces into the leg of Italy. They would be
wiser to fight only delaying actions, stimulating the Italians
in these regions and retiring to the line of the Po, reserving
their strength to hold the Riviera and the Balkans, which
[latter] are of value as a supply area. If the battle goes against
them in Russia and if our action upon or in Italy is also successful the Germans may be forced by events to withdraw
to the Alps and the Danube, as well as to make further withdrawals on the Russian front and possibly to evacuate Norway. All these results may be achieved within the present
year by bold and vigorous use of the forces at our disposal.
No other action of the first magnitude is open to us this year
in Europe.

*   *   *

We met again at Eisenhower's villa on the afternoon of May
31, Mr. Eden arrived in time to be present. I tried to clinch
matters, and, after referring to the paper I had circulated, said
that my heart lay in an invasion of Southern Italy, but the fortunes of battle might necessitate a different course. At any rate,
the alternative between Southern Italy and Sardinia involved
the difference between a glorious campaign and a mere con-
venience. General Marshall was in no way hostile to these ideas,
but he did not wish for a clear-cut decision to be taken at this
moment. He said that it would be better to decide what to do
after we had started the attack on Sicily. He felt it would be
necessary to know something of the German reactions in order
to determine whether there would be real resistance in Southern
Italy ; whether the Germans would withdraw to the Po, and,
for example, whether they could organise and handle the
Italians with any finesse ; what preparations had been made in
Sardinia, Corsica, or in the Balkans ; what readjustments they
would make on the Russian front. All these things would be
factors in deciding our 'Post-Husky' plans. There were two or
three different ways in which Italy might fall ; a great deal could

happen between now and July. He, General Eisenhower, and the Combined Chiefs of Staff were fully aware of my feelings about invading Italy, but their only desire was to select the 'Post-Husky' alternative, which would give the best results.

I said that the conclusions of the minutes of the last meeting did not represent my whole feeling. I very passionately wanted to see Italy out of the way and Rome in our possession, and I offered to send the eight additional British divisions from other parts of the Middle East if these were needed. There was a considerable discussion about these reinforcements and the shipping required to move them. I said it would be hard for me to ask the British people to cut their rations again, but I would gladly do so rather than throw away a campaign which had possibilities of great success. I could not endure to see a great army standing idle when it might be engaged in striking Italy out of the war. Parliament and the people would become impatient if the Army were not active, and I was willing to take almost desperate steps in order to prevent such a calamity.

General Marshall replied that he was not arguing against the particular commitment made in Washington to aim at the fall of Italy. He only wished to emphasise that we must exercise great discretion in choosing what to do after the conquest of Sicily.

*   *   *

An incident now occurred which, as it relates to matters which have become the subject of misunderstandings and controversy after the war, must be related. Mr. Eden, at my request, commented on the Turkish situation, and said that knocking Italy out of the war would go a long way towards bringing the Turks in. They would become much more friendly 'when our troops had reached the Balkan area'. Eden and I were in full agreement on the war policy, but I feared that the turn of his phrase might mislead our American friends. The record states, 'The Prime Minister intervened to observe emphatically that he was not advocating sending an army into the Balkans now or in the near future.' Mr. Eden agreed that it would not be necessary to put an army into the Balkans, since the Turks would begin to show favourable reactions as soon as we were able to constitute an immediate threat to the Balkans.

Before we separated I asked General Alexander to give his view. He did so in an extremely impressive speech. He said that he was optimistic. The fighting value of our troops and equipment was excellent, and so were our chances of success, although it might take a fortnight of very bitter fighting. Once we joined battle the slogging generally lasted from ten days to a fortnight, or even three weeks. Then the end came quickly. The most important points in Sicily were the airfields in the south-east corner of the island, and the ports. Once we had a firm grip on these we could ignore the remainder of the island for the time being. It should be possible to cross the Straits of Messina and secure a foothold on the opposite shore, which was the very windpipe of Sicily. He repeated his statement made at the meeting of May 29 that securing a bridgehead on the Italian mainland should be considered as a part of the plan. It would be impossible for us to win a great victory unless we could exploit it by moving ahead, preferably up into Italy. All this however would be clarified as the Sicily operation moved along. It was not impossible, although it seemed unlikely, that the toe of Italy would be so strongly held as to require a complete re-staging of our operations, and we should be ready to keep moving, with no stop at all, once the attack on Sicily was started. Modern warfare allowed us to forge ahead very rapidly, with radio controlling troops at a great distance and with air providing protection and support over a wide area. The going might become more difficult as we moved up the Italian mainland, but this was no argument against going as far as we could on the momentum of the Sicily drive. He stated that none of the possibilities he had discussed could be accurately foreseen. In war the incredible often occurred. A few months before it would have been impossible for him to believe what had actually happened to Rommel and his Afrika Korps. A few weeks since he would have found it difficult to believe that three hundred thousand Germans would collapse in a week. The enemy air forces had been swept out of the skies so completely that we could have a parade, if we chose, of all our North Africa forces on one field in Tunisia without any danger from enemy aircraft.

He was at once supported by Admiral Cunningham, who said that if all went well in Sicily we should go directly across the Straits. Eisenhower concluded the meeting by expressing appreciation of the journey which General Marshall and I had made to clarify for him what the Combined Chiefs of Staff had done. He understood it was his responsibility to get information regarding the early phases of the invasion of Sicily and forward them to the Combined Chiefs of Staff in time for them to decide on the plan which would follow, without a break or a stop. He would send not only information but also strong recommendations, based upon the conditions of the moment. He hoped that his three top commanders (Alexander, Cunningham, and Tedder) would have an opportunity to comment more formally on these matters, although he agreed completely with what they had said thus far.

* * *

On the two following days we travelled by plane and car to some beautiful places rendered historic by the battles of a month before. General Marshall went on a brief American tour of his own, and then travelled with General Alexander and myself, meeting all the commanders and seeing stirring sights of troops. The sense of victory was in the air. The whole of North Africa was cleared of the enemy. A quarter of a million prisoners were cooped in our cages. Everyone was very proud and delighted. There is no doubt that people like winning very much. I addressed many thousand soldiers at Carthage in the ruins of an immense amphitheatre. Certainly the hour and setting lent themselves to oratory. I have no idea what I said, but the whole audience clapped and cheered as doubtless their predecessors of two thousand years ago had done as they watched gladiatorial combats.

* * *

Our last meeting, on June 3, was largely concerned with the question of bombing the marshalling yards of Rome, and there was agreement that they were an important and necessary military objective, and that there was no valid reason for refraining from bombing this target, provided the attacks were made by day and due care was taken to prevent damage elsewhere. General Marshall and I understood that we must seek authority from our respective Governments authorising such action.

I now asked General Montgomery, who had joined us at this meeting, to say what he thought about the plan of invading Sicily, with the execution of which he had been entrusted. Montgomery said that all his commanders had complete confidence in the present plan, and that the troops would be filled with enthusiasm when they stepped ashore. Some administrative risks were involved, but they had been gone into very carefully and he felt that they were justified. He pointed out that although he had two airborne divisions he had only enough air transport for one. In the early stages he would be able to employ only about one-third of his airborne strength; the remainder should be brought in on D+2 or D+3. With 140 more aircraft he could employ another airborne brigade at the very first. However, he understood that these were not available and the limitation was accepted. His officers were completely happy about the whole thing. As regards 'Post-Husky', he felt it important that we should decide in what direction we wanted to go, and use our military strength to make the battle move that way.

I felt that great advances had been made in our discussions and that everybody wanted to go for Italy. I therefore, in summing up, stated the conclusions in a most moderate form and paid my tribute to General Eisenhower. I said I should take home the feeling of confidence and comradeship which characterised action in this theatre. I had never received so strong an impression of co-operation and control as during my visit. It would be impossible to embark on an undertaking under better augury. I said that I should not like to go away without reaffirming my full confidence in General Eisenhower, and without expressing my admiration of the manner in which he had handled his many great problems.

General Eisenhower replied that any praise which might be given belonged to the officers round the table, and stated that while there might be differences of opinion and discussion in his headquarters, these were never based upon national lines. General Marshall and General Brooke warmly concurred, and we all parted on the best of terms.

*　　　*　　　*

Eden and I flew home together by Gibraltar. As my presence in North Africa had been fully reported, the Germans were exceptionally vigilant, and this led to a tragedy which much distressed me. The regular commercial aircraft was about to start from the Lisbon airfield when a thickset man smoking a cigar walked up and was thought to be a passenger on it. The German agents therefore signalled that I was on board. Although these passenger planes had plied unmolested for many months between Portugal and England, a German war plane was instantly ordered out, and the defenceless aircraft was ruthlessly shot down. Thirteen passengers perished, and among them the well-known British actor Leslie Howard, whose grace and gifts are still preserved for us by the records of the many delightful films in which he took part. The brutality of the Germans was only matched by the stupidity of their agents. It is difficult to understand how anyone could imagine that with all the resources of Great Britain at my disposal I should have booked a passage in an unarmed and unescorted plane from Lisbon and flown home in broad daylight. We of course made a wide loop out by night from Gibraltar into the ocean, and arrived home without incident. It was a painful shock to me to learn what had happened to others in the inscrutable workings of Fate.

*   *   *

Here then we end this volume, which describes the turning-point of the Second World War. The entry of the United States into the struggle after the Japanese assault on Pearl Harbour had made it certain that the cause of Freedom would not be cast away. But between survival and victory there are many stages. Over two years of intense and bloody fighting lay before us all. Henceforward however the danger was not Destruction, but Stalemate. The Americans' armies had to mature and their vast construction of shipping to become effective before the full power of the Great Republic could be hurled into the struggle. But further successes lay right before us, and the Fall, or rather Liberation, of Italy was near. Hitler had still to pay the full penalty of his fatal error in trying to conquer Russia by invasion. He had still to squander the immense remaining strength of Germany in many theatres not vital to the main result. Soon the German nation was to be alone in Europe, surrounded by an infuriated world in arms. The leaders of Japan were already conscious that their onslaught had passed its zenith. Together soon Great Britain and the United States would have the mastery of the oceans and the air. The hinge had turned.